Ibn Qayyim al-Jawziyya on Divine Wisdom and the Problem of Evil

OTHER TITLES BY IBN QAYYIM AL-JAWZIYYA
AVAILABLE FROM THE ISLAMIC TEXTS SOCIETY

Medicine of the Prophet
Ibn Qayyim al-Jawziyya on the Invocation of God
Ibn Qayyim al-Jawziyya on Knowledge

Ibn Qayyim al-Jawziyya

ON DIVINE WISDOM
and the Problem of Evil

Translated by
TALLAL M. ZENI

THE ISLAMIC TEXTS SOCIETY

This edition published 2017 by
THE ISLAMIC TEXTS SOCIETY
MILLER'S HOUSE
KINGS MILL LANE
GREAT SHELFORD
CAMBRIDGE CB22 5EN, UK

British Library Cataloguing-in-Publication Data.
A catalogue record for this book is
available from The British Library.

ISBN: 978 191114 396 paper

Front cover Arabic calligraphy by Arabiccalligraphy4you.

CONTENTS

Acknowledgements VII
Translator's Introduction IX

CHAPTER ONE: A Glorious Exposition of the Secrets of God in Making Adam Descend from the Garden to this Earth 1
CHAPTER TWO: The Infallibility of the Divine Decree from Being Evil 19
CHAPTER THREE: Affirming the Exalted Lord's Wisdom in His Creation and Commandments 43
CHAPTER FOUR: A Response to Those Who Deny God's Wisdom and Causality 72
CHAPTER FIVE: A Response to Those Who Question God's Wisdom in Creating Disbelief, Wickedness and Sin 94
CHAPTER SIX: A Response to Those Who Question God's Wisdom in Creating Iblīs and his Army 130
CHAPTER SEVEN: An Exposition of Whether the Punishment of Hellfire is Eternal 164
CHAPTER EIGHT: A Response to Those Who Question God's Wisdom in Allowing His Enemies to Overpower His Saints 194
CHAPTER NINE: An Exposition of the Statement of the Predecessors that One of the Principles of Faith is Contentment with Predestination Whether Good or Evil, Pleasing or Painful 201
CHAPTER TEN: The Impermissibility of Stating that the Lord Intends Evil or Performs It 203
CHAPTER ELEVEN: An Exposition of the Secrets Within the *Ḥadīth* of the Prophet, 'O God, I seek refuge in Your pleasure from Your wrath, and in Your forgiveness from Your punishment. I seek refuge in You from Yourself. I cannot praise You enough; You are as You have praised Yourself.' 209
CHAPTER TWELVE: Faith in the Divine Determination and Decree, His Justice, Monotheism and His Wisdom are all Included in the *Ḥadīth* of the Prophet, 'Your judgment upon me will be carried out and Your decree for me is just.' 214

CHAPTER THIRTEEN: The Rulings Regarding Contentment with His Decree and the Correct Position 223
CHAPTER FOURTEEN: The Division of Matters into the Ontological Pertaining to God's Creating and to the Religious Pertaining to God's Commandments 229
CHAPTER FIFTEEN: An Exposition of God's Wisdom in Allowing People to Sin 237

Notes 265
Bibliography 305
Index 313

ACKNOWLEDGEMENTS

I would like to again thank Andrew Booso for his meticulous and excellent editing, as well as his exceptional advice. He has made many significant contributions, which improved the fluency of the text, and ensured that Ashᶜarī viewpoints were represented in the Introduction. I am also grateful for the recomendations of Khalid Williams on an early version of Chapter One. I must express my deep appreciation to Fatima Azzam, the Director of Islamic Texts Society, for her enduring patience, invaluable advice and endless support of this project as well as *Ibn Qayyim al-Jawziyya on Knowledge*. It has been a great joy to work with Fatima and Andrew and without their efforts these two books would not have been possible. Any errors within it are, of course, due to my inadequacies and faults.

May God reward them as well as my parents and family for all the good they have done. All praise and gratitude is due to God. I ask God to accept this work and make it a source of goodness for others. In the Name of God, Most Beneficent, Most Merciful, we begin.

TRANSLATOR'S INTRODUCTION

Abū ʿAbd Allāh Shams al-Dīn Muḥammad b. Abī Bakr b. Ayyūb b. Saʿd al-Zurʿī al-Dimashqī, better known as Ibn Qayyim al-Jawziyya, was born outside of Damascus, Syria in 691/1292.[1] Ibn al-Qayyim was one of the most important scholars of the late-Ḥanbalī school, along with figures like Ibn al-Jawzī and Ibn Taymiyya.

Ibn al-Qayyim's name is inevitably attached to that of his famous teacher Taqī al-Dīn b. ʿAbd al-Ḥalīm b. Taymiyya (1263–1328 CE) whom he dedicated himself almost exclusively to from the age of twenty-one until the latter's death. It was only after Ibn Taymiyya's passing that Ibn al-Qayyim became an earnest author on a multitude of subjects. Ibn al-Qayyim's writings[2] spanned over more than twenty years. His foremost goal was to explain and establish the primacy of the Qur'ān and the Sunna, and that reason and revelation are congruous. Moreover, he sought to repudiate groups that stripped God of His Attributes or denied His wisdom and causality. This book—being derived from *Cure for Those Ailed in Questions Concerning Divine Decree, Predestination, Wisdom and Causality* (*Shifā' al-ʿalīl fī masā'il al-qaḍā' wa'l-qadar wa'l-ḥikma wa'l-taʿlīl*) and *Key to the Blissful Abode: Proclamation of the Sovereignty of Knowledge and Willpower* (*Miftāḥ dār al-saʿāda wa-manshūr wilāyat al-ʿilm wa'l-irāda*)[3]—seeks to address the aforementioned issues, as well as the problem of evil itself. Jon Hoover states that 'Ibn Qayyim al-Jawziyyah may well be the most prolific optimist in the Islamic tradition',[4] and he 'provides a more fully developed optimism than does Ibn Taymiyya himself'.[5]

Ibn al-Qayyim on Divine Wisdom and the Problem of Evil

Ibn al-Qayyim begins, in Chapter One, by alluding to twenty-six wisdoms behind God's creating humanity and making them reside on earth. He then rejects any attribution of evilness to the Holy

Lord, whether in regards to His Names (*asmāʾ*), Attributes (*ṣifāt*) or actions (*afʿāl*). This reality is substantiated by affirming God's holiness, praiseworthiness, sovereignty and righteousness.

Ibn al-Qayyim starts to reconcile the existence of evil by stating, 'Although the existence [of a particular good] may be better than its non-existence, its existence [in all situations] may result in forgoing (*fawāt*) something that is more beloved to God. Likewise, although the non-existence of something evil may be preferable to its existence [in one aspect] it may be that its existence is a means or a cause that leads [indirectly] to something more beloved to Him.'[6]

He asserts that one of the greatest reasons for the creation of both good and evil is to manifest God's Names, Attributes and actions in a manner which is concordant with His wisdom: 'If the effects of His Names and Attributes cannot become manifest, except by [creating] opposing [entities], then His wisdom deems it to be inevitable that He bring them into existence. Had they not been created, then His Attributes would not have become manifested; and this is implausible.'[7]

Ibn al-Qayyim affirms the existence of causes and causality, and denies that their presence is purposeless: 'The Sublime has linked effects to their causes in both religious (*sharʿan*) and ontological (*qadaran*) matters.[8] Due to God's wisdom He has established causes within His religious commandments and Divine Law, His ontological laws and determination, and His sovereignty and administration. Denying causation, forces and natures represents a rejection of vital necessities, a deprecation of reason and the innate nature, an affront to experience and reality, and an obstinate rejection of the Divine Law and recompense [in the Hereafter].'[9] He adds later, 'If there are wisdoms, advantages and benefits in the creation of intermediaries then their intermediation is not frivolous. The wisdom that results from their presence is not equivalent to how it would have been if they had been absent.'[10] In this manner, Ibn al-Qayyim rejects the occasionalism of the Ashʿariyya and affirms God's great wisdom.

The Ashʿariyya (represented by Rāzī in many of Ibn al-Qayyim's books) state that events need not be due to His wisdom (*ghayr muᶜallala*), but rather are due to His will alone. They also deny causality because they claim that it necessitates attributing a need to God and that He gains perfection through the accomplishment of such an objective, which would then suggest that He was deficient before its attainment.[11] Ibn al-Qayyim responds at length to these claims in Chapter Four, in particular.

It should also be mentioned that Rāzī did adopt a crass determinism[12] unlike other Ashᶜariyya. Ibn al-Qayyim further mentions and rejects Rāzī's claim in the latter's *al-Mabāḥith al-mashriqiyya* that God acts out of necessity: '[Rāzī states that] there is no way to reconcile what exists except by explaining that the Sublime's actions necessarily emanate from Him—not by [His] intention or free choice (*fāᶜilan bi'l-dhāt*)... [Rāzī thus adheres] to the methodology of those [philosophers] who are enemies of the messengers and the Islamic doctrines... Rāzī has no further opinion [on this matter].'[13]

In addition, Ibn al-Qayyim—like Ibn Taymiyya—rejects the claim of Juwaynī, another Ashᶜarī theologian, that 'God loves even the unbelief and iniquity that He creates'. The opposition to Juwaynī's position was based on the argument 'that God hates these evils [and that] what God loves is the belief and obedience that correspond to His prescriptive or legislative will (*irāda sharᶜiyya*). God does create things that He hates, but He does this only for the sake of a wise purpose that He loves... Ibn Taymiyya [and Ibn al-Qayyim thus] subordinate God's will to God's love'.[14]

Ovamir Anjum explains the stance of Ibn Taymiyya (as well as Ibn al-Qayyim) in the following terms: 'He rejected the Ashᶜarī view that denied that God had any interests, and hence any purpose, in His acts: [...] [Ibn Taymiyya says] "He the Exalted and Glorified is Most Wise, places everything in a place appropriate for it, and it is not permissible for him (*lā yajūzu ᶜalayhi*) to equate the essence of truth and falsehood, or the just and the unjust, or the knowing and the ignorant, or the reformer and the corrupter."'[15]

Sherman Jackson takes issue though with Ibn Taymiyya's position in the following terms:

> [T]he going opinion in Ash'arism was also that God's ontological decree is separate and distinct from God's deontological

> decree. Thus, not everything God decrees ontologically could be said to reflect God's pleasure. Nor could one assume that because God prefers a particular thing that God would necessarily bring it into actual existence. Ibn Taymīya proceeds on the assumption, however, that this is *not* the position of Ash'arism and that according to them, God's will, love, pleasure, desire, displeasure, wrath, and the like are all synonymous. This is clearly an overstatement on his part. And he appears to have been compelled to this move in order to pull the rug out from underneath a particularly intractable form of antinomian Sufism that had located in the articulations of a few prominent Ash'arites a theological justification for antinomianism... [The] works of al-Ash'arī and al-Juwaynī contained language suggesting that there is no distinction between God's will, love, desire, and the like. Ibn Taymīya proceeds as if this represents the position of Ash'arism as a whole. Clearly, however, he could not have been unaware of other statements by these men—not to mention other Ash'arites—that flatly contradicted this view. Indeed, the very works he cites of al-Ash'arī and al-Juwaynī contain language that differentiates between God's will and God's preference.[16]

Indeed, late-Ashᶜarī doctrine seeks to defend itself against being misunderstood as denying God's acting with wisdom, as evidenced in the words of Ibrāhīm al-Bājūrī in his commentary on Sanūsī's *Umm al-barāhīn*: 'You should know that although His actions and judgments are transcendent and exalted beyond motives, they still contain wisdom [*ḥikma*], even if it does not reach our rational minds. If His actions were without wisdom, they would be futile, and that is impossible for Him, the Exalted.' Hence, a late-Ashᶜarī like Ibrāhīm b. Aḥmad al-Mārghanī further clarified that 'Wisdom is the *result* of an action or judgment and it is not a *motivator* for a particular thing.'[17]

Next, Ibn al-Qayyim moves on to affirm that what exists is either itself purely good, or preponderantly good, or indirectly leads to greater goods: 'God (Glory be to Him) has left out some things, which may have resulted in wise purposes had He created them, either because of the absence of His love for their existence, or because their existence would have prevented the existence of something more beloved to Him or led to its lapse. In these cases, His wisdom in not creating those entities preponderates over His wisdom in creating them... Consequently, God's creating and commanding are based upon attaining what is purely advantageous or what is preponderantly so, and allowing the lesser [good] to lapse; hence preventing what is purely harmful or what is preponderantly so.'[18]

Such a doctrine conforms to some writings of the Ashʿariyya. For instance, Ghazālī writes, 'There is no evil in existence which does not contain some good within it, and were that evil to be eliminated, the good within it would be nullified, and the final result would be an evil worse than the evil containing the good.'[19]

Ibn al-Qayyim also includes many of God's wisdoms in His permitting the existence of evil and Satan. Elucidation of these will be left to the text; however, for instance, Ibn al-Qayyim maintains that 'the creation of Iblīs and his army has [indirectly] led to the establishment of [waging battle and striving in His path] and their consequences,'[20] and 'Had those who were faithful and righteous been the overwhelming majority, then the possibility of waging battle [in His path]—which is one of the most eminent types of worship—would have eluded us.'[21] Ibn al-Qayyim emphasizes in many instances that the higher levels of Paradise can only be reached by 'traversing a bridge of hardships and tribulations'.[22]

The last chapter discusses thirty wise purposes and secrets associated with allowing people to sin. Prominent among them are that God loves repentance and loves to manifest His Attributes of forgiveness and mercy; so that the believer may become humble rather than proud; and so he may recognize that it is only his deficient nature, ignorance and injustice which results in sin. Finally, Ibn al-Qayyim emphasizes that 'We should recognize that everything that He has commanded encompasses far-reaching wisdoms. As for the detailed secrets of these wise purposes, they are not attainable for all of humanity. Rather, God provides insight to those whom He wishes of His creation to what He wills.'[23]

The Premise of the Problem of Evil

At this juncture, a brief survey of Muslim approaches to the problem of evil will help situate the point of departure for Ibn al-Qayyim, and his teacher Ibn Taymiyya, in this regard. Of course, it is important to remember that the latter two considered their methodology to be that of the Predecessors (*salaf*), so any perceived contravention of such principles was to be discussed and refuted. Ibn al-Qayyim quotes Ibn Taymiyya as saying,

> The basis for many people going astray—no matter their school—
> Is seeking out the reasons for God's actions.[24]

The first major break from the Predecessors came from the Qadariyya. The impetus for the Qadariyya doctrine was their attempt to explain that the existence of evil could not arise from God. Ibn al-Qayyim states that both the Qadariyya and Jabriyya claimed that God's actions are the same as what He enacts. The Qadariyya added that 'since His acts are not evil, then evil also cannot be enacted by Him; therefore, [in their opinion], evil is created by humans.'[25] Thus, in trying to justify the presence of evil, the Qadariyya placed its creation in the human realm. The Jabriyya, on the other hand, asserted a crass determinism as the basis for human works. They claimed that the 'Lord (Glory be to Him) wills evil and carries it out' and 'since evil exists, it is inevitable that there be someone to create it, and there is no Creator except God. God creates through His will, therefore every creature is willed by Him and is an act of His.'[26]

The Muʿtazila followed in the footsteps of the Qadariyya on this issue by claiming that humans are the creators of their acts, both evil and good. They obligated God to do what is beneficial and most advantageous (*al-ṣalāḥ wa'l-aṣlaḥ*) for humanity and to be omnibenevolent, thus denying His freedom of action. They claimed that if He were to act in a contrary manner then He would be deemed unjust. Hoover states, 'Muʿtazilī Kalām theology provides the primary instance of an Islamic free-will theodicy... Humans for their part have free will and create their own good and bad deeds apart from God's control.'[27] Ibn al-Qayyim is highly critical of this doctrine as well as their denial of God's wisdom.

The Ashʿarī doctrine came in response to the Muʿtazila. It began with its eponymous founder, Abū al-Ḥasan al-Ashʿarī, who rejected the Muʿtazilī doctrine after initially adhering to it.[28] In that light, Jackson states that 'when the Ash'arites deny, for example, that God *must* act in the interest of humans or that God *must* indemnify them for any unearned suffering God inflicts, they are not denying that God *may* or even *does* do these things. They are simply denying that God *must* do these things, especially on the basis of historically informed or socially constructed notions of justice or goodness that are independent of God's self-disclosure'.[29]

Shihadeh interprets Ashʿarī doctrine as advancing a 'theological voluntarism:[30] the view that God's will and acts are free and never subject to ethical considerations.' Yet he argues that 'classical Ashʿarism… did not subscribe to a simple divine command theory of ethics, but in fact grounded this theory in a fairly developed anti-realism,[31] which became the basis for the more sophisticated consequentialist ethics[32] advanced in neo-Ashʿarite sources [like Rāzī]'.[33]

That said, Hoover summarizes the Ashʿarī approach to theodicy in the following manner: 'The voluntarism of Ashʿarī Kalām theology rejects the question of theodicy as meaningless. God's unfettered will, sufficiency apart from the world, and exclusive power preclude asking why God does this or that. God is not limited by any necessity of reason, and His acts require no deliberation, rational motive or external cause. Thus, God's creation of injustice, unbelief and other evils is not susceptible to any explanation except that God wills it.'[34]

Of note, Ibn al-Qayyim initially held the Ashʿarī creed until meeting Ibn Taymiyya. As mentioned previously, Ibn al-Qayyim dedicates much of his discussion in this book to repudiating Ashʿarī doctrine. He also rebuts it in his books *al-Sawāʿiq al-mursala* and *al-Qaṣīdah al-nūniyya*. Despite that, Ashʿarī creed has been adopted by a majority of Sunni theologians. It could be posited that elaborations on the issue of theodicy or the problem of evil have been marginalized as a result of the Ashʿarī doctrine claiming that God's actions need not occur for a wise purpose. [35]

Now, Ibn al-Qayyim does not specifically mention Māturīdī doctrine in either *Shifā' al-ʿalīl* or *Miftāḥ dār al-saʿāda* (or in any of his other books for that matter). It may be due to the fact that Abū Manṣūr Muḥammad al-Māturīdī (d. 333/944) affirmed God's wisdom, which he defined as 'putting everything in its proper place' (*waḍʿu kulli shay'in mawḍiʿahu*).[36] This again is in contrast to many of the Ashʿariyya, who upheld divine omnipotence, contended divine command ethics and claimed that God could have done or commanded the opposite. Māturīdī also maintained that 'bringing into existence is not identical with what is brought into existence (*al-takwīn ghayr al-mukawwan*)', unlike the Muʿtazila and Ashʿariyya.[37] This formulation is similar to the Traditionalist viewpoint that God's actions are different than what He enacts. Finally, the Māturīdiyya (like the Traditionalists and the Ashʿariyya) maintained God's freedom to do as He wills (unlike the Muʿtazila, the philosophers, and Rāzī in some of his writings). Sherman Jackson's study of the Muʿtazilī, Ashʿarī, Māturīdī and Traditionalist doctrines in relation to the problem of black suffering concluded that divine omnibenevolence and omnipotence for the first two groups 'serve to exonerate God of evil', while the Māturīdiyya contended that God allows evil only if it can 'serve a wise end'.[38] Therefore, the Māturīdiyya affirmed that God creates everything, including evil, but that He allows evil for certain wise purposes. The Māturīdiyya did not, however, delve into those wisdoms[39] as much as Ibn al-Qayyim does in this book.

Before concluding this section mention should be made of Avicenna (Ibn Sīnā), the prominent Islamic philosopher who incorporated Neoplatonic elements into his notion of theodicy and philosophy. He claimed an emanative theory regarding this world, as explained by Michael Marmura: 'Al-Fārābī formulated a dyadic emanative scheme, [whereas] Avicenna transforms [it] into a triadic one. Accordingly after the emanation of the first intellect from God, the series that ensues is a series of celestial triads. Each triad consists of an intellect, a soul, and a sphere.'[40] This emanative scheme holds that God's creation necessarily emanates from Him, without His free will or choice (*mūjiban bi'l-dhāt*)—God is infallible above that.

According to Shams Inati, Avicenna's 'solution' for the problem of evil can be summarized as follows: 1) God is good and providential, but precisely because of His goodness, God cannot intend any good or evil in the world; 2) there is more good than evil in the universe—essential evil is rare, only non-essential evil is predominant; 3) evil is a necessary consequence of good, and to wish the removal of evil is to wish the removal of good; 4) evil is a necessary means for the good; 5) God is not omnipotent—that is, God cannot free the world from evil; 6) essential evil is privation of being, and therefore cannot be caused by God, who is the cause of being only; and 7) human evil is due to human free will, resulting from knowledge.[41]

Now, the most problematic aspects of Avicenna's 'solution' are the first, fifth and sixth positions, which limit God's power and creative ability. Denying God's omnipotence is heretical and contradicts the Qur'ān, which states in thirty-five verses that God is able to do all things. Inati states that Avicenna 'must have adhered to this thesis... [but he did not explicitly deny God's omnipotence] for fear of the theologians'.[42] This theory and the notion that God acts out of necessity both represent the Divine as being compelled—and God is again infallible above all these claims.

For these reasons, as well as many others, Ibn al-Qayyim characterizes Avicenna as 'the leader of the heretics' (*shaykh al-mulḥidīn*).[43] Likewise, Ghazālī[44] deemed Avicenna to be a disbeliever, as the latter claimed that the world is pre-eternal, denied God's knowledge of particulars, and denied bodily resurrection.[45]

Ghazālī and the Best of all Possible Worlds

Eric Ormsby investigated Ghazālī's statement, 'There is not in possibility anything whatever more excellent, more perfect, and more complete than it. For if there were and He had withheld it, having power to create it but not deigning to do so, this would be miserliness contrary to the divine generosity and injustice contrary to the divine justice. But if He were not able, it would be incapability contrary to divinity.'[46] This statement 'engendered a controversy that lasted from [Ghazālī's] own lifetime until well into the 19th century'.[47] Ormsby then went on to discuss the various positions held by the subsequent scholars of Islam.[48] In the pro-camp, Ormsby lists: Ibn

ʿArabī (d. 638/1240), Taqī al-Dīn al-Subkī (d. 756/1355), Jalāl al-Dīn al-Suyūṭī (d. 911/1505) and Murtaḍā al-Zabīdī (d. 1205/1791), among others. Prominent scholars in the contra-camp include: Abū Bakr b. al-ʿArabī (d. 543/1148), Ibn al-Jawzī (d. 597/1200) and Ibrāhīm b. ʿUmar Burhān al-Dīn al-Biqāʿī (d. 885/1480).

Suyūṭī wrote *Tashyīd al-arkān fī laysa fi'l-imkān abdaʿ mimmā kān* in support of Ghazālī's dictum.[49] Suyūṭī responds to those who contend that the dictum contradicts God's omnipotence by saying, 'It does not contradict [the belief] that God can create into existence something other than what exists, rather [it refutes the possibility] that the alternative be more wonderful than what exists. The "Proof of Islam" rejected that there could exist something more wonderful than what exists, despite affirming that He has the power to [create otherwise]. We also affirm that God is capable [of creating something better]. God (Exalted is He) has said, *And if thy Lord willed, all who are in the earth would have believed together* [Q.X.99]. But what Ghazālī has rejected is this possibility being more wonderful than what currently exists.'[50] Suyūṭī maintains that humanity's division into believers and disbelievers and the wide spectrum of people is deemed to be 'most wonderful'.[51] Suyūṭī then states, 'God knew all the possible states that a creature could be originated in, and therefore He selected the most wonderful aspect in which to do so… This is due to God's knowledge of the wisdom of creating it in such fashion.'[52]

Suyūṭī discusses Ghazālī's explanation of the dictum in the following terms: 'For if there were [anything more wonderful] and He had withheld it, having power to create it but not deigning to do so, this would be miserliness contrary to the divine grace and injustice contrary to the divine justice. But if He were not able [to fashion an alternative], it would amount to an incapacity that is contrary to divinity.'[53] Suyūṭī then argues,

> People were confused by this statement and said that it is more in line with the doctrine of the Muʿtazila who state that God is obligated to provide what is most advantageous. Ahl al-Sunna maintain that it is not necessary that God acts [always] in a manner that represents His grace, and He can remain just without

> doing so. I continued to think about this for many days until God granted and inspired me with the answer, and all praise is due to God. The 'Proof of Islam' (may God be pleased with him) wanted to make this dictum consistent with the doctrine of both groups. In regards to Ahl al-Sunna, it would have contradicted His grace had He withheld. As for the doctrine of the Muᶜtazila, had He withheld that would have contradicted His justice. Thus this dictum takes into account the doctrine of both groups...[54] Behind all this is the secret of [God's] determination (*sirr al-qadar*), which the vast majority have been perplexed by, while those who are unveiled to it are prohibited from elucidating it.[55]

So Suyūṭī argues that, in order to maintain our amazement with His determination, God keeps it a secret. In addition, he gives the example of al-Khiḍr, and how after he unveiled the secrets behind his actions, Moses' amazement with them ceased.[56]

Now, Ormsby did not include Ibn Taymiyya within the list of disputants. Nonetheless, Hoover mentions that Ibn Taymiyya commented on Ghazālī's dictum in three instances; in the first two, Ibn Taymiyya rejected it because it could be easily misinterpreted as limiting God's power or stating that God is necessitating in His Essence (*dhāt*). Subsequently, Ibn Taymiyya reinterpreted the dictum in his treatise *Qāᶜida fī maᶜna kawn al-Rabb ᶜādilan* stating, 'It could mean that no better (*aḥsan*) than this [world] or no more perfect (*akmal*) than this is possible (*yumkin*). This is not a defamation of power. Rather, it has established His power [to do] other than what He has done. However, it says, "What He has done is better and more perfect than what He has not done." This ascribes to Him (Glory be to Him) generosity, liberality and beneficence. He (Glory be to Him) is the most generous. No more generous (*akram*) [being] than He can be conceived.'[57]

Hoover states that Ibn Taymiyya thus 'accepts al-Ghazālī's statement on the condition that it is understood that God could have created other than He did. However, what God did create is the best of all possible worlds because He is the most perfect and generous being imaginable. With this, Ibn Taymiyya becomes one of the earliest scholars after Ibn ʿArabī to accept al-Ghazālī's dictum before it became widely accepted from the mid-eighth/fourteenth century onward.'[58]

Now, Ormsby did mention Ibn al-Qayyim's name in this regard; however, his position on the dictum was not elaborated upon.[59] To be sure, Ibn al-Qayyim does not comment directly on the matter; nonetheless, we may infer his stance from a few passages. Before that, it should be recognized that Ibn al-Qayyim's methodology is to never criticise some of the major scholars by name (Ghazālī being one of them). This is unlike Ibn Taymiyya who, for example, directly criticises Ghazālī for adopting Greek logic during most of his life,[60] for including many fabricated *ḥadīths* in his writings,[61] and for granting mystical unveiling more than its due in achieving religious knowledge.[62] Ibn al-Qayyim never mentions Ghazālī's name although he does agree with Ibn Taymiyya in these matters.

Ibn Kathīr reported that 'Ibn al-Qayyim was very loving, and he never envied others or caused harm to them. He never pointed out the inadequacies of others nor harboured envy of them... I do not know of anyone living in our time who is a greater worshipper than him. His custom in prayer was to prolong it greatly, including the bowing and prostrating. Many of his colleagues would occasionally criticize him for that, but he would not respond to them nor would he abandon [his practice]. May God (Exalted is He) have mercy on him!'[63]

Ibn al-Qayyim therefore only mentions Ghazālī by name when he agrees with him. For instance, in *Miftāḥ dār al-saʿāda*, Ibn al-Qayyim mentions that he agrees with Ghazālī that there is no need to discuss the branches of speculative theology and philosophy, because 'all the beneficial proofs found in speculative theology are encompassed within the Qur'ān and the Traditions of the Prophet... None of this existed in the first period [of Islam] whereby it was considered a [blameworthy] innovation to take up [speculative theology]'.[64]

Ibn al-Qayyim instead merely alludes to what he considers to be intellectual mistakes by the major scholars in a discrete manner. Ghazālī's dictum again is: 'There is not in possibility anything more wonderful (*abdaʿ*) than what exists.' Now, Ibn al-Qayyim uses the word 'dazzling/wonderful' (*badīʿa*) more than fifteen times in *Ibn Qayyim al-Jawziyya on Divine Wisdom*—all of these being in reference to God's wisdom (*ḥikmatuhu al-badīʿa*). Yet Ibn al-Qayyim never utilizes the word *badīʿa* to describe this world. For instance, he affirms 'the complete nature of His dazzling wisdom and overwhelming omnipotence';[65] and that the creation of 'opposites is in order to manifest His dazzling wisdom, vanquishing power, accomplished will, and perfect and complete sovereignty'.[66]

Next, Ibn al-Qayyim differentiates between God's actions versus what He enacts or wills: 'God's actions themselves (Glory be to Him) are not divided [into beloved or not], since all of His actions are beloved and pleasing to Him. Therefore, one must differentiate between His actions and what He enacts. His actions are all pure good, just, advantageous and wise—there is no evil within them from any aspect whatsoever. As for what He enacts, it is subject to division [into good or not].'[67] Consequently, it becomes clear, for him, that God's wisdom—which is an Attribute of His for He is the Most Wise—as well as His actions are dazzling, whereas that which He enacts, i.e. this world and what it contains, may be divided into aspects that are wonderful or not: 'God (Glory be to Him) created three abodes: one that is purely dedicated to bliss, pleasure, delight and joy; one that is purely dedicated to pain, suffering, calamities and evils; and one that is mixed having both good and evil, bliss and wretchedness, pleasure and pain.'[68]

Ibn al-Qayyim also mentions that if the Muʿtazilī claim that God is obligated to act in a manner that is beneficial and most advantageous (*al-ṣalāḥ wa'l-aṣlaḥ*) were correct, then His beneficence, kindness and grace must be granted to all in an equal fashion; however, he continues, higher degrees of benefit or advantage can always be postulated.[69] The fact of this reasoning can also be perceived in relation to Paradise where Ibn al-Qayyim states that God's 'wisdom dictated that He would create and structure Paradise with progressively higher levels, some on top of others, and that He will populate Adam and his offspring [who are believers] within it according to their deeds'.[70] God (Glorious is He) therefore could have created an even better Paradise—having all believers occupy an equivalent superior rank whereby they could enjoy the same bliss—but even in that case the level of bliss within that rank could be extended to a higher degree. Therefore, characterizing this world or even Paradise as being the 'best' is only congruent in some aspects—neither can be generally deemed as such. Ibn al-Qayyim thus maintains that God (Exalted is He) has, in reality, structured both this world and Paradise concordant with His divine wisdom.

To be clear, regarding this world, Ibn al-Qayyim states, 'The greatest injustice, clearest ignorance, most repugnant abomination, greatest insolence and shamelessness occurs in the case of one… who criticizes God's wisdom and thinks that something other than what He has determined and foreordained would have been more appropriate. Glory be to God, the Lord of the Worlds, for He is infallible in His sovereignty, divinity and greatness.'[71] By this, Ibn al-Qayyim means that God created this world in order to achieve the wise purposes He has dictated. These include manifesting His Names and Attributes in a fashion, which is consistent with His wisdom, mercy, beneficence and justice, as well as many other wisdoms that Ibn al-Qayyim has mentioned throughout this book.

In summary, characterizing existence, i.e. what God has enacted or willed, as being wonderful is ambiguous, for there is much suffering, evil and disbelief in this world. Ibn al-Qayyim avoids all that by maintaining that it is God's wisdom, which is dazzling/wonderful. It seems that the best way to reconcile Ghazālī's dictum and Ibn al-Qayyim's position is to state, 'What is good in this world is more wonderful than if good existed alone, and God has many dazzling wisdoms in mixing good and evil herein.'

Ibn al-Qayyim's Investigation on the Duration of Hellfire

There is agreement amongst Ahl al-Sunna that the believers who have perpetrated a major sin and enter Hellfire will exit it after being initially punished therein. The Khawārij though disagreed and claimed that such people will be eternally punished in Hellfire. The Muʿtazila accorded them an intermediary status whereby such a perpetrator is neither a believer nor a disbeliever; thus claiming that they will be punished forever in Hellfire but to a lesser degree than the disbelievers. Numerous scholars from the Ahl al-Sunna maintain that there is scholarly unanimity (*ijmāʿ*) that only the disbelievers will be eternally punished in Hellfire.[72]

Khalil states that 'like other Ashʿarites, Ghazālī maintains that true unbelievers will remain in Hell "forever" (*ʿalā al-taʾbīd*),' but then he adds:

> Yet I would be remiss not to mention Ghazālī's cryptic conclusion to his exposition of the divine names, the Compassionate and the Caring: 'Never doubt that [God] is "the most merciful of the merciful" [Q. 7:151], or that "His mercy outstrips His wrath," and never doubt that the one who intends evil for the sake of evil and not for the sake of good is undeserving of the name of mercy. Beneath all this lies a secret whose divulgence the revealed law [*al-sharʿ*] prohibits, so be content with prayer and do not expect that it be divulged.' Ghazālī goes on to state that this 'secret' is not discernable to most people. One can only wonder what it is. Given the available evidence, however, it would be difficult to aver that this is a sign of his being a closet universalist.[73]

Now, Ibn al-Qayyim, although fairly categorised within Ahl al-Sunna, investigates at length whether the punishment of Hellfire is truly eternal for the disbelievers. His arguments and the perception of his position have earned him a good share of scholarly attention.[74] Hoover has stated that, although the topic of Hell's chastisement for disbelievers being of 'limited duration' had been discussed before by Rāzī, Ibn al-Qayyim's arguments on the topic 'appear to be unprecedented in their thoroughness and length'.[75]

By way of context, Ibn al-Qayyim had requested Ibn Taymiyya to opine on this matter, and so the latter wrote *al-Radd ʿalā man qāl bi-fanāʾ al-jannah waʾl-nār*—this being his last work. Ibn al-Qayyim many years later engaged the matter in *Ḥādī al-arwāḥ ilā bilād al-afrāḥ*, but not to the extent of his discussions within *Shifāʾ al-ʿalīl*. He also addressed it further in *al-Ṣawāʿiq al-mursala*, and this will be discussed below.

In essence, Ibn al-Qayyim (as well as Ibn Taymiyya) maintained that many of the Predecessors held the opinion that the punishment of Hellfire will eventually end for the disbelievers. Since many Predecessors held that viewpoint, in their estimation, and since we know that God is the Beneficent and Merciful, Ibn al-Qayyim alludes to the conclusion that the punishment of the disbelievers may ultimately end.

Nāṣir al-Dīn al-Albānī, the pre-eminent *Ḥadīth* scholar, concluded that all of the traditions from the Predecessors mentioned by Ibn al-Qayyim arguing for the ending of Hellfire or the removal of the disbelievers from it are neither authentic nor sound, and therefore cannot be relied upon to render a judgment in this matter.[76] Regardless, Ibn al-Qayyim states at the end of his exposition on the matter,

> My position in this matter is the same as that of the Emir of the Believers ʿAlī b. Abī Ṭālib (may God be pleased with him). He mentioned the entrance of the inhabitants of Paradise into Paradise and the denizens of Hellfire into Hellfire, and he described that in the best manner. Then he said, 'Thereafter God will do what He wills with His creation.' [...] I likewise agree with the view of Qatāda as he said, regarding His statement, *Save for that which thy Lord willeth*,[77] 'God is more knowledgeable about the interpretation of this.' I similarly agree with the view of [ʿAbd al-Raḥmān] ibn Zayd [b. Aslam] as he said, 'God informed us about what He wills for the inhabitants of Paradise when He said *a gift unfailing*;[78] but He did not inform us regarding His [ultimate] will for the denizens of Hellfire.'
>
> The viewpoint that Hellfire and its punishment are eternal just as God is eternal represents a notification about what God (Almighty and Most Glorious is He) will do. If something is not concordant with what He has informed us, then it represents something that is said about Him without knowledge. The texts do not substantiate [the punishment of Hellfire being eternal], and God knows best.[79]

Of note, Ibn al-Qayyim also related, in *Shifāʾ al-ʿalīl*, the arguments of one group who claim that the disbelievers will be entered into Paradise after their punishment in Hellfire is concluded. This group states, 'God (Glory be to Him) informed us that His mercy encompasses everything, that His mercy prevails over His wrath, and that He has prescribed mercy upon Himself. Therefore, it is inevitable that His mercy encompass [even] those being punished. Had those [disbelievers] remained in the punishment for an unlimited [duration], then His mercy would never encompass them. This is patently obvious... The point is that [ultimately His] mercy will necessarily encompass the denizens of Hellfire. His mercy inevitably extends [to everything] just as [His] knowledge does. The angels said, *Thou comprehendest all things in mercy and knowledge*.'[80]

Moreover, one of this group's arguments is that God endowed humanity with an innate disposition (*fiṭra*), which is good and pure. They state, 'The secret of this question is that the original innate disposition must inevitably manifest itself, just as the extraneous incident did its work. This innate disposition is universal to all of Adam's offspring.'[81] They explain, 'Had the evil and unjust souls been returned to this world before being punished, they would have returned to what they were forbidden. They are not suitable to live in the abode of peace [i.e. Paradise] as it is incompatible with lies, denial, evils and injustices. But if these souls are punished in Hellfire such that they are expunged from their evils and wickedness, the wisdom of that would be considered reasonable. But the creation of souls whose evilness never vanishes whatsoever as they are pure evil and deserving of eternal and everlasting punishment—this is not consistent with [His] wisdom and mercy, even if He is capable [of punishing the denizens eternally].'[82]

As a consequence of Ibn al-Qayyim relating at some length the position of this aforementioned group, some have claimed that Ibn al-Qayyim held this viewpoint himself in *Shifāʾ al-ʿalīl*. Nevertheless, Ibn al-Qayyim's opinion in the *Shifāʾ* is only that the punishment of the denizens of Hell will end, and nothing further. Ibn al-Qayyim mentions that his opinion is in accordance with the stances of ʿAlī, Qatāda et al., as mentioned previously.

He subsequently writes that since most of humanity are disbelievers, this 'corroborates the viewpoint of the Companions and Successors regarding this issue [i.e. that the punishment of Hellfire will end], and that it all goes back to [His] mercy, which has encompassed everything, has preceded [His] anger, and will prevail over it'.[83]

Although Ibn al-Qayyim does investigate further issues regarding the innate disposition in the concluding chapters of *Shifāʾ al-ʿalīl* (not translated herein), he never goes beyond his aforementioned opinion.

One may think of the inclusion of this group's opinion in the same manner as Ibn al-Qayyim's exposition in *Miftāḥ dār al-saʿāda* of whether the Garden of Adam and Eve was in Paradise, in the heavens, or on this earth. Ibn al-Qayyim's inclusion of the opinion of those who hold that the Garden was in the heavens or on this earth (rather than Paradise) is because it, although incorrect in his view, does not contradict God's wisdom.[84]

The point is that, even though Ibn al-Qayyim mentioned the opinion of a group who claimed universal salvation, this does not indicate that he espoused those views at the time he wrote *Shifāʾ al-ʿalīl*. That said, by the time Ibn al-Qayyim writes *al-Ṣawāʿiq al-mursala*, he considers that group's opinion to be his own. In *al-Ṣawāʿiq* he also adds another argument:

> Hellfire was created to absolve people of their evils. How can these causes [i.e. evil sins] remain after the disbelievers have tasted its punishment and severe pain. At that point they become certain that their sins were harmful to them, will greatly regret them, will witness that they were unjust, and that God (Exalted is He) has justly punished them. In that context they will praise, thank and extol Him in accordance with His Names and Attributes, which they were innately disposed to. If all this is present in their hearts in reality, and God is content with that, then Hellfire will become cool and peaceful. Ibn Abī al-Dunyā related a tradition in his book *Ḥusn al-dhann bi'llāh*: 'Two men who entered Hellfire were screaming out loud so God (Exalted is He) commanded that they be removed. God then asks them, "Why are you screaming out loud?" They respond, "We did that so You would have mercy upon us." God then says, "My mercy entails that you both go back to where you were in Hellfire." One of them will go back, and at that point God will render it cool and peaceful. The other will not and therefore the Lord will say to the latter, "What prevented you from going back as your companion did?" He will respond, "My Lord, I

> hope that You will not return me to it after You had removed me from it." The Lord will then say, "Your hope will be fulfilled," and they will both be entered into Paradise together.'[85]

Therefore, the essence of Ibn al-Qayyim's argument is that since all of humanity possesses an innate disposition, which is good, after the disbelievers are punished in Hellfire—no matter how long—only their innate disposition will remain, and hence they will be ultimately saved.

This argument, however, is a rational one predicated mainly on God's mercy and is not substantiated in other aspects within the Qur'ān or the Sunna. On the other hand, consider for instance the verse, *Those who believe, then disbelieve and then (again) believe, then disbelieve, and then increase in disbelief, God will never pardon them, nor will He guide them unto a way.*[86] This pertains to those who ultimately die as disbelievers but freely chose to believe—possibly at two earlier points in their lives—and yet God states that He will never pardon them. Are not then those who only lived a life of disbelief—never freely choosing to believe, despite possessing an innate disposition which they were endowed with by God—less worthy of being pardoned? By way of seemingly ending the dispute, one can read God (Exalted is He) saying, *It does not behove the Prophet, and those who have attained to faith to pray that they who ascribed divinity (li'l-mushrikīn) to aught beside God be forgiven [by Him] even though they happened to be [their] near of kin—after it has been made clear unto them that those [dead sinners] are destined for the blazing Fire.*[87]

Now, Taqī al-Dīn al-Subkī, who was the chief judge in Damascus and an Ashᶜarī, wrote his letter *al-Iᶜtibār bi-baqā' al-janna wa'l-nār*[88] by way of addressing many of the arguments that Ibn al-Qayyim (as well as Ibn Taymiyya) had advanced on the question of Hell's eternality, albeit without referring to them by name (hence the confusion as to whom Subkī was directly responding to).[89] As a result, we might presume, Ibn al-Qayyim ultimately abandoned a position of universal salvation. In *Zād al-maᶜād*, considered to be Ibn al-Qayyim's last work,[90] he states, 'Since those who worship others [besides God] have a nature and essence which is wicked, they will never be purified through [the punishment of] Hellfire… For this reason, God (Exalted is He) has prohibited those who have worshipped others from entering Paradise.'[91] May God reward Taqī al-Dīn for his efforts in this regard! This, however, does not indicate that Ibn al-Qayyim abandoned his position that the punishment of the disbelievers will end.

Subkī, in addition to the aforementioned, went further stating, 'Whoever claims that Hellfire and Paradise will both be annihilated, or [contends that] only one of them [i.e. Hellfire] will be, is a disbeliever.'[92] For Subkī, the consensus on the matter precluded any individual scholarly deduction (*ijtihād*).[93] However, characterizing the latter contention as 'disbelief' appears to not be explicitly substantiated by the Qur'ān alone—the punishment of a disbeliever in Hellfire may end in light of God's mercy, some interpretations of verse 107 of Sūrat Hūd,[94] as well as other arguments advanced by Ibn al-Qayyim in Chapter Seven, and God knows best.

The Methodology of this Translation

The majority of *Ibn Qayyim al-Jawziyya on Divine Wisdom and the Problem of Evil* is derived from *Shifā' al-ʿalīl*. This was based on the critical edition edited by ʿAlī b. Muḥammad b. ʿAbd Allāh al-ʿAjlān and Aḥmad b. Ṣāliḥ b. ʿAlī al-Ṣamʿānī. It was published in Riyadh by Dār al-Ṣamayʿī in 2013. The text translated here is found in volume III, Chapters (*bābs*) 21–29, and it represents Chapters Two to Fourteen in *Ibn Qayyim al-Jawziyya on Divine Wisdom and the Problem of Evil*. Chapters One and Fifteen of this translation were derived from the beginning and end, respectively, of part I of *Miftāḥ dār al-saʿāda* published by Dār al-Ḥadīth, Cairo. A critical edition was also referenced: its second edition has been published in Mecca by Dār ʿĀlim al-Fawā'id and edited by ʿAbd al-Raḥmān b. Ḥasan b. Qā'id. The pages referenced in this book are to this critical edition of the *Miftāḥ*.

The headings for Chapters One to Three and Chapters Nine to Fourteen are derived directly from Ibn al-Qayyim's original choices (with occasional adaptation), while those for Chapters Four to Eight and Fifteen have been provided by us in order to better convey the content of a chapter (in particular, Chapters Four through Eight).

The English translations of the Qur'ānic verses were derived from Pickthall in the vast majority of cases, with his older English style often retained, although his use of 'lo!' was largely omitted. The translations of Yusuf Ali and Muḥammad Asad were utilized on occasions when they more accurately portrayed the meaning put forward by Ibn al-Qayyim in his text. Of note, as per the Islamic Texts Society usage, *God* is used in place of *Allah*.

The English translations of the six canonical books of *Ḥadīth*—Bukhārī, Muslim, Tirmidhī, Ibn Māja, Nasā'ī and Abū Dāwūd—published by Darussalam have also been utilized, adapted and referenced. *Ḥadīth*s were also found in the following collections: *Muwaṭṭa' al-Imām Mālik*, *Musnad al-Imām Aḥmad* and Aḥmad's *Zuhd*—references to 'Aḥmad' alone are indications of narrations found in the *Musnad*—*Sunan al-Dārimī*, Bayhaqī's *Sunan* and *Shuᶜab al-īmān*, al-Ḥākim's *al-Mustadrak ᶜalā'l-Ṣaḥīḥayn*, *Ṣaḥīḥ Ibn Ḥibbān*, Abu Nuᶜaym's *Ḥilya*, Mundhirī's *al-Targhīb wa'l-tarhīb*, Haythamī's *Majmaᶜ al-zawā'id*, Ibn ᶜAbd al-Barr's *Jāmiᶜ bayān al-ᶜilm wa-faḍlih*, Tabrīzī's *Mishkāt al-maṣābīḥ* and al-Khaṭīb al-Baghdādī's *Tārīkh Baghdād*. When quoted, the *ḥadīth* numbers are referenced to editions of these books which are included on the website shamela.ws or its application, and mentioned in the Bibliography. In addition, any chains of narrators have been shortened to only include the immediate Companion of the Prophet who narrates it. Furthermore, in order to prevent the referencing of *ḥadīth* from being over-bearing for the reader, if a tradition was found in either *Ṣaḥīḥ al-Bukhārī* or *Ṣaḥīḥ Muslim* then references were limited to the 'Six Books' and *Musnad al-Imām Aḥmad*. If not present in the two *Ṣaḥiḥ*s, then the aforementioned collections were also cited. Also, in the footnote references, there is usually only the mention of the collector's name and the number of the tradition; however, in other instances, in regards to some lesser-known collections, the author, page number and volume is given (with the Bibliography considered sufficient for clarifying publication details in both instances). Finally, all *ḥadīth*s other than those present in *Ṣaḥīḥ al-Bukhārī* and *Ṣaḥīḥ Muslim* were categorized as 'authentic' (*ṣaḥīḥ*), 'sound' (*ḥasan*), 'weak' (*ḍaᶜīf*) or 'fabricated' (*mawḍūᶜ*) according to the opinion of the pre-eminent *Ḥadīth* scholar Nāṣir al-Dīn al-Albānī wherever possible.

Ibn al-Qayyim's writing style has been correctly described by Ibn Ḥajar in the following terms: 'His writings can be long-winded and prolix in an attempt to clarify issues.'[95] Therefore in both the *Shifā'* and the *Miftāḥ* there are many instances of repetition, which Ibn al-Qayyim himself acknowledges. In order to shorten this book and make it more readable, repetition and digression not immediately relevant to a theme being discussed has been abridged. In addition, numerous grammatical discussions and many instances of poetry were also omitted. The outcome is that approximately fifteen per cent of the text has been abridged in this presentation.

CHAPTER ONE

A Glorious Exposition of the Secrets of God in Making Adam Descend from the Garden to this Earth

In the Name of God, the Beneficent, the Merciful

Praise be to God Who eased the path to His contentment for his pious servants, elucidated His guidance, and rendered their following of the Prophet to be an indication of His [contentment with them]. He accepted them for they are worshippers of Him. They affirmed their servitude to Him and relied on none other than Him. God wrote faith in their hearts and He assisted them with a spirit from Him once they were content with God as their Lord, Islam as their religion and Muḥammad as their Prophet. Praise be to God Who has appointed, in the absence of the messengers, those who are suitable for elucidating their teachings.

He has established within this Community (*umma*) a group of people who will always remain upon the truth; no harm will come upon them from their enemies or from those who oppose them until His decree comes,[1] even if both the humans and jinn fought against them. This group will call those who have gone astray to guidance and endure patiently the suffering they encounter. They will convey God's light to those who are blind and God's Book to those who are [spiritually] dead, thus bringing them back to [spiritual] life. They are the best of people in guidance and the best of them in speech. How many people were killed by Iblīs[2] [in a spiritual sense] yet this group was able to bring them back to life? How many were ignorant—unaware of the path to guidance—that this group was able to guide? How many innovators in God's religion did they pelt with blazes of truth? They strive in this manner for God's sake alone seeking His contentment. They will elucidate His proofs and signs to humankind due to their aspiration to become proximate to Him and attain His contentment and Paradise. They fight in God's path against those who: strayed from His true religion and Straight Path; introduced distorted innovations into the religion; seduced others with temptations; and opposed, deviated or abandoned His Book being content with falsehood.

I praise God, and He is praiseworthy for all that He has decreed and determined. I ask for His assistance for there is no lord or deity other than Him. I ask for His guidance to the [Straight] Path along with others whom He has blessed and chosen to accept the truth. I thank God, as being grateful ensures that He will bestow more. I ask His forgiveness for all sins since they act as a barrier between the heart and His guidance. I seek refuge with God from my evil self and sinful actions as I am His servant who [has no choice but to] flee to his Lord in such [a state]. I seek shelter with Him from destructive desires and innovations that only lead to deviance. No one who seeks refuge and shelter with Him will ever be disappointed.

I bear witness that there is no deity but God, alone without any partner, along with the believers who do so and in contrast to those who deny [that testimony]. I ask God to preserve this testimony in preparation for the Day of Judgment. I bear witness that the permissible is only what He has prescribed and the prohibited is only what He has forbidden; that the religion is only what He has ordained; that the Hour is coming without a doubt; and that God will resurrect those who are in their graves. I bear witness that Muḥammad is His chosen servant, His elect Prophet, and His truthful and trusted Messenger who *does not speak out of his desires but rather from inspired revelation.*[3] God sent him as a mercy [to both humans and the jinn], as guidance to the seekers, and as a proof to the entirety of humankind. He sent him after an interval between the prophets, and He guided through him to the most upright and lucid path. God has made it obligatory upon humankind to obey Muḥammad, laud him, respect him, and carry out his rights. God has closed all of the paths to Him except that of the Prophet Muḥammad.

God elevated Muḥammad's commemoration and eased him

from his burden, while He disgraced and humiliated those who opposed his message. The Messenger taught those who were ignorant, guided those who were astray, gave sight to those who were [spiritually] blind, gave hearing to those who were deaf and opened encased (*ghulfā*) hearts. The Prophet (may God bless him and grant him peace) continued to uphold the commandments of God—not allowing any hindrance or obstacle to dissuade him—and persisted in calling others to God until the earth was filled with light after its darkness, and people's hearts were brought back into harmony after they had been disparate. His message and God's religion will ultimately reach everywhere the sun rises.

Once God had perfected the religion and completed His blessings upon His believing servants through the efforts of Prophet Muḥammad, He preferred to raise the Prophet up to His Exalted Self out of His magnanimity. The Prophet will occupy the most brilliant and dignified level of God's highest Paradise. Thus, the Prophet departed this life with this Community upon the Straight Path such that only those who deserve punishment will go astray. May God continue to bless Muḥammad and grant him peace along with his pure and good family for as long as the heavens and the earth remain and thereafter eternally.

Now God (Glory be to Him) sent Adam (blessings be upon him)—the father of humankind—down from the Garden [in Paradise] in a manner which is concordant with wise purposes that minds cannot comprehend nor tongues describe [but we will allude to some]:

[1] Adam's descent from it became a method for perfecting him so that he would return to it in the best state. The Sublime willed to give him and his children a taste of the hardship, grief, distress and difficulties of this lesser world, so that they would appreciate the greatness [of Paradise] once they were admitted into it in the Hereafter. Since by comparing opposites the goodness of one is better shown, had they lived only in the blissful abode [of Paradise] they would not have appreciated its [true] worth.

[2] God (Glory be to Him) wanted to command and forbid them, and put them through tribulation and tests. Because Paradise is not the appropriate abode for responsibilities, God sent them down to

the earth so that they may achieve the greatest reward—this can only be attained by obeying His commandments and prohibitions.

[3] The Sublime wanted to establish within them prophets, messengers, saints (*awliyā'*) and martyrs—all whom *He loves and who love Him*.[4] Thus, God left them and His enemies to be tested altogether, such that when the saints and martyrs preferred Him and sacrificed their lives and wealth for His contentment and for what He loves, they were granted His love and pleasure, and bestowed proximity to Him—they could not have achieved all that in any other manner. To be a messenger or a prophet, or a martyr, or one who loves and hates for His sake, i.e. one who assists His saints and opposes His enemies, is considered amongst the most elevated levels in His sight. One cannot achieve that except by this manner, which He has [ontologically] determined and decreed, namely by descending Adam and his offspring to this earth and settling them here.

[4] God (Glory be to Him) is characterized by Beautiful Names, among which are the All-Forgiving (*al-Ghafūr*), the Merciful (*al-Raḥīm*), the Effacer [of sins] (*al-ʿAfū*), the Forbearing (*al-Ḥalīm*), the One Who lowers (*al-Khāfiḍ*), the One Who elevates (*al-Rāfiʿ*), the One Who honours (*al-Muʿizz*), the One Who abases (*al-Mudhill*), the Life-Giver (*al-Muḥyī*), the Life-Taker (*al-Mumīt*), the Inheritor (*al-Wārith*) and the Patient One (*al-Ṣabūr*)—these Names must inevitably become manifested. Thus, the Sublime's wisdom dictated that Adam and his offspring would descend to an abode in which those Beautiful Names would become manifest: where He might forgive those whom He wills; have mercy on those whom He wills; abase those whom He wills; exalt those whom He wills; honour those whom He wills; humble those whom He wills; take retribution against those whom He wills; bestow, deny and grace [those whom He wills]; as well as manifesting other Names and Attributes of His.

[5] Consider also that God (Glory be to Him) is the True and Righteous King. One must recognize that a king commands and forbids, rewards and punishes, abases and elevates, honours and humbles. Therefore, the Sublime's sovereignty dictated that Adam and his offspring would be settled in an abode where they would be

subject to His rulings as a King. Thereafter He will transfer them to another abode in which He will complete the meaning [of His sovereignty].

[6] The Sublime descended them to an abode where their faith would necessarily be based on the Unseen. Faith in the Unseen is the only beneficial type of faith [and is associated with righteousness]. On the other hand, faith in what is witnessed is something that everyone will have on the Day of Judgment, though it will not benefit them. If they had only lived in the blissful abode they would not have otherwise attained faith in the Unseen, and the subsequent pleasure and distinguished status achieved through it. Without that [faith] they would have only attained lesser types of pleasure and honour.

[7] Furthermore, God (Glory be to Him) created Adam from a handful that He took from the earth, which contains the good and the filthy, the easy-going and the rough, the noble and the base. The Sublime knew that some would not be worthy of being proximate to Him in His Paradise. Thus, God (Glory be to Him) descended Adam to a world wherein the good and evil of his progeny would be differentiated—each to their respective abode: the righteous proximate to Him in His Paradise, and the evil ones in the abode of punishment and evil. God (Exalted is He) said, *That God may separate the wicked from the good. The wicked will He place piece upon piece, and heap them all together, and consign them unto Hell. Such verily are the losers.*[5] This is all from His far-reaching wisdom and His executable will; He is the Eminent (*al-ʿAzīz*), the Omniscient (*al-ʿAlīm*).

[8] The Sublime said to the angels, *Lo! I am about to place a viceroy in the earth. They said, Wilt thou place therein one who will do harm therein and will shed blood, while we, we hymn Thy praise and sanctify Thee? He said, Surely I know that which ye know not.*[6]

Then God manifested His knowledge to His servants and angels, regarding those elite of His creation whom He will settle on this earth: His messengers, prophets, saints, those who seek to become proximate to Him, those who will sacrifice themselves for His love and contentment, and those who will struggle against their temptations and desires. [It is as if God said to the angels], 'They abandon their desires and temptations to become proximate to Me, sacrifice their blood and lives for what I love, and therefore I will grace them with knowledge that you do not have. They will glorify and praise Me throughout the night and day, and worship Me despite the obstacles of their desires, temptations, selves, and enemies. You [angels] worship Me without any obstacles or temptations hindering you, or enemies that I have allowed to overcome you. Indeed, your worship [O angels] is like breathing [for humanity]. Moreover, I want to manifest what has been hidden from you [O angels] regarding My enemy [i.e. Satan], and how he fights against Me, arrogantly disdains My commandments and pursues what displeases Me.'

These facts were all hidden and concealed within the father of humankind [Adam] and the father of the jinn [Satan]. Thus God descended them to the earth wherein what only God (Glory be to Him) knew at that time, within His [infinite] knowledge, became manifest along with His wisdom. His command was fulfilled and His knowledge became apparent to the angels, who previously were unaware of all that.

[9] The Sublime loves those who are patient, are pious, who wage battle in a unified manner in His path, are repentant, who purify themselves, and those who thank Him. Now, His love is the highest type of honour. His wisdom therefore dictated that He would settle Adam and his offspring in an abode wherein they could accomplish these characteristics, and be honoured with His love, which is His greatest blessing. Thus, their descent to earth was one of the most immense blessings upon them. *God chooseth for His mercy whom He will, and God is of infinite bounty.*[7]

[10] The Sublime wanted to take from amongst the offspring of Adam those whom He would support, show affection and love; and they would love Him in turn. Their love of Him is a sign of their ultimate perfection and great eminence. They can only achieve this majestic status by following what pleases Him, obeying His commandments and abandoning their desires and temptations as their Beloved dislikes the latter. Therefore, He descended them to an abode wherein He could command and forbid them, and they could carry out His commandments and prohibitions. They could thus

love Him, which allows them to be loved by Him. This is an indication of His perfect wisdom and mercy; and He is the Righteous Doer of Good (*al-Barr*), the Merciful.

[11] Since the Sublime formed the creation in stages and types, and it has preceded in His judgment that He would prefer Adam and his progeny over much of His creation, He made their worship the best grade; here I mean worshipping Him by their free choice rather than it being imposed or necessitated upon them.

God (Glory be to Him) sent Gabriel to the Prophet [Muḥammad] giving him the choice whether to be a king-Prophet or a servant-Prophet. He looked at Gabriel, seeking his advice, and the latter indicated to him that he should humble himself. Therefore, [Muḥammad] (may God bless him and grant him peace) said, 'I will be a servant-Prophet.'[8]

The Sublime described him as His servant in the most eminent of occasions: the occasion of the Night Journey (*isrā'*), the occasion of prayer, and on the occasion of challenging (*taḥaddī*). Of the occasion of the Night Journey, He said, *Glorified be He Who carried His servant by night from the Inviolable Place of Worship to the Farthest Place of Worship.*[9] God did not say 'Messenger' or 'Prophet' here, which indicates that the Prophet Muḥammad attained this great status due to the perfection of his servitude to his Lord. God said of the occasion of prayer, *And when the servant of God stood up in prayer to Him, they crowded on him, almost stifling.*[10] Finally, He said of the occasion of challenging, *And if ye are in doubt concerning that which We reveal unto Our servant (Muḥammad), then produce a sūra of the like thereof, and call your witness beside God if ye are truthful.*[11]

In the *ṣaḥīḥ* [collections of Bukhārī[12] and Muslim[13]], the *ḥadīth* concerning the intercession [to begin the Judgment in the Hereafter] relates that the Messiah (may God bless him and grant him peace) says, 'Go to Muḥammad, a servant whom God has forgiven his past and future sins.'[14] This reveals that the Prophet Muḥammad has achieved the highest rank because of his perfect servitude to God and the perfect forgiveness that God has bestowed upon him.

Since servitude to God has such a high status, His wisdom dictated that Adam and his offspring live in an abode which would allow them to achieve it by complete obedience to God, pursuing what He loves, and abandoning their desires for His sake. All of this indicates God's complete blessing and grace upon them.

[12] God (Glory be to Him) wanted His servants, whom He has blessed, to recognize the magnitude of His perfect blessings upon them, so that they would possess greater love, gratitude and enjoyment of them. The Sublime also wanted to demonstrate to them how He has dealt with His enemies and how He has ordained punishment and types of pain for them. In addition, He wanted to show the believers how He has saved them from all of that and then selected [and rewarded] them with the highest type of bliss. Thus their joy will increase, felicity will become perfect, happiness will intensify, and pleasure will become complete. This all illustrates His perfect blessings and love of them. None of this could have been achieved except by sending them down to the earth, testing them, and putting them through tribulations. Thereby He will grant those whom He wills success (as a mercy from Him and a blessing) and forsake those whom He wills (as a wisdom and justice from Him)—He is the Omniscient and Most Wise (*al-Ḥakīm*).

There is no doubt that when the believer sees his enemy and the enemy of his Beloved being punished with all types of punishment and pain, all while the believer is immersed in bliss and pleasure, the former's joy will increase, his pleasure will intensify, and his bliss will become perfect.

[13] God (Glory be to Him) originated the creation to worship Him, and that is the ultimate objective [of their existence]. The Exalted said, *I created the jinn and humankind only that they might worship Me.*[15] It is well known that the perfect [manifestations of] servitude required from humanity cannot occur in the eternal blissful Paradise, but can only occur in an abode of trial and tribulation. The eternal abode is one of enjoyment and bliss, and not one of tribulation, trial or obligation.

[14] God's wisdom (Glory be to Him) dictated that He create Adam and his offspring from a constitution that necessarily entails the existence of the urging of desires and anger on the one hand, and the appeal of the intellect and knowledge on the other. The

Sublime endowed them with intellect and desires and gave them their requisite appeals in order to establish His will and manifest to His servants His glory in His wisdom and might as well as the mercy, beneficence and kindness in His power and sovereignty. Therefore, His wisdom and mercy dictated that He would allow their father to taste the evil consequences of disobeying Him so that he would know the ramifications of following one's temptations and desires and, thus, would take precautions to a greater degree and be more apt to flee [from sinning].

This is akin to a person walking along a road while his enemies, unbeknownst to him, have hidden on the side, behind, and ahead of him, ready to ambush him. If he was harmed in the past, he will prepare himself better, take away any element of surprise from his enemies, and be ready with some [instruments] to repel them. Had it not been for his past experience of the pain and attack of his enemy, he would not have made preparations, taken precautions, and protected himself with instruments. Thus, it is from the full blessings of God upon Adam and his offspring that He allowed them to see what their enemy did to their father [Adam] and them so that the they could take precautions and prepare [for the Devil].

If it is said that it would have been possible to prevent any enemy from overwhelming [humankind], the reply is that it was mentioned previously that God (Glory be to Him) created Adam and his offspring in such a constitution and fashion that necessitates them to be susceptible to their enemy and thereby tested. If God had willed, He could have created them like the angels—who have intellects but no desires—so that their enemies could not overcome them whatsoever. But if humankind had been created as such, they would be another type of creation—certainly not the offspring of Adam. Instead, the progeny of Adam have been created with both intellects and desires.

[15] Since loving God alone is the ultimate objective—without which the perfection and bliss of the servant cannot fundamentally occur—and since true love is only achieved when one prefers the Beloved more than anything else, it is only through enduring great difficulties in His path and seeking His contentment that this love is achieved and known to be truly established within their hearts.

Therefore, the Sublime's wisdom decreed that they would descend to this abode, filled with temptations and with what humankind desires, such that if they prefer instead the True Beloved and turn away from all that, their love and preference for Him becomes a reality. If one endures extreme difficulties, undertakes perilous tasks, endures the criticism of others, is patient and struggles against the calling of transgression and going astray, then all of this will intensify the power of one's love, allow it to become more firmly rooted in one's heart, and will lead to fruitful actions. Sustained love in the face of many obstacles, barriers and distractions is the true beneficial love. On the other hand, a love that is contingent upon well-being, blessings, pleasure and attaining one's desires from the beloved is not a true love, and it will not hold up in the face of difficulties and obstacles. If something is contingent upon a condition, it becomes absent when the latter becomes null. 'Fair-weather friends abandon you when the wind changes.' Thus, there is an immense difference between one who worships God in times of joy, ease and well-being only, and one who worships Him in times of joy and hardship, ease and difficulty, well-being and tribulation.

[16] God (Glory be to Him) deserves perfect, absolute and infinite praise. Therefore, it is necessary to manifest the causes that affirm [His] praiseworthiness, and these are concordant with His praiseworthy essence. There are two reasons to praise the Exalted: firstly, for His grace; and secondly, for His justice. Thus, it is necessary to manifest the causes and requisites which lead to His justice, so that the perfect praise that He deserves can result. Just as the Sublime is praiseworthy for His benevolence, kindness, grace and reward, He is praiseworthy for His justice, retribution and punishment; these all proceed (*ṣādir*) from His majesty and wisdom.

God (Glory be to Him) points this out often in the Qur'ān. For instance, after each story concerning the messengers and their nations in Sūrat al-Shuᶜarā', God says, *Herein is indeed a portent; yet most of them are not believers. And thy Lord! He is indeed the Almighty, the Merciful.*[16] Thus, the Sublime notifies us that these events proceed from His majesty (which encompasses His perfect omnipotence) and His wisdom (which encompasses His perfect omniscience and putting of things in their appropriate places). God bestowed His blessing and salvation for His messengers and their followers, while He destroyed and exacted retribution against their enemies—this all was done appropriately, due to the perfection of His majesty and His wisdom. Furthermore, the Sublime states after describing His judgment between the blissful and the wretched, and their placement within their appropriate and respective abodes in accordance with His wisdom, *And they are judged aright. And it is said, Praise be to God, the Lord of the Worlds* (*Rabb al-ʿālamīn*)*!*[17]

[17] The Sublime's wisdom and praiseworthy [Essence] has dictated that He differentiate between His servants to such a great and clear degree so that those who are blessed may thank Him for [His] blessings and grace and recognise that they were selected specifically for them rather than others. Had everyone been given an equal share of blessings and well-being, then the blessed individual would not know its value and would not express his gratitude since he would see everyone in the same state. One of the strongest reasons and causes for gratitude to be expressed from the servant is him witnessing another in an opposite state of his perfect and successful state. In the well-known tradition, God (Glory be to Him) showed Adam (blessings be upon him) his offspring and their different levels. Adam said, 'O my Lord, why did You not make all of Your servants equal?' God replied, 'I love to be thanked.'[18] Thus, the Sublime, due to His love of being thanked, dictated that causes be created so that the gratitude of those who were thankful would become greater and more perfect. This is the essence of the wisdom which proceeds from [His] Attribute of praiseworthiness.

[18] Nothing is more beloved to God (Glory be to Him) than the servant being humble, submissive, needy and penitent before Him in addition to beseeching Him. It is well known that these only follow from causes, which they are dependent upon. It would be impossible for these [traits and actions] to occur in an abode of absolute bliss and perfect well-being.

[19] God (Glory be to Him) creates and commands; His commandments include His Divine Law, commandments and religion for which He sent His messengers and revealed His Books. Paradise is

not the abode for obligations (where the rulings and requirements of these obligations would occur); rather, it is one for bliss and pleasure. Thus, the Sublime's wisdom dictated settling Adam and his offspring in an abode where they could follow the rules of His religion and commandments. In that manner the requisites and requirements of His commandments would become manifest.

Just as God's actions and creative powers are manifestations of His perfect Beautiful Names and Exalted Attributes, so too are His commandments and Divine Law (as well as the rewards and punishments that result from them). The Sublime has guided us to this meaning in many places in His Book: *Thinketh man that he is to be left aimless?*[19] i.e. neglected and not commissioned, nor commanded nor forbidden, nor rewarded nor punished. This indicates that such would be inconsistent with His perfect wisdom, and that His lordship, majesty and wisdom all reject that. Therefore, the verse is worded in such a manner as to repudiate those who imagine that.

Furthermore, the verse indicates that the goodness [of God commanding and forbidding humanity] is established within people's innate disposition and intellects, and that the repugnance of leaving humanity neglected and not commissioned is also established in their innate disposition. Therefore, how can something that the innate disposition and intellect recognize to be repugnant be ascribed to the Lord? The Exalted said, *Deemed ye then that We had created you for naught, and that ye would not be returned unto Us? Now God be Exalted, the True King! There is no deity save Him, the Lord of the Throne of Grace.*[20] The Sublime has refuted this false claim as it opposes the requisites of His Names and Attributes, and it is not fitting to attribute such to His majesty. There are many other instances in the Qur'ān of this.

[20] God (Glory be to Him) loves that some matters, which are dependent upon the occurrence of causes, arise and follow. These cannot occur except in an abode of tribulation and testing. The Sublime loves those who are patient, who are thankful, who wage battle in a unified manner in His path, who repent, and those who purify themselves. There is no doubt that the occurrence of these things, which are beloved to Him, is impossible without their causes—just as end results cannot occur without their means.

God (Glory be to Him) rejoices at the repentance of His servant more than one who loses his riding animal—laden with his food and drink in a barren and dangerous land—and then finds it again. This has been related in the authentic *ḥadīth* of the Prophet (may God bless him and grant him peace): 'God is more pleased with the repentance of His servant than a man who [is forced to] encamp at a spot where his life is in jeopardy. This [individual's] riding animal carries his food and water, and he goes to rest and sleep for a short while only to wake up and find his riding animal gone. He starts looking for it and suffers from severe thirst. He then says, "I will go back to my [initial] spot to sleep and await my death." He lays his head down in anticipation of death, but awakes to find his riding animal standing there still laden with his provisions, food and drink. God is more pleased with the repentance of the believing servant than this person when he finds his riding animal.'[21]

This person's happiness represents the ultimate and highest type; however, God's happiness with the repentance of a believer is greater than that. God willing, this *ḥadīth* and the secret of His pleasure with the repentance of His servant will be discussed further later in this book.[22] The point is that God's pleasure does not occur except after the believer repents from a sin, which means that both the repentance and the sin are requisite causes leading to this pleasure. A necessary concomitant cannot occur in the absence of its requisite. Since this aforementioned pleasure only occurs after repentance from a sin, then its occurrence [had humankind only been created] in Paradise (where there are no sins or disobedience) is impossible. Since the Lord's pleasure (Glory be to Him) is more beloved to Him in this case than its absence, His love of it dictated that He [ontologically] create the causes that lead to it, thus resulting in an outcome, which is beloved to Him [i.e. repentance].

[21] God (Glory be to Him) has made Paradise the abode of recompense and reward, and He varied its levels amongst its inhabitants concordant to their deeds. To that end the Sublime created Paradise in accordance with His wisdom, which was dictated by His Names and Attributes. Paradise is composed of levels, some higher than others, and between two levels is the distance separating the heavens from the

earth. The Prophet (may God bless him and grant him peace) said in a *ḥadīth*, 'Verily in Paradise there are a hundred levels, between two levels is the distance separating the heavens from the earth.'[23]

The wisdom of the Lord (Glory be to Him) dictates that all of these levels be occupied, which can only occur if deeds [are varied]. This was stated by many of the Predecessors: 'The [pious] are rescued from Hellfire due to God's mercy and forgiveness, and they are admitted into Paradise due to His grace, blessings and forgiveness. But the levels they reach are determined by their deeds.' They also used the following verses to prove that entry into Paradise is determined by deeds, whereby the Exalted said, *This is the Garden which ye are made to inherit because of what ye used to do,*[24] and *Enter the Garden because of what ye used to do.*[25] Moreover, they [qualified] those [traditions] which negate that deeds [are alone sufficient] for entry into Paradise, such as the *ḥadīth* of the Prophet (may God bless him and grant him peace), 'One's good deeds will not make him enter Paradise.' They asked, 'Not even you, O Messenger of God?' He said, 'Not even I.'[26] Here, the Prophet informed us that entrance into Paradise is not in exchange for one's deeds, and were it not that God (Glory be to Him) enveloped His servant with His mercy, then He would not have admitted him into Paradise.

Thus, the servant's deeds, no matter how great, are not sufficient for entry into Paradise nor can they be exchanged for it. Even if the servant's deeds were completely beloved by God and absolutely concordant with His pleasure, they cannot rise to even the level of the blessings that He has bestowed upon him in this world. Indeed, were He to hold him to account, the entirety of his deeds would only make up for a tiny amount of His blessings, and the remainder of His blessings would still require gratitude. Therefore, if God were to punish him in that case it would not be unjust, and if He were to have mercy on him then His mercy would be better for him than his own deeds. It has been narrated by Zayd b. Thābit,[27] Ḥudhayfa[28] and others that the Prophet (may God bless him and grant him peace) said in a *ḥadīth*, 'If God were to punish those in the heavens and the earth, His punishment would not be unjust. And if He were to be merciful with them, His mercy would be better for them than their deeds.'[29]

The point is that the Sublime's wisdom dictated that He would create and structure Paradise with progressively higher levels, some on top of others, and that He will populate Adam and his offspring [who are believers] within it according to their deeds. This could only be achieved by settling them in an abode wherein they could work and strive.

[22] God (Glory be to Him) created Adam and his offspring to make them viceroys on the earth. The Sublime stated in His Book, *I am about to place a viceroy in the earth*;[30] *He it is Who hath placed you as viceroys of the earth*;[31] *[Moses] said, It may be that your Lord is going to destroy your adversary and make you viceroys in the earth.*[32]

Nonetheless, the Sublime intended to transfer Adam and his offspring from being viceroys to inheriting the everlasting Paradise. The Sublime knows in His eternal knowledge that humans, due to their weakness and shortsightedness, may select that which is immediate and contemptible rather than that which is delayed and priceless. This is a requisite of the fact that *Man is made of haste*;[33] and *man was ever hasty*.[34] The Sublime is well aware that man's nature is weak and languid. Therefore, His wisdom dictated that He enter Adam into Paradise so that he could know and see with his own eyes the bliss that He has prepared for him. Thereafter, he would yearn for it, aspire to it and desire it all the more ardently. If one encounters a good thing, enjoys and experiences it, one will barely be able to withstand being separated from it. Similarly, once the servant tastes the sweetness of faith and feels it happily in his heart, then his love of faith will become entrenched and he will not prefer anything else to it.

In the authentic *ḥadīth* narrated by Abū Hurayra[35] (may God be pleased with him) the Prophet said, 'God says [to the angels], "What do My servants ask of Me?" The angels will reply, "They ask You for Paradise." God says, "Have they seen it?" The angels then say, "No, O Lord! They have not seen it." God says, "How would it have been had they seen it?" The angels will respond, "Had they seen it, they would have had a greater desire for it."'[36]

Thus, God's wisdom dictated that He would allow Adam to see and live in Paradise and then tell his sons his story so that it would be as if they had witnessed and encountered it along with their father. Those who were created for it, and for whom it was created, will comply, will hasten towards it and will not be prevented by this immediate life from pursuing it. Instead, they will act as though they had once [lived] in it, before being captured by the enemy [and removed from it]. They will consider it to be their first home, and will always be nostalgic for it. They will not feel at peace until they see themselves again back there. A poet said,

> Move your heart wherever you may in accordance with
> its desires,
> But its love is only for its first love.
> How many homes exist on the earth that one may like,
> But one's yearning is always for his first home!

I also wrote some poetry that encompasses this meaning:

> Come to the Paradise of Eden (ʿ*adn*) since it is
> Your first home and it will be the encampment.
> But we have been taken hostage by the enemy so I ask you
> Will we be able to return to our homeland and be saved?

[23] The secret of all these principles is that it has preceded in God's judgment and wisdom (Glorious and Exalted is He) that desired objectives cannot be attained except through their means. God has made the latter to be causes leading to the former. One of the ultimate objectives is the highest and most eminent type of bliss [i.e. Paradise], and again it cannot be attained except through means, which He has established.

If lowlier ends are not achievable except through their means, such as obtaining food, drink, clothing, offspring, money and power in this world, then how can there be any doubt that the highest and most eminent objective can only be attained through means? Therefore, settling Adam and his offspring in this world, in which they may attain the means leading to the highest stations, represents the fulfilment of His blessings upon us.

[24] One of the secrets also is that the Sublime made carrying the message, prophethood, His friendship (*khulla*), His speech, loyalty and servitude [to Him] as the most honoured stations that He has created and the end objectives of perfection [for humanity]. Thus,

God sent them down to an abode wherein He could bring forth from amongst them prophets and send some of them as messengers, could speak directly to Moses, and establish amongst them friends, saints, martyrs, believing servants and elites whom He loves and who love Him. So sending them down to the earth represents the fulfilment of [His] great blessings and benevolence.

[25] Another secret is that God manifested the effects of His Names and Attributes as well as His rulings in a manner consistent with and dictated by His wisdom, mercy and knowledge.

[26] One of its secrets is that God revealed to His creatures His Names, Attributes and actions as a result of Him honouring and blessing His saints, while humiliating and bringing wretchedness upon His enemies. He has answered the prayers of His saints and taken care of their needs, has saved them from calamities and liberated them from tribulations, and has submitted them to His decree as He wills, and shifted them between different types of good and hardships. These are some of the greatest proofs that He is their Lord and King; that He is God, besides whom there is no other deity worthy of worship; that He is the Omniscient, the Most Wise, the All-Hearing (*al-Samīʿ*) and All-Seeing (*al-Baṣīr*); and that He is the True God while everything else is falsehood.

The proofs for His Lordship and Oneness have become manifest on this earth and established from every perspective. His servants who have been granted success know them and affirm His Oneness faithfully and obediently, while those who are forsaken have denied them, associated others with Him unjustly, and disbelieved. Therefore, whoever is ruined is only so after clear evidence [has been established against him], and whoever is saved is only so because of [His] clear signs [and grace]. God is the All-Hearing, the Omniscient.[37]

Whoever examines His signs on this earth, whether witnessed or heard, and experiences their effects, will acknowledge [His] perfect wisdom in settling Adam and his offspring in this abode until the appointed time. God (Glory be to Him) created Paradise solely for Adam and his offspring and made the angels their attendants therein. His wisdom though dictated that He create for them this abode in order to allow them to supply themselves with provisions for [Paradise in the Hereafter] that [He also] created for them, since they cannot reach it without supplies. The Exalted states, *And they bear your loads for you unto a land ye could not reach save with great trouble to yourselves. Your Lord is full of pity, merciful.*[38] This verse concerns travelling within this world from one place to another; so what, then, of moving from this world to the everlasting abode? *So make provision for yourselves; for the best provision is to ward off evil.*[39]

Hence, those who are deceived and are lost sold their homes within [Paradise] for a very low and trifling price. But those who have been granted success have sold themselves and their wealth for God's sake and made that their ticket into Paradise. Their trade was thus profitable and they were bestowed the greatest victory. God (Exalted is He) has said, *God hath bought from the believers their lives and their wealth, that Paradise will be theirs.*[40]

Therefore, the Sublime did not remove Adam from Paradise except that He willed to return him to it in a more perfect [state]. It is as if [God's] predestination (*ʿalā lisān al-qadar*)[41] had dictated, 'O Adam, do not despair because I told you to leave it, as I have created it for you. I am the Self-Sufficient (*al-Ghanī*) and not in need of it or anything else; and I am the Magnanimous (*al-Jawād*), the Most Generous (*al-Karīm*). I do not enjoy anything within it, but instead I sustain [the creation] and I am not in need of any sustenance. I am the Self-Sufficient, the Most Praiseworthy (*al-Ḥamīd*). Go down to the abode of cultivation; if you cultivate within it such that the crops stand upon their stalks and yield their harvest, then come back and I will recompense you with what you need the most. Each seed will be multiplied tenfold to 700 times, and even many times more. I am more knowledgeable than you about that which is good for you; and I am the Omniscient, the Most Wise.'

CHAPTER TWO

The Infallibility of the Divine Decree from Being Evil

God (Exalted is He) advised us to say, *O God! Owner of Sovereignty (Mālik al-mulk)! Thou givest sovereignty unto whom Thou wilt, and Thou withdrawest sovereignty from whom Thou wilt. Thou exaltest whom Thou wilt, and Thou abasest whom Thou wilt. In Thy Hand is the good. Thou art able to do all things.*[1] In this verse, God (Glory be to Him) expressed that He alone possesses the sovereignty (*mulk*); and secondly, that He bestows it upon whom He wills and withdraws it from whom He wills. Therefore, He alone disposes of it as He wills. It also mentions that He (Glory be to Him) exalts those whom He wills according to whatever types of glory He wills for them, and He abases those whom He wills by withdrawing that honour from them. All goodness is from Him—no one else [intrinsically] possesses any of that [goodness] along with Him. Finally, God concludes [the verse] by saying, *Thou art able to do all things.*

Thus, this verse encompasses a discussion of His supreme sovereignty, His disposition, and His universal power. It mentions that all of these actions (*taṣarrufāt*) are through His power and that they all are good. Therefore, His abasing or withdrawing sovereignty from those whom He wills is good—even if it is harmful for those who are deprived and humbled in particular. His actions revolve completely and only around [His] justice, grace, wisdom and beneficence. Furthermore, all of these are good—the Lord is praiseworthy and commendable for them, just as He is lauded and extolled for His infallibility from any evil. Finally, evil cannot be attributed to Him.

In *Ṣaḥiḥ Muslim*, the Messenger of God (may God bless him and grant him peace) said in his supplication commending His Lord,

'Here I am at Your service, all goodness is in Your Hands and evil cannot be attributed to You. My existence is due to You and my return is to You. Blessed and exalted are You.'[2]

God is most blessed and exalted, and is far above having any evil attributed to Him. Only good can be attributed to Him. On the other hand, something is evil or becomes evil because it is deprived of being associated and connected to Him. If something is associated with Him it is not evil. This will be discussed below.

God (Glory be to Him) has created both good and evil—evil exists within some of His creatures *not* in His act of creating or in His actions themselves. His act of creating and His actions, decrees and determinations are all good. It is for this reason that the Sublime has declared Himself infallible from any injustice. The reality of [injustice] is putting something in an inappropriate place. He does not place anything except in its concordant position; and this represents goodness. Evilness is to put something into an inappropriate position—if it is placed in its concordant position it is not considered evil. It is well established that evilness is not attributable to Him. His Beautiful Names all attest to that. Some of them are: the Holy (*al-Quddūs*), the One Who is faultless and bestows peace (*al-Salām*), the Almighty (*al-ʿAzīz*), the Irresistible (*al-Jabbār*), and the Proud (*al-Mutakabbir*).[3]

The Holy indicates One Who is infallible from any evilness, deficiency (*naqṣ*) or fault (*ʿayb*). This is the interpretation of the exegetes and the linguists. The basis of the word *quddūs* is derived from purity and righteousness. Also derived from *quds* is the Holy Mosque [in Jerusalem] (*bayt al-maqdis*), since it is a place where people are purified from their sins. Whoever goes there—not desiring anything except to pray there—will leave purified of all his sins like the day his mother gave birth to him [i.e. as if he was born again]. In addition, another name for Paradise is *ḥaẓirat al-quds*, because it is free from all of the evilness of this world. In addition, Gabriel is named the Holy Spirit (*rūḥ al-qudus*) because he is pure from any faults.

The statement of [*nuqaddisu* by] the angels [in the following verse] is also derived from it: *while we hymn Thy praise and sanctify*

Thee (*nuqaddisu laka*)?[4] It has also been said that the meaning is: 'We dedicate ourselves purely for Thee.' In this [alternative] interpretation [*nuqaddisu laka*] was converted into the transitive form—but this is an inadequate interpretation. Instead, the correct meaning is: 'We sanctify Thee and we declare that You are infallible from anything which is incongruent or evil being attributed to You.'

Ibn Jarīr[5] interpreted *sanctify Thee* to mean: 'We characterize You with only Your perfect Attributes that are devoid of any faults which the disbelievers have ascribed to You.'[6] He added that some like Abū Ṣāliḥ[7] and Mujāhid[8] have stated it means: 'We glorify and exalt You.' Therefore, the angels are declaring that God is infallible—not that they deem themselves to be so righteous that they would not attribute anything incongruent to Him.

My opinion is that *nuqaddisu laka* was juxtaposed to *while we hymn Thy praise,*[9] because glorification (*tasbīḥ*) is to declare that God (Glory be to Him) is infallible above doing any evil. Maymūn b. Mihrān[10] said that *subḥān Allāh* is a phrase by which the Lord is glorified and deemed far above any evil. Ibn ᶜAbbās[11] said, 'It is to declare that God is infallible above any evil.'

The basis of the word *subḥān* is 'being distant' (*mubāᶜada*), as in the statement 'We spread out (*sabiḥtu*) on the earth,' i.e. they distanced themselves from one another. Thus, whoever extols God and declares Him to be infallible above any evil has glorified Him. It is likewise said, 'They glorified God (*sabbaḥa Allāh*) or glorified for His sake (*sabbaḥa lahu*), and sanctified Him (*qaddasahu*) or sanctified for His sake (*qaddasa lahu*).'

God's Name *al-Salām,* the One Who is faultless and bestows peace, indicates that He is free from any faults or imperfections. Characterizing Him by using the word *salām* is more emphatic than using the word *sālim.* One of the necessary manifestations of this characterization is that His creation is safe from any injustice from Him. Therefore, God (Glory be to Him) is free from willing any injustice or evil.

It is also for this reason that the Sublime characterized the Night of Power (*laylat al-qadr*) as being safe (*salām*), Paradise as the abode of safety, and the salutation of the believer's therein as [spreading] freedom [from any injustice]. Finally, He praised His saints by saying 'peace' to them. These all proceed from One Who is faultless and bestows peace.

The Great One (*al-Kabīr*) and the Proud (*al-Mutakabbir*) are also Names of God. Qatāda[12] and others said that the latter indicates that He is proud above [performing] any evil or offense. Muqātil[13] said that the former indicates that He is too great to be characterized with any evil. Abū Isḥāq[14] said that He is too proud to perform any injustice to His servants.

One of His Names is the Almighty (*al-ʿAzīz*), which indicates that He is characterized by complete might. Some of the manifestations of His perfect might are that He is innocent of [performing or being characterized by] any evil, wickedness or fault.

One of His Names is the Most High (*al-ʿAlī*), which connotes that He is high above any fault, evil or deficiency. In addition, one of the manifestations of His perfect Highness is that nothing can be above Him—instead He is above everything.

God's Name of the One deserving of all praise (*al-Ḥamīd*) indicates that all praise is due to Him. His perfect praiseworthiness necessitates that no evil, misconduct or deficiency be attributed to Him—neither in His Names, actions or Attributes. His Beautiful Names preclude any attribution of evil, misconduct or injustice to Him.

God (Glory be to Him) is the Creator (*al-Khāliq*) of everything, and He has created people, their actions, movements and statements. If a person performs a repugnant and forbidden act then he has perpetrated evil and wickedness. Now, the Exalted Lord has allowed him to do so, and allowing a person to be an agent is good in and of itself, but the person's act is evil and repugnant (*qabīḥ*) in itself. The Sublime's allowance represents the putting of things in their appropriate place in a manner consistent with His far-reaching wisdom, which He is praiseworthy for. This [concordance] is good, wise and beneficial even though the performance of [that repugnant act] by a person is blameworthy, faulty and evil.

This is [all] rational and experienced. For example, if an experienced craftsman takes a crooked piece of wood or a broken piece of a rock but thereafter places them in the appropriate and correct place for each of them it is just and wise. He is, therefore, commendable for that. But if his placement is instead crooked, inadequate or blemished, then he will be criticized [rightly for that]. Whoever places a turban on the head, shoes on the feet, make-up on the eyelids and waste material in the rubbish has put everything in its appropriate place. Such a person has not done any injustice to the shoes or the waste, as those are the appropriate places for them.

The Sublime's Names also include the Most Just (*al-ʿAdl*) and the Most Wise (*al-Ḥakīm*); thus, He does not put anything except in its appropriate place. He is the Most Benevolent (*al-Muḥsin*), the Magnanimous, the Most Wise, and the Ruler (*al-Ḥakam*) in everything that He has created. He has appropriately placed and arranged everything.

God (Glory be to Him) creates and commands. Since He only commands that which is best and preponderantly good, His commandments only accrue what is advantageous and perfect. At the same time, they either annul harm completely or lessen it. But if two outcomes are not reconcilable, He preponderates that which is better and more advantageous. The Divine Law only contains commandments whose presence is better than their absence. It also does not prohibit actions unless their absence is better than their presence.

Should someone contend, 'If the existence [of some good] is better than its non-existence, why would He not always will its existence? Or if the non-existence [of some evil] is preferable to its existence, why would He ever will its existence? Indeed, the [notion of the] ontological (*kawnī*) will completely contradicts the aforementioned principle.'

I state that the existence of evil does not contradict [that principle]. Although the existence [of a particular good] may be better than its non-existence, its existence [in all situations] may result in forgoing (*fawāt*) something that is more beloved to God. Likewise, although the non-existence of something evil may be preferable to its existence [in one aspect] it may be that its existence is a means or a cause that leads [indirectly] to something more beloved to Him. A more complete discussion will follow in the chapter on the concordance between determination and Divine Law.[15]

If the Lord (Glory be to Him) commands something, then it indicates that He loves that thing, is pleased with it and wills it from a religious [but not necessarily ontological] perspective. The existence of everything that He loves is better than its non-existence. Moreover, God hates and dislikes everything that He has forbidden. The non-existence of anything He hates is preferable to its existence. Yet this only applies if the entities themselves are directly compared. However, when considering what these [entities] lead to, and whether He loves or dislikes those [indirect consequences], another conclusion must be considered.

God (Glory be to Him) commanded His servants to follow the best of [the guidance] revealed unto them.[16] Here, what is better is what they were commanded—this is better than what they were forbidden from. If this is God's methodology (*sunna*) regarding His commandments, prohibitions and Divine Law, it is also His custom (*sunna*) in His [ontological] creation, Divine will and predetermination. Whatever He wills to create or carry out is better than it not being created or done by Him and vice versa. If something's [absolute] non-existence is better than its existence then its evil is [considered to be preponderant], and He is infallible above allowing [or creating] that.

If it is asked, 'Why did He create something if it is evil?' I respond, 'Both His creation of it and His actions are good; they are not evil. The creative action subsists with God (Glory be to Him), and it is impossible that He would perform anything evil or be characterized by it. Whatever evil is present in a creature, it is because of its lack of association or connection to Him. Anything that He does not will to exist remains non-existent by definition. All [absolute and preponderant] evils are non-existent. In fact, [evils] are caused by ignorance (which is the absence of knowledge) or injustice (which is the absence of justice). All types of pain are caused by the lack of receptivity or acceptance of a place/receptacle for what [would otherwise] lead to goodness or pleasure.'

Many contend, 'All good is derived from existence and its necessary requisites, while all evil is derived from non-existence and its necessary requisites. Also anything that exists is good, while anything that is pure evil is non-existent.' My reply is that this wording is too generalized. If what is intended is 'Everything that God has created and brought into existence contains some good and its existence is better than its non-existence; and everything that He has not created or not willed remains non-existent because it is devoid of any goodness,' then this [interpretation] is correct.

But if what is intended [by that generalization] is 'Everything that exists is good, while everything that is non-existent is evil,' then that [interpretation] is incorrect. Instead, existence may entail evil that is preponderated [by good], while non-existence may entail good that is preponderated [by evil]. Examples of the first are fire, rain, heat, cold, snow and the presence of animals. All of these things exist and entail partial evils, which are subsumed in comparison to the good that exists within them. Similarly, commandments may necessarily require some pain and hardships that may be considered partly evil/harmful, but again that is subsumed in comparison to the good they contain.

The above is confirmed by considering that there are two types of evil: [1] absolute essential evil and [2] relative evil. The first does not even exist. If something exists it cannot be purely evil. Only the second exists. Entities that exist may run counter to life, permanence and perfection, like diseases and their causes or pains and their causes. Also included are entities that prevent good from occurring altogether or hinder it from reaching a receptive place. Examples include any bad entity that prevents food from reaching or benefitting the organs of the body, or any false beliefs and corrupted desires that prevent their opposites [which are good] from reaching the heart.

If the above is known, then evil is essentially the privation of what is required for something to come into existence, remain or to reach perfection. This privation also inevitably results in elements which are in themselves evil. For example, the privation of knowledge and justice results in ignorance and injustice, which are existent evils. The privation of health and moderation results consequently in pain and harm, which are also existent evils.

On the other hand, the non-existence of something non-essential, like the absence of excessive wealth or some types of knowledge (that would not lead to harm if one remained ignorant of them), are not evil in reality nor is their presence a [necessary] cause for evil. Thus, knowledge itself or wealth itself are not causes of evil. Instead, evil occurs because of the absence of some trait that would have rendered that entity to become good. For example, the absence of virtue, patience or justice in one who is affluent may lead to the occurrence of evil in his wealth. The absence of wisdom or the ability to put things in their appropriate place also [results in evil].

Thus, it becomes clear that evil is only a consequence of the non-existence [of another entity]. Evils in existence are not purely or essentially [evil]; rather, they are only relatively [evil] from the standpoint that they lack elements that are necessary [to allow them to become good] or beneficial. Evil actions will appear so from the agent's perspective, but may not be evil relative to other vantage points.

An example of this is injustice, which arises from an agent who desires to subdue and conquer using his power. His anger is only calmed after completing that act. The sole existence of this [anger or power] is not necessarily evil; rather, [greater] evil would occur if it did not [exist] or was not effective. In that latter case, one would be weak, incapable and vanquished. The existent evil that does occur [in this example] is relative to the victim due to the loss of his wealth, life or ability to act. The evil relative to the oppressor is not that he has conquered and subdued, but that he has carried that out against an inappropriate [person]. Had he utilized the power of his anger to subdue those speaking animals [i.e. humans] and beasts who harm and transgress then it would have been good. But he went astray by conquering others [who were innocent] instead of being just and moderate, and he imposed harshness instead of mercy.

Another example is a river that flows to a farm that it irrigates and benefits; it is perfect in that case. But if, instead, its stream deviates to another land, then that will result in harm and disintegration of the farm.

Another example consists of the desires and anger that a person is bestowed so as to assist him in attaining what benefits him and subduing those who try to harm or destroy him. If they are used to that end then their perfection is reached, and that is good. But if these powers are diverted and instead utilized in an inappropriate way, they become relative evils.

Another example is fire; it is considered perfect in its ability to burn. Thus, if it burns what it is supposed to burn, then it is considered good. But if it inadvertently encounters something, which it is not supposed to burn and destroys it, then it becomes a relative evil in that particular circumstance.

Another example is killing, which entails using a cutting tool that separates one part of the body from another. The power that a person possesses to utilize the tool is good, that the tool has a capacity to be effective is good, and that the object is susceptible to that is good; however, the evil may relatively occur due to putting this effect in an inappropriate place and by straying from an appropriate objective to an inappropriate one. This all is relative to the agent. As regards the victim, the evil is also relative from his vantage point due the pain or death that occurred to him. It may though be beneficial for another individual.

Another example is sexual intercourse: the power of the agent and the receptivity of the spouse are both deemed to be good. Yet evil occurs if deviation occurs from the appropriate place to an inappropriate and unsuitable one. Speech or bodily movements are considered similarly.

Thus, it becomes apparent that evil exists only in relation to and by its connection with something, rather than it being absolutely or essentially evil. Another example is prostration: it is not evil in essence; however, if it is done for any other than God then it is evil by this relation or association. Likewise, existent disbelief and polytheism is evil due to its association with aggrandizement of idols. The act of glorification itself is not praiseworthy or blameworthy until what it is associated with it is considered. Thus, if it is glorification of God, His Book, His religion and His Messenger then it is pure goodness. But if idols or the Devil are aggrandized, it is rendered evil similar to how prostration to other than God results in it being so classified.

It is also necessary to know that things which develop in stages, like plants or animals, are susceptible to becoming defective. Defects can be [harmful or] evil either during development or afterwards. The first type occurs [during development] because its elements are subjected to causes, which render them bad natured or inadequately prepared, thus resulting in evil. It is not because the Agent denied the object or took away some existent that [would have otherwise] rendered it perfect, but instead because the object did not accept that perfection or completion. This lack of acceptance is again an issue of non-existence, which is not due to the Agent—for the Agent has endowed all that is good in existence. Any deficiencies or evil that occur within something are due to that object not being provided with what would cause its perfection; thus, [that trait or entity] remains in its original non-existent state.

Through this, the secret of the Exalted's [following] statement can be understood: *Thou (Muḥammad) canst see no fault in the Beneficent's creation.*[17] All that He has originated exists to result in the perfection and completion of that creature. On the other hand, any blemish or deficiency is due to either lack of acceptance [of that creature] or to privation. [In the latter case], the Lord (Glory be to Him) did not create [that person] with the [requisite] preparedness; and therefore the disharmony that occurred was due to privation—it was not present within that creature itself. Deeply reflect on this. Creating is attributable to the Lord (Glory be to Him)—He is not the originator [of privation]. For instance, if a foetus fails to develop completely or attain perfection and well-being—only then does it become faulty. The same applies to plants.

As for the second—that is, evil which occurs after [a creature's] formation and development—it also consists of two subtypes. The first is that the provisions allowing it to maintain perfection cease. Examples include cutting off the supply of irrigation to a plantation or feed to animals. These also represent examples of [harm or] evil associated with privation.

The second [subtype] consists of something that negates the occurrence of its perfection; there are also two divisions here. The first of them is the occurrence of an obstacle that prevents otherwise beneficial causes from being effective. For example, sometimes bad mixtures prevent food from being beneficial. Likewise false desires and beliefs may preclude the heart from benefitting [spiritually] from guidance and knowledge. This type of evil, although existent, is also due to the privation of power and a firm will that would otherwise allow one to block that obstacle.

When corrupt desires overtake one it is only due to the weakness of one's chastity, courage or patience. Likewise, when false beliefs overcome one it is due to a lack of knowledge that one should have been aware of. Thus, every evil or fault that occurs is due to the absence of a cause to oppose it. The privation of that opposing cause does not lead directly to that [evil], but the fact that it is non-existent is sufficient.

The second division is an external obstacle like extreme cold, fiery heat or flooding, which afflicts animals and plants, thus resulting in their destruction. There is no doubt that this is an existent evil, but this evil is also relative and dependent on what it is associated with—it can be good when considered from other aspects. The presence of heat, cold or water in general accrues many benefits and goods, such that the [aforementioned] evils relative to [those goods] are few. Therefore, nullifying these causal entities completely in order to avoid those relative evils would result in greater evils and the lapse of many good outcomes. For instance, the goods that are accrued by the creation due to the sun, wind, rain, snow, heat and cold are many times greater than the relative harms that may occur. When compared to those goods the latter [harms] are like a drop in the ocean. Even if most people do not recognize the good, the Exalted Lord has decreed nothing in vain nor has He created anything wrongly.

Now it can be said that an entity can either be pure good, absolute evil, have good preponderate, have evil preponderate, have an equal amount of good and evil, or finally have neither good nor evil. Thus, there are six types. Some of them occur in reality while some do not.

As for the first type, which is pure good having no evil from any aspect, it is absolutely the most eminent, perfect and most dignified of all that exists. Any goodness or perfection that is thus characterized is essentially derived from God's goodness and perfection, not vice versa. It is in need of Him, and He is self-sufficient above it.

Everything asks God to grant it perfection. Thus, the angels request Him to allow them to be [spiritually] alive, and ask His assistance in remembering Him, thanking Him, worshipping Him with piety, carrying out His commandments and upholding what He has charged them with. All of this results in the well-being of both the heavenly and earthly worlds. They then finally beseech Him to forgive the offspring of Adam.

The messengers supplicate Him to assist them in conveying and fulfilling His message, and that He grants them victory over their enemies, in addition to other beneficial things for their livelihoods and Hereafter. All of the offspring of Adam appeal to Him for a various array of beneficial matters. All of the animals entreat Him for their sustenance, food, power, livelihood, and to repel away [harms]. Trees and plants entreat Him to sustain and complete them. In fact, everything in the universe asks Him to sustain them for their maintenance and livelihood: *All that are in the heavens and the earth entreat Him. Every day He exerciseth (universal) power.*[18]

God's Hand is outstretched to them in giving and favours; and His Right Hand is infinitely full and it is not diminished by any expenditure. Indeed, His giving and goodness are granted to both the righteous and the wicked. God is perfect in every aspect and every good is from Him. All praise is due to Him, the sovereignty is wholly His, and all glorification is due to Him. In His Hand is all goodness and all matters return to Him. Most blessed are His Names, Attributes, actions and Essence. All blessings are from Him.

As for the remaining five [entities], the only existent subtype is one wherein its benefit, wisdom and goodness preponderates over its evil. The remaining four subtypes do not even exist. Again, absolute evil remains absolutely non-existent and is unreal.

If it is contended that Iblīs, disbelief and polytheism are all absolutely evil, then some ask, 'What good results from their existence?' We reply: Many wisdoms, benefits and goods [indirectly] result from the creation of Iblīs—only God is fully aware of all of them, but we will allude to some.[19] God (Glory be to Him) did not create the Devil in vain nor did He aim, by creating him, to destroy His servants. How many dazzling wisdoms, overwhelming proofs, manifest miracles and abundant blessings does God have in creating him? Although the [parallel of Satan] for the religion and faith is like poison for the body, there do exist [greater] benefits and wisdoms in the creation of poisons than if they had lapsed.

In addition, a [hypothetical] entity that is neither good nor evil does not exist, for that would be vain. God is exalted above creating such a thing. If this subtype is barred from existing then, by extension, something wherein evil predominates should not.

Whoever deeply reflects on existence realizes that goodness predominates. Even if there are many diseases, health predominates; pleasures are greater than pains; well-being is greater than affliction; and although flooding, burning, destruction and the like are somewhat frequent [our lives] are predominated by safety from them. Had this type, wherein good predominates, not existed because of the incidental occurrence of evil then we would have missed out on many [goods]. The lapse of predominate good would then result in predominate evil. An example of this is fire: there are many benefits in its existence, yet there are also some associated harms. But if we compare them, its harm is deemed to be small relative to its overall benefit. The same applies to rain, wind, heat and cold. In general, the good constituents of this lower world are mixed in with evil ones, but the good predominates. On the other hand, the heavenly world is devoid of all those [evils].

If it asked: Why did the Most Wise not create this world devoid of evil such that it was only absolute good? It would have been possible [for God] to create it just like the heavenly world devoid of evil. Furthermore, even if we concede that good predominates over evil, what good or benefit results from allowing the existence of Iblīs, the head and source of all that is evil, and the leader of the disbelievers? And what good is there in allowing the Devil to remain until the end of time? And what predominant good exists in creating ninety-nine [percent of humanity] for Hellfire and only one for Paradise?[20] And what predominant good is there in removing our parents [Adam and Eve] from Paradise so as to allow what has occurred to their offspring? Had they remained in Paradise they would have been completely free from all evil.

And if God created us to worship Him, why did His wisdom dictate that most people would turn away and only a minority would be granted success? And what predominant good is there in creating disbelief, sinfulness, disobedience, injustice and transgression? And what good is there in allowing pain to occur to those who are not charged with obligations, such as children,[21] insane people [or animals]? [They further maintain] that if you claim that they will be compensated (*taʿwīḍ*) [with Paradise], then the pain animals endure [since they will not enter Paradise] contradicts that.

Moreover, [they continue], what good is there in creating the Antichrist[22] and enabling him to appear and seduce people? And if it was necessary that [His] wisdom dictate that, then what good occurs by allowing him to possess supernatural powers and wonders? And what good is there in magic, which results in corruption and evil? And what good is there in allowing people to become factions whereby some are injured by others? And what good is there in creating poisons, creatures that are endowed with these poisons, and animals that are by nature hostile and harmful? And what good is there in allowing the death of a young child after creating him in the best state or allowing him to reach an old contemptible age after being healthy and well? And what about the destruction of a home and the obliteration of its remnants?

Finally, if you ignore all of the above, then what predominant or preponderant good is there in the presence of Hellfire, for it is the abode of the greatest evils and severest afflictions? There is no way to account for all of these concerns except by: [1] denying His wisdom and causality, and instead attributing the [structure and events of this] universe to His will alone; or [2] claiming emanation from His Essence and that the Lord cannot do anything out of His free choice or will.

For these reasons, the groups who subscribe to the aforementioned two claims have resorted to denying causality altogether.[23] Otherwise, [they ask] how can you reconcile between maintaining [His] wisdom and causality and between these issues?

We reply by first saying: Glory be to God (*subḥān Allāh*); all praise is due to God (*al-ḥamd li'llāh*); there is no deity but God (*lā ilāh illā Allāh*); and God is the greatest (*Allāh akbar*). By affirming these phrases [and their deeper meanings] we possess the curative response: *Our Lord! Thou createdst not this in vain. Glory be to Thee! Preserve us from the doom of Fire;*[24] *And We created not the heaven and the earth, and all that is between them, in play. We created them not save with truth; but most of them know not;*[25] *And We created not the heaven and the earth and all that is between them in vain. That is the opinion of those who disbelieve. And woe unto those who disbelieve, from the Fire!*[26] *Deemed ye then that We had created you for naught, and that ye would not be returned unto Us? Now God be Exalted, the True King! There is no deity save Him, the Lord of the Throne of Grace.*[27] *God it is Who hath created seven heavens, and of the earth the like thereof. The commandment cometh down among them slowly, that ye may know that God is able to do all things, and that God surroundeth all things in knowledge;*[28] *God hath appointed the Kaʿba, the Sacred House, a standard for humankind, and the Sacred Month and the offerings and the garlands. That is so that ye may know that God knoweth whatsoever is in the heavens and whatsoever is in the earth, and that God is knower* (*ʿalīm*) *of all things.*[29] *The doing of God Who perfecteth all things,*[30] *Who made all things good which He created.*[31] *Thou* (*Muḥammad*) *canst see no fault in the Beneficent's creation.*[32] There is no disharmony in the Sublime's creation. Instead, everything is exceptionally harmonious, exists in the most perfect manner, and fulfils its praiseworthy objectives and intended wise purposes.

Only God (Glory be to Him) knows these wisdoms and objectives in detail, yet He enlightens those whom He wills of His servants to the slightest aspects of them. The proximate angels asked Him some questions, which were fundamentally the same type [as the aforementioned ones], whereupon He responded, *Surely I know that which ye know not.*[33] They then acknowledged that His knowledge and wisdom are perfect, and that all His actions are upon the Straight Path. They said, *Be glorified! We have no knowledge saving that which Thou hast taught us. Thou, only Thou, art the Omniscient, the Most Wise.*[34] Furthermore, once some of His wisdoms became apparent to them, *He said, Did I not tell you that I know the secret of the heavens and the earth? And I know that which ye disclose and which ye hide.*[35]

We will now, God willing, recount some important principles through which the answer to these questions will become clear. Many of the speculative theologians (*mutakallimīn*) have again claimed that one cannot account for those [aforementioned questions] except by [first] arguing that His actions emanate from His Essence, or [second] by negating [His] wisdom and causality. According to the latter, the Sublime does not do anything for a reason, nor does He command anything for a wise purpose, nor does He render one thing a cause for the occurrence of another. Instead, they claim that everything is exclusively due to His absolute will and power. Moreover, they claim that one cannot ask: Why? How? For what reason or for what wisdom does He act in a particular manner? Nor [do they claim that it can be said] that His actions are principally done to result in what is most advantageous.

Now Rāzī[36] said in *al-Mabāḥith* [*al-mashriqiyya*],

> If it is asked, 'Why did the Creator not create things devoid of evil?' I would reply that if He would have made it as such, then everything would have been of the first type, i.e. pure good, which we have already discussed. But reason would allow another type wherein good predominates over evil. We have already indicated that the existence of this type is appropriate. But this answer does not appeal to me because those who claim this must state that everything, whether good or evil, only exists due to the free choice and will of God. For example, the combustion that occurs due to fire is not a requisite of fire itself, but instead God (Exalted is He) freely chooses to create that [burning] after the fire contacts [some object]. Now, if fire causes burning only as a result of the free choice of God and His will, He could have chosen to create its capacity to burn when beneficial and not [combust] when evil/harm [ensues]. Thus, there is no way to reconcile what exists except by explaining that the Sublime's actions necessarily emanate from Him, not by [His] intention or free choice (*fāʿilan bi'l-dhāt*). Ultimately, in short, this issue goes back to the question of pre-eternity and temporal origination (*al-qidam wa'l-ḥudūth*).[37]

Observe how Rāzī acknowledges that there is no way to reconcile these issues except by disbelieving in all of what the messengers [conveyed] from the first of them to the last, by negating [fundamental principles of] all of the revealed Books from God, and by contradicting what clear reason (*ṣarīḥ al-ʿaql*) knows [to be true], i.e. that the Creator (Glory be to Him) of this universe wills and chooses freely, that whatever He wills exists by virtue of His will, and whatever He does not will is non-existent due to the absence of His will for it. Thus, Rāzī has avowed that there is no way to reconcile these issues except by adhering to the methodology of those [philosophers] who are enemies of the messengers and the Islamic doctrines. These [enemies] claim that God did not create the heavens and the earth in six days, nor did He originate the universe into existence after it was non-existent, nor will He annihilate it afterwards. They [also claim] that whatever proceeds from Him is not due to His free choice or will.

Rāzī has no further opinion [on this matter]. Then there is the viewpoint of the Jabriyya, who deny causality and His wisdom. Finally, there is the viewpoint of [some] Muʿtazila, who affirm [the existence of] wisdom, but [claim] that it does not originate from the Agent. They then obligated Him to have [divine] providence for what is advantageous—in doing so they anthropomorphized the Creator. These [Muʿtazila] also prescribed canonical laws in accordance with their reasoning. In doing so they commanded and prohibited laws concordant to what they obligated or forbade upon Him. These three opinions waver in Rāzī's chest—their waves launch him around just like a ship cast about in a stormy tempest. A rational person would not accept any of these doctrines, since they contradict reason, revelation and the innate disposition.

We respond by the grace of God, and all praise is due to Him: The middle ground viewpoint is ours and it is the correct one. On the other hand, the enemies of the messengers deny the Agent's free choice and will; [secondly] the Jahmiyya[38] and Jabriyya deny [His] wisdom, causality and reason; and [thirdly] the Qadariyya[39] (who are the Zoroastrians [of this Community])[40] deny the Exalted Lord's universal power, will and wisdom, which encompass what He loves and dislikes. They also deny what are necessary [concomitants] of His praiseworthiness, as well as the requisites, meanings and effects of His Names and Attributes. We absolve ourselves in front of God (Exalted is He) of all of those claims.

The first key principle is to affirm that God (Glory be to Him) is omniscient and knows particulars, that there is nothing hidden from Him, nor anything that escapes Him whether in the heavens or the earth. Two groups have denied this principle:

The first are those who are the enemies of all of the messengers. These include the philosophers [such as Ibn Sīnā] who deny God's knowledge of particulars. Their doctrine ultimately leads to the conclusion that He does not know anything in existence—since everything in existence is a particular. If He is not knowledgeable about particulars, then He [in their doctrine] is not knowledgeable about anything in the heavenly world, nor in this earthly one.

The second group are the fanatical Qadariyya, who claim that God does not know the actions of the servants until after their occurrence. Furthermore, the Qadariyya maintain that not only was God unaware of [their actions] until then, but He also did not inscribe [those actions in the Preserved Tablet], determine, will nor create them.

The opinion of this group is well known to be false by necessity according to the religion of all of the messengers and revealed Books of God. Furthermore, the *ḥadīth*s of the Messenger [Muḥammad] (may God bless him and grant him peace) are replete in rejecting and negating their viewpoint. The *ḥadīth*s affirm [the first principle] that He is omniscient and that His creation is not privy to any [of His knowledge] except for what He has willed to reveal and teach. Moreover, what they know compared to what God has hidden and not revealed to them is like a drop in the ocean. Al-Khiḍr said to Moses—and they were the two most knowledgeable human beings on earth at that time—'Your knowledge and mine compared to God's knowledge comprise nothing more than what this bird has taken from this sea.'[41]

It is sufficient to say about God's knowledge that *If all the trees in the earth were pens, and the sea, with seven more seas to help it, (were ink), the words of God could not be exhausted.*[42] Moreover, the knowledge of the creation compared to His knowledge is like their power compared to His power, their capability compared to His capability, and their wisdom compared to His wisdom. The most knowledgeable of the creation [Muḥammad] used to say, 'I cannot praise You enough; You are as You have praised Yourself.'[43] He also used say in the supplication of seeking guidance (*istikhāra*), 'You have power while I do not; You have knowledge while I do not; and You know all hidden matters.'[44]

God (Glory be to Him) said to the angels, *Surely I know that which ye know not.*[45] And the Sublime said to the most knowledgeable of nations, the Community of Muḥammad (may God bless him and grant him peace), *Warfare is ordained for you, though it is hateful unto you; but it may happen that ye hate a thing which is good for you, and it may happen that ye love a thing which is bad for you. God knoweth, and ye know not.*[46]

God said to the People of the Book, *And of knowledge ye have been vouchsafed but little.*[47] On the Day of Judgment, when He asks His prophets regarding the people's acceptance [of their message], they will say, *We have no knowledge. Thou, only Thou art the knower of things hidden.*[48] This is the only manner that humanity should adopt, since their knowledge is trivial and insignificant when compared to that of God (Glory be to Him). Another similitude is a faint light in comparison to the sun.

The greatest injustice, clearest ignorance, most repugnant abomination, greatest insolence and shamelessness occurs in the case of one whose knowledge is insignificant compared to that of other people—which in itself is insignificant compared to the knowledge of the messengers, and the latter itself is insignificant compared to the knowledge of the Lord of the Worlds—who criticizes God's wisdom and thinks that something other than what He has determined and foreordained would have been more appropriate. Glory be to God, the Lord of the Worlds, for He is infallible in His sovereignty, divinity and greatness above anything not befitting which the ignorant and unjust disbelievers attribute to Him.

Glory be to God (*subḥān Allāh*) is a phrase by which God is deemed far from and far above anything that contradicts His perfection, whether it be an evil, a deficiency or a fault. He is completely and absolutely infallible in every aspect and in every regard from any imagined deficiency. Affirming His praiseworthiness, perfection and divinity, and that His Essence, Attributes and actions are greater than anyone or anything else— these all negate [any imaginary faults that the ignorant attribute to Him].

This [first] principle, i.e. that the intellect, gnosis, knowledge and wisdom of all of humanity is inadequate in understanding the details of the Exalted Lord's wisdom to even the slightest degree is one that we should adhere to in this matter.

The second principle is that God (Glory be to Him) is truly eternal and His life is the most perfect and complete life. It is a life that necessarily results in [His] actions, which are derived from [His] free choice. Every living being acts; the more perfect a being, the more perfect and powerful are his actions. It is for this reason that the Exalted Lord is omnipotent (*ᶜalā kulli shay'in qadīr*), and He does that which He wills.

Bukhārī mentioned in his book *Khalq afᶜāl [al-ᶜibād]* that Naᶜīm b. Ḥammād[49] said, 'Being alive (*ḥayy*) indicates that one is an agent, and every living being acts.'[50] Therefore, the only difference between a living being and a dead one is the former's ability to act and sense.

The third principle is that [His] actions must be freely chosen and willed—they cannot conceivably occur otherwise. Furthermore, whatever emanates from an essence in the absence of its ability or choosing is not named an 'action' by any rational person—even if it was an effect [of that essence] or originated from it. Examples include the effects of: fire burning, water drowning or the sun warming. These are all effects that occur as a result of these entities, but they are not considered to be actions of theirs (even though they are due to the power or nature that God has endowed them with).

The actions and deeds of a knowledgeable living being do not occur except through his will and power. The fact that the Exalted Lord is living, acting, freely choosing and willing is agreed upon by all the messengers and Books, and is proven by reason and the innate disposition. Whoever denies that the actions of the Lord occur by His will and free choice has stubbornly rejected his Lord and Creator, and has denied that this world has a Lord.

The fourth principle is that the Sublime has linked effects to their causes in both religious (*sharʿan*) and ontological (*qadaran*) matters. Due to God's wisdom He has established causes within His religious commandments and Divine Law, His ontological laws and determination, and His sovereignty and administration. Denying causation, forces and natures represents a rejection of vital necessities, a deprecation of reason and the innate nature, an affront to experience and reality, and is an obstinate rejection of the Divine Law and recompense [in the Hereafter].

The Sublime has established and linked everything—whether people's livelihoods or the Hereafter, their reward or punishment, legal limits and expiations, commandments and prohibitions—to their respective causes. Indeed, the characteristics and actions of a servant cause what arises from him. Moreover, everything that exists represents cause and effect. All of the Divine Law represents cause and effect; and every determination is a result of cause and effect.

The Qur'ān is replete with examples that affirm causation: *What ye used to do;*[51] *What ye used to earn;*[52] *(And unto him it will be said), This is for that which thy two hands have sent before.*[53] *Whatever of misfortune striketh you, it is what your hands have earned;*[54] *(And it will be said unto those therein), Eat and drink at ease for that which ye sent on before you in past days;*[55] *Reward proportioned (to their evil deeds).*[56]

Because of the wrongdoing of the Jews We forbade them good things which were (before) made lawful unto them, and because of their much hindering from God's way, And of their taking usury when they were forbidden it, and of their devouring people's wealth by false pretenses, We have prepared for those of them who disbelieve a painful doom;[57] *Then because of their breaking of their covenant, and their disbelieving in the revelations of God, and their slaying of the prophets wrongfully, and their saying, Our hearts are hardened—Nay, but God set a seal upon them for their disbelief, so that they believe not save a few—And because of their disbelief and of their speaking against Mary a tremendous calumny; And because of their saying, We slew the Messiah, Jesus son of Mary, God's messenger;*[58] *And because of their breaking their covenant, We have cursed them and made hard their hearts.*[59]

It was by the mercy of God that thou wast lenient with them (O Muḥammad);[60] *That was because their messengers kept bringing them clear proofs (of God's Sovereignty) but they disbelieved; so God seized them.*[61] *Those who swallow usury cannot rise up save as he ariseth whom the Devil hath prostrated by (his) touch. That is because they say, Trade is just like usury;*[62] *That is because those who disbelieve follow falsehood and because those who believe follow the truth from their Lord;*[63] *And they disobeyed the messenger of their Lord, therefore did He grip them with a tightening grip;*[64] *So they denied them, and became of those who were destroyed;*[65] *But Pharaoh rebelled against the messenger, whereupon We seized him with no gentle grip;*[66] *But they denied him, and they hamstrung her, so God doomed them for their sin and razed (their dwellings);*[67] *So, when they angered Us, We punished them and drowned them every one. And We made them a thing past, and an example for those after (them).*[68]

And We send down from the sky blessed water whereby We give growth unto gardens and the grain of crops;[69] *And He it is Who sendeth the winds as tidings heralding His mercy, till, when they bear a cloud heavy (with rain), We lead it to a dead land, and then cause water to descend thereon and thereby bring forth fruits of every kind;*[70] *Whereby God guideth him who seeketh His good pleasure unto paths of peace;*[71] *Fight them! God will chastise them at your hands, and He will lay them low.*[72]

Moreover, in every instance wherein He followed some act with a religious ruling or punishment, He notified us that the former were causes for the latter. Examples include His statements: *As for the thief, both male and female, cut-off their hands. It is the reward of their own deeds, an exemplary punishment from God. God is almighty, most wise;*[73] *The adulterer and the adulteress, scourge ye each one of them (with) a hundred stripes.*[74]

And as for those who make (men) keep the Book, and establish worship—We squander not the wages of reformers;[75] *For those who disbelieve and debar (men) from the way of God, We add doom to doom because they wrought corruption.*[76] Examples of this are so numerous that it cannot be adequately covered here.

Again, in every instance of a condition and consequence, He notifies us of the causative nature of the former, and that it resulted in the latter. *O ye who believe! If ye keep your duty to God, He will give you discrimination (between right and wrong);*[77] *And when your Lord proclaimed, If ye give thanks, I will give you more; but if ye are thankless, lo! My punishment is dire.*[78] Every instance where God declared the wisdom of a ruling or its final objective also represents evidence of causality. The final objective is the reason for the effective cause.

If we listed all the instances where causation is affirmed in the Qur'ān and the Sunna, they would exceed 10,000. This is not an exaggeration but rather the reality. It is sufficient that the senses, reason and innate disposition all attest to it. Some scholars said, 'A group has denied causality leading those who are rational to ridicule the former's reasoning. The former thought that they were affirming His Oneness, but instead they resembled the Muᶜaṭṭila (those who stripped away the Attributes and perfect characteristics of the Lord, denied His exaltedness above His creation and highness above His throne, and His revelation of His Books to His angels and servants).

One of the greatest offenses against the Divine Law, the prophets and His Oneness is to deceive people into thinking that [affirmation of] His Oneness cannot occur except when causality is denied. If those theologians do not think that they can affirm the Oneness of the Lord (Glory be to Him) except by denying causality then they have misunderstood both His Oneness and the prophets who conveyed it.

You will not find any book that affirms causality more than the Qur'ān. By God, is it so surprising that God has created both cause and effect, has made the former result in the latter, and made them both subject to His will, power and wisdom? But if He wills to annul the effectiveness of something He could do so just like He negated the ability of the fire to burn His friend Abraham and the ability of water to drown [Moses] and his people. If He wills He can establish barriers that obstruct the manifestation of those causes. And finally, if He wills He can allow [the cause] to be effective. The Sublime has allowed all of these scenarios to occur.

In what manner does [causality] negate His Oneness? How does polytheism result from [affirming causality]? If those who have weak intellects hear that the fire does not burn, water does not drown, bread does not satisfy, the sword does not cut, and that they are not effective or causative, but rather it is only the Creator who chooses and wills the occurrence of each of these effects each time,[79] then they may have doubts [about the religion itself].

This group claims that only their [doctrine] affirms His Oneness and that the Lord is solely responsible for creating the effects [of causes in every instance]. But they do not realize that this is the wrong interpretation of monotheism, and it instead empowers the enemies of the messengers over the religion the latter conveyed.

The Exalted said about Dhū al-Qarnayn, *We established him securely on earth, and endowed him with [the knowledge of] the right means to achieve anything [that he might set out to achieve].*[80] The [interpretation of *sababā* ([*the knowledge of*] *the right means*)] is 'knowledge', according to Ibn ʿAbbās[81]. Qatāda, Ibn Zayd,[82] Ibn Jurayj,[83] al-Ḍaḥḥāk[84] and Abū Isḥāq al-Zajjāj said that it is 'knowledge that results in what one desires'. Al-Mubarrad[85] said, 'A cause (*sabab*) is any entity that allows one thing to result in another.' Many exegetes interpreted the cause that God bestowed Dhū al-Qarnayn as every type of knowledge that the creation would need from him.

Also God (Glory be to Him) named the 'road' (*ṭarīq*) as a cause in His verse, *And he followed a road*,[86] according to Mujāhid.[87] The Sublime also named the paths to heaven as 'causes' (*asbāb*). The Exalted said in the verse narrated from Pharaoh, *O Haman! Build for me a tower that haply I may reach the roads (asbāb), the roads of the heavens.*[88] A 'rope' is also named a 'cause' because it allows one to reach his goal. The Exalted said, *Let him stretch a rope (sabab) up to the roof (of his dwelling).*[89] Some linguists maintained that a 'rope' can only be named a 'cause' if it is strong and allows one to utilize it to ascend and descend.

The Sublime also named the ties between people as 'causes' because they are the causes by which they can mutually achieve their needs. The Exalted said, *Then would those who are followed clear themselves of those who follow (them): They would see the penalty, and all relations (asbāb) between them would be cut-off.*[90]

In summary, God (Glory be to Him) named all of these things 'causes' because they allow one to reach a desired goal. Those who deny causality deem these to only be figurative expressions rather than being realities. We ask God for guidance.

CHAPTER THREE

Affirming the Exalted Lord's Wisdom in His Creation and Commandments

Pure reason and the sound innate disposition have corroborated what the Qur'ān and the Sunna prove: that God (Glory be to Him) is the Most Wise and He does not do anything in vain or without purpose, benefit or wisdom. Instead, all of the Sublime's actions have intended objectives and proceed from His far-reaching wisdom. Likewise they are originated through causes. His words and those of His Messenger all substantiate the above. There exist such a great number of instances that they cannot all be listed individually, but we will recount some.

The first type occurs when He clearly states the word 'wisdom' (*ḥikma*): *Effective wisdom*;[1] *God revealeth unto thee the Book and wisdom*;[2] *He giveth wisdom unto whom He will, and he unto whom wisdom is given, he truly hath received abundant good.*[3] Wisdom is comprised of beneficial knowledge and pious deeds. It is also named 'wisdom' because the knowledge and deeds therein lead to praiseworthy ends and beneficial objectives. But if a speaker does not intend to [firstly] benefit those whom he is addressing or lead them to their guidance and happiness; nor [secondly intend to] show them the means that would lead them to those [two] or obstacles [that would hinder them] from being [guided or blissful]; and furthermore [thirdly] does not send the messengers or reveal the Books, nor [fourthly] establish the reward or punishment predicated on the above; then that being is not wise, his words are not considered to reflect wisdom, nor [would his wisdom be] effective or far-reaching.

The second type is that He notifies us that He commanded something for a particular reason, like His statements: *That is so that ye may know that God knoweth whatsoever is in the heavens and whatsoever is in the earth;*[4] *God it is Who hath created seven heavens, and of the earth the like thereof. The commandment cometh down among them slowly, that ye may know that God is able to do all things, and that God surroundeth all things in knowledge;*[5] *God hath appointed the Kaʿba, the Sacred House, a standard for humankind, and the Sacred Month and the offerings and the garlands. That is so that ye may know that God knoweth whatsoever is in the heavens and whatsoever is in the earth, and that God is knower of all things.*[6]

Messengers of good cheer and of warning, in order that humankind might have no argument against God after the messengers;[7] *We reveal unto thee the Book with the truth, that thou mayst judge between humankind by that which God showeth thee;*[8] *That the People of the Book may know that they control naught of the bounty of God, but that the bounty is in God's Hand to give to whom He will;*[9] *And We appointed the qibla which ye formerly observed only that We might know him who followeth the Messenger, from him who turneth on his heels.*[10]

Save unto every messenger whom He hath chosen, and then He maketh a guard to go before him and a guard behind him. That He may know that they have indeed conveyed the messages of their Lord.[11] God has notified us of this to indicate that He has established [angels] to guard and protect the messengers [from the jinn demons] so as to allow them to convey His message.

When He made the slumber fall upon you as a reassurance from him and sent down water from the sky upon you, that thereby He might purify you, and remove from you the fear of Satan, and make strong your hearts and firm (your) feet thereby.[12] *That He might cause the Truth to triumph and bring vanity to naught;*[13] *God ordained this only as a message of good cheer for you, and that thereby your hearts might be at rest;*[14] *Say: The Holy Spirit hath delivered it from thy Lord with truth, that it may confirm (the faith of) those who believe;*[15] *We have appointed only angels to be wardens of the Fire, and their number have We made to be a stumbling-block for those who disbelieve; that those to whom the Book hath been given may have certainty, and that believers may increase in faith;*[16] *Thus We have appointed you a middle nation, that ye may be witnesses against humankind, and that the Messenger may be a witness against you.*[17]

We have revealed unto thee the Remembrance that thou mayst explain to humankind that which hath been revealed for them;[18] *This is a clear message for humankind in order that they may be warned thereby, and that they may know that He is only One God, and that men of understanding may take heed;*[19] *We verily sent Our messengers with clear proofs, and revealed with them the Book and the Balance, that humankind may observe right measure; and He revealed iron, wherein is mighty power and (many) uses for humankind, and that God may know him who helpeth Him and His messengers, though Unseen;*[20] *Thus did We show Abraham the kingdom of the heavens and the earth that he might be of those possessing certainty;*[21] *And horses and mules and asses (hath He created) that ye may ride them, and for ornament. And He createth that which ye know not.*[22] There are many similar verses in the Qur'ān.

But if it is contended that the letter *lām* is only used to indicate the consequence and effect of the action (i.e. *lām al-ʿāqiba*) rather than being *lām al-taʿlīl*—where the latter indicates that what was intended and desired [was done for a reason or wise purpose][23]—then the response is twofold. Firstly, *lām al-ʿāqiba* is only used regarding [1] those who are either ignorant of the [true] consequences [of their actions] or [2] those who cannot repel the [effects] of them. God's statement [about Pharaoh] illustrates [1]: *And the family of Pharaoh took him up, that he might become for them an enemy and a sorrow.*[24] The following poetry exemplifies [2]:

> Even though you may try to resist death
> You and everything you construct will inevitably perish.

It is, on the other hand, impossible for *lām al-ʿāqiba* to be used in the case of God as He is omniscient and omnipotent. Instead, only *lām al-ḥikma* [and *lām al-taʿlīl*], which indicate the wisdoms and intended objectives, are used.

We will now respond to each instance [in which the Ashʿariyya and others argued in favour of *lām al-ʿāqiba* rather than *lām al-taʿlīl*]. His statement, *And the family of Pharaoh took him up, that he might become for them an enemy and a sorrow,*[25] indicates the reason for the predestination and decree of God (Glory be to Him) that Moses would [ultimately] become an enemy [to Pharaoh and his people], and a cause for their sorrow. God mentioned the action [of Pharaoh's family] rather than His predestination because it is more emphatic.

Those who freely choose their own actions, which then ultimately lead to their destruction, incur greater sorrow, grief and regret than those who must suffer due to [forces] outside their control.

The Sublime wanted to manifest to Pharaoh, his people and to others of His creation: His Omnipotence, perfect knowledge and dazzling wisdom. Despite the fact that Pharaoh was killing the [Israelite] children in order to pursue Moses, he [and his family] would eventually raise Moses in his own home, and by his own free choice and desire.

As for the statement of the Exalted, *And even so do We try some of them by others that they say, Are these they whom God favoureth among us?*[26] there is no doubt that this explains the reasoning for His mentioned action, i.e. the tribulation of some of His creation through others. Once the leaders and nobles see that the slaves, weak ones and destitute become believers, their pride and racism may prevent them from becoming Muslims themselves. They may think to themselves, 'How can it be that [the latter] have beaten us to something good or beneficial while we have lagged behind. Had it been something good or led to bliss, they could not have done so.' Their statement is evidence of the wisdom and desired objective of this tribulation as it epitomizes their stubbornness, haughtiness and refusal to follow the truth even after fully comprehending it.

Now the above [tribulation] is a cause leading to another desired objective. Sometimes causes have objectives which are desired for themselves, and sometimes they are desired for other [indirect ones]. In the latter case, [the cause ultimately] becomes a means to reach something directly desired. Therefore, this statement of theirs manifests [God's] justice, glory, power, reign and wisdom in favouring those who are suitable [for His guidance], while denying those who are not and instead deserve [to remain astray].

It is for this reason that the Exalted said, *Is not God best aware of the thanksgivers?*[27] This refers to those who have recognized and thanked Him for His great blessings and favours, which He bestowed upon them. Conversely, others did not acknowledge nor thank their Lord for those blessings. Therefore, this tribulation of some by others is a cause, which allows the occurrence of their differentiation.

As for His verse, *That He may make that which the Devil proposeth a temptation for those in whose hearts is a disease, and those whose hearts are hardened,*[28] this is similar in that it involves the use of the letter *lām* to indicate wisdom and causality. God (Glory be to Him) has notified us that He has made that which Satan proposes—in regards to the aspirations of the Messenger—a tribulation and test for people. Thus, those whose hearts are [spiritually] diseased and hardened become seduced [by those Satanic calumnies]. On the other hand, the believers are certain that the Qur'ān and the Messenger are the truth, while the proposition of Satan is falsehood. Therefore, their hearts submit in humility.[29]

God also informed us that those who have been given knowledge recognize the truth from their Lord in the matter of allegories. They state, *We believe therein; the whole is from our Lord.*[30] Thus, in both of these instances mentioned [i.e. Satanic calumnies in the prior verse and allegories in this verse there existed some obscurity], but the believers' faith only increased, while those whose hearts strayed from the truth were seduced.

God (Glory be to Him) perfectly established His verses[31] in contrast and in opposition to that which Satan has proposed. In a similar vein, the clear-cut verses counter the [misinterpretations of the] allegorical ones. Here the established prescriptions are akin to the clear-cut revelations, while the abolishment of that which Satan proposes is like rejecting what is [misinterpreted of the] allegorical [verses] and instead following what is clear-cut.

Now, *iḥkām* has three meanings. Firstly, it means 'clear-cut' in contrast to allegories (*mutashābih*). God has said, *He it is Who hath revealed unto thee (Muḥammad) the Book wherein are clear revelations—they are the substance of the Book—and others (which are) allegorical.*[32]

Secondly, it means that His revelation is established, in contrast to what Satan has proposed. God has said, *But God abolisheth that which Satan proposeth. Then God establisheth His revelations.*[33] This type is generalized to all of His verses for they are established, arranged and elucidated. Another example is His statement, *(This is) a Book the revelations whereof are perfected.*[34]

Thirdly, it indicates that His revelation is established in contrast to the verses which are abrogated. The Predecessors would often say, 'This verse is established (*muḥkama*), not abrogated.'

Ultimately, the point is that the verse, *That He may make that which the Devil proposeth a temptation for those in whose hearts is a disease,*[35] contains *lām al-taʿlīl*, which indicates that this trial and test manifests the three different types of hearts. The [1] hardened and [2] diseased hearts manifest the doubts and disbeliefs, which are hidden within them. On the other hand, the [3] humble hearts may now manifest their faith and guidance, which was previously veiled. The [believers'] hatred of disbelief and polytheism as well as their desire to avoid them also increases. Thus, great wisdoms occur as a result of [God allowing] Satan's calumnies.

Furthermore, His statement, *That he who perished (on that day) might perish by a clear proof (of His sovereignty) and he who survived might survive by a clear proof (of His sovereignty),*[36] includes the *lām al-taʿlīl*. It is mentioned to manifest His wisdom in gathering His saints and enemies together even though there had been no prior appointment[37]. God then gave victory to His saints, despite their smaller numbers, weakness and lack of preparation, over [His enemies] who were more powerful, greater in number and better armed. Indeed, no one would have conceived of the former prevailing. Thus, this is one of the greatest miracles of the Lord (Glory be to Him), Who fulfilled His promise in His Book to His Messenger to destroy those who have chosen disbelief and stubbornness despite receiving clear guidance, and to grant [spiritual] life to those who have faith in God and His Messenger. The disbelievers will therefore have no excuse in front of God for themselves, while the believers will have no further doubts or uncertainties after the manifestation of these clear proofs. God (Exalted is He) said similarly, *And We have not taught him (Muḥammad) poetry, nor is it meet for him. This is naught else than a Reminder and a Lecture making plain, to warn whosoever liveth, and that the word may be fulfilled against the disbelievers.*[38]

His statement, *That the hearts of those who believe not in the Hereafter may incline thereto* to the end of the verse,[39] also includes a *lām al-taʿlīl*. It indicates the reason for the whisperings of the [devils of humankind and jinn]: they are trying to deceive others through guile, and the latter's hearts deviate towards it, take pleasure in it, and act accordingly. Thus, God (Glory be to Him) has tested their intentions through [His allowance of] these mentioned whisperings.

Now if it is viewed from the Lord's perspective (Glory be to Him), [then it should be known that] He has predestined that each of His prophets will have enemies so as to result [indirectly] in end objectives and wisdoms that are beloved to Him. Had [these enemies not existed] other more beloved things to Him [which will be discussed later] would not have occurred. Regardless, the *lām* indicates the reason and wisdom from both perspectives.

The third type involves the use of [the word] *kay*, which explicitly indicates the reason (*taʿlīl*). An example is the Exalted's statement, *That which God giveth as spoil unto His Messenger from the people of the townships, it is for God and His Messenger and for the near of kin and the orphans and the needy and the wayfarer, that it become not* (*kay lā*) *a commodity between the rich among you.*[40] Thus, the Sublime has given the reason for the division of the spoils in this manner: so that it does not become a commodity for only the rich and powerful, and so that it is distributed amongst the destitute and weak.

The [following] statement of the Sublime [is also to be considered]: *Naught of disaster befalleth in the earth or in yourselves but it is in a Book before We bring it into being—that is easy for God—That ye grieve not* (*li-kay lā*) *for the sake of that which hath escaped you, nor yet exult because of that which hath been given. God loveth not all prideful boasters.*[41] God (Glory be to Him) has notified us that He has predestined all of the adversities afflicting them before He created their souls, the hardships themselves, or this earth. This is all easily done by Him due to His omnipotence, [omniscience] and far-reaching wisdom. In addition, it becomes easier for His servants to avoid being grieved for what has eluded them since they recognize that these afflictions were predestined by Him and inscribed in His [Preserved Tablet] before they themselves were created.

Since hardships involve [1] the lapse of what was beloved [in the past] or a fear that [what one loves] will escape one [in the future], or [2] the occurrence of what is disliked or the fear that it will occur, He advised the one who has had something beloved escape him not to grieve, and [cautioned] against exulting if [what is beloved] does occur. Instead one should prepare for the loss [of what is beloved] prior to attaining it, and be patient and endure [some hardship] if it does occur.

The fourth type involves mentioning the reason for an action and its cause. An example is His statement, *And We reveal the Book unto thee as an exposition of all things, and a guidance and a mercy and good tidings for those who have surrendered (to God).*[42] Also the verses, *And We destroyed no township but it had its warners for reminder, for We never were oppressors.*[43] *By those who bring down the Reminder, to excuse or to warn*[44] refer to the purpose of establishing a justification against [the disbelievers] or as a warning [to them]. He also stated, *We gave the Book unto Moses, complete for him who would do good, an explanation of all things, a guidance and a mercy, that they might believe in the meeting with their Lord.*[45] Thus, all of that was done for those reasons.

As for His verses, *Have they not then observed the sky above them, how We have constructed it*... to His statement *A vision and a reminder for every penitent servant*,[46] they indicate that [His creation exists] for the purpose of enlightening [humanity] and [enabling them] to remember Him. The difference between the two is that enlightenment (*tabṣira*) results in knowledge and gnosis, whereas remembrance (*dhikran*) leads one to be penitent and submissive. Guidance occurs through both [enlightenment and remembrance].

The fifth type occurs by using the word 'lest' (*an*) followed by some [statement of the disbelievers]—the reason for [His action] therefore becomes clear. For example, His statements, *Lest ye should say, The Book was revealed only to two sects before us*;[47] *Lest any soul should say, Alas, my grief that I was unmindful of God.*[48]

Another example is the statement of the Exalted, *And (remember) when thy Lord brought forth from the Children of Adam, from their reins, their seed, and made them testify of themselves, (saying), Am I not your Lord? They said, Yea, verily. We testify. (That was) lest ye should say at the Day of Judgment, Of this we were unaware; Or lest ye should say, (It is) only (that) our fathers ascribed partners to God of old and we were (their) seed after them.*[49] Thus God (Glory be to Him) mentioned that the wisdom of making them testify is so that they would not make excuses on the Day of

Judgment, whether it be claiming ignorance of His command or that they were just following their forefathers.

Also consider His statement, *Remind (humankind) hereby lest a soul be destroyed by what it earneth.*[50] This indicates that the Qur'ān should be used [to remind people]; but if they disbelieve (*an tubsala*), that will be the reason for their destruction and punishment.

The sixth type is to mention clearly the reasoning by saying 'for that reason/cause or because' (*min ajl*). An example is God's statement (Exalted is He), *For that cause We decreed for the Children of Israel that whosoever killeth a human being for other than manslaughter or corruption in the earth, it shall be as if he had killed all humankind.*[51] One group thought that the *cause* referred to in this verse was [Cain's] regret after murdering his brother [Abel], but this is misleading as it goes against the ordering of the verse, diminishes the lofty reason for the decree that was mentioned, and minimizes the calamity that murder results in.

Some will ask: How can it be that one of the sons of Adam murdering another is the reason for His ruling upon other nations? And even if it is the reason, how can it be that murdering only one is like killing all of humanity? My response is that the Lord (Glory be to Him) has made His predestined ontological will a reason for His religious commandments. Since He considers murder to be one of the greatest types of injustice and corruption, He stressed its [evil] nature and deemed its evilness greater than any other [sin]. Therefore, He drew a parallel between murdering one person and killing all of humankind. It is not required that this comparison be the same in all aspects. But since both the killer of all of humankind and the murderer of one will go to Hellfire, from [this aspect] the analogy is appropriate.

Similarly, the person who drinks one drop of alcohol or has committed fornication once is sinful just as one who drinks a tremendous amount or has committed fornication repeatedly even though there is a difference in the degree of sinfulness. Mujāhid stated, 'Whoever murders one person goes to Hellfire just like the killer of all of humankind.'[52] Therefore, the basis of this comparison is in the occurrence of the punishment, not its extent. There are many other interpretations of this verse.

The seventh type involves mentioning the reason using the wording 'so that' (*laʿalla*). It is used in the words of God (Glorious and Exalted is He) to indicate the [definitive] reason. When *laʿalla* is said by a human though, there is an element of hope [or uncertainty] attached to it. An example is His statement, *O humankind! Worship your Lord, Who hath created you and those before you, so that ye may ward off (evil).*[53] Essentially, *so that ye may ward off evil* is the reason for His religious commandment of *O humankind! Worship your Lord* and for creating us. Also derived are His verses: *O ye who believe! Fasting is prescribed for you, even as it was prescribed for those before you, that ye may ward off (evil)*;[54] *So that he might bethink himself or [at least] be filled with apprehension.*[55]

The eighth type is where God mentioned an ontological or religious ruling after the reason for it. The [first example] follows utilizing *inna*, the [second] is preceded by the letter *fā'*, and the [third] is mentioned alone. The first example is illustrated in His verses: *And Zachariah, when he cried unto his Lord, My Lord! Leave me not childless, though Thou art the best of inheritors. Then We heard his prayer, and bestowed upon him John, and adjusted his wife (to bear a child) for him. They used to vie (innahum) one with the other in good deeds, and they cried unto Us in longing and in fear, and were submissive unto Us*;[56] *Those who keep from evil will dwell amid gardens and watersprings, taking that which their Lord giveth them; for aforetime (innahum) they were doers of good*;[57] *Thus it was, that We might ward off from him evil and lewdness. He was (innahu) of Our chosen servants*;[58] *And as for those who make (men) keep the Book, and establish worship—We (innā) squander not the wages of reformers.*[59]

As for [using *fā'*] it is represented in His verses: *As for the thief, both male and female, cut-off their hands. It is the reward of their own deeds*;[60] *The adulterer and the adulteress, scourge ye each one of them (with) a hundred stripes*;[61] *And those who accuse honourable women but bring not four witnesses, scourge them (with) eighty stripes.*[62]

As for the third example it is contained in His verses: *Those who keep from evil will dwell amid gardens and watersprings*;[63] *Those who believe and do good works and establish worship and pay zakāt, their reward is with their Lord.*[64] The Qur'ān and the Sunna are filled with more than 1000 instances of this.

If it is claimed, 'The above only helps to illustrate that these actions represent causes for their effects, but they do not necessitate that the Lord's actions or commandments entail causality,' we reply: Since the Lord (Glory be to Him) made those characterizations as reasons and causes for their respective rulings, this proves that He rules in both a religious and ontological fashion, and that He did not rule without reason or wisdom. Therefore, whoever rejects causality and rulings has not permitted causes, wise purposes or final objectives to be involved in the ontological and religious rulings of the Lord.

Whoever examines the religion of the Lord, His determination and His recompense becomes absolutely certain that those who deny [His wisdom and causality] are wrong. God (Glory be to Him) has arranged all of [His] rulings based on respective causes and reasons. He clearly illustrated them [to be correct using many means], including through knowledge, the senses, innate disposition and rationality. If we were to mention this in detail, it would take many volumes.

The ninth type is that God (Glory be to Him) will state that the presence of a barrier is the reason for the absence of an ontological or religious ruling. An example is His statement: *And were it not that humankind would have become one community, We might well have appointed, for those who disbelieve in the Beneficent (al-Raḥmān), roofs of silver for their houses and stairs (of silver) whereby to mount;*[65] *And if God were to enlarge the provision for His servants they would surely rebel in the earth, but He sendeth down by measure as He willeth. He is informed, a seer of His bondmen.*[66]

They say, Why hath not an angel been sent down unto him? If We sent down an angel, then the matter would be judged; no further time would be allowed them (for reflection). Had we appointed him (Our Messenger) an angel, We assuredly would have made him (as) a man (that he might speak to men); and (thus) obscured for them (the truth) they (now) obscure.[67] Thus, the Sublime informed us of the barrier—i.e. His wisdom and divine providence for His creation—that prevented the sending down of an angel whom they could clearly see. Had they disbelieved after seeing an angel, their punishment would have been hastened without delay.

Another example is God's statement (Exalted is He): *Naught hindereth Us from sending portents save that the folk of old denied them.*[68] Thus, the Sublime informed us of His wisdom for not sending His messengers with the miraculous portents that they desired—it is because these [portents] do not necessarily result in faith. The prior generations had been granted them, but continued to disbelieve, and were destroyed as a result. Since there was no benefit in sending [portents] to those [prior nations], it was completely inconsistent with His wisdom (Glory be to Him) [to grant them to the Quraysh].

The tenth type involves God mentioning His wisdoms and objectives that He has endowed His creation with or commanded things for. Examples include His statements: *Who hath appointed the earth a resting-place for you, and the sky a canopy; and causeth water to pour down from the sky, thereby producing fruits as food for you;*[69] *And God hath given you in your houses an abode, and hath given you (also), of the hides of cattle, houses which ye find light (to carry) on the day of migration and on the day of pitching camp; and of their wool and their fur and their hair, caparison and comfort for a while. And God hath given you, of that which He hath created, shelter from the sun; and hath given you places of refuge in the mountains, and hath given you coats to ward off the heat from you, and coats (of armour) to save you from your own foolhardiness.*[70]

And of His signs is this: He created for you helpmeets from yourselves that ye might find rest in them;[71] *God is He Who created the heavens and the earth, and causeth water to descend from the sky, thereby producing fruits as food for you, and maketh the ships to be of service unto you, that they may run upon the sea at His command, and hath made of service unto you the rivers; And maketh the sun and the moon, constant in their courses, to be of service unto you, and hath made of service unto you the night and the day.*[72] *God it is Who hath made the sea of service unto you that the ships may run thereon by His command, and that ye may seek of His bounty, and that haply ye may be thankful.*[73]

All of these verses, in addition to many more of them, are included in the Qur'ān, and they indicate conclusively—to any one who has a minimum ability to reflect on them—that God (Glory be to Him) acts in accordance with wisdoms and benefits, some of which He mentions and some of which He does not.

And thy Lord inspired the bee, saying, Choose thou habitations in the hills and in the trees and in that which they thatch; Then eat of all fruits, and follow the ways of thy Lord, made smooth (for thee). There cometh forth from their bellies a drink divers of hues, wherein is healing for humankind. Herein is indeed a portent for people who reflect;[74] *And the cattle hath He created, whence ye have warm clothing and uses, and whereof ye eat; And wherein is beauty for you, when ye bring them home, and when ye take them out to pasture. And they bear your loads for you unto a land ye could not reach save with great trouble to yourselves. Your Lord is most kind, merciful. And horses and mules and asses (hath He created) that ye may ride them, and for ornament. And He createth that which ye know not.*[75]

How can all these [creations] be deemed sound and correct if the One originating them does not do so for wise purposes, benefits or specifically intended objectives? It is necessarily evident that affirmation or denial [of His wisdom] represents two extremes of the spectrum.

The eleventh type is that God (Glory be to Him) criticizes those who think that He has not originated the creation for any objective or wise purpose. Examples include His statements: *Deemed ye then that We had created you for naught, and that ye would not be returned unto Us?*[76] *Thinketh man that he is to be left aimless?*[77] *And We created not the heavens and the earth, and all that is between them, in play. We created them not save with truth.*[78] The *truth* here connotes the commandments and praiseworthy objectives that all of these entities were created for. They include:

[1] Knowing God (Exalted is He) as well as His Names, Attributes, actions and signs.

[2] [Showing] that He is to be loved, worshipped, thanked, remembered and obeyed.

[3] [Emphasising] that He is able to command, forbid and prescribe the Divine Law.

[4] [Highlighting] that He is able to regulate all affairs and administer His kingdom concordantly.

[5] [Making clear] that He will reward the devout for their righteousness, and punish the sinners for their disobedience. As a result, His justice and grace are witnessed. He is praiseworthy for [both His justice and grace] and will be thanked [by the believers].

[6] Enabling His creation to know that there is no other deity or Lord but Him.

[7] Making manifest His various Names and Attributes in both the intellectual and material realms. Thus, His servants will not only know [His Names and Attributes], but also witness their manifestation in reality.

[8] Enabling the faithful to act truthfully, so that He may bestow upon them His magnanimous reward. On the other hand, the sinners will spread falsehoods; and therefore, they will deserve to be disgraced by Him.

[9] Granting the opportunity to all of His creation to bear witness that He alone is their God, that He alone deserves to be worshipped, and that He is their Lord, Creator and Sovereign Owner.

[10] Manifesting the signs of His holy perfection. Creating and originating are necessary requisites of His perfection as He is living, omniscient and omnipotent. Whoever is characterized as such can only be an Agent who is freely choosing.

[11] Displaying the signs of His wisdom amongst His creation by putting everyone in a place appropriate [to his deeds]. Humankind will thus witness God's greatness and His dazzling wisdom to be concordant with their rationality and innate disposition.

[12] The Sublime loves to be magnanimous, to bestow His blessings, to forgive, to have mercy and to pardon; therefore, it is inevitable that the necessary concomitants of all these exist both from the ontological and deontological perspectives.

[13] God also loves to be lauded, praised, extolled, glorified and exalted.

[14] Allowing the manifestation of many proofs for His lordship, Oneness and divinity.

In fact, there are many other wisdoms encompassing His creation, for God originated His creation based upon the truth. The basis [of His creating] is the truth, the purpose of it is the truth, and it is permeated with the truth. God (Exalted is He) commends those believing servants of His who deem Him to be infallible above bringing creatures into existence without any reason or objective. The Exalted said, *Such as remember God, standing, sitting and reclining, and consider the creation of the heavens and the earth, (and say), Our Lord! Thou createdst not this in vain. Glory be to Thee!*[79] He also informed us that only His enemies claim that [His creation is in vain], not His saints: *And We created not the heaven and the earth and all that is between them in vain. That is the opinion of those who disbelieve.*[80]

How can anyone who knows Him say that He has not created for wise ends that He intends, or commanded and prohibited things for wise reasons. They claim instead that His creating and commandments emanate solely as a result of His will and power devoid of any wisdom or intended objective. Does this not represent anything but a rejection of the reality of His praiseworthiness? In actuality, His creation and commandments were established for wise purposes and objectives that are manifestations of His praiseworthiness and His wisdom. Thus, to deny [His] wisdom is to deny the reality of His creating and commandments.

These deniers have instead claimed that [His] creation and commandments are devoid of mercy, benefit or wisdom—the Lord is infallible and exalted above this being attributed to Him. It is possible in their doctrine that He would command something having no benefit whatsoever to those who are charged with it, or that He would forbid something which is beneficial. Everything [in their thinking] is equal in His estimation. Furthermore, in their doctrine He could have instead commanded what He has forbidden and vice versa; there is no [determining factor except His will]. It is also possible in their doctrine that He could punish someone who never disobeyed Him, but instead spent his whole life in obedience, thankfulness and remembrance of Him; or that He could grant His blessing [and reward] to someone who never obeyed Him, but instead spent his whole life in disbelief, polytheism, committing injustice and immorality. They [claim that the] only way to reject their doctrine is if the message of the Prophet [explicitly denies it]—otherwise all of the aforementioned is permissible. These are again the most repugnant and worst types of thoughts regarding the Lord (Glory be to Him).

Declaring Him infallible of this [doctrine] is just like deeming Him above committing injustice or oppression. Their [doctrine] represents in fact the essence of injustice that God is exalted above.

It is most amazing that many of those who are part of this school of thought avoid describing Him with the perfect and glorious Attributes that He has characterized Himself with. They do so thinking that would anthropomorphize Him (*tashbīh*) or make Him corporeal (*tajsīm*). Yet they refuse to deem Him infallible above this injustice and oppression. They believe that their version of monotheism cannot occur except through this doctrine, just as it does not occur [in their thinking] except by denying: His highness above the Throne (*istiwā'ihi*), His loftiness above His heavens, His speaking and speech, and His perfect Attributes. We depend on God for success.

The twelfth type is that God (Glory be to Him) rejects equating two opposites, or differentiating between two same entities because of His wisdom and justice. As for [not equating two opposites] it is represented by His statement, *Shall We then treat those who have surrendered as We treat the guilty? What aileth you? How foolishly ye judge!*[81] Thus, He informed us that this treatment would be false and unjust. It is impossible to attribute that to Him, just like it is impossible to attribute poverty, need or injustice to Him. Those who deny wisdom and causality permit this attribution to Him [i.e. that He could reward the disbelievers]—they even affirm it.

The Exalted said, *Shall We treat those who believe and do good works as those who spread corruption in the earth; or shall We treat the pious as the wicked?*[82] *Or do those who commit ill-deeds suppose that We shall make them as those who believe and do good works, the same in life and death? Bad is their judgment!*[83] Thus, the Sublime has characterized this judgment as an evil one. God is exalted and holy above it even being a possibility for Him, much less Him ruling in such a fashion.

What is more profound than that is His rejection of the claims of those who thought that they could enter Paradise without being tested or obligated in a manner that would manifest their patience and thankfulness. His wisdom (Exalted is He) rejects that: *Or deemed ye that ye would enter Paradise while yet God knoweth not those of you who really strive, nor knoweth those (of you) who are steadfast?*[84] *Or think ye that ye will enter Paradise while yet there hath not come unto you the like of (that which came to) those who passed away before you? Affliction and adversity befell them, they were shaken as with earthquake.*[85] *Or deemed ye that ye would be left (in peace) when God yet knoweth not those of you who strive, choosing for friends or protectors none save God and His Messenger and the (Community of) believers?*[86] Thus, God rejected this belief or calculation, because it is inconsistent with His wisdom.

As for [the inappropriateness of] differentiating between two similar entities, He states, *Whoso obeyeth God and the Messenger, they are with those unto whom God hath shown favour, of the prophets and the saints and the martyrs and the righteous. The best of company are they!*[87] *The hypocrites, both men and women, proceed one from another. They enjoin the wrong, and they forbid the right.*[88] *And their Lord hath heard them (and He saith), I suffer not the work of any worker, male or female, to be lost. Ye proceed one from another.*[89] *And when he reached his prime, We gave him wisdom and knowledge. Thus, We reward the good.*[90] *God wiped them out. And for the disbelievers there will be the like thereof.*[91] *(Such was Our) method in the case of those whom We sent before thee (to humankind), and thou wilt not find for Our method aught of power to change.*[92] *It is the law of God which hath taken course aforetime. Thou wilt not find for the law of God aught of power to change.*[93]

Thus, God's methodology (*sunna*) (Glory be to Him) is His custom, which is known to His saints and enemies, whereby He honours the former by granting them victory and glory, while He disgraces the latter by humiliating and abasing them. The Exalted said, *Those who oppose God and His Messenger will be abased even as those before them were abased.*[94]

The Qur'ān is replete with examples of this [type]. The Exalted informs us that His ruling regarding matters is in accordance with His wisdom and justice, and that it is the same for something similar or comparable. If we were to enumerate every example therein it would require a separate book.

The thirteenth type is that God (Glory be to Him) commanded us to ponder and contemplate His words, commandments, prohibitions and legal limits. Had these not contained wisdoms, advantages, desired objectives and praiseworthy outcomes, there would have been no reason to do so. In fact, He urged us to contemplate and ponder them so that He could reveal to us His far-reaching wisdoms and how they lead to advantages and praiseworthy objectives.

Whoever understands the latter will affirm that they were sent down by the Most Wise and Most Praiseworthy.

Now, a corollary of these deniers' doctrine (as they claim that [His commandments and prohibitions] are solely due to His power and will) is that one who is a false [prophet] may be given miracles and granted victory and supremacy, while the true [messengers] may be humiliated, humbled and destroyed. Had what they claimed been correct then pondering and contemplating as to the truthfulness of His messengers would have been pointless, and there would have been no reason for Him to establish His evidence against [the disbelievers]. Thus, by denying [His] wisdom and causality, these groups have barred faith and guidance from reaching them, and have instead affronted reason and rejected necessities.

Instead, everything which God has created and commanded has wise purposes, intended benefits and praiseworthy objectives—these are witnessed by those whose innate disposition is sound and those who are wise. Now, some of the [deniers] do not completely deny [His wisdom], but instead claim that [wise purposes] have occurred by accident, not by intention. An example [of theirs] is a great timber falling and coincidentally killing a predatory animal on its way to injure a human. Another example [they claim] is of a person who distributes a dirham for no reason or benefit, but simply because he is capable or wills to do so; and it just accidentally happens to fall into the hands of someone in need, and hence benefits him. Again, this is way the deniers approach the issue of wisdom and benefit.

There is no doubt that this [doctrine] fails to duly praise the Lord (Glory be to Him) for the occurrence of benefits and wisdoms, since they contend that these occurred accidentally, not by His intention and will.

The fourteenth type is when He informs us that His creating and commanding proceed from His wisdom and knowledge. He thus mentions two of His Attributes when He informs us of the origin of His Divine Law and creation. He states, *The revelation of the Book is from God, the Almighty, the Most Wise.*[95] Thus, He mentioned [first] His Almightiness, which comprises His absolute omnipotence and administration, and [second] His wisdom, which denotes His perfect praiseworthiness and knowledge.

As for the thief, both male and female, cut-off their hands. It is the reward of their own deeds, an exemplary punishment from God. God is almighty, most wise.[96] One of the Bedouins heard another recite [this verse] incorrectly [by saying], 'God is forgiving, merciful.' The former said, 'These are not in the Book of God.' The latter said, 'Have you disbelieved in the Qur'ān?' The former said, 'No, but what [you have recited] is inappropriate.' Once the latter went back [to the Qur'ān], saw his mistake, and read it as, *God is almighty, most wise*, he said, 'You have spoken the truth.'

If you reflect on His Book, you will find that His Names and Attributes at the end of many verses are appropriate to the context therein. It is almost as if the verse was mentioned as a proof and reason [for His Attribute]. Another example is His verse [as stated by the Messiah on the Day of Judgment], *If Thou punish them, they are Thy servants, and if Thou forgive them (they are Thy servants). Thou, only Thou, art the Almighty, the Most Wise.*[97] Thus, His forgiveness occurs in the context of His Almightiness, which represents His perfect omnipotence, and His wisdom, which is associated with His omniscience—it does not [proceed] from any incapacity or ignorance.

His statement, *Such is the judgment and ordering of (Him), the Almighty, the Omniscient,*[98] is mentioned in three places in the Qur'ān.[99] He informed us that [His] precise and well-planned order proceeds from His might and knowledge. It is not something that occurred by accident, for the agent in such cases is neither praiseworthy nor commendable.

In addition, the Sublime ends each story of a prophet and his nation in Sūrat al-Shuʿarā' with, *And lo! thy Lord! He is indeed the Almighty, the Merciful.*[100] God's judgment in support of His messengers and their followers against their enemies is in accordance with His might and mercy. He reserved and placed His mercy in its concordant place, i.e. for the messengers and their followers, and took revenge against His enemies through His might. He also rescued His messengers and their followers through His mercy. His wise purpose is intended and desired, and it is the ultimate objective of [His] action, and not something that just occurred by accident.

The fifteenth type is that He informed us that His rulings and arrangement are the best—had they not been wise and beneficial, they would not have been characterized as such. If it had been that [His rulings] were good just because they were determined [by Him] and existent (as the deniers claim), then they or their opposites would have been equivalent; but this [claim is false and] impossible. The Exalted stated, *Who is better than God to give judgment to a people who have certainty (in their belief)?*[101] *Who is better in religion than he who surrendereth his purpose to God while doing good (to men).*[102] It is impossible that God would choose for people another religion or be pleased with it, just like it is impossible that He has any faults or carries out any injustice.

The Exalted also stated, *Thus We arranged. How excellent is Our arranging!*[103] *So blessed be God, the best of creators!*[104] There is nothing better than His determination, arrangement and creation as they have occurred in accordance with His wisdom, mercy and knowledge.

The Exalted also stated, *Thou (Muḥammad) canst see no fault in the Beneficent's creation.*[105] Had it not been in the most beautiful and perfect manner, and in accordance with praiseworthy objectives and desired wisdoms, everything would have been disparate and faulty. Alternatively, if it is claimed that it is not faulty by accident, then again the agent would not be praiseworthy since he did not will or intend it.

The sixteenth type is exemplified where God informed us in two verses of His Book that He is on the Straight Path. In the first instance, He relates a statement said by the prophet Hūd: *I have put my trust in God, my Lord and your Lord. There is not an animal but He doth grasp it by the forelock! My Lord is on a straight path.*[106]

The second instance is His statement, *And God coineth a similitude: Two men, one of them dumb, having control of nothing, and he is a burden on his owner; whithersoever he directeth him to go, he bringeth no good. Is he equal with one who enjoineth justice and followeth a straight path (of conduct)?*[107]

Abū Isḥāq [al-Zajjāj] opined, 'Although God can carry out whatever He wishes due to His omnipotence, He only wills what is just.'[108] Ibn al-Anbārī[109] said that the verse *but He doth grasp it by the forelock* indicates that nothing is outside of His grasp and He has subdued all animals by virtue of His omnipotence; and that the statement *My Lord is on a straight path*[110] means that God is upon the truth. He stated that the latter is well known in Arabic usage.

There are other interpretations of this verse, which are corollaries of this meaning, like the statement of some, 'My Lord guides to the Straight Path.' His ability to guide others to the path is a corollary of the fact that He Himself is upon the Straight Path. His guidance and direction to it is due to His complete mercy, beneficence, justice and wisdom.

As for the Sublime's characterization that He is on the Straight Path, it is because He states the truth and does what is right. His words are all true and just, while His actions are all righteous (*ṣawāb*) and good. *But God saith the truth and He showeth the way.*[111] He only says that which confirms His praiseworthiness, and [His words] are necessarily true, just, righteous and wise.

If God being on the Straight Path is understood properly then it necessarily follows that He does not do anything except for wise purposes, which confirm His praiseworthiness, and objectives, which are associated with His [free] will. His actions all proceed from His wisdom, beneficence, mercy, justice and righteousness. His words likewise proceed from His justice and truthfulness.

The seventeenth type is the Sublime's praise of Himself for everything He does. God also commanded His servants to praise Him. This is due to the fact that His actions encompass many praiseworthy objectives and outcomes that make Him deserving of that praise. He is praiseworthy for His intention of the act, for His action itself, and for the occurrence of His praiseworthy objective [of that act]. The deniers of His wisdom and causality do not consider Him praiseworthy for His intention nor for the occurrence of the objective, because they consider it impossible for Him to intend it, rather it occurred only by accident.

It is self evident that an agent is not praiseworthy for an action or objective if he does not intend it. The sole occurrence of an action—which emanates from an agent having no intended objective—is not praiseworthy. It is impossible that One Who is omnipotent, Who can freely choose and is Most Wise would carry out an act in this manner. Only one who is faulty would do so, and God is infallible above any fault. The Sublime's praiseworthiness is one of the greatest evidences of His perfect wisdom and that His intended actions are beneficial to His creation and are [evidence of His] mercy upon them. If [His wisdom and free will] are negated then that would nullify the reality of His praiseworthiness.

The eighteenth type is that God has notified us of His blessings and beneficence upon His creation. He has created all that is in the heavens and the earth, and bestowed upon us hearing, sight and our hearts in order to complete His blessings. It is well known that one who blesses and is benevolent is not deserving of those attributes unless he freely intends them. Had God (Glory be to Him) not intended to carry these actions out with the purpose of granting blessings and being beneficent then in reality He would be neither a benefactor nor benevolent.

This also becomes clear after considering that, when God (Glory be to Him) mentions His blessings of creation and Divine Law, He does so in association with the wisdoms, advantages and benefits they were established for. An example of His creation is His statement at the end of Sūrat al-Naḥl, *And God hath given you, of that which He hath created, shelter from the sun; and hath given you places of refuge in the mountains, and hath given you coats to ward off the heat from you, and coats (of armour) to save you from your own foolhardiness. Thus doth He perfect His favour unto you, in order that ye may surrender (unto Him).*[112] Again, this pertains to the creation.

In regards to the Divine Law, God commanded us to face the Kaᶜba: *Whencesoever thou comest forth turn thy face toward the Inviolable Place of Worship; and wheresoever ye may be (O Muslims) turn your faces toward it (when ye pray) so that men may have no argument against you, save such of them as do injustice—Fear them not, but fear Me!—and so that I may complete My grace upon you, and that ye may be guided.*[113] And He said regarding His commandment for ablution and dry ablution (*tayammum*), *God would not place a burden on you, but He would purify you and would perfect His grace upon you, that ye may give thanks.*[114]

The nineteenth type is that God is characterized by mercy, and He is the Most Merciful (*arḥam al-rāḥimīn*). His mercy encompasses everything, and this can only be accomplished if He intends mercy for His creation through what He has created for them and what He has commanded them to do. Had His commandments not comprised mercy, wise purposes, advantages and beneficence, then they could not be considered to be a mercy for us. And if mercy only occurred by accident, then this would not necessitate that He Who commands (Glory be to Him) is the Most Merciful. Stripping away His wisdom and intended objectives that He acts for represents a denial of His mercy in reality.

The head of this school, Jahm b. Safwān, [exemplified the deniers] by saying after he witnessed a leper suffering, 'How can the Most Merciful do something like this?' Jahm is indicating [his viewpoint] that God is not merciful in reality, and instead what exists is determined by His will alone, devoid of any wisdom or mercy.[115]

The twentieth type is that God's response (Glory be to Him) to those who ask about the wise purposes of [some] specific actions of His is that only He knows them. For example, after the angels inquired, *Wilt thou place therein one who will do harm therein and will shed blood, while we, we hymn Thy praise and sanctify Thee*? God's response to them was, *Surely I know that which ye know not.*[116] If His actions were devoid of any wisdoms, objectives or advantages, the angels would have known better than to ask this type of question.

Furthermore, His response to them was that only He knows the wisdoms and benefits that will occur as a result of the creation of this vicegerent, and they do not.[117] Thus, their question was posed [to understand] the wise purpose [of this vicegerent] as it appeared to them that the creation of this vicegerent was contrary to wisdom or reason—[it was] not an objection to the Lord (Exalted is He). Even if it was considered an objection, it remains evidence of their recognition that everything He does is for a wise purpose.

Another example is His statement, *And when a token cometh unto them, they say, We will not believe till we are given that which God's messengers are given. God knoweth best with whom to place His message.*[118] Thus, God responded to them that due to His wisdom and knowledge, He rejects placing His message in an inappropriate place or person. Had this issue been solely dependent upon His will, then this response would not have been given. Instead, the response would have been that His actions are without reason or that He preponderates one [messenger] over another without a preponderator, or that everything is only due to His power [or will alone] as the deniers [of His wisdom] claim.

Similarly, there is His statement, *And even so do We try some of them by others that they say, Are these they whom God favoureth among us? Is not God best Aware of the thanksgivers?*[119] Thus, when some questioned and rejected God's favouring [and selection of the messengers], the response was that God is more knowledgeable as to who is best able and appropriate to carry out His message. Only those who acknowledge the value of His blessings and thank Him are appropriate [for selection]. Again, had this issue been merely a function of His will, the response would not have been suitable.

It is also for this reason that whenever God distinguishes one [person or place] specifically, He (Glory be to Him) mentions that it is a result of His knowledge. The Exalted said, *And unto Solomon [We made subservient] the stormy wind, so that it sped at his behest towards the land which We had blessed—for it is We who have knowledge of everything.*[120] God mentioned His knowledge after mentioning that He had given Solomon the ability to subdue the wind, and that He selected for him the blessed land.

Consider also: *God hath appointed the Kaʿba, the Sacred House, a standard for humankind, and the Sacred Month and the offerings and the garlands. That is so that ye may know that God knoweth whatsoever is in the heavens and whatsoever is in the earth, and that God is knower of all things.*[121] Thus, He mentioned His Attribute of knowledge that necessitated the selection of that particular place and time, in preference above any other.

Finally, consider the Sublime's statement, *Then God sent down His peace of reassurance upon His Messenger and upon the believers and imposed on them the word of self-restraint, for they were worthy of it and meet for it. And God is aware of all things.*[122] Thus, He informed us that He granted [self-restraint (*taqwā*)] to those who were suitable and worthy of it.

He alone is most knowledgeable of those who are most deserving. One who distinguishes things only as a result of his will—not for some reason or objective— would not be characterized as such.

The twenty-first type is that the Sublime informed us that He disregarded some of those whom He has [created] and determined because of their corrupt nature, and because doing so is more beneficial. If it had been that the issue solely pertained to His will, there would be no reason to differentiate between [creatures]. The Exalted stated, *The worst of beasts in God's sight are the deaf, the dumb, who have no sense. Had God known of any good in them He would have made them hear, but had He made them hear they would have turned away, averse.*[123]

Thus, the Sublime gave the reasons that they could not hear with comprehension and thereafter derive benefit: [first] they had no goodness within them and [second] because their pride and stubbornness formed obstacles that prevented them from comprehending what they heard. Therefore, the reasoning for the first is the absence of a requisite, while the second is due to the presence of an obstacle.

The above can only be deemed appropriate in the case of One Whose commandments and prohibitions result in wisdoms and benefits. On the other hand, one whose actions are devoid of [wisdom] will only rule in some manner predicated on his ability to bring about effects. But God has declared Himself infallible above performing many actions that He is capable of because they do not conform to His wisdom, perfect [Attributes] and praiseworthiness. Examples of this are included in the Exalted's statements: *It is not (the purpose) of God to leave you in your present state till He shall separate the wicked from the good. And it is not (the purpose of) God to let you know the Unseen;*[124] *But God would not punish them while thou wast with them, nor will He punish them while they seek forgiveness;*[125] *It was never God's (part) that He should send a folk astray after He had guided them until He had made clear unto them what they should avoid;*[126] *In truth, thy Lord destroyed not the townships tyrannously while their folk were doing right;*[127] *And never did thy Lord destroy the townships till He had raised up in their mother(town) a messenger reciting unto them Our revelations.*[128]

The deniers do not consider the Lord infallible above carrying out actions inconsistent with His [holy] perfection, wisdom and praiseworthiness, since He is indeed capable of performing them. Instead, [they claim] that He is only infallible above not being capable of something. Furthermore, [they claim] that these [types of actions] do not occur because of the absence of His will for them—[in other words], not because of the repugnant nature of those actions.

The twenty-second type is that a wisdom or desired objective may not occur in an action [due to many reasons]: [first], because of the agent's lack of knowledge about it or its particulars. This is of course impossible in regards to One Who is omniscient. [Second], due to one's inability to fashion it—and this is impossible in regards to One Who is omnipotent. [Third], due to the lack of His wish or will to be beneficent to others or to bestow some favours upon them. This is also impossible with regards to the Most Merciful as His beneficence is a necessary concomitant of His Essence. [Fourth], due to some obstacle that prevents them from carrying out their will or intent. This is impossible in regards to One Who cannot be prevented by any obstacle from doing anything He wills. [Fifth], because doing so would connote some inadequacy, not perfection. This is also falsehood. Furthermore, it is a vitiation of the truth and contradicts what the innate disposition and reason [know to be true], which is that whoever does something for a wisdom or a desired objective is more praiseworthy than someone who carries out something for no reason whatsoever. Likewise, One Who can create is more perfect than those who cannot create, and One Who is omniscient is more perfect than those who are not. One who can speak, is capable, has a will, can hear and see, becomes pleased or displeased, and loves or dislikes is more perfect than those who are not characterized as such. [Knowledge of] this is embedded within the innate disposition and reason. Denying His wisdom is like denying those above-mentioned Attributes from Him. [Stripping Him of all of those] necessitates characterizing Him with the opposite Attributes, and deeming Him faulty and deficient.

Many of the deniers, like [the Ashʿarīs] Juwaynī[129] and Rāzī, openly stated that one cannot use rational evidence to deny faults from God—instead denial is only based on the traditions [of the Qur'ān and the Sunna] and the consensus. It can be said to them, 'If affirming [His] wisdom results in no fault being attributed to Him then it is impermissible to deny it. But if it is a [sign] of faultiness, then where is the [proof] in the traditions or in the consensus that it should be denied?'

All of the Imams agree in affirming God's wisdom (Glory be to Him) and that His actions lead to praiseworthy objectives. The deniers [of His wisdom] have no basis for their claim, whether in the traditions, reason or by consensus. Instead, all of these, as well as the [sound] innate disposition, attest to the falsity of their doctrine. Only God guides to the truth.

In conclusion, the perfection of the Exalted Lord and His glory, wisdom, justice, mercy, omnipotence, beneficence, praiseworthiness, magnificence and the real meanings of His Beautiful Names all reject the occurrence of any action [from Him] that would not be associated with wise purposes or desired objectives. We have pointed out some evidences from the Qur'ān; however, there are many more that we have not mentioned. Everything in existence attests to His wisdom and divine providence. Even if one were to spend a whole life trying to enumerate and compile this all one could not.

Likewise, the proofs for God's existence (Exalted is the Creator) are infinite. The same can be said for the veracity of His prophets and messengers, especially the seal of them Muḥammad (may God bless him and grant him peace). Despite that many arrogantly reject those [proofs]. Indeed, you will find a person who is completely immersed in [God's] blessings, yet he is always complaining about his situation or may even deny those blessings. The delusions and temptations of people are endless, especially those who are ignorant and unjust.

One of the most amazing things is that some will allow themselves to deny the wise purposes, final objectives and benefits that this perfect Divine Law encompasses. It represents the greatest of proofs for the veracity of the one who conveyed it, and that he is truthfully the Messenger of God. Had he not brought forth any other miracle [than the Divine Law of Islam] it would have been sufficient and unequivocal. This [Divine Law] encompasses so many wisdoms, benefits, praiseworthy objectives and justified outcomes, all of which attest that only the Most Wise and Most

Merciful could have been the One Who prescribed and revealed them.

Glory be to God! How can anyone allow himself to presume that the Lord of the Worlds and the Most Wise would punish most of those He created with the severest of punishments, eternally [in Hell], for no objective, reason or cause. Instead, [the deniers claim] that the punishment is solely due to His will devoid of any wisdom or cause. Is not this the worst of presumptions about the Lord (Exalted is He)?

If we were to mention the wisdoms of God present in His creation and commandments, which are easily apparent to the likes of us, they would exceed 10,000 instances—this despite the limitation of our minds, inadequacy of our intellects and knowledge. Even if all of humanity's knowledge was combined, it would come to almost nothing compared to the knowledge of God. It would be just like the light of a firefly compared to that of the sun. This is just a metaphor, but in reality the difference is much greater. One should not minimize the importance of this matter for it is great, and the dangers associated with it are even greater.

The speculative theologians deny causality, attributing [His actions] solely to His will and power. They claim that the freely-choosing Agent prefers one thing over another without taking into consideration any deciding factor, reason, wisdom or objective. They negated causes, forces, natural dispositions, instincts, wisdoms and objectives. Some who only affirmed one quiddity claimed that the rotating celestial bodies, planets and the like always break up during their rotation but that the Omnipotent One freely chooses to return them back to their initial state [of rotation]; that the colours, measures, forms and attributes become non-existent every moment, but the Omnipotent One freely chooses to return them back every moment; and that the saltiness of the oceans becomes non-existent every moment, but that the Omnipotent One freely chooses to return it back. All of these things occur, [for them], without a cause, and for no wisdom or final objective. The speculative theologians deemed that they could not rid themselves of the doctrines of the philosophers—who are the enemies of the Messengers—except through this argument.

These two groups [i.e. the speculative theologians and the philosophers] were not guided to the truth, which is that God (Glory be to Him) acts according to His will, omnipotence and wish, and that He carries out what He wills through causes for wise purposes and praiseworthy objectives. He established His creation and commandments in this world through forces, natural dispositions, instincts, causes and effects. This is the viewpoint of the multitude (*jumhūr*) of the Muslims; most of the speculative theoreticians (*nuẓẓār*); and the viewpoint of all of the jurists except for those who adopted the principles of those deniers, and even abandoned the tenets of Islamic law and thus opposed [sound] religious doctrine.

CHAPTER FOUR

A Response to Those Who Deny God's Wisdom and Causality

[Rāzī's First Argument]

The deniers state, 'You have mentioned your imagined and improvised proofs, so now consider our refutation of them and respond if you can.' Thus, I will relate what the most clever of the latter's group, Muḥammad b. ʿUmar [Fakhr al-Dīn] al-Rāzī, has said [in his book *al-Arbaʿīn fī uṣūl al-dīn*], 'Any agent who performs an action to attain some benefit or to prevent some harm—assuming that the accrual of those advantages takes precedence over not doing so—has benefitted by carrying out that action. But whoever is like that has an essence which is deficient, and therefore needs to derive perfection from another. This is impossible with regards to God. But if [performing such or not] is considered to be equivalent by Him, then there is no preponderant one, and therefore it will not occur.' Then he relayed a question: 'What about the case in which it is equivalent to Him, yet the servant prefers its occurrence, and due to that preference God (Glory be to Him) preponderates its existence over non-existence?' He responded to his own question by saying, 'The occurrence of these benefits or their absence is either considered to be equivalent by God or not. In the latter case it goes back to the previously-mentioned division.'[1]

Those who affirm [His wisdom and causality] state that there are many ways to respond to this specious argument:

1. As for the statement that any agent who performs something for some purpose possesses an 'essence which is deficient, and therefore needs to derive perfection from another', do you mean [first]

that he lacks some type of perfection which he should have possessed before his intent [to carry out that action]? Or [second] do you mean that he lacks some type of perfection before the existence [of that act]? Or are you suggesting a third meaning?

If the first [is your position], this claim is false. One performing something for some purpose (which takes precedence over its absence) is not necessarily lacking in some requisite type of perfection before his intent to do that action. Indeed, intent is not described as being perfect before it becomes existent.

If the second [is your position], its absence is also not considered to be a deficiency. A purpose cannot perfect something else before its existence; and if something is not perfect in one instance it cannot be considered to represent a deficiency should it be absent. The absence of some entity before its creation [obviously] takes precedence over its existence; but after its origination its existence takes precedence over its non-existence. Thus, its non-existence before its existence should not be considered to be a deficiency nor should its existence after its non-existence. Instead, perfection entails the non-existence [of that entity] before its existence, and its existence after it is originated.

The intended wise purposes and objectives are of that sort. Their existence when existent is considered to be perfection. Had they been non-existent at that time, then that could be considered to be a deficiency. Likewise, their non-existence when it should be so is considered perfect, and had they been existent in that case it would be considered a deficiency. For this reason, the denier is the one who attributes faults to God, not the one who affirms [His wisdom]. Finally, if you intend a third [option], you must elaborate before we can discuss it further.

2. Do you mean by that [same] statement that the wise purpose, which should be existent, occurs from a source other than Him? Or do you mean that He does not possess that wise purpose itself or that He derives perfection from it only [after its existence]?

If the first [position is advanced] then this is false, since there is no other Lord or Creator besides Him. God (Glory be to Him) has not derived any perfection from a creature [of His] in any aspect whatsoever. Instead, the whole of creation gains any perfection it has from Him. The Sublime has not derived any perfection from others, just as He is not dependent upon anything else for His existence.

If the second [position is advanced], [then we respond that God's] wisdom is an Attribute of His (Glory be to Him) and His Attributes are not derived from others. His wisdom is self-subsisting and He is the Most Wise. Likewise, He is the Omniscient, the All-Hearing and the All-Seeing.

3. If God (Glory be to Him) performs something, the existence of which is more beloved to Him than its non-existence, then it is required that His objective, which He loves and has done the action for, must occur—this is the ultimate perfection. If the latter does not become existent then that would be considered to be a deficiency. Whoever is capable of attaining something that he loves, at the time that he loves, and in accordance with the manner that he wishes, is truly perfect. On the other hand, one who loves nothing or is not capable of achieving what he loves [is one who is imperfect].

4. Rāzī has mentioned in his books (following the viewpoint of Juwaynī and others) that no rational proofs exist to deny faults from God—it is only through [the Qur'ān and the Sunna] that rejecting any particular fault to God (Almighty and Most Glorious is He) can be done. But they have not used reason or any transmitted evidence from the Messenger (may God bless him and grant him peace) to deny [His wisdom]—they have only relied on their 'consensus'. God's acting through His wisdom has not been denied by the consensus [of Ahl al-Sunna wa'l-Jamāʿa].

This Community is also not unanimous in denying causality. If they state [correctly] that the consensus reject faults from being attributed to Him, however [incorrectly claim that causality] represents a deficiency, our response is that those who have affirmed [causality] agree that it is not a fault, but instead a sign of [His] perfection. Moreover, denying [causality] would lead to attributing faults [to Him].

5. This Community unanimously agrees in rejecting any faults from God. The knowledge which God (Exalted is He) has revealed concerning [His being exonerated of faults] is one of the great-

est and most essential types; and it is well established within the innate disposition. Had His actions been devoid of wise purposes and praiseworthy objectives then that would have required [attributing] faultiness [to Him], but doing so is impossible. Reason, the innate disposition and knowledge—both the requisite and theoretical types—all confirm by necessity that denying His wisdom, rather than affirming it, would result in faults being attributed to Him.

6. Being faulty is either a possibility or impossibility. If it is a possibility then their proof is invalidated [because they have characterized God as being deficient]. If [attributing faults to Him] is impossible then their argument [denying His wisdom and causality] is also invalidated. Therefore, their proof is invalid in both instances.

7. Attributing faults to God (Almighty and Most Glorious is He) is known to be invalid through reason, just as well as by transmitted evidence. Reason and transmitted evidence both necessitate characterizing Him with Attributes of perfection. Having knowledge, power, will, hearing, vision, speech and life are all attributes of perfection, while [being characterized by any] opposites of those constitute being faulty. It is required to declare Him to be infallible above any [opposites of perfection], because they would nullify His perfection. The occurrence of that which God (Exalted is He) loves in the time frame that He loves is perfection, since it occurs in a fashion that He loves. Its non-existence beforehand does not represent a fault, since He did not love that it should exist anterior to that time.

8. The perfection that God (Glorious and Exalted is He) deserves is either a possible or impossible [type]. The first is indisputable (*musallam*), while the second is absolutely false. So why do you [deniers] claim that it is possible for an event to occur in a time other than it should have, while you affirm that the existence of an event in pre-eternity is impossible? Why do you claim that only in the latter case is the non-existence [of a particular event] not a [sign of] deficiency?

9. The non-existence of that which is impossible is not an indication of imperfection. That which is impossible does not exist in reality, and if it is a non-entity then its non-existence is not faulty. Therefore, if it is determined that created entities are only to be created gradually, and their existence in pre-eternity is impossible, then

their non-existence is not faulty. Perfection is instead characterized by their origination into existence when it is possible for them to be existent.

10. There is no doubt that God (Exalted is He) originated things after having willed their non-existence. Even those [philosophers] who claim that celestial bodies are pre-eternal and not dependent upon a necessary cause affirm that. They acknowledge that He originated those events through intermediaries.

We maintain that this origination is either a perfect attribute (*ṣifa kamāl*) or not. If it is a perfect attribute then [according to their claim] He would have lacked it beforehand; and if it is not [then in their doctrine] He is faulty. Now if you argue that it is neither a perfect attribute nor a fault, we would reply: Why do you not say likewise regarding causality [and acknowledge that it could possibly be involved in His originating the creation and is not a sign of faultiness]?

Moreover, [attributing faults] to the Lord (Exalted is He) is impossible since everything that He does is deserving of praise, and all His Attributes are perfect attributes, whereas their opposites are faults.

The speculative theoreticians may disagree about effectiveness (*fāʿiliya*)—is it a perfect attribute or not? All Muslims, regardless of their doctrine, maintain that it is a perfect attribute. One group though, consisting of most of the Ashʿariyya, claimed it is neither a perfect attribute nor a fault. It is said to those who hold this viewpoint: It is well known from pure reason that whoever creates is more perfect than one who cannot. The Exalted said, *Is He then Who createth as him who createth not? Will ye not then remember?*[2] The question [in that verse] represents a criticism of those who equate between those two alternatives—God is teaching us that He [the Creator] is absolutely more perfect [than the creation]. There is no doubt that the One Who creates is superior to one who cannot, for this is affirmed in the innate disposition and reason. In addition, preference is given to one who is knowledgeable over one who is not, one who is capable over one who is not, one who can hear and see over one who cannot.

Since this is well established in the innate disposition of the offspring of Adam, God (Exalted is He) made it a way to establish His Oneness and His evidences upon His servants. The Exalted said, *God propounds [to you] the parable of [two men]—a man enslaved, unable to do anything of his own accord, and a [free] man upon whom We have bestowed goodly sustenance [as a gift] from Ourselves, so that he can spend thereof [at will, both] secretly and openly. Can these [two] be deemed equal? All praise is due to God [alone]: but most of them do not understand. And God propounds [to you] the parable of two [other] men—one of them dumb, unable to do anything of his own accord, and a sheer burden on his master: to whichever task the latter directs him, he accomplishes no good. Can such a one be considered the equal of [a wise man] who enjoins the doing of what is right and himself follows a straight way?*[3]

Therefore, whoever equates between the ability to create and lack thereof—whereby the former represents perfection, and the latter represents a deficiency—has invalidated the evidences of God and the proofs for His Oneness.

11. Why is it not possible that His actions could entail wise purposes, and that in His sight it is equivalent whether or not the latter are present? Since the deniers consider that origination/existence and non-existence are equivalent to Him and that He is an Agent Who has intentions, but the presence or absence of His intent is equivalent in His sight (even though there is no way for us to know His intention), then why is it not permissible in their doctrine for His actions to entail wise purposes, and their presence or absence likewise be equivalent in His sight? Especially since they consider that [His] acts are distinct enactments of His, they should allow [Him to act] for wisdoms distinct from Him. But instead they have claimed [that His acts do not entail wise purposes] in order to escape from saying that events subsist in Him and from infinite regress (*tasalsul*). Therefore, they should at least maintain [the possibility of Him acting for] wise purposes.

12. Pure reason dictates that whoever does not possess a wisdom or intended objective for an action of his is more deserving of being characterized by faults than someone who performs an act for wise purposes, even if [that wisdom] was previously absent and then becomes present only at the time that his wisdom decreed to

originate that action. Therefore, how can a rational person claim that God's performance of an action for a wise purpose necessitates faultiness [being attributed to Him], while actions that are devoid of wisdom do not result in Him being considered faulty?

13. The deniers say that the Sublime performs whatever He wills without consideration of the wisdom of doing so. Thus, they make it permissible for Him to do anything, which is a possibility (*mumkin*)—even to command polytheism, lying, injustice, abominations, or to forbid monotheism, honesty, justice and legal retribution. In that case we say: Deeming it permissible for Him to [command those abominations] and claiming that there is no deficiency [attributable to Him] in intending those represents the worst attribution of faultiness to Him.

Now the claim that whoever performs [an action] for a reason [or a benefit or to prevent some harm] is considered to be deficient without [that action] is an absolute claim not a general one. Some will contend that whoever honours those who are ignorant, unjust and corrupt, yet dishonours those who are knowledgeable, just and benevolent, is an unjust fool. But the deniers allow and permit saying this about God, and they do not consider Him to be unjust or foolish in general.

Similarly some say, 'Whoever allows his slaves and servants to be sinful and kill each other, while he is able to prevent them, is foolish.' They acknowledge that God has allowed that, and yet He is not considered by them to be [foolish or] encompassed in that general claim. Therefore, their absolute claim [i.e. that one who does something for a reason is deficient without it] is more likely to be false, and it contradicts [their general claims].

14. If we concede that He becomes more perfect through some event that is originated, then [we must also concede that] it is something intended by Him. In the doctrine [of the deniers of His wisdom] everything that occurs is intended by Him, and therefore it is not repugnant. They only consider disobedience of what is commanded or forbidden to be repugnant. Since there is no one above God to command or forbid [Him], He can carry out anything, which is a possibility except for that which He explicitly informed

us that He would not do. But they only declare Him infallible from carrying out something in opposition to what He has informed us of, not something that contradicts His wisdom. And they do not consider anything He is capable of carrying out to be repugnant, nor does [that action] lead to Him becoming faulty.

15. If something impermissible necessarily follows from allowing Him to act in a manner consistent with His wisdom, His acting for no wise purposes results in greater impermissibilities. Also if they consider that the barriers, which would prevent Him acting in a manner consistent with His wisdom to be impossible, then the obstacles leading them to deny [His wisdom] are more likely to be impossible.

16. It is unreasonable and even impermissible to claim that the freely-chosen actions of one who is living and knowledgeable are done for no objective or purpose. These [aimless actions] do not arise except from an insane person, one who is sleeping, or one who is unreasonable. Having wise purposes and final objectives are what makes one having a will described as such. If one knows the advantage, benefit and objective of an action, then he will intend it. But if one does not recognize any advantage, truthful objective or any motive whatsoever that calls him to that action, yet one carries it out, it is only because of vanity. This is how anyone who is rational thinks of this issue.

In conclusion, denying that the actions of the Most Wise incorporate wise purposes and final objectives only represents in reality a rejection of His ability to freely choose them. This [denial] therefore leads to [attributing to Him] the greatest of faults, as has been mentioned. We depend upon God alone for success.

[Rāzī's Second Argument]

Those who have denied [His] wisdom now state, 'Supposing that our first argument is invalid, it does not necessarily mean that our doctrine is false. We can mention another argument: "Had the Exalted's actions been done for reasons then those reasons would be pre-eternal (*qadīm*), in which case the action would also be required to be pre-eternal, and that is impossible. On the other hand, if the reasons were temporally originated, this would require them to be dependent upon another reason [thus necessitating infinite regress], and this would also be impossible."'[4]

Stated in another way they claim,

> If the Exalted's actions are for wise purposes then that wisdom is either pre-eternal or temporally originated. If it is pre-eternal then that would necessitate that the action be either pre-eternal or not. The former is impossible because an action cannot be pre-eternal. If, on the other hand, [His wisdom] is pre-eternal but the action is not, then [His wisdom] exists without that action. If [His wisdom] is not pre-eternal yet the action exists without it, then no wise purpose is associated with that action. If something is not dependent upon a wise purpose for its existence then it may occur in the latter's absence, and that is what we desire [to prove].
>
> But if wisdom is temporally originated with the onset of the action, then either it is dependent upon an Agent or not. If it is not dependent then that necessitates it occurring without an Agent, and this is impossible. But if it is dependent upon an agent, then that agent is either God or someone else. However, it is not possible that it be someone else, since there is no creator other than God. In that case either He has, in His actions, a purpose or not. If it is the former then we have already addressed this, and it necessitates infinite regress. But if it is the latter then His actions are devoid of purpose, and that again is what we desire to prove.

The deniers continue by stating, 'If some maintain that His action for some purpose only represents the purpose in and of itself, and therefore it does not necessitate infinite regress, the response is that it would necessitate the same for every created action, i.e. that the purpose of it is itself, and not some need for any another purpose. And that is also what we desire [to prove, i.e. that there are no other associated wisdoms or purposes for His actions].'

They feel that this is an amazing argument that is sufficient regarding [the issue of] purpose. Those who affirm His wisdom maintain it is untenable and invalid from many aspects. The detailed response is as follows:

1. An action is either [I] pre-eternal in essence, [II] pre-eternal in type, or [III] neither. If the action is either pre-eternal in essence or by type then it is possible that the wisdom that led to the action also be [pre-eternal]. But if the action is neither then if His action is temporally originated in essence or by type then that wisdom is also [temporally originated]. The wise purpose follows suit to the action; whatever is possible for the former is possible for the latter, and whatever is impossible for the former is impossible for the latter.

2. Whoever says, 'He is the Creator Who originates things in pre-eternity even before they become existent' maintains that it is akin to saying, 'He wills things in pre-eternity before they become existent.' Based upon that we can maintain that His wisdom, which He utilizes to create and will things, is also pre-eternal. It does not necessarily follow that if His wisdom is pre-eternal then [the timing of] His action should also be pre-eternal, just like it is not a necessary concomitant that the pre-eternity of His will leads to pre-eternality of what He has willed. Likewise, it is also not a necessary concomitant that the pre-eternal nature of His Attribute of being the Creator leads to [asserting] the pre-eternality of the entities He creates.

Therefore, our statement that His wisdom is pre-eternal, yet the action is temporally originated, is akin to their statement regarding the pre-eternality of His will and creative ability. What is incumbent upon us is likewise incumbent upon them.

This is not inconsistent with any principle held by any group. Even the philosophers who say that His actions are pre-eternal and lead to what is enacted maintain that His wisdom is pre-eternal. The Karrāmiyya,[5] on the other hand, state that just as that which is enacted by the Lord is temporally originated, so too is His wisdom. Even others who say that the type of action is temporally originated, but not carried out by the Lord, maintain that [His actions proceed from] His wisdom. Regardless, affirming that the Sublime's wisdom results in His actions does not contradict any of the principles of any of those mentioned groups.

3. Their argument that His temporal origination of one particular cause renders it dependent on another cause is incorrect. This would only be correct if it was said, 'Every temporally-originated

thing (*ḥādith*) inevitably is a result of a cause.' But we do not contend that. Instead we maintain that He acts [and enacts] for wise purposes. It is well known that anything an agent enacts is intended by him and beloved to him. Sometimes that which is beloved is enacted for itself, and sometimes another [benefit] is intended from it. The latter will inevitably result in some intrinsic benefit by regress. We maintain the same about His creating through causes, i.e. that He creates an [effect] through such-and-such a cause until that matter ends up returning to the first cause: the will of the Lord. Similarly, God creates for wise purposes, one wisdom regressing to another until the matter returns to His ultimate wisdom.

4. The deniers claim that every created entity is intended for itself, and not for another. But it is not impermissible to maintain that some creatures are intended for others initially, yet that matter regresses to being intended for itself. Moreover, this is more suitable and likely than making each creature intended for itself. Commandments and other beloved things can be considered similarly.

5. The deniers have held their opinion, in part, because of their contention that infinite regress would otherwise necessarily result [if the position contrary to theirs was true]. But which of the two types of infinite regress—the impossible type or the possible one—is necessitated? As for the latter, infinity in regards to future effects is possible and will occur. There are two opinions regarding infinite regress when it pertains to past effects, but infinite regress involving all causes and agents is impossible by the agreement of all sages (*bi'ttifāq al-ʿuqalā'*). Yet it is not impossible that there be One Eternal Agent Who has been perpetually acting and will continue to be so.

If that becomes known then the wise purpose He acts for occurs posteriorly. If a further wisdom should transpire thereafter, then it continues to result in events which are endless. This is possible, and occurs by the agreement of Muslim [scholars]. There is no disagreement regarding this, except by some innovators like the Jahmiyya and the Muʿtazila.

Now if it is claimed that [perpetually occurring wisdoms] can never lead to desired ultimate outcomes, then we reply that intended outcomes can occur perpetually. This matter is rational and experienced. A person will do something for a wise purpose, which results in a beloved thing occurring. The occurrence of that beloved thing will make him pursue another beloved thing and so on. If one could do so in perpetuity then that would represent a state of perfection. What is beloved to Him occurs perpetually. God is the only One deserving of this perfection (Glorious and Exalted is He). His will is perpetual and it results in what is beloved to Him in a manner that He wishes. God is absolutely self-subsistent from everything else, while everything is completely dependent upon Him. Can perfection be considered anything other than this? Deficiency is considered to be inherent to any entity lacking [a self-subsistent nature and the ability to attain what is beloved to it].

Now God's mercy and beneficence are requisites of His Essence. Moreover, God (Glory be to Him) commanded His servants to do what He loves and what pleases Him. He intended His beneficence and mercy for them in accordance with what He loves and is pleased with. But there is a difference between God's acts and what He wills to create, which result in wise purposes beloved to Him, and between what He wishes or loves for people to carry out of His commandments, yet has not willed their creation. There is a difference between what God has willed to create and between what God has commanded yet not willed to create.

God (Glory be to Him) creates and commands:[6] creating regards His actions, whereas commandments are His statements. The latter are connected to the actions of His servants. The Sublime may command His servant and may will Himself to assist His servant to carry out His commandment so as to achieve His wisdom and what He loves. Conversely, God may also command others but not will that He assist them to carry out His commandment due to some wisdoms; this represents His abandonment (*tark*) of those people. Nonetheless, God commands them so that they will no longer have any excuse to claim 'No warner came to us, for had God commanded us we would have rushed to obey Him.' Moreover, God did not will to assist those people because they are not appropriate for that blessing. Absolute wisdom dictates that blessings should not be bestowed upon those who are unsuitable for it, and likewise that [favours] should not be withheld from those who are appropriate for it.

The Exalted said, *And [We] imposed on them the word of self-restraint, for they were worthy of it and meet for it;*[7] *Is not God best aware of the thanksgivers?*[8] *Had God known of any good in them He would have made them hear.*[9] It cannot be argued, 'Why did He not make all of His creation equal and appropriate for those [blessings], since He is able to do so,' for that is like asking, 'Why did He not make their forms, images, ages, sustenances and livelihoods all the same?' Even though that is within His ability, the diversity that has occurred is a requisite of His far-reaching wisdom, as well as His absolute sovereignty and lordship.

His wisdom dictated that He should command everyone, but that He should differentiate between them in terms of His assistance. It is similar to how He contrasted between people in regards to their [level of] knowledge, ability, wealth, beauty, eloquence and other [characteristics]. The individual specifications [particular to each creature] in His kingdom do not contradict His wisdom; rather, they are the greatest proofs of the perfection of His wisdom. Had it not been for those [blessings] His grace would not have become manifest. The Exalted said, *But God hath endeared the faith to you and hath beautified it in your hearts, and hath made disbelief and lewdness and rebellion hateful unto you. Such are they who are the rightly guided.* (*It is*) *a bounty and a grace from God;* [*and God is omniscient, most wise*].[10]

God is the Omniscient and the Most Wise [for all]: those who are appropriate to be bestowed with [His] blessings, as well as those who are not suitable and are thus denied. The Exalted said, *O ye who believe! Be mindful of your duty to God and put faith in His Messenger. He will give you twofold of His mercy and will appoint for you a light wherein ye shall walk, and will forgive you. God is forgiving, merciful; That the People of the Book may know that they control naught of the bounty of God, but that the bounty is in God's Hand to give to whom He will. And God is of infinite bounty.*[11]

The Exalted also said, *He it is Who hath sent among the unlettered ones a messenger of their own, to recite unto them His revelations and to make them grow, and to teach them the Book and wisdom, though heretofore they were indeed in error manifest, along with others of them who have not yet joined them. He is the Almighty, the Most Wise. That is the bounty of God, which He giveth unto whom He will. God is of infinite bounty.*[12] *O ye who believe! Whoso of you becometh a renegade from his religion, (know that in his stead) God will bring a people whom He loveth and who love Him, humble toward believers, stern toward disbelievers, striving in the way of God, and fearing not the blame of any blamer. Such is the grace of God which He giveth unto whom He will. God is all-embracing, aware.*[13]

The messengers said to their people, *We are but mortals like you, but God giveth grace unto whom He will of His servants.*[14] The Exalted also said, *And they say, If only this Qur'ān had been revealed to some great man of the two towns? Is it they who apportion thy Lord's mercy? We have apportioned among them their livelihood in the life of the world, and raised some of them above others in rank.*[15]

In a *ḥadīth* which depicts that [God's grace upon the] Muslim believers is [greater] than [that granted to the] Jews or Christians, God will say to the People of the Book, 'Have I wronged you as regards your rights?' They will respond no. Then God will say, 'Then that is My grace which I grant to whomsoever I will.'[16]

The Exalted also said, *Whoso obeyeth God and the Messenger, they are with those unto whom God hath shown favour, of the prophets and the saints and the martyrs and the righteous. The best of company are they! That is bounty from God, and God sufficeth as knower.*[17] There are many examples in the Qur'ān whereby He mentions selecting only some with His grace and mercy. Had He made all creatures equal then the degrees of His grace, blessing and mercy would not have become apparent. Indeed, blessed is God, the Lord of the Worlds and the Most Wise.

Moreover, it is not obligatory upon Him to permit others to [completely] share in His wisdom—nor is it possible. Rather, the knowledge which people can attain is like a drop of water that a bird drinks from a large ocean. Where is the deficiency if His wisdom is perpetually revealed—one instance after another—just like His will, speech, actions, beneficence, magnanimity and blessings are? Is not this perpetual sequence perfect?

6. If the Lord (Most Blessed and Exalted is He) creates an entity

then it is incumbent that its necessary concomitants exist. The existence of a necessary concomitant without its requisite is impossible; and the existence of two opposites at the same time and place is also impossible. What is considered impossible and implausible is non-existent, and the mind cannot conceptualize its existence in reality. If the [occurrence of] perpetual sequence is a necessary concomitant of His creation and wisdom, then holding our doctrine is not impermissible; rather, what is prohibited is denying it.

7. There is no rational or transmitted proof [in the Qur'ān or the Sunna] that deems actions of the Lord being perpetual, whether in the past or future, to be impossible. On the other hand, all of the claims of the deniers against [perpetual sequence] are invalid. They have been sufficiently refuted by Rāzī himself and Āmidī[18] in most of their books, as well as by others.

The veracity of affirming His wisdom has been established by reason, transmitted evidence and the innate disposition, as well as many other types of proofs, some of which were previously pointed out. How can such well-known and correct proofs be denied, while no definitive proof exists to substantiate the contrary?

8. Sequential actions can either be possible or impossible. If possible, then [the deniers' claim against them] is rendered null. If impossible, then we can plausibly say, 'What is willed ultimately results in an objective for itself alone—not for another—and thus the sequence ends.'

9. Why is it unreasonable to maintain that the reason for [His] action be pre-eternal? Their contention that a pre-eternal [reason] would necessitate an eternal effect is invalid, since [His] will is eternal and yet it does not necessarily follow that what is willed is eternal.

Now if they maintain that [His] eternal will is only attached to and leads to an event at the time of the latter's temporal origination, why then did they not affirm that [His] eternal wisdom is likewise attached to and leads to an event at the time of its temporal origination? If they claim that [His] will is selective, then our response to them is: [His] wisdom is similar, as it represents selecting some entity at [the appropriate] time, place and specification. That selection proceeds from [His] wisdom, will, knowledge and omnipotence. Now if [His] wisdom being eternal necessitates that [His] action be pre-eternal, then [His] will being eternal would also require that [the action] be pre-eternal. If [they do not consider] the latter to be necessary then neither is the former.

10. Had His actions not been for wise purposes and ultimate objectives then He would not be characterized as having a will. It is not rational to deem one to have a will unless his will is attached to purposes and wisdoms. If wisdoms or purposes [to His actions] are denied then [by extension they deny that He is] characterized by a will. In that case [events only occur] because they emanate from [His] essence [with Him having no free will] (*mūjiban bi'l-dhāt*). This represents a complete cause in pre-eternity that necessarily results in its effect. This [will] must therefore accompany all of its effects by necessity. This, then, would necessitate that all events be eternal [and since this is impossible their doctrine is false]. However, a detailed exposition of that is beyond our scope here.

[Rāzī's Third Argument]

Those who deny [His] wisdom state, 'The purpose of [creatures doing anything] is twofold: [first] attainment of pleasure and joy, and [second] avoidance of pain, grief and distress. God (Exalted is He) is capable of attaining those two without intermediary [causes]. Whoever is able to attain such results without intermediary causes is frivolous (*ʿabath*) if he seeks to attain it through intermediaries. But it is impossible that God be characterized as being incoherent (*ʿabath*).'[19]

Those who affirm His wisdom respond to this ambiguity by maintaining:

1. There is no doubt that God is omnipotent, but this does not necessitate that the desired wisdoms behind possibilities within His power should be attained without [intermediaries]. That which is dependent on another cannot occur if the latter is absent—such as the impossibility of a son without a father [or naming the former as such]. The existence of something is impossible without its necessary concomitant. Likewise, the existence of two opposites [at the same time and place] is impossible. It cannot be claimed that [creat-

ing intermediaries] necessitates [that God is] incapable, since what is impossible is [characterized as being] non-existent, and it is not related to [His] power. God is omnipotent, so nothing possible is outside of His capability.

2. The claim that one entity being an intermediary, a condition or a cause for another represents incoherence on His part is false and invalid. Describing something as frivolous is only [valid] when it is devoid of benefit. But it is not incoherent to have a condition, a cause or a form serving as an intermediary for the origination of some event.

3. The purposes and characteristics originated by God (Glory be to Him) in their forms are required for the materialization of those forms—the latter's existence without the former cannot be conceptualized. The intermediation of the former is an inevitable necessity. Therefore, their 'proof' is instead [evidence] against them.

We would also ask, 'Can the Sublime bring about the existence of those events [i.e. purposes] without the intermediation of their respective forms?' If they say that it is possible then intermediation *is* pointless (*ʿabath*). But if they claim that He cannot then they have [attributed] incapability to Him. Now if they say that these are impossible hypotheticals, then we would agree and inform them that they have spoken the truth. This is the essence of our position—what is dependent upon another for its existence cannot occur without the latter. Therefore, intermediation is not frivolous.

4. If there are wisdoms, advantages and benefits in the creation of intermediaries then their intermediation is not frivolous. The wisdom that results from their presence is not equivalent to how it would have been if they had been absent. For example, when God (Glory be to Him) makes the sustenance of some people occur through [intermediaries], this requires creating the tools for those who would need them. Some would benefit from the use of those tools, while others from the sale of them. Thus, both groups derive advantages. If you deeply reflect on existence you will find that it is established upon [intermediaries]. This is a testament against those who deny His wisdom. God (Glory be to Him) has many wisdoms and benefits in originating those intermediaries for His servants.

Had these intermediaries been null then those wisdoms and benefits would not have existed.

5. We would respond to their statement that [the presence of intermediaries] would necessitate incoherence by replying that it would be more appropriate that He not do or command anything except for an advantage or wisdom. Therefore, their position is self-contradictory. If incoherence is impossible then their argument [denying God's wisdom] is false. Hence, we have shown [their doctrine] to be invalid either way.

6. What prevents us from maintaining that God (Glory be to Him) carries out some acts for reasons and some not, the latter being just for themselves. If it is permissible to contend that, then maintaining that only some intermediaries are not intended for reasons is also permissible. But they have denied causality altogether. At most, though, this line of argumentation, if it was correct, can only prove that it is not necessary for a reason or cause to exist in every instance.

Some jurists maintain—while affirming causality [in regards to His commandments]—'We may not be able to infer the reason for some rulings.' Why, then, do [the deniers] not say the same about His creation? The truth, though, is that all of His actions and Divine Law are prescribed and enacted for wisdoms and ultimate objectives—even if the creation is unaware of them in detail. Just because they do not know [the reasons and wisdoms in every instance] does not mean that they do not exist.

7. At most, this ambiguity can only claim that the Sublime is capable of attaining these wise purposes without intermediaries, just as He is able to attain them with intermediaries. If both are possible, then it would not be incoherent for Him to pursue one rather than the other, unless both were equivalent in all aspects. It is impossible for a rational person to claim that the absence of those intermediaries is equivalent in every aspect to their presence. To claim so is one of the greatest types of blasphemies and falsehoods, as it encompasses rejecting the senses, reason and the Divine Law just as it rejects [His] wisdom. Those who deem equivalent the presence of His messengers and their absence; the presence of the sun, moon, stars, rain, plants, animals and their absence equivalent; or the presence of all

intermediaries and their absence—they have completely affronted reason.

8. As for the statement [of the deniers] that the purpose of any being is either to attain pleasures or to avoid distress and grief, [we would ask], 'Does this only concern [I] animals or are you referring to the [II] wise purpose for which God (Glory be to Him) enacts things, or do you mean [III] something even more general than that?'

If you intend the first, then that does not lend support to your position whatsoever. If you intend the second or the third then those are untrue claims. The wisdom of the Lord (Exalted is He) is above attaining [material] pleasures or avoiding distress and grief. There is nothing akin to His wisdom, and He is exalted. Likewise, He is characterized by a will, which is unlike that of animals, since they desire something so as to attain some [direct] benefit or avoid some harm. Likewise, His wrath is not similar to the anger of His creation as theirs is due to a physiologic reaction that results in seeking revenge; God is exalted above that. Just as His will, contentment, wrath, mercy and Attributes do not resemble those of His creation, His wisdom is not likewise similar [to theirs].

His wisdom is more glorious and eminent than for some to claim that its [purpose] is the attainment of some [material] pleasure or avoidance of some grief. Creatures only act in this manner due to their deficient [nature]—their well-being cannot occur otherwise. God (Glory be to Him) is Self-Sufficient, and He does not derive any type of perfection from His creation. Instead, creatures acquire their perfection from Him.

9. Revelation along with reason have both proven that God (Glory be to Him) loves and hates. As for revelation, the Qur'ān is filled with examples of that. As for reason, we say that that His saints and obedient servants are honoured, while His enemies and the sinners are humiliated. This attests to His love and contentment with the former, and His hatred and criticism of the latter. It is well known with absolute certainty that those who love and hate manifest those preferences to a higher degree if they are able to attain what they love. Therefore, God performs His actions because they

lead to what He loves, and He leaves aside others because He does not love them. And if He allows what is disliked to Him it is only because it [ultimately] leads to something that He loves [to a greater degree].

Now, if they intend pleasure, joy, distress and grief by 'love' and 'hate', then although the Exalted Lord loves and hates, it is not permissible to claim that the Lord's love and hatred are for those reasons. In addition, just because He enacts those things for wise purposes, it does not mean that He is characterized by those.

10. If the Sublime is able to attain [objectives] both with and without intermediaries, then doing so in both ways indicates His power, sovereignty and lordship to a greater degree. It is also more perfect and farther reaching than if He were only able to do it in one way. The Exalted Lord varies His actions in accordance with His omnipotence, perfect wisdom and lordship.

11. The Lord (Glory be to Him) is perfect in His Attributes, Names and actions. It is inevitable that their effects become manifest in this world. The following Names of His require entities to which they must be attached, as well as effects by which they can be manifested: the Beneficent (*al-Raḥmān*), the Provider (*al-Razzāq*), the One full of Forgiveness (*al-Ghaffār*), the Forbearing, the Magnanimous, the One Who is kind with His servants (*al-Laṭīf*), the Benefactor (*al-Mannān*), the One Who bestows (*al-Wahhāb*), the One Who constricts (*al-Qābiḍ*), the One Who is munificent (*al-Bāsiṭ*), the One Who lowers, the One Who elevates, the One Who honours, and the One Who abases.

Intermediation inevitably occurs so as to manifest the effects and realize the meanings of those Names and Attributes. Therefore, how can it be said that [intermediaries] are frivolous and lacking in benefit? It is only God who grants success.

[Rāzī's Fourth Argument]

Now, those who have denied His wisdom state,

> Had it been necessary that God's creation and commandments be for some wise purpose or reason, then His creation of this world at a particular time—instead of an anterior or posterior

> one—could only be due to providence of some purpose or advantage. This purpose or advantage could either occur anterior to that time or not. If the [purpose] that God created this world for at a particular time existed anteriorly, then it would be necessary to say that He created it anterior to actually creating it, and this is impossible.
>
> But if either that purpose and advantage did not occur anterior to that time, but rather was originated at that particular time, then its occurrence is either dependent upon an Originator or not. If it is not dependent, then that thing would have been originated without a Creator or Originator; and this is impossible. But if it is dependent upon an Originator, and that purpose at that particular time is connected to another purpose, then this returns to being like the first subtype, thus necessitating infinite regress. But if it is not dependent on providence for another purpose, then God's power to originate and create entities is not in need of any purposes or advantages. And this is what we desire to prove. Know that this argument, which is predicated on specifying that this world must have been created at a particular time, is predicated upon specifying that each temporally-originated thing occurs at its appointed time.[20]

In conclusion, [they claim that] if these events are originated at their [particular] time for a purpose that can be attained anteriorly, then it becomes necessary to originate those [events] earlier—the fact that they were not is due to not being originated. If [events] are originated for some purpose then that would lead to infinite regress. But if not for [a purpose] then [no infinite regress results] and in this manner the [deniers feel] that they have 'proven' their doctrine.

Those who affirm His wisdom state that this argument is the same as what was mentioned within [Rāzī's] second argument. It is as if they are impressed with repeating false [arguments]. All that we used to respond to them previously can be used here. At most, [their argument] indicates that infinite regress would occur in past effects, but not in originated events in the future. But [infinite sequences in the future] are deemed permissible and necessary by the agreement of the Muslim [scholars]—all except Jahm [b. Safwān] and [Abū Hudhayl] al-ʿAllāf.[21]

Ultimately, this matter regards temporally-originated events that are either willed for themselves or for other reasons. A wisdom that is intended for itself is not dependent upon others. Their argument, even if its presumptions were correct—but they are far from that—only proves that the Exalted's actions do not necessarily need to have reasons. But one cannot deduce that [His actions] are done in the absence [of wise purposes]. Again, at most, [their argument] only proves the absence of a reason [or wise purpose] for *some* temporally-originated events—but not *all*.

What has preceded is sufficient—there is no need to make it any longer. The secret of this issue is the perpetuity of His agency into the future, and this is agreed upon. The Predecessors are also in agreement about the perpetuity [of His agency] in the past, although many of the speculative theologians (*ahl al-kalām*) disagreed with that.

CHAPTER FIVE

A Response to Those Who Question God's Wisdom in Creating Disbelief, Wickedness and Sin

[POINTS 1–23]

The deniers of His wisdom state: It has been proven that God is the Creator of everything, but what wisdom or advantage accrued from creating disbelief, wickedness and sin? What wisdom is there in creating those whom He knows will disbelieve, be wicked, commit injustice, and corrupt other people's livelihood and religion?[1] What wisdom is there in creating many of the inorganic materials or inert metals, since it makes no difference whether they exist or not; or trees, plants, and useless animals—mind you that some are predatory and injurious?[2] What is the wisdom in creating poisons and other harmful things?

What is the wisdom in creating Iblīs and the devils?[3] And if there is a wise purpose in their creation, then what is the wisdom in allowing Iblīs to remain alive until the Day of Judgment, while the messengers and prophets are made to die?[4]

What is the wisdom in making Adam and Eve exit the Garden, and submitting them and their offspring to this great tribulation—they could have remained in the greatest well-being therein?[5] What is the wisdom in allowing animals to suffer?[6] Even if you assume that there is a wisdom in allowing those who are charged [with religious responsibilities] to suffer, then what is the wisdom in allowing those who are not charged—like grazing animals, children and the insane—to suffer? What is His wisdom in creating those whom He will punish with a variety of everlasting punishments (*bi-anwāʿ al-ʿadhāb al-dāʾim*) which are eternal (*alladhī lā yanqaṭiʿ*)?[7]

What is His wisdom in allowing His enemies to afflict His saints with painful torments, whether by killing them, taking them hostage, punishing them or taking them as slaves?[8] What is the wisdom in charging humans and jinn and subjecting them, as a result of these obligations, to many types of hardships and afflictions?[9]

They continued: We, as rational people, know by necessity that the denizens of Hellfire are [punished] therein eternally by the act of God. And we know by necessity that He accrues no benefit [from punishing them in Hellfire], nor [is there any benefit] to those being punished, nor to any others.'

They also said: It is sufficient to consider the debate between Ashᶜarī[10] and Abū Hāshim al-Jubbā'ī.[11] The former postulated to the latter three [hypothetical] brothers: the first died as a Muslim before reaching puberty; the other two reached puberty, and one of them died as a Muslim, while the last [died] as a disbeliever. They were gathered in front of the Lord of the Worlds. The Muslim who attained puberty reached one of the highest levels [in Paradise] because of his actions and Islam. His brother says, 'O my Lord, why did You not elevate me to the rank of my Muslim brother?' God replies, 'He has done some actions which you have not.' Then he asks, 'O my Lord, why did You not allow me to live so that I may perform similarly?' God responds, 'I knew that your death as a child would be better for you, because if you had reached puberty you would have thereafter disbelieved.' Then the third brother screams out from the depths of Hellfire, 'O Lord, why did you not cause me to die as a child before I reached puberty just as you did with my brother?' Then Ashᶜarī asks [Jubbā'ī], 'How would you respond [since you claim that God is obligated to do what is beneficial and most advantageous]?' At that point, Jubbā'ī became confounded and could not reply.

The deniers of His wisdom state that this [hypothetical anecdote] definitively proves their doctrine without a doubt. They continued by maintaining that the Exalted has said, *He punisheth whom He will and showeth mercy unto whom He will;*[12] *Unto God (belongeth) whatsoever is in the heavens and whatsoever is in the earth; and whether ye make known what is in your minds or hide it, God will bring you to account for it. He will forgive whom He will and He will punish whom He will;*[13] *He will not be questioned as to that which He doeth.*[14] Therefore, [they contend that] He notified us that matters return back to His will alone [and not His wisdom].

Another group who [denied His wisdom] mentioned that the basis for many people going astray is that they seek to find the reasons for all of the Lord's acts. Of note, the Shaykh of Islam [Ibn Taymiyya, although not a part of that group,] affirmed this in his poem *Tā'iyya*:

> The basis for many people going astray—no matter their school—
> Is seeking out the reasons for God's actions.

When such people sought to find out the reasons for His actions they found that their knowledge was inadequate. They thereafter they split into [different groups]. One group attributed [events] to nature and the celestial bodies.[15] Another group [like some of the Muᶜtazila] denied [some aspects of] reality and reason by saying that the fact that the denizens of Hellfire are [punished] there eternally is more beneficial and more advantageous for them than being in Paradise; that keeping Iblīs alive to deceive humanity and lead them astray is more beneficial for them than making him die; that making the prophets die is more advantageous for their nations than keeping them alive [conveying the message]; that causing torment to children is better for them than sparing them of that, as well as other impossibilities[16] that they were led to because they sought out the reasons for His actions, even though He is the One Who *will not be questioned as to that which He doeth.*[17] That is why some [deniers of His wisdom] maintain, 'The correct opinion is that there are no reasons [for His actions]. This absolves us of all of the snares and traps that others have fallen into.'

Those who affirm His wisdom state: Those questions and objections that you have raised [to deny] the wisdom of the Most Wise are not any stronger than those that the atheists have used to question the existence of God (Glory be to Him). They have raised some forty points, which they claim put into doubt and nullify His existence. Recall also the objections of those who disbelieved in His messengers—some have mentioned eighty points in this regard. Consider also the objections by which the Muʿaṭṭila used to strip away His Attributes of perfection—their nature and number are well-known. Recall also the objections which the Jahmiyya used to deny His transcendence above His creation and His establishment above His throne, His speaking of His Book or [conversing] with His servants [such as Gabriel or Moses]. Recall also the objections that the philosophers have used [to deny that] He created this world in six days, that He will resurrect people from their graves to either the abode of bliss or wretchedness, and that He will change this world and replace it with another. Recall also the arguments of those who deny His predestination. The objections and questions of those groups are many times greater than those who deny His wisdom and [reject] that His actions have intended purposes.

The wisdom of the Most Wise has dictated that He allow in this world for each truth [or bearer thereof] one who stubbornly rejects it, just as He has allowed for each blessing one who envies it, and for each evil one who carries it out. This is due to the complete nature of His dazzling wisdom and overwhelming omnipotence so that He may fulfil His Word[18] and enact His will upon them. He will manifest His wisdom amongst them and judge between them using His divine rulings. He will favour some with His knowledge, and He will manifest amongst them the effects of His Exalted Attributes and Beautiful Names. In addition, it will become clear to His saints and His enemies on the Day of Judgment that He did not leave out any wise purpose, nor did He originate His creation in vain, neglect them to be aimless, and that He did not create the heavens and earth and what is within them without purpose. [Finally, it will become clear] that all praise is due to Him for everything that He has created, determined and decreed; commanded and forbidden; rewarded and punished; and that He has placed everything in its appropriate and suitable place.

The Exalted said, *And they swear by God their most binding oaths (that) God will not raise up him who dieth. Nay, but it is a promise (binding) upon Him in truth, but most of humankind know not. That He may explain unto them that wherein they differ, and that those who disbelieved may know that they were liars.*[19] After God has implemented His definitive judgment and just ruling, the entire universe will speak out in praise of Him. The Exalted has said, *And they are judged aright. And it is said, Praise be to God, the Lord of the Worlds!*[20]

Now there are many ways in which to respond to these questions and they include:

POINT 1: God's wisdom is connected to what exists and what is temporally originated. Disbelief, evils and some types of sins are due to disobeying the prohibitions of God and His Messenger, and abandoning what He has commanded. Thus these [sins] are not connected to what exists [since they are due to privation]. We have only addressed [until now] that God has enacted and created things for intended wisdoms and purposes. Although God (Glory be to Him) has wise purposes in what He has left out and not enacted, this is not considered in our discussion here; and therefore, it cannot be used to repudiate our opinion.

We have already mentioned [in Chapter Two] that evil cannot be attributed to God in any manner whatsoever. Evil is the privation of good and [non-existence] of that which leads to good. Non-existence is nothing as its name implies. When we state that the actions of the Exalted Lord result in praiseworthy wisdoms and purposes, what He has left out cannot be used against us. This is clarified by the second response.

POINT 2: God (Glory be to Him) has left out some things, which may have resulted in wise purposes had He created them, either because of the absence of His love for their existence, or because their existence would have prevented the existence of something more beloved to Him or led to its lapse. In these cases, His wisdom in not creating those entities preponderates over His wisdom in creating them. It is impossible to reconcile two opposites; and therefore, the Sublime has preferred the greater of the two wisdoms and allowed the lesser one to elapse. This results in the highest type of wisdom. Consequently, God's creating and commanding are based upon attaining what is purely advantageous or what is preponderantly so, and allowing the lesser [good] to lapse; hence preventing what is purely harmful or what is preponderantly so. To do differently would represent the opposite of what is wise and correct.

POINT 3: If we assume that one [of those aforementioned] examples is devoid of some wise purpose, then how does that necessitate universally denying His wisdoms and purposes? How can you do so when some of His wisdoms and praiseworthy ends are so well known to those who are enlightened and firmly rooted in knowledge? We will illustrate some of these subsequently, God willing.

POINT 4: We do not claim that people necessarily are privy to or are even able to understand the details of His wisdom. God's wisdom is greater and more eminent than that. Why can it not be that only God knows the wise purposes present in the aforementioned examples? Recall God's response to the angels when they questioned Him about [the wisdom of creating humanity]: *Surely I know that which ye know not.*[21] Maintaining that His actions and rulings necessarily contain wisdom does not concomitantly necessitate that His creation must share in His knowledge of them.

POINT 5: There is nothing like God (Glory be to Him), whether in His Essence, His Attributes or His actions. He possesses many wise purposes in the examples they mentioned and [His wisdom] is not like that of His creation. Likewise, His actions are not similar to theirs. Moreover, His power, intent, will, love, contentment and wrath are not similar to the characteristics of people.

POINT 6: Wisdom is a corollary of knowledge and power. Whosoever is more knowledgeable and more powerful is characterized by actions that are wiser and more perfect. The Lord (Exalted is He) alone possesses perfect knowledge and omnipotence; and therefore, His wisdom follows suit. As was established previously, His wisdom is present within everything, which His knowledge and omnipotence encompass.

POINT 7: It has been definitively proven that He is Most Wise when it comes to His actions and rulings; and therefore, one must affirm what necessarily follows. The lack of our knowledge about His wisdom in regards to [some of] the aforementioned examples does not warrant one to repudiate those definitive proofs. Moreover, our lack of knowledge about something does not necessarily render that thing to be non-existent.

POINT 8: God's perfect Holiness rejects deeming even those

aforementioned examples to be devoid of wisdom. Nonetheless, His perfection and wisdom also refuse allowing His creation to be privy to all of His wisdoms. Indeed, one of us would be considered an ignorant fool if he allowed others to be aware of all of his affairs and matters. The eminence of the Lord is greater than to allow every one of His creation to be privy to the details of His wisdoms.

POINT 9: You either have to acknowledge that He has some wisdoms in His creation and commandments or you must deny all that. If you deny that—and only those who are unjust would do such—then you have disbelieved in all of God's Books and messengers, and have [rejected] rational arguments, the innate disposition and reality. The stubborn rejection of God's dazzling wisdoms in His creation and commandments is like rejecting [the presence] of the sun and moon, day and night. Still, it is not unusual [to see] that many groups of the speculative theologians stubbornly rejected such necessary [precepts].

If, on the other hand, you affirm His wisdom in some of His creating and commanding, then it can be posed to you, 'Which is more appropriate—the presence of His wisdom or its absence?' If you say that it being absent is more appropriate than its presence, then that represents the ultimate denial and heresy; and that is an impossible supposition. But if you maintain that the presence [of His wisdom] is more consistent with [Him being] perfect then we ask, 'Is He capable of permeating all of His creation and rulings [with wisdom] or is He not?' If you say that He is not then you have contended a grave error from a rational and religious perspective, and you have cast away your reason and intellect. But if you acknowledge that He is capable of that, then it is posed, 'If He is capable of something and that thing [i.e. creating and commanding in accordance with His wisdom] is perfect in essence, and its existence is better and more preferable than its non-existence, then how can you negate [His wisdom]?'

If the deniers contend that they have negated it only because they are not privy to the reality [of His wisdom], then we would reply, 'You have spoken the truth. Your only basis for denial is that you did not understand deeply the creed conveyed by the messengers or its reality.'

POINT 10: All sages unanimously agree that if an agent repetitively enacts actions, which manifest his wisdom in the most complete manner and always lead to the most advantageous outcomes, but then acts in a manner that they cannot grasp, they have no choice but to accept [his latest action] as being wise because of what they previously witnessed. Therefore, they do not allow what they are uncertain of to render null what they definitively know to demonstrate his wisdom.

We find the apprentices of each labour act in a similar manner with their masters. Even the deniers [of His wisdom] follow the same exact way with their imams and shaykhs. If they encounter from their imams some ambiguity regarding the [firmly-established] principles (*qawā'id*) and doctrines (*madhāhib*) that they had previously learned, they submit themselves saying that the latter are more knowledgeable than them and have higher degrees of knowledge, gnosis and wisdom. Why, then, do they not follow that same way with their Lord and Creator Whose wisdom has dazzled all those who are rational? Their ability to perceive God's wisdom is less than the degree to which a bat can see the sun's light.

If a distinguished well-known scholar, whose knowledge encompasses many sciences, is criticised and defamed by someone who is not in the same field (nor is he even competent) then the latter would not be considered rational or knowledgeable, but rather deficient and foolish. Then [how can the deniers question] the Most Wise, the Omniscient and the Omnipotent?

POINT 11: Wisdom is only manifested by creating opposites, like night and day, heights and depths, pleasant and repulsive, light and heavy, sweet and bitter, cold and heat, pleasure and pain, life and death, and health and illness. Therefore, the creation of these opposites is in order to manifest His dazzling wisdom, vanquishing power, accomplished will, and perfect and complete sovereignty.

To imagine the absence of these created opposites results in stripping away the requisites of His Attributes, their rulings and their effects—and this is impossible in essence. Each eminent Attribute of His manifests rulings, requisites and effects that illustrate its perfection. It is not permissible to strip any of those away.

His Attribute of being omnipotent requires things to be enacted, and His Attribute of being the Creator requires creation and His Attributes of being: the One Who bestows, the One Who provides, the One Who grants (*al-Muʿṭī*), the One Who withholds (*al-Māniʿ*), the One Who causes harm (*al-Ḍārr*), the One Who grants benefit (*al-Nāfiʿ*), the One Who advances (*al-Muqaddim*), the One Who defers (*al-Mu'akhkhir*), the One Who honours, the One Who abases, the Effacer [of sins] and the Most Kind (*al-Ra'ūf*)—they all result in their respective manifestations.

Had all of [His] creation been obedient servants who praised Him, then the effects of many of His Exalted Attributes and Beautiful Names would not have become manifested. How can the effects of His Attributes of being the One Who pardons, forgives, overlooks, and forgoes, or is almighty, has vanquishing power, and takes retribution be manifested appropriately in the absence of His justice and wisdom? It is only through [His justice and wisdom] that things are put into their respective place. Moreover, had all of creation been one nation then many praiseworthy wisdoms, signs, morals and purposes would have lapsed.

In addition, His perfect sovereignty and administration would not have been realized. If a king's disposal is limited to only one of his powers, then it is either because he is incapable of enacting the others or because of his ignorance regarding their advantageous natures. As for the One Who is the Omnipotent, the Omniscient and the Most Wise, His disposition of affairs within His kingdom is not limited to one type of power, as that would imply a deficiency in His sovereignty. Absolute perfection occurs in granting and barring, abasing and elevating, rewarding and punishing, being magnanimous and humiliating, bestowing glory and subjecting, bringing some proximate and forsaking others, harming some and benefitting others, and favouring and preferring some over others. Had God enacted all these in the context of only one type of human [creature], then that would have been inconsistent with His wisdom. His wisdom is exalted above not being able to differentiate between two equals or equating two disparate entities.

Indeed, God has criticized those who do [not differentiate

between two unequals] and has renounced those who attribute that [inability] to Him. The Qur'ān is filled with His criticism of those who do such a thing. Thus, how can servants attribute to Him a false analogy that they, in their innate dispositions, would hate to be characterized by?[22] The Lord (Glory be to Him) only considered that to be blameworthy because it represents a deficiency. Clearly, it is more fitting that He be infallible above it.

If the effects of His Names and Attributes cannot become manifest, except by [creating] opposing [entities], then His wisdom deems it to be inevitable that He bring them into existence. Had they not been created, then His Attributes would not have become manifested; and this is implausible. This is clarified in the next point.

POINT 12: Some of His Names are paired like the One Who honours and the One Who abases, the One Who lowers and the One Who elevates, the One Who constricts (*al-Qābiḍ*) and the One Who is munificent (*al-Bāsiṭ*), the One Who grants and the One Who withholds. Some of His Attributes include opposing ones, like contentment and displeasure, love and hatred, forgiveness and retribution. These Attributes are all perfect; otherwise, He would not be characterized by them or named in accordance with them. If [His wisdom was absent], then [those Attributes of His] would result in inappropriate outcomes; and this would represent a deficiency and inadequacy, which He is exalted above. Therefore, [it is clear] that these [Attributes] are designated so as to result in appropriate outcomes. This response should suffice one who has a deep understanding regarding His Names and Attributes.

POINT 13: One of His Names is the King (*al-Malik*). The true meaning of God (Glory be to Him) being the King must be firmly established in every aspect. This Attribute includes all the other Attributes of His perfection as necessary concomitants. It is impossible to affirm one's kingship in reality if one is not alive, is powerless or does not have a will, does not possess hearing and vision, cannot speak, or cannot carry out freely-chosen actions. How can one who does not command and forbid, reward and punish, bestow and withhold, grant glory to some and abase and humiliate others, honour/bless some and take revenge against others, lower and raise others, or send messengers throughout his kingdom be characterized as a king? What kind of king in reality is someone who lacks these?

This shows that those who strip away His Names and Attributes have made His servants more perfect than Him. One of them would disdain that these characterizations of the Lord be said about his ruler or king. The true reality of God's kingship necessitates the existence of that which can be administered. Everything is created by God (Glory be to Him), and therefore His perfect sovereignty is not dependent upon any other. Everyone is dependent upon Him; their existence is dependent upon His will and [act of] creation. This is clarified further by the next point.

POINT 14: The perfection of His kingship occurs by it being associated with praise of Him. The kingdom is His and all praise is due to Him. People are divided into three groups in this regard: [the first group includes] the messengers and their followers, who have affirmed that the kingdom is His and all praise is due to Him. This is the doctrine of those who have affirmed His predetermination and wisdom, as well as the realities of His Names and Attributes. They have declared Him infallible above any deficiencies or anthropomorphization. Ahl al-Sunna is alone in this matter as they refused to follow any doctrine forwarded by the speculative theologians.

The second group includes those who affirmed His kingship, but stripped away the reality of the praise due to Him. They include the Jabriyya for they denied His wisdom and causality. They claimed that He may perform anything that is possible, and that He is not infallible above doing something repugnant. Instead, anything that is a possibility [for Him] cannot be considered to be evil if done by Him. They defined repugnance as only that which is essentially impossible, such as combining two opposites. They declared it possible for Him to punish His angels, prophets, messengers and obedient believers, and yet honour Iblīs and the devils in eternal everlasting bliss. They also said that there was no way to deny the impossibility of that unless the Creator Himself has informed us so.

The Jabriyya claim that it is possible that He could command us to blaspheme Him or curse His prophets, to prostrate to idols, to lie, to be wicked, kill others, and to steal money. They [further claimed that He could] forbid benevolence, truthfulness, righteousness and chastity. They claim that there is no difference between what He has commanded and what He has forbidden except due to His will alone—not that what He has commanded is characterized by goodness that results in His love for it and His commandment of it, or that what He has forbidden is characterized by repugnance that results in His dislike and prohibition of it. In reality, these [Jabriyya] have stripped Him of the praise due to Him despite affirming His sovereignty. Some have gone further and have not affirmed even His sovereignty by stripping away His perfect Attributes, which are necessary requisites of Him being a King and Lord in pre-eternity and in future eternity—He cannot [in their doctrine] carry out any actions at all. In this manner, that group did not affirm either His sovereignty or praiseworthiness.

The third group are the Qadariyya who affirmed some types of praise due to Him, but negated perfection of His sovereignty. They affirmed some types of His wisdom, but negated perfection of His omnipotence. In reality, though, they have neither affirmed the essence of His praiseworthiness nor His wisdom.

The only type of wisdom that they really affirmed was that proceeding from creatures, and not [that which occurs due to] God's wisdom (Glory be to Him). Although they seemingly affirmed His sovereignty, they stripped away those Attributes of His which are necessary to establish Him as the Righteous King, as well as His ability to carry out freely-chosen actions. In their doctrine, God is not characterized by any Attributes nor can He execute any acts; this represents the ultimate in negating His sovereignty and praiseworthiness. One who is characterized as being incapable and not acting, lacking a will, being unable to speak, hear or see, nor able to love or hate has in reality been stripped of all of the realities of being a true king worthy of praise.

The point is that for His sovereignty to be universal and absolute it is necessary to affirm His determination, such that nothing occurs within His kingdom in the absence of His will. God is greater and more glorious than [to have something occur without His will]. In addition, for His praiseworthiness to be universal and absolute it is necessary that nothing in His creation or commandments be devoid of wisdom or praiseworthy ends. God is greater and more glorious [than anything existing without a wisdom or praiseworthy end]. This is clarified further in the next point.

POINT 15: An act that is done by an agent without intention, wise purpose or advantage is not considered praiseworthy, nor is such an agent deemed to be worthy of praise. The agent is not deserving of praise if there is no intent on his part to attain some advantage—even if the latter occurs. One who intends an act for an advantage, wisdom or praiseworthy end, but is incapable of carrying out his will, is more deserving of praise than one who is capable but does not carry out actions for a wise purpose, advantage or with the intent of being benevolent. This is well established in people's innate disposition.

Praise of the Sublime Lord has filled the heavens, earth, what is within them, and what is beyond them. It permeates the heavenly congregation and the worldly one in this life and the Hereafter. Praise of Him extends to everything His knowledge encompasses. He is perfectly praiseworthy for everything that He has created and judged—both ontologically and religiously. No atom or larger object moves, no drop falls, nothing in the heavenly congregation or worldly one changes from one state to another, nor do the celestial bodies revolve except in a manner consistent with His praiseworthiness.

The inhabitants of Paradise do not enter Paradise and the denizens of Hellfire do not enter Hellfire except through His praise. Al-Ḥasan [al-Baṣrī][23] (may God have mercy on him) said, 'The denizens of Hellfire will not enter Hellfire except that praise of Him is in their hearts—they cannot find any way to avoid it.' God (Glory be to Him) revealed the Books and sent the messengers through His praiseworthiness; and He brought death upon His creation and will resurrect them through His praiseworthiness.

God has praised Himself for His all-encompassing lordship: *Praise be to God, Lord of the Worlds*;[24] for revealing His Book: *Praise be to God Who hath revealed the Book unto His servant*;[25] for creating the heavens and the earth: *Praise be to God, Who hath created the heavens and the earth, and hath appointed darkness and light*;[26] and for the perfect nature of His sovereignty: *Praise be to God, unto Whom belongeth whatsoever is in the heavens and whatsoever is in the earth. His is the praise in the Hereafter, and He is the Most Wise, the Aware* (*al-Khabīr*).[27]

Therefore, praise of Him has filled all times, all places, all substances, and all states: *So glory be to God when ye enter the night and when ye enter the morning. Unto Him be praise in the heavens and the earth! And at the sun's decline and in the noonday.*[28] How can God not be praiseworthy for all that He has created when He is the One *Who made all things good which He created;*[29] and has perfected His design: *The doing of God Who perfecteth all things.*[30]

God [is worthy of praise] for all of His commandments, which encompass wisdom, mercy, justice and advantage, as well as all of His prohibitions, as everything that He has forbidden is evil and corrupt. He [is praiseworthy] for His reward as it represents His mercy and beneficence, as well as His punishment, since that represents what is just and deserved. All praise is due to God and the sovereignty is all His. In His power is all goodness and all matters revert back to Him.

The point is that the more an agent is characterized by wisdom, the more deserving he is of praise. If wisdom is absent or if he does not intend [wise purposes] through his actions or commandments, then he is not deserving of praise.

POINT 16: It is obligatory that we thank God (Glory be to Him). This is known rationally, through the Divine Law, and in our innate disposition. The obligation to thank Him is more obvious than any other obligation. How can it not be obligatory that the servants praise Him, declare His Oneness, love Him, remember His blessings and beneficence, glorify Him, declare His greatness, submit themselves to Him, mention His blessings and affirm them in all possible manners?

Thanking Him is the most beloved thing to Him and it affords the greatest reward; and God has originated the creation, revealed His Books and prescribed His Divine Law for this reason. It requires the creation of causes that lead to a more perfect [level] of gratitude to Him. Part of this is that He differentiated between His servants in regards to their characteristics, whether apparent or hidden, in their physiques, moral ethics, religions, provisions, livelihoods and lifespans. If one who is healthy sees another who is ill, or one who is wealthy [sees] one who is poor, or the believer [sees] a disbeliever, then the [former types] will be more grateful to God. The former will acknowledge the great extent of His blessings upon them, and realize that God has selected and distinguished them over others. They will be more thankful [to Him], become more submissive [to Him] and acknowledge His blessings to a greater degree. In a tradition mentioned by Imam Aḥmad, 'Moses asked, "O Lord, why did you not make all of Your servants equal?" God said, "I love to be thanked."'[31]

If it is said, 'It would have been possible for Him to bless them equally and make their degree of gratitude [to Him] equivalent, just as He has done with the angels,' we would respond: Had God done that then the resultant type of gratitude would have been different than the type that results from being distinguished and selected—the latter is greater and superior. For this reason, the gratitude, submission and humility of the angels to God's greatness and glory was greater and more perfect after they witnessed what came about from Iblīs or Hārūt and Mārūt.[32] This is all due to the Lord's wisdom (Exalted is He).

In addition, the gratitude of the prophets and their followers is greater and more perfect after seeing with their own eyes the retribution of the Lord leading to their enemies' destruction. Similar is the case with the gratitude of the inhabitants of Paradise after reaching Paradise and witnessing His enemies—those who disbelieved in His messengers and associated others with Him—being punished [in Hellfire]. There is no doubt that their gratitude, contentment and love of their Lord will be more perfect and greater at that time than had God decreed that all of the creation share in the eternal bliss [of Paradise].

The goodness/beauty of something is illustrated and revealed more clearly by comparing it to its opposite. If it was not for the creation of what is repugnant then the virtue of beauty and goodness would not have been recognized. If it was not for darkness, the excellence of light would not be known. If it were not for the creation of many types of afflictions, then the value of well-being would not have been realized. Had it not been for Hellfire, then the worth of Paradise would not be [completely] appreciated.

Had God (Glory be to Him) made the daytime continual, its value would not have been known; and if He had made the night-time enduring, its worth would not have been recognized. The most knowledgeable person about the excellence of a blessing is the one who has tasted affliction. Likewise, the person who realizes most the value of wealth is the one who has endured the bitterness of poverty and need.

Had all people been [created] in the same image of beauty, the value of beauty would not have been known. Similarly, if all people were believers, the worth and blessing of faith would not have been recognized. Most blessed is He Who imparts far-reaching wisdoms and abundant blessings in His creation and commandments.

POINT 17: It is obligatory to worship God (Glory be to Him) in a number of different manners. The highest and loftiest type is through loyally supporting and loving [the believers] for His sake, [directing] enmity [towards His enemies] for His sake, waging battle in His path, and sacrificing one's blood to attain His pleasure. Waging battle [for His sake] represents the apex of worship, and it is the most beloved type in His view. It is dependent upon things without which it could not occur, such as creating the souls that will loyally support Him, thank Him and believe in Him, while [also creating] the souls that will oppose and disbelieve in Him. In this manner, what is beloved to Him will occur more completely, and His saints will become more proximate to Him in [the process of] fighting against, resisting, humiliating, subduing and opposing His enemies. In addition, His Word and Message is the loftiest, and it will prevail over false beliefs and messages.[33] Had falsehood, disbelief and polytheism not existed, then over what would His words and message become exalted? Something towering over itself is impossible.

POINT 18: Some types of servitude to God are setting slaves free, giving charity, preferring others, consoling others, forgiving others, overlooking [others' mistakes], patience, suppressing one's anger, enduring hardships, and other similar things, which cannot occur except in the presence of their respective attachments and causes.

If it was not for the presence of disbelief, then worshipping [God] by freeing a slave would not have occurred, since slavery is a by-product of disbelief. Had it not been for injustice, maltreatment and oppression, then worshipping [Him] through patience, forgiveness and suppression of one's anger would not have occurred. Had it not been for poverty and need, the worship [of God] by giving charity, giving preference to others and consoling them would not have occurred. Had God made all of His creation equal then these types of worship—which are some of the most beloved to Him—would not [have been legislated] to be. It is for these that He created humans and jinn, prescribed the Divine Law, revealed the Books, sent the messengers, and created this world and the Hereafter.

POINT 19: God (Glory be to Him) is happier with the repentance of His servant than can be measured or imagined, even if one continually reflected on it. The occurrence of [God's] happiness is dependent upon repentance, which is in itself dependent on the existence [of a sin] to repent from. If something is dependent on another entity, then the former cannot exist without the latter. The existence of a necessary concomitant in the absence of its cause is impossible. There is no doubt that the existence of this happiness is more perfect than its non-existence.

It is from [His] complete wisdom that He determined causes and their necessary concomitants. The most knowledge person about God [i.e. the Prophet Muḥammad] pointed out this same exact meaning when he said in the authentic *ḥadīth*, 'If you did not commit sins, God would dispense with you and create another group of people who would commit sins. They would ask for forgiveness, and He would forgive them.'[34] Had He not [ontologically] determined the occurrence of sins and disobedience, then unto whom would He show mercy and forgive, whose repentance would He accept, whom would He pardon and save [from Hellfire]? Against whom would He set aside His rights so as to manifest His grace, magnanimity, forbearance and generosity [if there were not sinners]? His forgiveness is vast, thus how can that Attribute not be manifested? How can it be realized without there being something and someone to be forgiven, someone to repent and something to be repented of? Had there been no other wisdom and praiseworthy end for the [ontologic] determination of sins, disobediences and lapses [besides the aforementioned] it would have sufficed. Yet, in fact, beyond that there are many more wisdoms, advantages and praiseworthy objectives that can be imagined.[35]

One of the worshipers used to repeat in his circumambulations [around the Kaᶜba] the supplication 'O God, safeguard me from sins.' It was then said to him in a dream, 'You ask Me to safeguard you, and My servants ask Me to allow them to be sinless. But if I safeguard you from sins, then whom would I forgive, whose repentance would I accept, and whom would I pardon?' Had it not been that asking for repentance is one of the most beloved things to Him, then He would not have allowed one of the most distinguished people in His sight [i.e. Adam] to commit a sin (*dhanb*). This is clarified by the twentieth aspect.

POINT 20: Many of His dazzling wisdoms and manifest signs only occur as an [indirect] result of creating some people who disbelieve in Him, declare associates with Him and oppose His [religious commandments]. For instance, had it not been for the disbelief of Noah's people the sign of the flood would not have occurred, and subsequent generations would not have continued to mention it [as one of His greatest signs]. Had it not been for the disbelief of the people of ᶜĀd, the sign of the fatal tempest which destroyed everything would not have occurred. Had it not been for the disbelief of Ṣāliḥ's people [i.e. Thamūd], the sign of destroying them by the [boom of an awful] sound would not have happened. Had it not been for the disbelief of Pharaoh and his people, all those signs and wonders, which nation after nation have discussed, would not have occurred. Many have become guided, by God's will, through these clear signs. God destroys [those whom He wills], and guides to [spiritual] life those whom He wills.

These [events] have also manifested God's grace, justice and wisdom, as well as being [a means to establish] the signs of His messengers and their truthfulness. The messengers' ability to respond, disprove, invalidate and shatter [the disbelievers'] arguments, followed by God's destruction [of the disbelievers due to their stubborn rejection], all represent the greatest proofs for the veracity [of the messengers] and [God's] evidences.

Had it not been for the fact that the polytheists [of Quraysh] came forth in great numbers with strength [armed] with swords in the Battle of Badr, the great signs, faith, guidance and goodness associated with [that battle] would not have occurred nor existed. By God, how many people became believers after hearing the story of Badr? How many doors were opened as a result for those with intellects, so as to allow them to reach guidance and certainty? How many things occurred which are beloved to the Beneficent but a source of vexation (*ghayẓ*) for Satan? The harm which befell the disbelievers is insignificant compared to all the advantages and wisdoms that resulted. It is similar to the harm that rain may cause if it disrupts a traveller, soaks one's clothes, or destroys some houses, when compared to its generalized benefit.

Deeply reflect on how the flooding and drowning of Pharaoh and his followers [indirectly] led other nations to attain guidance and faith. The destruction that the former suffered becomes insignificant in relation to the advantages resulting from God's signs, as they include many wise purposes, miracles, evidences, insights and reminders.

God (Glory be to Him) commanded His messengers to remind their nations [about His signs]. The Exalted said, *We verily sent Moses with Our revelations, saying, Bring thy people forth from darkness unto light. And remind them of the days of God. Therein are revelations for each steadfast, thankful (heart). And (remind them) how Moses said unto his people, Remember God's favour unto you when He delivered you from Pharaoh's folk who were afflicting you with dreadful torment, and were slaying your sons and sparing your women; that was a tremendous trial from your Lord.*[36] Therefore, Moses reminded the Israelites about the 'days of God', His blessings, being saved from their enemies, and how they were destroyed as the Israelites watched. It came to pass that even the death of the [Israelites'] sons was small as compared to the remembrance of Him, gratitude to Him, love of Him, and exaltation and glorification of Him which occurred. The Israelites eventually found comfort and became relieved of being enslaved and humiliated by Pharaoh. Moreover, the pain that the [Israelite] parents endured when [their first born sons] were slaughtered was much less than that of [Pharaoh's] enslavement of them as both the parents and their offspring had to share in being [slaves].

God (Glory be to Him) also willed to show His servants one of His greatest signs, which was that Pharaoh—who had killed so many children (only God knows how many) in pursuit [of Moses]—ended up raising Moses in his own home. There is so much wisdom, advantage, mercy, guidance and insight encompassed within this sign. It is, of course, dependent upon the presence of many necessary concomitants and causes; and this [sign] could not have existed without them—that would have been impossible. The benefits and wisdoms of this sign overwhelm the harm of those [first-born] children being killed.

Likewise, consider the signs that God manifested through the actions of the honourable one [Joseph], son of the honourable one [Jacob], son of the honourable one [Isaac], son of the honourable one [Abraham]. The wonders, wisdoms, advantages and benefits in his story, which exceed 1000, could not have occurred without that cause [i.e. Joseph's brothers throwing him into the well and separating him from his father], although it was a source of harm and grief for both Jacob and Joseph. In the end, that harm turned into so many advantages such that it was as if the [harm] vanished away completely in comparison [to those wise purposes].

It became a cause for great advantages appreciated by Jacob, Joseph, his brothers, the wife of the minister, the inhabitants of Egypt, as well as the believers until the Day of Judgment. The gnostics have reaped much knowledge, wisdom and insight about God, His Names and His Attributes, as well as about His messengers, from this story.

The same can be said about the harm that Job suffered from Satan afflicting him with distress and torment.[37] That suffering is insignificant relative to the advantages and benefits received by him and others when this affliction finally ceased and was substituted with blessings. Moreover, his suffering was the reason and formed the path that allowed him to reach [those blessings]—it was the tree that resulted in the fruits of those blessings.

Consider also other causes, such as the disbelief of Abraham's people and their polytheism, which led him, the friend of the Beneficent, to break their idols. His action resulted in them becoming angered; they therefore lit up a great fire and threw him into it, but it became cool and peaceful like a green garden. It became a sign, evidence, lesson and proof for other nations—generation after generation. How many far-reaching wisdoms, vast blessings, mercies and clear evidences does God (Glory be to Him) have in this sign? Had those causes been null then those resultant wisdoms, advantages and signs would have never occurred. God's wisdom and perfect Holiness refuse their [lapse].

The establishment of Abraham as the leader of the believers until the Day of Judgment could not have occurred in the absence of the aforementioned harms. Those trivial harms are even lesser than the harm that heat, cold, rain and snow pose when compared to their greater advantages. But human beings are as God mentioned: *Lo! he hath proved a tyrant and a fool.*[38] They are unjust to themselves and ignorant of their Lord and His greatness, glory, wisdom and perfect works.

There is such a great difference between the Messenger of God (may God bless him and grant him peace) emigrating from Mecca in his state and later conquering it in a manner that humanity would be delightfully happy with it for God's sake. At that time, the Prophet entered His Sacred House accompanied by all the Emigrants [from Mecca], the Supporters [from Medina], while the angels were above all of them, and the revelation of God was coming down upon him. Therefore, the harm of that expulsion [by Quraysh] was rendered insignificant comparatively, and it was as if it never happened.

It is of the complete manifestation of the Exalted Lord's signs, perfect power and wisdom that He created Gabriel (may God bless him and grant him peace), who is the most noble, purest, most virtuous and most eminent heavenly spirit. He is the ambassador of every good, guidance, faith and righteousness. And on the other hand, God created the damned spirit of Iblīs, who is the most wicked, filthiest and most evil spirit. The Devil is the caller to evil and is the basis and root element of all [wickedness].

It is also from God's absolute wisdom and power that He created light and darkness, the earth and the heavens, Paradise and Hellfire, the lotus tree [in the seventh heaven] and the tree of *Zaqqūm* [in Hellfire], the Night of Power and the night of epidemic, the angels and the devils, the believers and the disbelievers, the righteous and the wicked, as well as cold and heat, remedy and disease, pleasure and pain, joy and grief. God (Glory be to Him) brought forth from amongst all of the aforementioned some of the most beloved types of worship to Him, and [through them] made Himself known to His creation.

Had it not been for the creation of the devils, desires and the self that incites one [to evil], then worship [of Him] through patience, striving against oneself and against the devils, and abandoning what one desires for God's sake, would not have occurred. These types of worship occupy a [greater] rank than others.

If it was not for the presence of disbelievers then worship [of Him] through waging battle would not have occurred nor would some of those fighters attain the status of martyrdom. Likewise, those who prefer the love of their Originator (*Fāṭir*) and Creator over themselves, their relatives, and their offspring would not have become apparent, nor differentiated from those who would rather prefer some trifling share [of this world]. The patience of the messengers and their followers, their striving, their enduring many types of adversities and hardships for God's sake, as well as the various types of worship connected to calling others [to Islam] and showing them [the Straight Path], could not have occurred if not for the existence of the disbelievers. This type of worship leads to a [high] rank in [Paradise]; but without such worship, that [rank] cannot be reached. The Lord (Exalted is He) loves that His messengers and their followers reach [that high rank]—therein He will allow them to witness His blessings, grace and wisdom. This will then result in them praising, thanking, loving and being pleased with God [to a greater degree].

POINT 21: The Sublime's wisdom has settled on the fact that bliss, luxury and relaxation cannot be attained except by traversing a bridge of hardships and fatigue. The former cannot be reached except by going through a door which requires patience in the face of adversities and endurance of hardships. It is for this reason that Paradise is surrounded by adversities, while Hellfire [is enveloped by] desires.

It is also for this reason that God made His chosen one, Adam, exit Paradise although He created it for him. His wisdom dictated that Adam would not re-enter it and settle in it again except after fatigue and hard struggle. God did not [temporarily] make him descend from it except to return him to it eternally. By God, there is such a vast difference between his first entry and the second.

How vast is the difference between the entry of the Messenger of God [into Mecca] (may God bless him and grant him peace) along with al-Muṭʿim b. ʿAdī [after returning from Ta'if][39] and between his entry into it on the Day of Conquest? How vast is the difference between the relaxation and bliss of the believers in Paradise after enduring what preceded it [in this world] and the pleasure [they would have experienced] had they only remained [in Paradise from the beginning]? How great is the happiness of one who becomes healthy after being afflicted with disease, one who becomes wealthy after poverty, one who becomes guided after being astray, and one who collects his heart after it was scattered? Indeed, the happiness of the former types is much greater compared to those who did not encounter those adversities [and overcome them].

It has preceded in God's divine wisdom that adversities are causes that [indirectly] lead to pleasures and goodness. The Exalted has said, *Warfare is ordained for you, though it is hateful unto you; but it may happen that ye hate a thing which is good for you, and it may happen that ye love a thing which is bad for you. God knoweth, ye know not.*[40] [A poet said],

> It may be that something that the soul dislikes is a cause
> which leads to something beloved in a manner that nothing else can.

POINT 22: All sages unanimously deem tiring one self to attain one's perfection as good, whether that includes beneficial knowledge, righteous deeds or a virtuous character. Whoever tires himself more in this pursuit reaches a better state and occupies a more elevated rank. They also deem tiring one self to attain wealth, glory and honour as good, while they criticize those who are lazy and classify them as having an inferior resolve, a contemptible soul and a lowly status.

Although this hard work is associated with fatigue, pain, adversity and suffering, it is the only pathway to reach those perfections. The [sages] never maligned the wisdom of those who withstood those [hardships], nor did they consider them to be deficient—instead they are [considered] to display full intelligence. And whoever recommends others [to endure hardships to attain those perfections] is considered to be wise, whereas one who discourages others from that is considered to be a fool and one who has betrayed them.

This concerns matters which are beneficial to one's livelihood, therefore how about those which concern the eternal and everlasting life and bliss? How can it not be that one who encourages others to endure hardship—for a limited amount of time so that they may attain eternal goodness—be considered a wise, merciful, beneficent and sincere advisor? This individual also discourages others from relaxation and pleasure, as these hinder them from attaining their perfection, eternal pleasure and joy.

Now, the commandments of the Lord (Exalted is He) are all merciful, benevolent and curative. The [commandments] sustain their hearts, adorn them both outwardly and inwardly, and [spiritually] enliven their hearts and bodies. Following [those commandments and prohibitions] results in much joy, happiness, pleasure, delight, bliss and consolation.

[God's Divine Law], which some consider to only be obligations, leads to delight for the soul, life for the heart, light for the mind, perfection for the innate disposition, absolute beneficence and consolation for the human species—these being much greater than His blessing them with health, well-being, food, drink and clothing. His blessings upon His servants through sending His messengers, revealing His Books, making known to them His commandments and prohibitions, and what He loves and hates are the greatest, noblest and most eminent types of blessings. Moreover, there is no comparison between His compassion upon people by [creating] the sun, moon, rain and plants and between His mercy by [bestowing upon them religious] knowledge, faith and the Divine Law. How can it be said, 'What wisdom is there in [His Divine Law] if it represents only hardships and ordeals that accrue no benefit'? By God, those who suspect and imagine that regarding the [Law of the] Most Wise are more astray than grazing animals and are in a worse state than donkeys. We seek refuge in God from being forsaken and being ignorant about the Beneficent, His Names and Attributes.

Has not that which is beneficial for humanity been established by His commandments and prohibitions, by the sending of the messengers and revelation of His Books? Had it not been for all of that, then all of humanity would have been like grazing animals clowning around in the streets, cohabiting with others like animals, not recognizing anything good, not deeming anything abominable as bad, not abstaining from anything which is repugnant, nor being guided to anything which is good. You can see for yourself the condition of people when the traces of prophethood vanish—ignorance, oppression, disbelief in the Creator, associating other creatures [in worship with Him], and deeming good that which is repugnant. Indeed corrupt doctrines and deeds predominate their affairs. The Divine Law was revealed and prescribed by the Most Wise and Omniscient, and He knows its benefits [in detail]. They result in bliss for [His] servants in this worldly life and the Hereafter.

God did not command us due to any need of His nor are [His commandments] frivolous. Instead, they are a mercy, beneficence and benefit [for us]. Nor did He forbid us with prohibitions due to any miserliness; instead, they are for our protection and preservation from that which would otherwise harm and come back to hurt us. How can it be imagined by anyone who has the slightest degree of intelligence that [His Divine Law] is devoid of wisdoms and praiseworthy purposes?

It is for this reason that many rational people used the Divine Law to prove the prophethood [of Muḥammad] and did not need any inimitable prophetic miracle (*muʿjiza*). The message (*daʿwa*) of the prophets (may God bless and grant them peace) is one of the biggest testaments to their veracity. Anyone who posseses intelligence and a sound innate disposition, has knowledge (*khibra*) of the words and message of the prophets, and reflects on the Divine Law [of Islam] would be definitively certain that the one [i.e. Muḥammad] who conveyed this Divine Law is a truthful messenger, and that the One Who prescribed it is Most Wise. Even some intelligent philosophers have attested to its perfection and complete nature, and that the world has not seen a more perfect or wiser moral law. This is the testimony of the enemies [of religion].

On the other hand, some who imagined themselves to be saints claimed that the Divine Law was not prescribed for any wise purpose or advantage. They stated, 'What wisdom is there in obligating people to carry out these hard and tiring obligations,' and 'What advantage or purpose is there for the One Who obligates?' They [claimed] that the Divine Law is only due to His will, which is devoid of intending any purpose or wisdom. Had those [who considered themselves to be saints] felt any shame from the intelligent [philosophers], they would have been prevented from writing down things like that and harbouring iniquitous hearts. Did the Divine Law leave out anything that is good and advantageous except that it included, commanded and charged [people] to do it? Or did it leave out any evil or harmful thing except that it prohibited it? Or did it [not describe the] objections of those who stubbornly reject, or [leave out any] request from those who asked? *Who is better than God for judgment to a people who have certainty (in their belief)*?[41]

Those who deny [His] wisdom claim that it is possible that He could have judged the opposite in every aspect, and that it is only His judgement and will which led to the Divine Law. Had the wisdom of all wise men from the beginning of time to the end been compared to the wisdom contained within the Divine Law—which is perfect and superior—theirs would have been like a drop of water compared to the ocean.

We mean by this Divine Law that which was revealed by God upon His Messenger and which He prescribed for this Community and called them to, and not incorrect or altered interpretations of it. These latter two types may include and are the source of much corruption and evilness occurring in this Community.

It is sufficient for an intelligent and enlightened person—who has a heart that is [spiritually] alive—to contemplate about just one [pillar of His] commandments, which is the prayer. It includes many dazzling wisdoms and advantages both hidden and apparent, as well as benefits that are connected to the heart, spirit and body. Had all the sages of this world gathered and depleted all of their powers and thoughts, they could not thoroughly comprehend the details of its wisdoms, secrets and praiseworthy objectives. They cannot even fully comprehend the secrets of the opening chapter, Sūrat al-Fātiḥa, and what it encompasses of divine knowledge and lordly wisdoms.[42] It affirms His absolute Oneness, extols God through His Names and Attributes, and identifies the divisions of humanity in accordance with their objectives and means.

In addition, prayer is conditional upon the purification of the bodily organs, clothing and place; adorning oneself; facing towards His [Sacred] House, which He made a leading direction for humankind; purifying one's heart and intention for God's sake alone; beginning it with His words, which combine all of the meanings of servitude that prove the principles and branches of extolling [Him]; and [finally] removing from one's heart any preoccupation with others than Him. There are many wonderful wise purposes in all of that.

One stands with an aware heart before the Exalted and Most Glorious, Who is greater and more exalted in His magnificence than any other entity in the heavens, earth or multiverse. All faces are humbled before Him, all necks are subservient to Him, and all tyrants are submissive to Him. He is omnipotent over His servants and is watching over them. God knows what they hide in their chests, hears their discussions, and sees their whereabouts—nothing of their matters is hidden from Him.

Then the servant starts glorifying, praising and remembering Him [by saying], 'His Name is the Most Blessed and exalted is His glory,' as well as declaring that He alone deserves to be worshipped. Then one extols Him in the best manner by praising Him, mentioning His lordship over this world, and His beneficence and mercy upon [humanity]. Then one exalts Him as all sovereignty is His on the Day [of Resurrection] as He will gather all generations from the first to the last in one plain, and judge them in accordance with their deeds. Then the servant will declare that He alone is deserving of worship; this includes Oneness of His lordship, such that He alone should be relied upon, and Oneness of His divinity, such that He alone should be worshipped.

Then one asks Him for the greatest and most glorious thing to be requested, which is that God guide him to the Straight Path that He has established for His prophets and messengers, and their followers. He made it to be the Path by which the travellers can reach Him and His Paradise. He has selected them [for His Path] and blessed them, revealed the truth to them, and allowed them follow it. This is unlike the nation which deserved His wrath, as they recognized the truth but did not follow it, and the nation that went astray and remained ignorant, and therefore could not follow [the Straight Path].

Thus, Sūrat al-Fātiḥa has made known to us: the Lord, the Path leading to Him, and the objective after reaching [Him]. It includes extolling and supplicating [to Him], as well as the most eminent objective: worshipping [Him]. The best means to achieve the aforementioned is by relying on Him. God mentioned [the objective] before the means, i.e. the One Who is worshipped is the One Whom we depend upon for [success in performing our] actions. This is a declaration that God alone is able to help us, and no one else but Him is suitable (Glory be to Him).

It also mentions His divinity, lordship and mercy. We extol Him and worship Him due to His divinity. He creates and sustains, grants life and death, administers His kingdom, leads astray those who deserve to go astray, and is angered with those who deserve His wrath. All this occurs through His lordship and wisdom. He blesses, shows mercy, is magnanimous, forbears, forgives, guides, and accepts repentance; all this occurs due to His mercy. By God, how much gnosis, knowledge, monotheism and realities of faith are contained within this *sūra*?

Thereafter the servant moves to recite the words of the Lord of the Worlds, which enliven the hearts and spirits, cure the chests and enlighten the insights. The prayer now takes him to pleasing and wonderful gardens containing blooming flowers and good fruits. One reaps from them the good that he is commanded to do, and the avoidance of evil, which he is forbidden from. The recitation includes many wisdoms, lessons, morals, insights and remembrance. It also affirms the truth, refutes falsehood, removes doubts, answers questions, and clarifies what is unclear. It also makes one yearn to pursue the causes that lead to success and bliss, and avoid those that lead to loss and wretchedness. It invites one to guidance and drives one back away from destruction.[43]

The heart becomes satisfied with the nourishment [from prayer], and takes its provision and ample share of medication so that it can resist [evil]. The prayer encompasses many [spiritual] states and [levels of] gnosis. It includes all of the stations and levels that are used to journey to God (Exalted is He). How can it be said that prayer is only an obligation, and that it was not prescribed for any wise purpose that the Lawmaker intended? Or that it is only an obligation and hardship that is predicated purely on His will? Or that it is an obligation that results in nothing beneficial in this world or the Hereafter? Deeply reflect on the gateways, means and end objectives of the Divine Law, and you will find that the prayer is loaded with wise purposes and praiseworthy objectives that it was prescribed for. Had it not been for the Divine Law, the state of humankind would have been like that of grazing animals or even worse.

There are also many wisdoms and benefits in ablution. For instance, it cleanses the heart, spirit and body. Deeply reflect on how ablution involves the limbs, which are the place of acquisition (*kasb*) and action. It also involves the face, which possesses hearing, sight, speech, smell and taste, which are the doors to all sins and disobedience. And since washing the head would otherwise entail difficulty and hardship, He prescribed that one only wipe it. As a consequence, God made ablution result in the removal of sins from these sites. It has been authentically narrated by Abū Hurayra that the Prophet (may God bless him and grant him peace) said, 'When a Muslim or a believer performs ablution and washes his face, every sin that he has looked at with his eyes leaves from his face with that water, or with the last drop of that water. When he washes his hands, every sin that he committed with his hands leaves from his hands with that water, or with the last drop of that water. When he washes his feet, every sin to which he walked with his feet leaves from his feet with that water, or with the last drop of that water. He, therefore, emerges cleansed of his sins.'[44]

Also in *Ṣaḥīḥ Muslim*, ʿUthmān b. ʿAffān narrated that the Messenger of God (may God bless him and grant him peace) said, 'If one performs ablution well, his sins are removed—even from beneath his nails.'[45] This is one of the greatest wisdoms and benefits of ablution.

Those who deny His wisdom claim that ablution is solely an obligation, hardship and difficultly, devoid of any advantage or wisdom that it was prescribed for. He [Ibn al-Qayyim] states that had there been no advantage or wisdom in it other than it being a mark and sign for this Community's faces and limbs on the Day of Judgment from amongst all of the nations [that would be sufficient]. What greater advantage, wisdom or mercy is there than the fact that ablution purifies the hands and allows the heart to seek repentance, so that one may prepare oneself to stand in front of one's Lord, as well speak and supplicate to Him with a pure body, clothes and heart?

By God, had Hippocrates or one of his students advised his followers with something similar to this, the [philosophers and deniers] would have all yielded to him, aggrandized him to the greatest extent, and expressed that he exhibited great wisdom.

To return, since one neglects his extremities [spiritually] outside of prayer using them instead to indulge in temptations and desires, the Lord commanded the servant to worship Him with all of his extremities so that they may all participate in worship. A person submits his heart, body, extremities, senses and power to his Lord (Almighty and Most Glorious is He). One stands in God's presence facing Him and neglects all others besides Him. One renounces ever turning away from Him or perpetrating any sins against His rights.

Moreover, God commanded one to repeat the prayers and face Him time after time. The stretch of time in between them is not too long such that one forgets his Lord leading him to become totally cut-off from Him.

Prayer is one of the greatest blessings of God and one of His best gifts that He bestowed upon us. The Divine Law in its entirety contains wisdoms and advantages; therefore, use what is apparent to you as proof for what is hidden from you. It may even be that what you do not know of something's wisdom is greater than what you do know. What you know correlates to the degree of your intellect and understanding, while that which is hidden from you is beyond your insight and comprehension. If we wanted to detail all [of God's wisdoms present within the prayer] we would have to write several volumes. We have sufficed with what is clearest. We depend on God.

POINT 23: Inanimate and animate objects have many different forms, quantities, characteristics, benefits and powers, as is the case with foods and plants; and there are many wise purposes and benefits behind them. Despite that people have only recognized the simplest and least [types of wise purposes derived from them]. In addition, they include many great lessons and manifest proofs regarding the existence of the Creator, His will, selection, knowledge, power and wisdom.

One element could not in itself have possessed all those unusual forms, different shapes, benefits and characteristics—even if one was added to another. Therefore, the occurrence of this diversity, differentiation and variety in animals and plants represents some of the greatest signs of the Exalted Lord; proofs of His lordship, power, wisdom and knowledge; and that He carries out that which He wishes by His free choice and free will. The diversity of His creatures and His temporal origination of them gradually, bit by bit, are the clearest proofs for all of the aforementioned. Deeply reflect on how the Qur'ān informs us of that in many places.

The Exalted said, *And in the earth are neighbouring tracts, vineyards and ploughed lands, and date-palms, like and unlike, which are watered with one water. And we have made some of them to excel others in fruit. Herein verily are portents for people who have sense;*[46] *And of His signs is the creation of the heavens and the earth, and the difference of your languages and colours. Herein indeed are portents for men of knowledge.*[47]

The Exalted also said, *God hath created every animal of water. Of them is (a kind) that goeth upon its belly and (a kind) that goeth upon two legs and (a kind) that goeth upon four. God createth what He will. God is able to do all things.*[48] Deeply reflect here on how God (Glory be to Him) apprised us of how the various animals walk. Even though they share the instrument, they are diverse in their shapes, strengths and actions. They differ in the foods [they eat] and homes [they live in]. Those animals which move on their bellies share in that regard, but their species differ. Those animals which walk on two feet share in that regard, but their species also differ greatly. Many of these animals possess certain types of knowledge, perception and vigour, which then allow them to pursue what is beneficial and avoid what is harmful. Even humankind is incapable of many of those [abilities].

One of the greatest and most evident wisdoms that prove the omniscience of the One Creator Who is omnipotent and Most Wise is that all [animals] are compliant and harmonious with what His will and wisdom created them for. Moreover, God (Exalted is He) said, *And He createth that which ye know not;*[49] *But nay! I swear by all that ye see. And all that ye see not.*[50]

Now, the ultimate objective of His actions and wisdoms of His creation and commandments are to prove His Divine Oneness, and that any other [claimed] divinity is false and impossible. Worshipping Him alone is the ultimate objective. Following that are other objectives, which are essentially the means [to truly worshipping Him] alone, and they are themselves considered to be objectives in relation to what is beneath them. *And that thy Lord, He is the goal.*[51] Any knowledge, pursuit or remembrance not attached to God is [in reality ultimately associated] with non-existence.

In essence, only God and the things that He enacts (*mafʿūlātihi*)—which are the effects (*āthār*) of His actions (*afʿālihi*)—exist. His actions are the effects of His Attributes; and His Attributes self-subsist as necessary concomitants of His Essence.

The point is that the intended objective of all of this is to know that One Knower possesses all knowledge, One Agent carries out all [types of good] actions, One Who is omnipotent possesses and exhibits all [types of] power, and One Who is Most Wise displays all [types of] wisdom. This is all evident despite the wide variety [of creation in existence]. All of the purposes of His actions and commandments end in one ultimate objective [i.e. so that we may worship Him alone]. This is one of the clearest proofs of His Divine Oneness: everything is originated by One Creator and One omnipotent Lord.

The one order and wisdom that encompass all of these different and numerous types—which also includes opposites—prove the Oneness of His lordship and divinity. The fact that they are dependent upon each other, are intertwined, assist one another, and are connected proves that they are the work of One Agent and one Lord.

Had there been any other deity or lord alongside Him then those other deities would have alone taken possession of what they had created, and subsequently departed. These [false deities] would not have been content to allow their creatures to be in need of another creature [or deity]. A king of this world would not be pleased in having one of their servants in need of another, due to the fact that it would indicate his deficiency and faultiness.

The ordered existence[52] [of creation within this universe] in the most perfect and beautiful manner—despite their different varieties—proves that they all end in one ultimate objective and intent: the One True God and Sublime Deity. There is no other god or deity besides Him.

Furthermore, if a person deeply reflects on the organs [of the body], their actions, benefits, and what each one of them includes of wise purposes, and their placement within him, he will know with certainty that all of this proceeds from One Creator and One Designer Who is Most Wise.

Now if we move from this to taking note of all the individual human beings in this world, one by one, you will find His wisdom manifested amongst those many individuals such that some benefit others and some assist others. There is a ploughman to aid the planter, a farmer to aid a harvester, a weaver to aid the tailor, and a tailor to [clothe] the carpenter so that he can build. One assists another by using his hands, another using his feet, another using his sight, hearing or speech, and another using his wealth.

Since a person is not capable of carrying out all of his interests or needs, and cannot have all of the characteristics of his kind, many individuals end up carrying out what is advantageous for others.

One cannot accumulate all of the virtuous types of knowledge, fulfil all actions and be completely powerful, so these were distributed amongst all of the human species.

God (Glory be to Him) has dispersed perfect [characteristics] amongst the individuals of humanity and made each inclined and disposed to some. He is magnanimous by essence, and they are [bestowed] in accordance with His will and wisdom. His magnanimity and goodness has inundated the entire world over the ages, and His grace is much greater. He will grace the inhabitants of Paradise much more, and will even originate other creatures to live in what remains unoccupied [by the believers].

Since His magnanimity and grace are vaster than the needs of the creation, it is inevitable that much of what is existent remains unused. For instance, consider the light of the sun: the well-being of animals cannot occur without it, yet it shines in many places in excess of where humans and animals are in need of it. It is likewise for the rain, plants and the rest of His blessings. Nevertheless, the presence of even these [excesses] is not devoid of wisdoms, benefits, lessons and proofs.

Consider the rising of the sun and its setting. There are many wisdoms and advantages in that. The wisdom in the rising [of the sun] is obvious, but deeply reflect on the wisdom in its setting. Had it not been for that then people would never have peace, rest or relaxation. Bodies are no match for continual labour—this would quickly lead to their demise. Moreover everything on this earth, whether plant or animal, would have been burned due to the sun's continual shining. Therefore, light and darkness, even though they are opposites, assist each other to clearly result in the well-being of this world, its establishment and its order.

Also consider the wisdom in the movement of the sun. Had it been still in one place, many benefits for this world would have lapsed, and its rays would not have reached many regions, since the mountains and walls would have shaded them. God's dazzling wisdom dictated that it rise in the morning from the east and pass over one region after another until it ends up setting in the west. Therefore, all regions share in benefitting from it. Likewise, consider

His dazzling wisdom in limiting the length of night and day: had the length of one of them increased greatly, the interests, well-being and order would have become null and corrupted.

Furthermore, consider His wisdom in the moon starting out as a fine [crescent] then subsequently waxing until full. Then it wanes until it returns to its first state. There are many wisdoms, advantages and benefits for creation in that. They can keep track of the months and years, months of pilgrimage, historical dates, their ages, lengths of business transactions, as well as other things. Even though this can all be documented through the sun, the use of the moon is better.

Moreover, consider His wisdom in lighting up the night using the moon and the stars. Despite the need for the night, He did not make it absolutely dark without any light such that one could not travel or work in it at all. Thus, people are able to do many things using the light of the moon. He made [the moon's] light cool in opposition to the heat of sunlight; therefore, the nature of one of them tempers the other and dissipates its harm.

Then, consider His wisdom in creating the stars as they guide [humanity] both on land and sea. One can use them to derive the times [of the year], and they are ornaments for the heavens. There are also many other [wisdoms] present therein that could not have occurred by accident (which the deniers of His wisdom claim). There are also many other wisdoms and advantages to the creation [of the stars] that people are not aware of. God has not created anything in vain.

The deniers of His wisdom claim that [the orbit and motion of the stars] is an accidental matter having no wisdom or intended purpose to them. But one of the wisdoms is that had all of them been ordered similarly then no patterns could be deduced regarding their movements within constellations. Many matters and events can be kept track of by using the movements of the sun, moon and orbiting bodies. Therefore, had they all been orbiting similarly, none would have had a station specific to it nor would there be any distinct pattern that could be deduced from it. In conclusion, had they all been of one state, then the order as dictated by His wisdom would have become null. This is all the determination of the Almighty

Lord Who is the Omniscient and Most Wise. How can one who is enlightened doubt that?

Affirming [His] wisdom does not negate causality, nor is wisdom negated by [affirming] causality. Finally, [affirming] His will does not negate either causality or His wisdom. [If you negate the latter two] then you are one of those who have only a crude share of rationality or [knowledge of] transmitted evidence.

Likewise, consider His wisdom in creating fire in such a manner that it is hidden within its carrier. Had it been apparent like air, water and the earth then it would have burned the entire world and what was within it. It is thus stored within bodies, and only kindled when needed. It remains [burning] within that matter or firewood as long as needed, but dies out once it is no longer required. It is created in a determined and measured manner so as to result in enjoyment and benefit, while also allowing security from its harm.

There is another peculiarity to fire, and that is that it is [used] specifically by humanity and not other animals. Since humanity's need for it is great, they were endowed with many tools and means to either bring it about or to extinguish it. Lamps allow people to attain many of their needs. Had it not been for them then half of our lives would have been [spent in the dark] like those in their graves. Its obvious benefits include cooking food, the preparation of medications, as well as staying warm. The Exalted pointed to these when He said, *Have ye observed the fire which ye strike out; was it ye who made the tree thereof to grow, or were We the grower? We appointed it a memorial and a comfort for the dwellers in the wilderness.*[53] It is a reminder of the [existence of] Hellfire in the Hereafter; thus, leading us to guard ourselves from it. It is there also so that the *muqwīn*, who are those dwelling in the desert or wilderness, can enjoy it. God mentioned them specifically because of their great need for fire when baking or cooking as they cannot buy [food].

Had we continued on this topic it would have taken us many volumes. Likewise, we would be incapable of completely exploring in detail the creation of humankind and what that includes of wise purposes and objectives. We will therefore return to responding to those who deny His wisdom and causality.

CHAPTER SIX

A Response to Those Who Question God's Wisdom in Creating Iblīs and his Army

[POINTS 24–36]

POINT 24: Regarding their statement, 'What is the wisdom in creating Iblīs and his army [of followers]?' [we respond] that there are many wisdoms therein. Only God knows them in detail—[but we will allude to some of them]:[1]

[I] God perfects His prophets and saints [by allowing them to attain] the [highest] levels of worship through fighting against [Iblīs], the enemy of God, and his party; by opposing [Satan] and striving against him for God's sake; by vexing him as well as his supporters; by seeking refuge with [God] and His protection from [the Devil], his evil and his snares. Therefore, many advantages—both for this world and the Hereafter—are a consequence of that; and these could not have occurred otherwise. We have already explained that something dependent upon another cannot occur without the latter.

[II] The fear that the angels and the believers feel as a result of their sins becomes stronger and more complete as a result of witnessing Iblīs' fall from [being alongside] the angels to a Satanic level. There is no doubt that the angels attained another [degree] of servitude and submission to the Exalted Lord, as well as fear of Him thereafter. This is like what is experienced when the servants of a king observe him humiliating one of them greatly; and there is no doubt that their fear and caution only increase as a result.

[III] The Sublime made Iblīs' disobedience a warning to those who disobey His command, those whose pride prevents them from obeying Him, and those who persist in sinning. God likewise made the sin of the father of humankind a moral lesson for those who perpetrate a prohibition of His or disobey a commandment of His, as Adam then repented from and regretted [his lapse], and returned back to his Lord. Therefore, He tested both the fathers of jinn and humankind with sins. He made one of the fathers [i.e. Iblīs] a warning to those who stubbornly persist in their sins, while He made the other father [i.e. Adam] a moral lesson for those who seek repentance and return back to their Lord. By God, how many dazzling wisdoms and manifest signs are encompassed within this!

[IV] Satan is a touchstone by which God tests His creation so as to differentiate those who are wicked from those who are good. The Sublime created the human species from the earth, which contains the smooth and rough, the good and the filthy. Therefore, it is inevitable that their original composition becomes manifest amongst them. In the *ḥadīth* narrated by Tirmidhī, which is traceable [to the Prophet], [we read], 'Indeed God created Adam from a handful that He took from the entire earth. So the children of Adam come in accordance with that: some of them good and some bad, some smooth and some rough...'[2] Now whatever was present in the original component became concealed within the created being.

Divine wisdom dictated the bringing out and manifestion [of the aforementioned]. It is necessary, as a consequence, that there exist a cause for manifesting and differentiating the wicked from the good—Iblīs is that touchstone. It is just like [the opposite case whereby] God made His prophets and messengers touchstones for the differentiation [of good from the wicked]. The Exalted said, *It is not (the purpose) of God to leave you in your present state till He shall separate the wicked from the good.*[3]

God sent His messengers to those who are obligated. As a result, the good became manifested as such and the wicked became manifested as such. His far-reaching wisdom dictated that they be intermingled in this abode of tribulation; however, once they reach the abode of permanence they will be separated—each to their respective residence [either Paradise or Hellfire]. That is due to His far-reaching wisdom and omnipotence.

[V] God manifests the perfection of His abilities in creating those like Gabriel and the other angels versus Iblīs and the devils. This is one of the greatest signs of His power, will and might. He is the Creator of all opposites in the heavens and the earth: the light and darkness, Paradise and Hellfire, water and fire, air and iron,[4] good and evil, cold and heat, the righteous and the wicked.

[vi] God created opposites whereby the goodness of one becomes more apparent due to the other's [evilness]. If it was not for the ugliness of one, the beauty of the other would not be recognized completely. Had it not been for poverty, the value of wealth would not be appreciated fully. This was explained in detail previously.

[vii] God (Glory be to Him) loves to be truly thanked in every way. There is no doubt that His saints exhibit—due to the presence of the enemies of God, Iblīs and his army of followers, as well as being tested through Iblīs—a greater number of ways of showing gratitude to Him, which would not have occurred otherwise. There was such a vast difference between the gratitude of Adam (peace be upon him) before his descent from the Garden and after he was tested through his enemy, for thereafter his Lord chose, forgave and accepted him.

[viii] Love of Him, returning to Him, depending on Him, patience [for His sake] and contentment [with His determination and decree] are the most beloved [types] of worship of God (Glory be to Him) in His sight. These types of servitude are not realized except through striving and waging battle, sacrificing oneself for God's sake, and preferring His love over everything else. Waging battle [in His path] is the apex of worship, and the most beloved to the Lord. Therefore, the creation of Iblīs and his army has [indirectly] led to the establishment of [waging battle and striving in His path] and their consequences. Only God can recount the wisdoms, benefits and advantages of all that.

[ix] The creation of those who oppose His messengers, deny them and show hostility towards them leads to the complete manifestation of His signs, wondrous powers and subtle works. The existence of those [signs] is more beloved to Him and more beneficial to His saints than their absence. Some of these signs were mentioned previously, like the flood [drowning Noah's people], the staff and hand

[of Moses], the parting of the [Red] Sea, and [the salvation of] His friend [Abraham] after being thrown in the fire. These, in addition to many of His other signs, are proofs of His omnipotence, omniscience and wisdom. The existence of causes leading [indirectly] to those [signs] is necessary, as was previously explained.

[x] Fire contains [the properties of] burning, rising above and destroying, but also shining, illuminating with warmth and lighting. God (Glory be to Him) brought out both of these [groups of properties]. Likewise, the earth contains the good and the filthy, the smooth and the rough, and the red, black and white. These were all brought forth by virtue of [His] dazzling wisdom and omnipotent power. These are signs that prove that *Naught is as His likeness; and He is the All-Hearing, the All-Seeing.*[5]

[xi] God's Names include the One Who lowers, the One Who elevates, the One Who honours, the One Who abases, the Ruler, the Most Just, and the One Who takes retribution (*al-Muntaqim*). These Names require attachments so as to manifest their consequences. They are like [His] other traits of beneficence (*iḥsān*), bestowing sustenance and mercy. So, it is necessary that those respective attachments be present.

[xii] God (Glory be to Him) is the King and His sovereignty is perfect. This includes His universal administration as well as His various types of reward and punishment, honouring and disgracing, grace and justice, granting of glory and humiliation. Just as He has created those who are attached to the former type, it is inevitable that there exist those who are connected to the latter.

[xiii] One of God's Names is the Most Wise, and wisdom is one of His Attributes (Glory be to Him). His wisdom necessitates putting everything in its appropriate place. Furthermore, His wisdom dictated creating opposites and selecting rulings, characteristics and criteria which are fitting to each [opposite]. Can wisdom be achieved in any other manner? This all manifests His perfect wisdom and omnipotence.

[xiv] God's praiseworthiness (Glory be to Him) is perfect and absolute in every aspect. He is praiseworthy for His justice, His barring, His abasing, His retribution, and His disgracing [of those

deserving such] just as He is praiseworthy for His grace, bestowal, raising and honouring. Perfect and absolute praise is due to God for both groupings [of His actions]; and God praises Himself for all of that. His angels, messengers and saints praise Him, as well as all of those standing [on the Day of Judgment]. If something is a necessary concomitant of His perfect and absolute praiseworthiness, then He has complete wisdom in creating and bringing it into existence, and He is absolutely praiseworthy for it. It is not permissible to strip away His praiseworthiness, just as it is not permissible to deny His wisdom.

[xv] The Sublime loves to manifest His forbearance, patience, perseverance, vast mercy and generosity to His servants. That dictated the creation of those who would worship others, oppose His rulings, issue legal rulings which contradict His [Divine Law], pursue what He dislikes, and anthropomorphize Him. Yet despite all that He bestows upon them good things, sustains them, grants them good health, enables them to enjoy a plethora of blessings, answers their supplications, removes harm from them, and deals with them in a manner consistent with His beneficence and benevolence. This represents the opposite of the manner that they treat Him, as they disbelieve in Him, associate other partners with Him, and curse Him. By God, how many wisdoms are present in that and [how much] praise [does God deserve for that]!

The Prophet (may God bless him and grant him peace) said, 'No one is more patient than God in bearing offensive things that are heard. They ascribe a son to Him, yet He still grants them provisions and good health.'[6] The Prophet (may God bless him and grant him peace) relates that his Lord says, 'The son of Adam curses Me, and he should not do so; he tells a lie against Me, and he should not do so. As for his cursing Me, it is that he says that I have a son, even though I am the eternally besought of all, Who begetteth not, nor was begotten, and there is none comparable unto Me.[7] As for his telling a lie against Me, it is his statement that I shall not resurrect him just as I have originated him beforehand. It is just as easy for Me to resurrect him as it is to originate him.'[8]

Despite the blasphemies and lies [of the disbelievers], God (Glory be to Him) grants them provisions and good health, and protects them [from harm]. [God] continues to invite them to His Paradise, and He will accept their repentance if they do so and replace their evil sins [in that case] with good deeds. He treats them with kindness, prepares them to receive His messengers, and commands [His messengers] to speak softly and be gentle with them.

Fuḍayl b. ʿIyāḍ states, 'There is no night except that the Most Glorious (*al-Jalīl*) calls out, "Who is more magnanimous than I. Although the creation is disobedient to Me, I continue to preserve them in their beds as if they have not done so. I take charge of protecting them as if they have not sinned. My grace is great, [even] upon the disobedient ones and sinners. Who has supplicated Me, yet I have not granted? Who has asked Me, yet I have not bestowed? I am the Magnanimous, and magnanimity is from Me. I am the Most Generous, and generosity is from Me. Part of My generosity is that I bestow upon the servant that which he asks from Me and that which he does not ask of Me; and [another] part of My generosity is that I treat the one who seeks repentance as if he never disobeyed Me. Why have the creation fled [from Me]? Before which gate besides Mine do the sinners stoop?'[9]

In a divine tradition [it is narrated], 'The relationship between Myself, humankind and jinn deserves a great announcement. I have created them, yet others are worshipped. I have granted them provisions, yet others are thanked.'[10] Another [divine] tradition [states], 'O children of Adam, you have not treated Me fairly. My good is bestowed upon you, yet you continue to worship others alongside Me. How many [blessings do I bestow upon you] so that you may love Me (even though I am Self-Sufficient), and how many sins, which I dislike, do you perpetrate (even though you are in need of Me)? The noble angel continues to ascend to Me with your repugnant deeds.'[11]

In the authentic *ḥadīth* [we read], 'If you did not commit sins, God would dispense with you and create people who would commit sins. They would ask [God] for forgiveness and He would forgive them.'[12] Due to the Sublime's perfect love of His Names and Attributes, His praiseworthiness and wisdom dictated that He originates creatures to manifest the rulings and effects of them. Due to His love of pardoning, He created those whom it would be appropriate to pardon. Due to His love for forgiveness, He created those whom He would forgive, forbear, be patient with and not rush. He loves to grant them security in order for them to take their time. His love of His justice and wisdom is such that He created those upon whom He would manifest them. Due to His love of magnanimity, beneficence and benevolence, God created those who would deal with Him in an unjust and disobedient manner; whereupon He (Glory be to Him) would treat them with forgiveness and beneficence.

Had it not been for the creation of those who did various types of sins and offenses then these wisdoms, advantages and many multiples of them would have lapsed. Most blessed is God, the Lord of the Worlds and the Most Wise, for His blessings are vast. His wisdom is far-reaching—it has extended to all that His power reaches. Just as His power is omnipotent, His wisdom is dazzling in everything that occurs. We have only mentioned what represents a drop in an ocean since the minds of humankind are incapable, too weak and limited in being able to comprehend the complete [reality] of His wisdom in even one thing that He has created.

[xvi] Consider how many beloved things to the Most Blessed and Exalted have occurred as a result [of the existence] of this hated and despised creature [Iblīs]. Although Iblīs' actions are hated by God, they have [indirectly] led to what is beloved to Him. One who is most wise and whose wisdom is dazzling allows the occurrence of something disliked, hated and despised if it leads to the attainment of a greater and more beloved good. The existence of something without its necessary concomitant is impossible. Although many evils and sins have occurred due to the existence of Iblīs, the enemy of God, many pious deeds have also resulted [indirectly]. These [pious deeds] include waging battle in His path, denying oneself of one's desires and temptations, and enduring hardships and adversities in order to attain His love and contentment—these are all more beloved and pleasing to God [than their absence]. The most beloved thing for someone is to see another who loves him enduring harm for his sake. That suffering repre-

sents the confirmation of the other's love for him. [A poet said],

> For your sake I have rendered my cheek to be a ground on which
> Those who curse and are jealous [can step] until you are content

A divine tradition says, '[One of] My goals is [to see] those who suffer for My sake endure.'[13] By God, how beloved is it to Him to see those who love Him endure the harm of His enemies for His pleasure! It will be very beneficial for them in the end and they are praiseworthy for it. They will attain much honour from the Beloved. But those who deny that will be prohibited from smelling the scent [of Paradise], entering its gate or tasting its drinks.

[A poet said],

> Tell those who are blind that others can [in fact] see the sun
> Setting and rising
> Tolerate those whom you do not feel love for
> It is not possible for everyone to be chosen.

Although this creature [Iblīs] has angered his Lord; God's prophets, messengers and saints have pleased Him. The pleasure from the latter is greater than that former anger. Although His displeasure with sins and offenses is great, God (Glory be to Him) is happier with the repentance of His servant than one who has lost his ride, upon which is his food and drink, in a perilous desert but later finds it. Even if He is angered by what His enemy [Iblīs] does to His prophets and messengers, God is joyful and pleased with what His prophets have done in shaming, opposing, striving against, quelling and vexing him. His pleasure with these [actions] is so great that it will not allow the lapsing of the former hated things, since the latter beloved things would have also failed to occur as a result. Even though God was displeased with Adam eating from the tree, He was pleased with his repentance, return back to Him, submission, brokenness and humility in front of Him. Even if God was angered by the expulsion of His Messenger [from Mecca] by His enemies, He was more pleased with Muḥammad's return to it [victorious].

Even though God is displeased with [His enemies] when they kill His saints and beloved [believers], tear apart their bodies and spill their blood, He is more pleased with the fact that the believers have attained the most beautiful, blessed and pleasurable life in [Paradise in] proximity to Him. Even though He is displeased with the sins of His servants, He is more pleased with His angels, prophets, messengers and saints witnessing the vastness of His forgiveness, pardon, beneficence, generosity and magnanimity, in addition to extolling and praising Him for all that. Their praise and exaltation of His Attributes is more beloved and pleasing to Him than had those sins lapsed, as that would have led to the failure of those beloved things occurring.

Know that praise of Him is the fundamental principle behind His creation and commandments. The Lord (Exalted is He) deserves all praise, in all of its facets, respects and ways. He did not create nor judge anything except that He is praiseworthy for it. Praise of Him extends to everything that He has created and commanded, in a real and essential manner. It includes loving and being content with Him, extolling Him, and affirming His far-reaching wisdom in everything that He has created and commanded.

Denying His wisdom is no different than stripping away praise of Him, as has been discussed previously. Just as God is praiseworthy, He is Most Wise [in all affairs]. His praiseworthiness and wisdom are necessary concomitants of His Essence just as are His knowledge, power and eternal life. It is not permissible to strip away any of His Attributes or Names from their requisites or effects, as that would result in [attributing to Him] deficiencies, which would then negate His perfection, majesty and greatness.

POINT 25: Just as God's perfect Attributes and praiseworthy actions, which we should extol, entail that He grants magnanimously, bestows and confers favours, they also entail that He grants refuge, gives victory and aid. He loves to grant refuge to those seeking it and He loves to grant sanctuary to those asking for it. A king's [power] becomes absolute only when he can grant refuge and sanctuary to those asking for it. This was mentioned by Aḥmad b. Ḥusayn al-Kindī:[14]

> O he whom I seek refuge with when I am hoping for something
> And whom I seek shelter [to protect me from] those I am wary of
> People cannot set bones that you have broken
> Nor can they shatter a bone which you have set.

Had al-Mutanabbī said the above in reference to his Lord and Originator, he would have been more blissful than had he [intended] a person who is created just like him.

The point is that the King of all kings loves to grant refuge to His subjects and to have them ask Him for sanctuary. He commanded His Messenger in many places in His Book to ask Him for sanctuary from the damned Satan. In this fashion, the perfect blessing that He bestows upon His servant by granting him sanctuary and shelter from his enemy becomes clearer. God (Exalted is He) loves to complete His blessings upon His believing servants by granting them victory over their enemy, protecting them and making them triumphant. How great is this blessing [of God] as it makes their joy and bliss become complete! It is also represents His justice that He imposes against His enemies and opponents.

[A poet said],

> There is nothing but that He has wise purposes in it
> But those who search are limited [in their capacity] to comprehend them.

POINT 26: Regarding the [deniers'] statement, 'What is the wisdom, which is imperceptible to us, in allowing Iblīs to remain alive to the [Day of Judgment], whereas the messengers die?' we respond there are many wisdoms that God has in that but [human] estimation is of too narrow a scope [to perceive it]. One of them is that since God (Glory be to Him) made the Devil a touchstone and test to differentiate those who are wicked from the good and His enemies from His saints, His wisdom dictated that He allow Satan to remain alive so as to fulfil that purpose. Had Iblīs died that purpose would have ceased.

Likewise, God's wisdom dictated that His disbelieving enemies remain on this earth until the Day of Judgment. Had He destroyed them all absolutely, then many wisdoms in keeping them alive would have not occurred. Just as His wisdom dictated the testing of the father of humanity [Adam], it dictated the tribulation of His offspring after him through Satan. Bliss is only attained by those who oppose and show enmity to Satan, while those who follow and support Iblīs will be aligned with him [in Hellfire].

Next, since God had already judged and dictated through His wisdom that Iblīs would have no share in the Hereafter [except Hellfire], and since he had previously been obedient and worshipped [Him], He recompensed Iblīs by allowing him to remain alive in this world until the Day of Judgment. The Sublime never fails to take into consideration any good deed done by someone. God rewards the believers for their pious deeds both in this life and the Hereafter. As for the disbeliever, He recompenses them for any good they have done only in this world. Therefore, once the latter reach the Hereafter they have nothing left. This has been indicated in the authentic *ḥadīth*s of the Prophet (may God bless him and grant him peace).

Next, allowing Satan to remain alive is not a form of honouring him—it would have been better for him had he died, for his sins would have been lesser in that case and so would his punishment. But Iblīs remained obstinate and stubborn after his initial sin, detracted from God's wisdom and was antagonistic towards the One Whose wisdom he should have submitted to, and then promised to work to bar humanity from worshipping God alone; due to all that obstinacy the punishment for Satan's sins was magnified. So God's keeping Satan alive in this world and granting him respite is so that the Devil will continue to increase in sinfulness—that will result in a greater punishment for him than anyone else. Satan's punishment is foremost amongst the evildoers, just as he was their leader in [promoting] evil and disbelief.

Since Satan is the root of all evil and it arises from him, he is recompensed in Hellfire accordingly. Every punishment that falls on the denizens of Hellfire starts with him and then spreads to his followers. This all represents [God's] justice and far-reaching wisdom.

Next, Satan said while antagonizing his Lord, *Seest Thou this (creature) whom Thou hast honoured above me, if Thou give me grace until the Day of Judgment I verily will seize his seed, save but a few.*[15] God (Glory be to Him) knew that many of Adam's offspring would not be appropriate for proximity to Him in His abode. They are not appropriate for anything, just like thorns and dung are not.

It is as if His predestination (*lisān al-qadar*) had dictated, '[Iblīs], these are your companions and supporters, so await their arrival. So every time one of them passes by you, pay attention to him. Had they been righteous, I would not have allowed you to overcome them. I support only those who are righteous and are worthy of [being proximate] to Me. [Satan], you are the leader of the criminals, who have forgone My support and have not sought My pleasure.' The Exalted said, *[Iblīs] hath no power over those who believe and put trust in their Lord. His power is only over those who make a friend of him, and those who ascribe partners unto Him (God).*[16]

As for death overtaking the prophets and messengers it is not due to their insignificance in His sight, but rather so that they may reach [Paradise] wherein God will honour them. They will also take rest from the hard and tiring work of this world, and from enduring the suffering [perpetrated against them] by His enemies. It is also so that other messengers will come and live after them. Thus, their death is more advantageous for them and their nations.

Again, as for the prophets, it is so that they can reach the Most High Friend (*al-Rafīq al-aʿlā*), whereby they will [be honoured] with the most perfect pleasures and joys. As for their nations, it is so that it may be known that they did not just obey [the prophets] during their lives, but that they also obeyed them after their deaths. Also, [it is so that it may be known] that the [prophets'] followers did not worship them, but instead worshipped God in accordance with their commands and prohibitions. God is the Ever-Living One (*al-Ḥayy*) Who never dies.

Therefore, many wisdoms and advantages occur with the death of the messengers both for them and their nations. In addition, they are human beings and God did not create humans with a nature which would be able to remain alive forever in this world. Instead, He made them succeed one another on this earth. Had He allowed them to remain living, then the advantages and wisdoms in making them successors would have failed to occur. Furthermore, the earth would have become too confined for all [of humanity].

Finally, death leads to the perfection of every believer. Had it not been for death, people would not have found this life to be agreeable or delightful. Therefore, the wisdom in allowing death is similar to the wise purpose in allowing life.

POINT 27: Regarding the statement [of the deniers], 'What wisdom or advantage is there in making Adam exit Paradise to the abode of tribulation and testing?' we respond by saying: God (Glory be to Him) has many wise purposes in that. There are also many blessings and advantages that human minds are incapable of knowing in detail, even if they were to exhaust themselves in trying to find them out.[17]

Although it would have been possible for them to attain everlasting bliss in [Paradise without being sent down to this earth], the attainment of it after tribulation, testing, enduring death and what follows all that (including the frights of the [Day of] Resurrection and traversing the pathway [over Hellfire]) represents a [greater] degree of bliss—the value of which cannot be grasped. This bliss is more perfect than that of those who will be created in Paradise, whether the youths or fair wives. In fact, there is no comparison whatsoever between the two groups.

One of the wisdoms is that the Sublime wished to establish amongst the offspring of Adam: messengers, prophets and martyrs whom He loves and who love Him; to reveal unto them His Books; and to entrust them with His covenant. In addition, God wanted to make them worship Him in both times of ease and hardship; and to make them prefer what He loves and is pleased with over their own temptations and desires. God's wisdom dictated that He descend them down to an abode where He would test them so that they may perfect the levels of servitude to Him—through tribulations—and worship Him [despite having to endure] what their souls dislike. This represents pure servitude [to Him]. Otherwise, those who only worship God [in ways that] they love or desire are in reality only worshipping themselves. God (Glory be to Him) loves that His saints loyally support [the believers] for His sake, take [the disbelievers as] enemies for His sake, and sacrifice themselves to attain His pleasure and what He loves. None of this can be attained in an abode of absolute bliss.

In addition, they were descended down to such an abode in order to achieve a complete faith. Faith includes speech, deeds, striving, patience and enduring [suffering]. These can only be achieved in an abode of tribulation, not in the blissful Paradise.

Many of the scholars, like Abū al-Wafā' b. ʿAqīl,[18] have mentioned that the deeds of the messengers, prophets and believers in this world are superior to the bliss of Paradise. They said that is because the bliss of Paradise represents their good fortune and enjoyment. There is no comparison of [enjoyment with] faith, [good] deeds, prayer, reciting the Qur'ān, waging battle in the path of God, sacrificing themselves for His pleasure, and preferring Him over their desires and temptations. Faith is connected to God (Glory be to Him) and it is His right upon them, whereas the bliss of Paradise is attached to them as their good fortune. They were created to worship [Him], whereas Paradise is an abode of bliss, not an abode of obligations and worship.

Now, God had predestined before He had created Adam that he would descend from the Garden [in Paradise] and be settled on this [earth]. This predestination occurred through causes [in order to attain certain] wise purposes. One of its causes was [God's] prohibition of that tree, as well as His leaving Adam and his enemy alone until Iblīs whispered to him to eat from it, and also leaving Adam alone to himself until he fell into sin. Yet praiseworthy and intended outcomes predicated on Adam's descent from Paradise did follow from these causes. Further causes were then arranged to lead to outcomes that accounted for other wise purposes. One of these outcomes is that Adam and the believers will return [to Paradise] in the most perfect state.

God's predestination, as well as those causes and end outcomes, indeed proceed from [His] absolute and far-reaching wisdom, which those in the heavens and earth praise Him for both [in this world] and in the Hereafter. The Most Wise did not determine all that based on falsehood, nor did He arrange that aimlessly, nor did He leave His far-reaching wisdom and perfect praiseworthiness out of that.

In addition, the angels were unaware of God's [plan] to bring about from Adam's offspring those who would become His saints, beloved ones (*aḥbāb*), messengers and prophets, as well as those who would become proximate to Him through various types of worship and [those who would] sacrifice themselves to attain His love and pleasure. No adversity, tribulation, poverty or disease distracts them away from remembering, thanking and worshipping Him. They worship Him despite the opposition posed [to it] by their temptations (*shahwa*), overwhelming desires (*hawā*) and natural dispositions (*ṭibāʿ*), in addition to the opposition posed by other people. [It is as if God said to the angels], 'Your worship of Me is not [susceptible] to any opposing factors or barriers, yet [humankind's] worship of Me is characterized by [overcoming] these opposing factors, barriers and distractions.'

Moreover, the Sublime willed to manifest to the angels what was hidden from them regarding Iblīs—whom they previously thought well and highly of, not knowing that he harboured pride, jealousy and evil in his soul. Similarly, the goodness and evilness latent in the souls [of people] are also concealed. Therefore, they must inevitably be brought out and exposed so that the wisdom of the Most Wise is evident when He recompenses each one appropriately.

Moreover, the Sublime originated His creation in stages and in various types. It preceded according to His judgment and wisdom that He would favour Adam and his offspring over much of what He has created by making their worship of Him more perfect than that of other [creatures]. Their worshipping [God] manifests their best state and represents the highest level [they can attain], since they worship Him by following [His commandments] by their free choice, not out of compulsion or some necessity.

God's absolute sovereignty and perfect praiseworthiness dictated that He bring them into an abode wherein what He (Glory be to Him) loves may occur, even if many of those [beloved] things [necessitate] pathways and causes that He dislikes. What is dependent upon something else cannot occur without it. Bringing into existence the necessary concomitants of wisdom is wise in itself, just like originating the necessary concomitants of justice represents justice in itself. We will acquaint ourselves with this further, God willing, in the section on the suffering that children undergo.

POINT 28: God (Glory be to Him) originated His creation from non-existence into existence so that He may put into effect the rulings of His Names and Attributes [in a manner] that would manifest His perfect holiness. Now God is eternally perfect and His perfection dictated that He manifest the effects of His perfection in regards to His creation and commandments, decree and determination, promise and warning, depriving and bestowing, honouring and humiliating, justice and grace, pardoning and retribution, the vastness of His forbearance and the might of His power.

God's perfect holiness (Glory be to Him) dictates that He disposes matters every day. Some of these matters are that He forgives sins, relieves calamities, cures those who are ill, liberates those who are suffering, gives aid to those who are oppressed, delivers those who are distressed, enriches those who are poor, answers supplications, cancels out offenses, strengthens one who is weak, humiliates one who is arrogant, breaks a tyrant, grants death and life, grants laughter and sorrow, lowers and elevates, sends His messengers (both angels and humans) to carry out His commandments, and administers His determined measure at the appropriate time. None of this could have occurred in the abode of permanence. Instead, His far-reaching wisdom dictated that it occur in an abode of testing and tribulation.

POINT 29: The absolute perfection of His sovereignty dictated His complete administration of various things. It is for this reason that God (Glory be to Him) created three abodes: one that is purely dedicated to bliss, pleasure, delight and joy; one that is purely dedicated to pain, suffering, calamities and evils; and one that is mixed having both good and evil, bliss and wretchedness, pleasure and pain. People will intermingle in this world and make requests of each other; and He populated the first two abodes [i.e. Paradise and Hellfire] predicated on this [worldly] abode. He brought about His rulings upon His creation in these three abodes in accordance with His lordship, divinity, knowledge, glory, wisdom, justice and mercy. Had He settled them all in the abode of permanence from the time they were created then the rulings and effects from [His previously-mentioned] Attributes would not have occurred.

POINT 30: The Day of the Great Return is the day when His Beautiful Names, exalted Attributes, great sovereignty, and their rulings will become [completely] manifested. For this reason, the Sublime says, *Whose is the sovereignty this day? It is God's, the One (al-Wāḥid), the Invincible (al-Qahhār)*;[19] *The sovereignty on that day will be the true (sovereignty) belonging to the Beneficent*;[20] *A day on which no soul hath power at all for any (other) soul. The (absolute) command on that day is God's.*[21] God (Glory be to Him) will even make Himself known to His servants on that Day using Names and Attributes that they were unaware of in this [worldly] abode.

Deeply reflect on what God and His Messenger have informed us about the Day [of Judgment] and its rulings, as well as the manifestation of the Exalted's almightiness, His greatness, justice, grace, mercy and the effects of His Holy Attributes. Had humankind only been created in the abode of permanence [this manifestation] would not have occurred—His perfection (Glory be to Him) rejects that. This is an independent proof for those who recognize God's Names and Attributes (Exalted is He), that the Return will occur and that the messengers have been truthful in what they have us informed us from God. Thus, the rational and transmitted proofs conform with each other.

POINT 31: God (Glory be to Him) loves to be worshipped in all manners. This is only fitting for His greatness and majesty, and it is only appropriate for Him alone. It is well known that the various types of worship that occur in this abode of tribulation and testing do not exist in the abode of recompense. Even if there is some recompense in this abode, it only occurs perfectly and completely in the Hereafter. On the other hand, the [Hereafter] is not the abode of actions, but rather that of recompense and reward. His perfect holiness made it necessary to recompense those who perpetrated evil accordingly and [reward] those who acted righteously in the best [manner].

POINT 32: God (Glory be to Him) has made some of His servants as a test for others. The Exalted said, *And even so do We try some of them by others*;[22] *And We have appointed some of you as a test for others.*[23] The Sublime has made some of His saints as a test for His enemies; some of His enemies as a test for His saints; the kings as a test for their subjects and vice versa; men as a test for women and vice versa; and affluent ones as a test for those who are poor and vice versa. He tested each group with its opposite. Our parents had not even settled on this earth before their opposite [i.e. Iblīs] faced off with them. This matter will continue amongst Adam's offspring until God folds up this world and those within it.

God (Glory be to Him) has many far-reaching wisdoms and vast blessings in tribulations and tests like these. There are also many valid rulings, commandments and prohibitions, and dispositions that illustrate His lordship, divinity, sovereignty and praiseworthiness. Likewise, testing His servants with [ease or hardship] in this abode is due to His perfect wisdom, and is a requisite of His absolute praiseworthiness.

POINT 33: Had it not been for these tribulations and tests, then the virtues of patience, contentment with and reliance on God, waging battle [in His path], chastity, courage, forbearance, pardoning and forgiveness would not have occurred. God (Glory be to Him) loves to honour His saints by granting them these perfections and allowing them to manifest these [characteristics]. As a result, God and His angels will commend them for possessing these characteristics, and they will attain the ultimate distinction, pleasure and joy. Even if [their lives] started out bitter, there is no sweeter end.

God (Glory be to Him) has executed His wisdom such that the end outcome follows according to the strength and perfection of its causes. If the causes are weak, the end outcome will be deficient. Whoever has perfectly fulfilled the causes [that will lead] to bliss and pleasure will have completely achieved that outcome. Those who refuse to do so will be deprived of it, and those who are inadequate will [only attain] an end outcome which is deficient concordantly. In this manner, recompense is just—whether reward or punishment. The manner of this world's [existence as it is] sufficiently attests to that. The Lord of this World and the Hereafter is One. There is uniformity to His wisdom in both: *His is all praise in the former and the latter (state), and His is the command, and unto Him ye will be brought back.*[24] This is clarified by the thirty-fourth point.

POINT 34: The most superior and glorious type of [God's] bestowal [upon His servants] is faith and its recompense—without exception. Indeed, it is not actualized except through testing and trials. The Exalted said, *Do men imagine that they will be left (at ease) because they say, We believe, and will not be tested with affliction? We tested those who were before you. Thus, God knoweth those who are sincere, and knoweth those who feign. Or do those who do ill-deeds imagine that they can outstrip Us? Evil (for them) is that which they decide. Whoso looketh forward to the meeting with God (let him know that) God's reckoning is surely nigh, and He is the All-Hearing, the Omniscient. And whosoever striveth, striveth only for himself, for God is altogether independent of (His) creatures.*[25]

God (Glory be to Him) thus informed us in Sūrat al-ʿAnkabūt how it is inevitable that He test and put to trial His creation, so that a clear differentiation may occur between those who have true [faith] from those who try to deceive; the believers from the disbelievers; and those who thank and worship God from those who deny, stubbornly reject Him and worship others besides Him.

God mentioned the state of those tested in this immediate [world] as well as the Hereafter, and that those who are most tested in this world are the messengers and their followers. He also described their end outcome and what they will attain. Then He mentioned the tribulations of the enemies and deniers [of the messengers] and their end. God began [this *sūra*] by criticizing those who imagine that they will not have to undergo testing and trials in this abode after claiming that they possess faith. His wisdom (Glory be to Him) and His will in creating [humanity] both reject that.

God informed us the secret reason for these trials and tests: it is to differentiate clearly those who have true [faith] from those who try to deceive, and those who are believers from the disbelievers. Even though God (Glory be to Him) knows all that occurs before it happens, His justice and praiseworthiness dictated that He does not recompense the servants in light of His knowledge regarding them, but only after His knowledge is manifested in existence and actualized. Trials are what manifest [people's true natures] into existence. In this manner, His recompense becomes most justified.

Then the Sublime rejected those who failed to be faithful to Him or follow His messengers, due to their fear of the trials and testing which the messengers and their followers [inevitably] undergo.

The [disbelievers] imagine and suppose that by shunning away faith and denying His Messenger that they will avoid trials and tests. In reality, He possesses in His power [the ability to put them through] greater and more difficult trials, tests and punishments than what they escaped from.

A person who is charged with obligations has only two choices after the messengers are sent to him: either one says, 'I believe', or he refuses and continues to do evil. Those who say that they have believed are tested by the Exalted Lord and undergo tribulation so that their faith can be manifested and established. It also proves that their faith is not limited to times of well-being and ease; but is, instead, a firm faith, which endures in both times of comfort and in times of affliction.

Those who do not believe should not suppose that they are beyond the capability or reach of their Lord (Exalted is He). Rather, they are within His grasp and their forelocks are within His Hand; and God can afflict them with much greater tribulations than what is experienced by those who have said that they believe.

It is inevitable that those who have believed in Him and His messengers will be afflicted by His enemies and the enemies of His messengers in a painful and difficult manner. But it is also inevitable that those who did not believe in Him and His messengers shall be punished by Him. Thus, the latter [i.e. disbelievers] will incur much more pain and hardship than the believers. It is inevitable that every believing and disbelieving soul will endure some pain, but the believers will only encounter pain in this world, which will be limited and followed by the greatest [types of] pleasure. On the other hand, the disbelievers will attain some pleasure and enjoyment [in this world] but that will end and be followed by the greatest pains and hardships.

The condition of those who follow their temptations is similar: they derive pleasure initially but it is followed by pain that is commensurate with their experiencing of [that initial temptation]. On the other hand, those who patiently avoided [temptations] will initially endure pain due to its loss, but this pain will be followed by pleasure and enjoyment commensurate with what they abandoned with fortitude.

Pain and pleasure are necessary elements of being a human. There is a major difference though between the immediate, insignificant and transient abode versus the everlasting and great Hereafter. It is for this reason that one of the special characteristics of the mind is that it can reflect on end outcomes and objectives. Those who imagine that they can completely avoid pain are deluded.

Human beings have been created susceptible to pleasure and pain, joy and grief, happiness and sorrow. This is due to two reasons: [first], due to their intrinsic build, natural disposition and form. They are created from a variety of opposing mixtures, and it is impossible or at least very difficult for them to be completely balanced. That imbalance will inevitably lead to pain. [Second], humans are social by nature, and are unable to live in isolation. They all have wants and needs that are opposing and conflicting, and they cannot be reconciled. If one objective occurs, then others will have to be forgone. A person wishes that others would agree to his demands and desires, and others wish the same from him. If a person agrees to the [desires] of others he will experience pain and hardship in accordance with the desires which he has forgone. But if he does not agree to their desires, they will harm, torment and strive to concordantly deny him of his desires. Therefore, he will experience pain and torment either way.

One will sometimes experience pain and hardship as a result of false doctrines, corrupt desires, and actions that he knows will harm him in the end. By succumbing to them one will be recompensed with greater pain [in the Hereafter], but by avoiding them some pain will still occur [in this world]. Rational thought, religious [principles], valour and knowledge all bid a person to endure the lesser of two pains in order to free himself from the greater one, and to prefer the transient [pain] in order to be saved from the eternal perpetual [pain of Hellfire].

Whoever supports the criminal oppressors in their injustice, aids those who follow their desires in order to achieve their passions, assists heretics to produce their innovations, and helps those who are wicked and lewd [to spread] their wickedness and lewdness, so that he can avoid their harm—he will be afflicted with other pains both in this immediate life and the Hereafter, which will be many times greater than what he tried to escape. God's custom in His creation is that He will punish those who supported and aided [the oppressors, innovators and wicked people] by the latters' same hands. But if a person patiently endures such pain as will be inflicted upon him from opposing and avoiding them, then that [pain] will be followed by a pleasure both immediately [in this life] and in the Hereafter that is much greater than the pleasure [that would have occurred] had he conformed to their desires. God's custom is also that He will elevate those who remain patient and pious, those who rely on Him, and those who are sincere [to Him].

Since it is inevitable that one will encounter pain and torment, it is more fitting that it be for God's sake, for His pleasure, and in following His Messenger rather than for people's sake, their whims or desires. The Sublime informed those being tested that their afflictions will be only temporary. In this manner, He has consoled them and made it easier for them to carry their burdens. God also reassured them that there will come a time when they will finally meet Him. The Exalted said, *Whoso looketh forward to the meeting with God (let him know that) God's reckoning is surely nigh, and He is the All-Hearing, the Omniscient.*[26] If the servant considers the short and transient nature of his tribulations, as well as the appointed time in which he will then meet God (Glory be to Him), then he will find what he endures to be manageable and his burdens lighter.

Again, these [tribulations] involve striving against one's [desires], the Devil and other people. The person who is carrying out these deeds recognizes that the fruits of his deeds and toil will be his alone, so he will strive and struggle more fully. The Exalted said, *And whosoever striveth, striveth only for himself, for God is altogether independent of (His) creatures.*[27]

In addition, one should not imagine that this striving, patience or endurance accrues benefit to God (Glory be to Him), for He is Self-Sufficient from His creatures. He did not command them with His commandments due to some need of His, nor did He forbid them with His prohibitions due to miserliness. Instead, His commandments are more beneficial for them in their livelihoods and

Hereafter. [The avoidance of] His prohibitions should [be understood] in a similar manner, as [perpetrating them] leads to harm and insolence in their livelihoods and Hereafter. Therefore, the fruits of these afflictions and tests are theirs alone.

God's wisdom dictated that He set up causes that would lead to the differentiation of those who are righteous from the wicked, the pious from those who are seduced, and those who are fit [to worship] Him from those who are not suitable. The Exalted said, *It is not (the purpose) of God to leave you in your present state till He shall separate the wicked from the good.*[28] Therefore, God (Glory be to Him) submitted them to tribulations by sending the messengers to them [to convey] His commandments and prohibitions. Through His messengers the righteous become differentiated from the wicked, and the good from the bad. His [eternal] knowledge thus becomes manifested through those tribulations and tests, which then allows His just reward and punishment to occur.

Moreover, since the one being tested will deviate away without fail from the path of patience and striving due to the demands of his nature and desires, and his weakness in resisting what he has been afflicted with, the Sublime promised [the believer] that He would overlook and remit him of those [sins].[29] Since he had faith in God and obeyed Him [to a certain extent], His mercy dictated that He would remit [the believer] of his sins and recompense him with the best reward.

Then the Sublime mentioned the testing that a servant undergoes in regards to his parents, and how he is commanded to obey them. But one must not obey them if they fight against him in [the hope] that he would worship others alongside [God].[30] One should be patient in this test and trial, and should be kind and respectful. Nevertheless, one should turn away from them [in this matter] and follow the path of His messengers.

Then the Sublime mentioned the condition of those who have entered into this faith, yet have a weak resolve, lack patience and do not stand firm [in the face of] tests and tribulations.[31] Now, God's custom and wisdom dictated that His enemies will afflict His saints, and will [sometimes] overpower them and [subject them to] many types of adversities and harms. If one is harmed because of having faith in God, but is not able to be patient, becomes distressed by [adversities], and tries to escape from these [afflictions]—in a manner similar to how one should instead flee from [what would lead to] God's punishment—then all that indicates is that one lacks insight, and that one's heart does not have true faith and has not experienced its sweetness. This person considers the trials of people against him, due to his faith and obedience of God's messengers, to be like the punishment of God for polytheism or opposing His messengers. This is the state of those who worship God on the verge: their feet are not firmly rooted in faith and the worship of God. These people are seduced and they will be punished [by God], even if they manage to escape people's torment. God then mentioned this person's state when the believers are made triumphant: in that case, he returns to them and says that he was with them [all along]. God (Glory be to Him) knows that what is in his heart contradicts that [statement].

Then God (Glory be to Him) mentioned the tribulation of Noah with his people for 950 years. His people were tested [and were commanded] to obey him but they disbelieved. God, therefore, afflicted them [in this world] by drowning them in the flood, and burning them [in the grave and in the Hereafter]. Then He mentioned the tribulation of Abraham with his people, how they [did not] respond to him, and how they were tested by being commanded to obey and follow him. Then He mentioned the tribulation of Lot with his people and vice versa, and how their matter ended. Then He mentioned the tribulation of Shuᶜayb with his people and vice versa, and the state they ended up in. Then He mentioned how He tested ᶜĀd, Thamūd, Korah, Pharaoh, Hāmān and their armies [by commanding] them to have faith in Him and worship Him alone; He thereafter afflicted them with many types of punishments [due to their disobedience].[32]

Then He mentioned the tribulation of His Messenger [Muḥammad] (may God bless him and grant him peace) by the many disbelievers, including both the [Arab] polytheists and the People of the Book. God commanded the Prophet to debate with the People of the Book in the best way.[33]

Then He commanded His servants who are being afflicted by His enemies to migrate from their country to another one within His vast earth, so that they may worship Him [freely] therein. After pointing out the lesser move from one country to another, God reminded them of the greater journey from this worldly abode to that of the Hereafter, and that they will return to Him.[34]

Then God clarified that He will settle those who are patient—in the face of these tribulations for His sake—in eternal Gardens of Paradise through which rivers flow. This represents Him consoling them after they had to leave their lands and homes for His sake. Paradise is far better than this worldly abode, and it will encompass every type of good, pleasure and bliss, in addition to being eternal and everlasting. This is all due to their patience in enduring [worldly] tribulations and their reliance on their Lord.[35]

God informed them that He will guarantee their provisions in the [foreign] land just as He used to provide sustenance for them in their [native] land. They should not worry about carrying their provisions [to the foreign land] as many animals [such as birds] migrate from one place to another without doing so.[36]

Then God (Glory be to Him) mentioned the end outcome of those who did not believe in Him [as a result of] their afflictions, and that any pleasure they happen to experience [will be limited] to this [worldly] abode. They will come to realize that the eternal bliss will elude them and that their lot [in the Hereafter] will only be the painful punishment. He then indicated that the end outcome of those who believed in Him, obeyed His messengers, struggled against their [desires and fought] against His enemies in this abode of tribulation will be His guidance and bestowal of victory.[37]

Thus, God (Glory be to Him) informed us that the most superior and eminent grace in this world and the Hereafter is reserved for those who were tested with afflictions, yet remained patient and relied on Him. He also informed us that the greatest and most difficult punishment is reserved for those who were not patient in [the face of] His tribulations, but instead tried to escape from them and preferred comfort.

This *sūra* therefore comprises the secret of His creation and commandments. It clearly illustrates the state of those undergoing tribulation and testing in this world and their [recompense in the] Hereafter. Whoever deeply reflects on its beginning, middle and end realizes that [this *sūra*] revolves around being patient and relying [on Him] in the face of tribulation and testing, and that this will ultimately lead to [His] guidance and granting of victory. We depend on God.

POINT 35: God (Glory be to Him) informed us that He created the heavens and the earth and the heavenly and the lower world to test us so as to [manifest] those who are the best in deeds. He also informed us that He adorned the earth with animals, plants, metals and the like for this tribulation. He also created death and life for this tribulation. Therefore, this tribulation is the objective of His creation and commandment.

It is thus inevitable that there exist an abode wherein this tribulation occurs, i.e. this [worldly] one of obligations. His wisdom [has dictated] that Paradise is an abode of bliss, not an abode of tribulation or testing; therefore, He created an abode of tribulation before it as a bridge that one must traverse in order to reach Paradise. One [can also consider] it as a plantation wherein one sows [and will reap in the Hereafter], or a port wherein one can supply oneself with provisions.

God should be worshipped alone through His commandments that were conveyed by His messengers. He commanded and prohibited us; thus, He did not create us aimlessly. He promised to reward us; therefore, He did not abandon nor neglect us. Instead, we were created to be commanded and prohibited, rewarded and punished. His wisdom and praiseworthiness [have dictated all that] and nothing else is fitting. This is, in truth, why and what He originated the creation for.

The aforementioned allows one to know the response to the [following] questions: What is the wisdom in creating the soul desiring both good and evil? Why was it not created desiring good alone? Why did His wisdom dictate that one be able to do evil, since He is capable of preventing one from doing such? What is the wisdom in granting [the soul] power and ability, when the One Who bestows is aware that they may be used to perpetrate evil? What is the wisdom in allowing [evil] souls to carry out seduction, injustice, and oppression? [The deniers of His wisdom further claim], 'It is well known that one who does something for wise purposes does not act in such a manner nor would his wisdom permit him to neglect his servants if he is able to prevent them from corrupting, oppressing and killing one another. Either [I] he is unaware of what they are doing, or [II] he is not able to prevent them, or [III] he is not one who acts for wise purposes and wisdoms. The first two are impossible in regards to the Lord (Exalted is He); therefore, it must necessarily be the third.'

[Ibn al-Qayyim responds]: This ambiguity is based on a corrupt principle, which is drawing an analogy between the Lord and His creation, and anthropomorphizing His actions [to theirs]. It is for this reason that the Qadariyya [are considered to] anthropomorphize His actions. The later [Qadariyya] theologians went further and stripped away His Attributes while anthropomorphizing His actions.

This corrupt principle has been refuted by all sages who said that drawing an analogy between the actions of the Lord and those of His servants is invalid. Similarly, drawing analogies between His wisdom and theirs or between His Attributes and theirs [is also false]. It is well known that the Lord (Exalted is He) knows that His servants will disbelieve, and perpetrate injustice and wickedness. He is capable of not bringing them into existence, and is [capable] of creating them all as one nation in accordance with what He loves and is pleased with, or intervening to prevent those who transgress against others from doing so. But His far-reaching wisdom refuses to do that and dictated creating them in such a manner.

God (Glory be to Him) created the souls into different groups: one group desires only good, and they are the angels; another desires only evil, and they are the devils; and finally one that desires both types, and these are the souls of human beings. [Humans] are [judged] in accordance with which characteristic predominates: if good predominates they are united with the first group [i.e. the angels], while if evil predominates they are joined with the second group [i.e. the devils]. If His wisdom allowed the existence of the second group, then dictating the existence of the third is worthier and more appropriate.

The Exalted Lord's power, majesty and wisdom dictated bringing into existence opposite essences, attributes and actions, as has been discussed previously. God has [originated] His creation in many varieties, which all illustrate His perfect power and lordship. Claiming that it would have been more appropriate or perfect had He created all as one type—such that the entire world [for example] would be heavenly or all light, or that all of the animals were [instead created as] angels—indicates great ignorance and misguidance.

POINT 36: Regarding the [deniers'] statement, 'What is the wisdom in animals feeling pain since they are not obligated?' this is an issue on which people have disputed in the past as well as nowadays, and their solutions have varied. Those who deny that God can freely choose His actions [respond by] attributing [the susceptibility of animals to experience pain] to pure nature, and that it is a necessary concomitant and prerequisite of it. They deny that it could result from the [freely-chosen] actions and will of the Agent, or the power of One Who is omnipotent.

Those who deny His wisdom and causality attribute the [occurrence of animal suffering] completely to His will and administration similar to [the prior viewpoint]. They do not require that there be a necessitating cause, end objective or intended wisdom. They suspected that they could rid themselves of this question and close this door. Instead, they only closed the gateway to knowing the Lord, His perfection, as well as His perfect Names, Attributes and actions; and they stripped away His wisdom and the reality of His divinity and praiseworthiness. They were like those who jumped out of the frying pan into the fire.

Those who affirmed that wisdom and causality are valid but only in how they apply to people, and not the Creator, argued that [humans], who will be resurrected for reward and punishment, will be compensated for those pains. They will be compensated and rewarded for their patience and suffering on the Day of Judgment. Their response to [the reason] animals suffer, since they are neither rewarded nor punished [...][38]

As for those who affirmed the realities of the Lord's Names, Attributes and wisdom, and that these have led to His creation and commandments, they are the most knowledgeable in this issue. Their path is the most correct one, and it is free from contradiction and incongruity. They reconciled affirmation of His omnipotence, universal will and all-encompassing wisdom with His Names and Attributes. Thus, only they were able to make transmitted evidence, rational proofs, religious verdicts and innate dispositions concordant. They recognized that [animal suffering] is a requisite of His far-reaching wisdom.

Know that there are two relevant issues here:

Firstly, there are souls which are moved as a result of their will and free choice, and there are beings in nature which are not. Evil originates from these two movers and these two movements. The soul and nature were created in this fashion; and both move to attain their respective perfection. Good and evil originate from these two movements, just like benefit and harm result from the movements of the sun, moon, wind, water and fire. The goods that originate from these movements are either intended for themselves or as a means to result in greater goods. The evils that originate from them are not intended for themselves, but instead only as an inevitable means or a necessary concomitant [towards a greater good].

If there are some evils that come about from bringing these souls into existence, it is only relative and partial when compared to the totality of good which they indirectly result in. Furthermore, their existence is better than their non-existence. Had souls like these not been created, existence would have been deficient. Many wisdoms and great advantages, which are dependent on the creation of souls like these, would have passed.

When the angels objected to the creation of human beings, saying, *Wilt thou place therein one who will do harm therein and will shed blood*,[39] God (Glory be to Him) responded that there are many wisdoms and advantages to their creation, which they are unaware of. If the angels did not know those wisdoms and advantages, then others are less likely to be able to grasp that knowledge. The creation of human beings, therefore, is absolutely wise, merciful and advantageous. Although [humankind's] presence necessarily results in some evil, that evil is inundated by the greater good that results.

Likewise, the righteous deeds that God has commanded are preponderantly good and advantageous. Even though they may [indirectly result in] some harm, their good overwhelmingly inundates that [harm]. Similarly, the evilness and harmful effects of repugnant deeds and statements, which He has prohibited, preponderate and inundate any good in them. Again, God's custom (Glory be to Him) in His creation and commandments is to enact and command what is purely or preponderantly good. But if the goodness and evilness of something conflict, and it is impossible to reconcile between these two opposites, He prefers the causes that lead to greater goods over those [resulting in] lesser ones. Forgoing the lesser ones in that case is not evil. God also prevents the causes that lead to greater evils by using other causes. The occurrence of the lesser evil is preferable to the greater evil. This is something which is well known in general to the gnostics of God, but they vary in their knowledge of its particular details.

If this is understood, then the reasons for pains and hardships are either: beneficence and mercy; justice and wisdom; reformation and a preparation for some good that will occur later; to prevent some greater pain, which may occur as a requisite of pleasure; or are necessary concomitants of justice, grace or beneficence. In that last case, it is one of the necessary concomitants of goodness. Had [pain] become null then the greater good would have also become null.

The Divine Law and determination truly attest to the aforementioned. There is harm even in the falling of rain, as mentioned by God (Exalted is He): *If you are troubled by rain.*[40] There is also [some] harm in the heat of the sun, cold and wind which results in causing pain for many species of animals. Indeed, the greatest pleasures in this world include eating and drinking, sexual intercourse, the wearing of clothing and ruling [over others], but most—if not all—of the pains suffered by those living on this earth originate and arise from these as well.

Moreover, human perfections cannot be achieved except through pain and hardship. These include attaining knowledge, courage, asceticism, chastity, forbearance, valour, patience and righteousness. It has been said [by al-Mutanabbī],

> Had it not been for hardship then anyone could have become a master
> Being magnanimous [may] lead to poverty, and advancing [towards the enemy may] result in one's death.

If pains are [necessary] causal factors for pleasures that are greater and more permanent, then rationality dictates that they be endured. In many cases, pains may be causes for well-being—had the former not occurred, the latter would have also failed to occur.

This is the case for most of the bodily diseases. Consider fever as it contains so many benefits for the body that only God knows them all. It dissipates away what would otherwise be ruinous, and removes it [from the body]. Many medications cannot do what it does. It is such that the doctor is delighted when fevers occur in many diseases. As for the benefits for the heart and the spirit due to pain and diseases, it is a matter which is not sensed except by those who are [spiritually] alive. The benefits of diseases have been recounted and they are more than 100.

God (Glory be to Him) has veiled the greatest pleasure [i.e. Paradise] with many types of adversity. He made these [hardships] a bridge that one [must traverse] to reach [Paradise]. Likewise, He veiled the worst pain [i.e. Hellfire] with temptations and [worldly] desires. It is for this reason that all rational sages have said, 'Bliss cannot be achieved via ease, relaxation cannot be attained via rest, and those who prefer [worldly] desires have forgone the pleasures [of Paradise].' So, pain, disease and hardship can be [considered to be] some of the greatest blessings, since they are causes for bliss [in the Hereafter]. Now, whatever animals, who are not obligated, endure of them is overwhelmingly inundated by their advantages and benefits. Examples include what they endure of the summer's heat, the winter's cold, the lack of rain or snow, the pain of pregnancy or delivery, or their pursuit of sustenance. But the pleasures [of animals] are many times greater than their pains. What they attain of benefits and goods are many times greater than what they endure of evils and pains.

Most blessed is God, Who due to His perfect wisdom and omnipotence, brought forth entities from their opposites. He brought forth the living from the dead, the dead from the living, the animate from the inanimate, and the inanimate from the animate. Likewise, He brought forth pleasure from pain and pain from pleasure. The greatest pleasure [i.e. Paradise] results [from enduring] pain, while the greatest pain [i.e. Hellfire] is a consequence of following one's desires.

Now, pleasure and joy, goodness and blessing, well-being and health, as well as mercy, exist to a much greater degree and by many multiples than their opposites. The pain of animals [is much less] relative to their pleasures; the same can also be said regarding their illnesses compared to their health, their hunger and thirst relative to their being satiated and feeling quenched, and their fatigue compared to their relaxation. The Exalted said, *But with hardship goeth ease, lo! with hardship goeth ease.*[41]

One hardship will not overcome two eases.[42] [His] mercy overcomes [His] wrath, [His] pardon precedes [His] punishment, and [His] blessings come before trials. Goodness characterizes [His] Attributes and actions, while evilness is only [attributable to] things that are enacted, and not [to His] actions themselves. All of His Attributes are perfect and His actions are all good. The pain that animals endure does not eliminate their ability to enjoy well-being; nor their preparedness to become stronger, healthier or complete; nor does it represent 'compensation' for something totally unrelated to that pain whatsoever.

All of the pains of this world when compared to the pleasures and goods of the Hereafter are much less than [the weight of] an atom compared to all the mountains of this world. Likewise, all of the pleasures of this world [are insignificant] compared to the pains of the Hereafter.

God (Glory be to Him) did not create pain and pleasure in vain nor did He determine them aimlessly. Due to the perfection of His power and wisdom, He made each one of them result in the other. It is impossible to eradicate the necessary concomitants of creation, just like it is impossible to eliminate a creature's dependence, need and deficiency. A creature is necessarily dependent, needy and deficient when it comes to knowledge and power.

Had human beings and other animals not experienced in this world hunger or thirst, nor pain or harm, then they would not be animals. Moreover, God did not make this abode one of permanent, absolute and complete pleasure. Instead, He made it an abode wherein its pains are mixed in with pleasures, its joy with grief and sorrow, and its health with disease. Indeed, all of this is due to His far-reaching wisdom.

But most souls are so ignorant about God, and His wisdom, omniscience and perfection, that they conjecture impossibilities, which they consider to be rational, thinking that these are more perfect than what is real and existent. Despite that, their Lord has mercy on them because of their [inevitable faults, which include] ignorance, incapability and deficiency. If they acknowledge their faults, while affirming His perfection and praiseworthiness, and carry out the requisites of these two acknowledgements, then they will still be able to attain an abundant share of His mercy.

God began creation with His praise, and ended the matter of this world with His praise. He said, *Praise be to God, Who hath created the heavens and the earth*;[43] *And they are judged aright. And it is said, Praise be to God, the Lord of the Worlds!*[44] God revealed His Book, prescribed His Divine Law, and necessitated His reward and punishment through His praiseworthiness. Praise of Him is a necessary concomitant of His Essence. His praiseworthiness is infinite, just as His knowledge and mercy are [infinite]. Everything is encompassed within the Lord's mercy and knowledge; and everything that He has created and prescribed leads to praiseworthy end objectives. They must inevitably be accompanied by their necessary concomitants as well as the concomitants of the latter.

There are many types of praise that God (Exalted is He) is deserving of: praise for His lordship, and that He alone [is the Lord]; praise for His divinity and Oneness; praise for His blessings; praise for His favours; praise for His wisdom; praise for His justice [in dealing] with His creation; praise for His Self-Sufficiency in not having a son, associate or supporter due to a need; and praise for His perfection, which no one else possesses.

God is praiseworthy in every state, in every moment, and in every breath. He is praiseworthy for everything He does, everything He has prescribed [through His Divine Law], for all of His Attributes, for all that He is infallible from, and for everything that is in existence (whether good or evil, pleasure or pain, well-being or affliction [as they lead to greater goods and are evidence of His dazzling wisdom]). Just as sovereignty, power, majesty, knowledge and beauty are all His, praiseworthiness is also all His. This is mentioned in a tradition: 'O God, all praise is dedicated to You, the sovereignty is all Yours, in Your Hands is all good, and all matters return to You. You alone are deserving of all praise.'[45]

CHAPTER SEVEN

An Exposition of Whether the Punishment of Hellfire is Eternal

If it is asked, 'What pleasure or good emanates from a severe, eternal and everlasting punishment that never ends or lets up? [For in the punishment of Hellfire] every time their skin is burnt off it is exchanged [with fresh skin]; and they are never allowed to expire such that they die, nor does [the punishment] ease up for even a moment.'

We respond: By God, this is a question that shakes the mountains let alone the hearts of men. Due to this question some who initially affirmed the wisdom of the Almighty and Most Wise subsequently denied [His wisdom] and causality, denied that matters have [wise] purposes, and instead [claimed that they are solely a result of His will]. This group [which includes some of the Ashʿariyya] also deemed it permissible for God to punish those who obey Him and are His saints in the lowest levels of Hellfire; and to reward His enemies who associate others with Him, raising them to the highest levels of blissful Paradise eternally. [This group further claimed] that He could punish those whom He wills in Hellfire without any reason, cause or [evil] deed. [They then claimed] that He could vary [the punishment for Hell's] denizens even if their [evil] deeds are equivalent, that He could punish them in an equal fashion even if their deeds are disparate, and that He could punish a person with the sins of another; or that He could annul all the righteous deeds of a person, not reward him, and instead reward another for those [same deeds]. They deemed all of those things permissible to Him [claiming] that it cannot be known that He does not do these unless there is an authentic tradition [that states otherwise]. [They claim that] God doing those or their opposites is all the same to Him.

They also claimed that there is no way to escape from this question except by using this principle. Yet they may just be holding on to this principle superficially, without really understanding its deeper implications. Nonetheless, they did not reconcile between [this principle] and the proofs indicating [His] justice and wisdom, or the connections of [effects] with their causes and that the former follow suit, balance and compensate for them. They misunderstood the Qur'ān just like they erred in describing the Lord with what is not befitting to Him—instead characterizing Him with impossibilities.

Some of the Qadariyya (who affirm causality and [His] wisdom) claimed that they could escape from this repugnant principle because of their affirmation of [His] wisdom and causality. But they fell into something similar or even worse, since they obligated God (Glory be to Him) to eternally punish a Muslim—who spent his whole life obeying Him, but then perpetrated one major sin and died without [repenting]—in Hellfire along with His enemies.

Again, the doctrine [of this subgroup of Qadariyya] is even more evil than the Jabriyya as the latter did not obligate God to judge in that manner. Rather, the Jabriyya declared that it was permissible for Him to judge either way. Due to the [Qadariyya's] mistaken interpretation of the Qur'ān and the Sunna and what they deemed permissible or impermissible for the Lord, they succumbed just like the Jabriyya.

Others [like Ibn Sīnā] speculated and investigated, and thereafter supposed that the Resurrection [and the sending of a faction to Hellfire]—which the messengers informed us of—contradicts wisdom, mercy, justice and advantage. Therefore, they [claimed] that the [warning of Hellfire] is only to make us fearful, that it is only imaginary and not real, and that it is to restrain those whose nature is animalistic and beastly from perpetrating their temptations. Hence, they claimed that this [warning] is advantageous for existence, [but is not true].[1]

One of the greatest reasons for falling into heresy and disbelief in God and the Hereafter is the attribution of false doctrines and corrupt viewpoints to the messengers. Other groups similarly succumbed in the question of the temporal origination of this world.[2] They claimed that the messengers notified us that God had been pre-eternally stripped of acting, and that [His creative ability] transformed from being essentially impossible to becoming possible (*inqalaba min al-iḥāla al-dhātiya ilā'l-imkān al-dhātī*) at the initiation [of His creation] without a renewed cause or event (*bi-lā tajaddud sabab wa-lā amr*) which subsists in the Agent's [Essence][3] (*qām bi'l-fāʿil*).[4] They claimed that whoever does not have faith in that is not a believer nor does he believe in the messengers. Therefore, the latter [heresy] concerns the origin [of this world] while the former regards the Resurrection.

Then another group came along and denied [His] creation and commandments altogether. They claimed that all of that is not true, but is instead deceitful. Then they claimed that there is only one existence:[5] there is no Creator and created being, no Lord and creatures submissive to His lordship, and no obedience or disobedience; rather, everything is one order. [In addition, they argued that] disassociating these represents only imagination and fantasy. [For them], the heavens and the earth, this world and the Hereafter, pre-eternity and eternity, and the good and the repugnant are all one and the same. Later, they revised [their inconsistency] and claimed that they are instead one essence.

People—knowing nothing other than these viewpoints and doctrines—were initiated into these four groups, except those whom God willed. Their harm became rampant and the calamity was great. Some of the smartest scholars became atheists. Only those who were dull and simple-minded were able to avoid this, but these people were also far away from rational thought and transmitted evidence.

We state after asking God for success, depending on God, and relying on Him: The Qur'ān, the Sunna, innate disposition and rational proofs all prove that God (Glory be to Him) created the heavens and the earth, and what is in between them with the truth. He did not create anything aimlessly, nor in vain and falsehood. The Truth is an Attribute and Name of His, and His statements and actions are also [the truth]. God (Glory be to Him) is the Clear Truth, and thus nothing proceeds from Him except the truth. He does not say anything but the truth, nor does He carry out anything but the truth. He does not command anything but the truth, nor does He recompense anyone except with the truth.

Falsehood cannot be attributed to Him. Moreover, falsehood is anything that is not attributable to Him; for example, a false judgment; a false religion that He did not permit nor prescribe, as it was not conveyed by His messengers; a false deity who is not deserving or suitable to be worshipped, and therefore worship or supplicating to it is falsehood; false speech that consists of lies and slander; and statements which are impossible and are not connected to any existent, but instead are attached to something false, which is not real.

God (Glory be to Him) originated the creation only so that they may worship and know Him. Worshipping Him is predicated on loving Him for His favours and blessings, and for His perfection and glory. God made His creation with this innate disposition; and, therefore, they were created affirming His [existence]. The messengers (may God bless them all) said to their nations, *Can there be doubt concerning God, the Originator of the heavens and the earth?*[6]

The creation is innately disposed to acknowledge Him and worship Him alone. If they were left alone to this innate disposition they would have grown up knowing Him and worshipping Him alone. This innate disposition is a created entity that they were originated upon—there is no altering His creation. People lived upon this innate disposition for many generations, but then succumbed to the consequences of their corruption and dissented from righteousness and uprightness. It is similar to what occurs to a healthy body and nature that results in them becoming diseased. Therefore, God sent His messengers to return people back to their original innate disposition.

Nonetheless, people divided into three groups after [the messengers conveyed their message]. Some of them responded completely and followed [the messengers] totally, and thus their innate disposition returned to its original perfection. That resulted in complete knowledge and righteous deeds. Thus, their innate disposition became even more perfect than before. This group will not need reformation or chastisement in the Hereafter nor Hellfire to remove from them their wickedness or purify them from their dirt or filth. Their submission to the messengers eliminated the need for all that.

The [second] group complied in some respects but not in others, and therefore they retained some dirt and filth that were in contrast to the truth that they were created to pursue. Hence, the Omniscient and Most Wise prepared medications for them consisting of tribulation and trials [to cure] the diseases that had taken hold of them. If they are able to completely purify themselves in this abode [then that is good], but if not then they are [punished] in the grave. If this [latter punishment] is not sufficient then standing on the Day of Judgment and [enduring] its shocks may absolve some of them from their remaining [sins]. If this is not sufficient then they inevitably must be cured with the greatest type of remedy, which is by being burned. They will therefore enter the bellows [of Hellfire] to be purified and absolved until they are completely reformed and there is no further benefit [or need] for it. At that point, they will be removed from the infirmary to the abode of those who are healthy. This has been indicated in multiple *ḥadīth*s narrated from the Prophet (may God bless him and grant him peace). He said it explicitly in his statement, 'After they are cleansed and purified, they will be admitted into Paradise.'[7] The Exalted said, *Peace be unto you! Ye are good, so enter ye (the Garden of delight), to dwell therein.*[8] Therefore, God did not permit them to enter [Paradise] until after they became pure—it is only the abode of the pious, in which there is no wickedness whatsoever. They will only remain in Hellfire in accordance with their need to become purified and absolved of their wickedness.

The third group are those who did not submit to nor follow the messengers. Instead, they continued to deviate away from their innate disposition, and they never returned to it. Corruption consolidated itself within them completely, such that they could never become righteous. This world, the afflictions of death and what follows it, and the shocks of the [Day of] Resurrection are insufficient to dissipate away their filth and dirt. So it is not befitting according to the wisdom of the Omniscient and Most Wise to settle them next to the righteous in the abode [of Paradise]. And since they were not created to be annihilated, they will go to the abode of afflictions and suffering. They will remain in it as long as their filth [composed] of disbelief and polytheism remains with them. Hellfire was fired up to the degree of their wicked deeds; therefore, their punishment within it is to the same degree as their evil sins. Their punishment will continue as long as the consequences of those [evil] deeds remain, as well as what was instigated by them. As long as the requisites remain, the punishment also remains.

Now [some maintain that] we should investigate [the following]: 'Did the original innate disposition vanish completely [in such people] so that its effect became non-existent and completely null? If yes, then it is their evil that obliterated their innate disposition and became all that remained. In that case there is no way that they can be saved from the punishment. Or can it be said that their innate disposition did not become [completely] anulled, but instead the illness and corruption due to [their evilness] took hold of them, just like a disease of the body that afflicts a person yet he remains alive (even though it may not be a life he derives benefit from)? However, if a medication becomes available that can rid him of this disease and return him to his health—even though it is bitter, difficult to swallow, and must be taken over and over—then the original innate disposition can become manifest once again. At that point no further treatment is needed. This is the secret of this question.' Those who argue this second proposition say that rational thought does not prove the impossibility of such [an argument], as [reason] does not deem it to be inherently impossible [for the innate disposition to be the only entity left after a disbeliever is absolved of all of his evilness and wickedness through the punishment of Hellfire].

They then state, 'Rational thought, transmitted evidence and the innate disposition have instead all proven that the Exalted Lord is wise and merciful. God's wisdom and mercy rejects maintaining these [evil] souls in the punishment forever (*sarmad*) and eternally (*abad*), such that this punishment remains existent alongside God's Eternal [existence]. This [eternal punishment] is inconsistent with [God's] wisdom and mercy.'

They also said: 'Many textual or contemplative proofs have indicated that the punishments and penalties, which God has prescribed and determined in this abode, are only to chastise souls and purify them from the evil that they have within them, to attain the benefit of restraining and warning them, to make them abstain from returning back [to sins], in addition to many other wise purposes. Once these [wise purposes] occur then punishing them becomes devoid of any further wisdom or advantage; and therefore, [that punishment] no longer remains necessary. [Do not forget that] this is the punishment of One Who is knowledgeable, most wise and merciful—He does not punish in vain or due to any benefit that He will gain, as that is impossible. Hence, [His] punishment only occurs to accrue some advantage to either the one being punished or someone else. It is well known that He derives no advantage—nor does anyone else—in keeping a [disbeliever] in the punishment forever and eternally.'

They maintained that the Qur'ān and the Sunna have proven that the types of pains [that exist] are for humankind's benefit. The Exalted said, *That is because neither thirst nor toil nor hunger afflicteth them in the way of God, nor step they any step that angereth the disbelievers, nor gain they from the enemy a gain, but a good deed is recorded for them therefore;*[9] *And that God may prove those who believe, and may blight the disbelievers.*[10] Thus, God notified us that the pain from death and wounds incurred in His path is a *tamḥīṣ*, i.e. as purification and cleansing for the believers. He gave glad tidings to those who are patient [in the face] of the pain from hunger, fear, poverty, losing beloved ones and others by [reminding them] that He will bless them, have mercy on them and guide them.

The Exalted also said, *He who doeth wrong will have the recompense thereof.*[11] Abū Bakr al-Ṣiddīq said, 'O Messenger of God, we have sustained a mortal blow—who amongst us has not done evil?' The Prophet said, 'O Abū Bakr, do you not become fatigued? Do you not become grieved? Do you not encounter harm?' He replied yes. The Prophet then said, 'This is what you are recompensed and expiated (*tujzawna*) with.'[12]

Furthermore, the Exalted has said, *Whatever of misfortune striketh you, it is what your hands have earned.*[13] There are glad tidings as well as a warning [in this verse], since He has informed us that the misfortunes of this world represent punishments for our sins. In addition,

He is too merciful to repeat a punishment upon His servant [in the next world] for a sin after having already done so in this world. The Prophet (may God bless him and grant him peace) said, 'Whoever perpetrates some filthy [sins], but God conceals it, then his matter returns back to God. If He wills, He punishes him; and if He wills, He forgives him. Whoever is punished for them in this world, then [know that] God is too beneficent to punish His servant again.'[14] In another *ḥadīth*, [we read], '[I do not know if (*wa-mā adrī*)] legal punishments expiate those who perpetrated [major sins].'[15] ᶜUbāda narrated the following *ḥadīth*: 'Whoever among you falls into any [sins] and is punished for them in this world, then that represents an expiation for him.'[16]

The Prophet (may God bless him and grant him peace) said, 'No suffering, fatigue, sorrow, sadness or harm befalls a Muslim—even the prick of a thorn—but that God expiates some of his sins for that.'[17] He also said, 'Tribulations will continue to afflict the believer, whether in his family, wealth or children, until he meets God absolved of all his sins.'[18] In another *ḥadīth*, 'After the believer is cured of his illness he becomes pure, just like hail is clear and colourless.'[19] In another *ḥadīth*, 'Fever erases sins just like the bellows of fire remove the impurities of iron.'[20] In another *ḥadīth*, 'Do not revile fever, for it removes away the sins of the offspring of Adam.'[21] In fact, one of the names of fever is 'the expiator of sins'.

In an authentic *ḥadīth*, 'God (Almighty and Most Glorious is He) will say on the Day of Judgment, "O son of Adam, I fell ill and you did not visit Me." He will say, "O Lord, how could I visit You when You are the Lord of the Worlds?" God will say, "Did you not know that My servant so-and-so was ill, but you did not visit him? Do you not know that if you had visited him you would have found Me at his side?"'[22] This last expression is more profound than His statement [earlier in the same *ḥadīth* regarding those who were hungry or thirsty] who asked for food or drink: 'You would find that [reward] with Me.' God (Glory be to Him) is at the 'side' of one afflicted by disease out of His mercy and goodness. It is also to console him due to his heart being broken as a result of his disease. God is always with those whose hearts are broken.

This issue is greater than what can be mentioned. The Lord of this world and the Hereafter is One, and His wisdom and mercy are present in both this world and the Hereafter. Moreover, the manifestation of His mercy in the Hereafter is far greater. The punishment of the believers in Hellfire in the Hereafter is [to purify them], just like their punishment in this world with afflictions and legal punishments serves the same purpose. Similarly, [some of them] are held in-between Paradise and Hellfire in order to chastise them until they are purified. It is known using the authentic explicit texts that the punishment [of the believers] in Hellfire varies in degree and time in accordance with their sins. In addition, the believers will not be all removed [at the same time]; instead, one after another [will be removed] until the last will be taken out.

The punishment of the disbelievers in Hellfire also varies greatly, whereby the hypocrites occupy its lowest level. On the other hand, Abū Ṭālib is the least punished of its denizens: he is in the shallowest part of Hellfire, yet his brain still boils.[23] Furthermore, Pharaoh's people are in the severest punishment.[24]

Now they also contend that if the punishment in this abode amounts to only one part of [God's] mercy, beneficence and kindness from amongst one hundred [parts], then what about the abode wherein [ninety-nine out of] the one hundred mercies are implemented? [Remember that] each mercy fills the heavens and earth. The Exalted has said, *And verily We make them taste the lower punishment before the greater, that haply they may return.*[25] God therefore informed us that He will punish them out of His mercy so that they may return to Him. It is like a compassionate and merciful father who punishes his son if the latter flees from him to his enemy, so that the child may return to treating his parents kindly and honourably.

God (Exalted is He) also said, *What concern hath God for your punishment if ye are thankful (for His mercies) and believe (in Him)?*[26] Therefore, God's punishment does not accrue any benefit to Him or any gain in His kingdom, nor is it aimless or devoid of any wisdom or advantage. Again, if a person disbelieved, instead of being grateful and having faith, then his punishment will be a [direct] result of his disbelief. Otherwise, no objective or benefit reaches Him in punishing [the disbelievers].

They continued: [His] wisdom dictates that these souls, who are evil, must inevitably be punished to chastise them in accordance with what they perpetrated. This is proven by transmitted evidence and rational thought. But this would necessitate [that the punishment] end, and not be permanent.

They continued: God (Exalted is He) did not create human beings in vain nor to punish them, but instead He created them to have mercy upon them. They only acquired the requisites that led to their punishment after being created by Him. Therefore, His mercy preceded His wrath. The necessary manifestation of His mercy precedes that of His wrath and prevails over it. His punishment is not the objective of His creating; rather, [the objectives of] His punishment are wise and they represent [requisite steps leading to His] mercy. [His] wisdom and mercy reject making His punishment eternal and unending.

It is self-evident that [His] mercy [would not allow eternal punishment]. As for [His] wisdom, He only punishes an [evil] that befalls the innate disposition and changes it—not something that He created in humanity originally, and it was not created for that. Humanity was not created to worship others nor to be punished. Instead, they were created to worship [Him alone] and to be shown [His] mercy. But their [innate disposition] ended up [being characterised] by the requisites for punishment, and thus they were deserving of that punishment. This requisite feature is not permanent, though, since it is [based in] falsehood. This is in contrast to the truth, which is the requisite for [His] mercy—it is everlasting just as the Truth (Glory be to Him) is Eternal. Now the [truth] is an end objective. On the other hand, the punishment and its requisites are not end objectives; but [His] mercy and its requisites are end objectives. Deeply reflect on this well as this is the secret to this question.

They continued: The Lord (Exalted is He) named Himself the One who Forgives and the Merciful. He did not name Himself the Punisher (*al-Muʿadhdhib*) nor the Penalizer (*al-Muʿāqib*); instead, He only rendered punishments and penalties to be part of His actions.

The Exalted said, *Announce, (O Muḥammad) unto My servants that verily I am the All-Forgiving, the Merciful, and that My doom is the dolorous doom.*[27] The Exalted also said, *Verily thy Lord is swift in prosecution and verily He is all-forgiving, merciful;*[28] *The punishment of thy Lord is stern. It is He Who creates from the very beginning, and He can restore life, and He is the All-Forgiving, Full of Loving-Kindness (al-Wadūd);*[29] *The revelation of the Book is from God, the Almighty, the Omniscient, the forgiver of sin, the accepter of repentance, the stern in punishment.*[30]

There are many examples of this in the Qur'ān. God (Glory be to Him) extols Himself for pardoning, forgiving, being merciful and being generous, as well as for His forbearance. He named Himself with these [Names]. He never extolled Himself for being the One Who penalizes, Who is wrathful, Who punishes, or Who avenges (*al-muntaqim*)—although [the last is reported] in an unauthentic *ḥadīth* that enumerates other Beautiful Names [of God].[31]

In addition, God has prescribed for Himself mercy and inscribed upon a Book [on His Throne] that His mercy precedes His wrath.[32] They maintain that this also applies to the denizens of Hellfire. His mercy for them has preceded His wrath as He has shown them many types of His mercy before they angered Him by associating others in worship with Him. He has shown them mercy in their state of polytheism by [revealing] and establishing the evidence. God has also shown them mercy by [continuing to call] them to His religion after they angered Him, harmed His messengers and disbelieved in them. He also granted them respite and did not hasten [their punishment]. Instead, His mercy encompassed them, and therefore, again, His mercy preceded His wrath. Had it not been for that, the world would have been destroyed, the heavens would have toppled over the earth, and the mountains would have disintegrated. Now since [His] mercy prevails over [His] wrath and precedes it, it is impossible that the requisites of that wrath eternally prevail over His mercy.

They continued: Punishment is either in vain or for some advantage and wisdom. The Most Wise is infallible from it being in vain. Indeed, attributing that to Him would represent a great deficiency in His regard. But if it is advantageous, then that would connote benefits, necessary concomitants and requisites. Either those [advantages] are accrued by the Lord—but He is exalted and sanctified above that—or they are secured by a creature: either [1] by the person being punished, or [2] by another, or [3] by both of them. The first is impossible as there is no advantage to an eternal and endless penalty. Yet another advantage, which is the warning or restraining of that person, has also occurred. If it is to perfect another's pleasure, delight and joy, since he sees his enemy in that state while he is in ultimate bliss [in Paradise]; even if he was the most cruel individual, he would [ultimately] have compassion on his enemy due to the long length of the latter's punishment and suffering. Therefore, the [true objective of Hellfire] is to break tyrannical, stubbornly obstinate and evil souls. This will allow their evil illnesses and diseases to be curatively ridden from them. Again, those [evils] are incidental to their original innate dispositions.

They continued: The possible types of creation are five and no more: pure good, [absolute evil], preponderant good, [preponderant evil], and one where good and evil are equivalent. [His] wisdom dictates the presence of two types of them: pure good and preponderant [good]. As for absolute evil or preponderant [evil], [His] wisdom rejects these. Everything that God (Glory be to Him) created is for a wise purpose, and its existence is more appropriate than its non-existence. He created these evil [people who act like] animals and [their] evil actions due to them [indirectly] leading to beloved goods. He did not create those entities as pure evil or unable to [indirectly] result in any type of good; that is absolutely impossible. Therefore, good is intended for itself, but evil is only allowed as a [indirect] means and originator [to good]. Evil itself is not intended as an objective or end.

Now, once the intended objective of creating some entity or means occurs, its existence is no longer necessary. This is well known by experience and rational thought. So, punishment [in Hellfire] is evil and it is only a means to an objective. Once that objective is fulfilled, it becomes like a road that leads to its destination. Once a traveller reaches his destination, there is no longer any benefit to taking [the road that was necessary for the journey].

The secret of this issue is that the objective of [His] creation and commandments is mercy, not punishment. The punishment [of Hellfire] is one of His creations; and therefore, that would indicate that He has created it for a praiseworthy objective. It is inevitable that His Names and the effects of His Attributes become manifest, both universally and absolutely. This represents perfection. The Lord (may His glory be exalted) is characterized by perfection and He is infallible above any deficiency.

They also maintained that the Exalted has said, *As for those who will be wretched (on that day) they will be in the Fire; sighing and wailing will be their portion therein, abiding there so long as the heavens and the earth endure save for that which thy Lord willeth. Thy Lord is doer of what He will;*[33] *He will say, Fire is your home. Abide therein for ever, save him whom God willeth. Thy Lord is wise, aware.*[34]

Abū Saᶜīd al-Khudrī[35] said, 'God's statement [*save him whom God willeth*] takes precedence over all the other verses of the Qur'ān and qualifies them [regarding the punishment of Hellfire].'[36] ᶜAbd Allāh b. Masᶜūd[37] said, 'There will come a time when there will be no one left in Hellfire. This will be after they have remained therein for a long period (*aḥqāba*).'[38] A similar [statement has been narrated] from ᶜUmar b. al-Khaṭṭāb and Abū Hurayra. This requires that no denizens will remain in [Hellfire] after a long period [of punishment]. ᶜAbd al-Raḥmān b. Zayd b. Aslam said, 'God informed us about what He wills for the people in Paradise. The Exalted said *a gift unfailing;*[39] but He did not inform us of His [ultimate] will for the denizens of Hellfire.'[40]

They continued: What is in Sūrat al-Anᶜām is sufficient. God states, *In the day when He will gather them together (He will say), O ye assembly of the jinn! Many of humankind did ye seduce. And their adherents among humankind will say, Our Lord! We enjoyed one another, but now we have arrived at the appointed term which Thou appointedst for us. He will say, Fire is your home. Abide therein for ever, save him whom God willeth. Thy Lord is wise, aware.*[41] Then [consider] His statement, *O ye assembly of the jinn and humankind! Came there not unto you messengers of your own who recounted unto you My tokens and warned you of the meeting of this your day? They will say, We testify against ourselves. And the life of the world beguiled them. And they testify against themselves that they were disbelievers.*[42]

The [above verse] addresses the disbelievers [not sinful believers]. This can be proven in many ways. Firstly, it describes them being seduced, and that is due to them being deceived and going astray. This only applies to the disbelievers. Secondly, there is His statement, *and their adherents among humankind will say*;[43] their supporters are only the disbelievers. The Exalted said, *Lo! We have made the devils protecting friends for those who believe not*.[44] Satan's group are his friends. Third is His statement, *And they testify against themselves that they were disbelievers*.[45] Despite that, God said, *Fire is your home. Abide therein for ever, save him whom God willeth*; then He concluded the verse by saying, *Thy Lord is wise, aware*.[46] Their punishment is connected to His knowledge and wisdom; and likewise, this exception [i.e. *save him whom God willeth*] proceeds from [His] knowledge and wisdom. He knows what He will do with them, and it will be [concordant] with [His] wisdom.

They continued: When God (Glory be to Him) mentions in the Qur'ān both the recompense of those He will have mercy on and those whom He is angered by, He describes the former as being everlasting (*abad*), whereas He leaves open the latter's [final fate]. An example is His statement: *As for those who will be wretched (on that day) they will be in the Fire; sighing and wailing will be their portion therein, abiding there so long as the heavens and the earth endure save for that which thy Lord willeth. Thy Lord is doer of what He will. And as for those who will be glad (that day) they will be in the Garden, abiding there so long as the heavens and the earth endure save for that which thy Lord willeth: a gift unfailing*.[47]

Another example is His statement: *Those who disbelieve, among the People of the Book and the idolaters, will abide in fire of Hell. They are the worst of created beings. (And) those who believe and do good works are the best of created beings. Their reward is with their Lord: Gardens of Eden underneath which rivers flow, wherein they dwell forever (abadan). God hath pleasure in them and they have pleasure in Him. This is (in store) for him who feareth his Lord*.[48]

Another example is His statement: *On the day when (some) faces will be whitened and (some) faces will be blackened; and as for those whose faces have been blackened, it will be said unto them, Disbelieved ye after your (profession of) belief? Then taste the punishment for that ye disbelieved. And as for those whose faces have been whitened, in the mercy of God they dwell forever.*[49]

On the other hand, the disbelievers may be mentioned alone whereby He dictates that they are [punished] forever, like His statement: *And whoso disobeyeth God and His Messenger, lo! his is fire of Hell, wherein such dwell forever;*[50] *And whoso disobeyeth God and His Messenger and transgresseth His limits, He will make him enter Fire, where he will dwell forever (khālidan); his will be a shameful doom.*[51]

They maintain that solely mentioning [the punishment being] 'forever' (*khulūd*) and everlasting (*ta'bīd*) does not require it to be unending. Instead, *khulūd* means 'remaining there for a long time' (*al-makth al-ṭawīl*). It is like saying [one is] 'imprisoned forever'. The Exalted said about the Jews [and their statement regarding this world], *But they will never long for [death] (abadan), because of that which their own hands have sent before them.*[52] Now it is well known that they would hope [for death] in Hellfire, as they will say, *And they cry, O master! Let thy Lord make an end of us.*[53]

That the bliss of Paradise never ends can be derived from His statements: *This in truth is Our provision, which will never waste away;*[54] *a gift unfailing;*[55] and *for theirs is a reward unfailing (ghayr mamnūn),*[56] which means 'never cut-off'. Whoever claims that it instead means 'He will not make them recognize His favour upon them' has erred repugnantly. Regardless, none of these descriptions were used in regards to the punishment of the denizens of Hellfire.

As for the statements of the Almighty and Most Glorious, *And they will not emerge from the Fire;*[57] *nor will they be expelled from thence;*[58] *it taketh not complete effect upon them so that they can die, nor is its torment lightened for them;*[59] *Whenever they desire to issue forth from thence, they are brought back thither;*[60] and His statement, *As often as their skins are consumed We shall exchange them for fresh skins;*[61] these are the truth, and they cannot be construed otherwise [or interpreted allegorically].

They maintained that leaving the verses [concerning the disbelievers] open-ended still requires them to be subject to verses that describe [His] will. Thus, the [former verses] specify the general nature of the latter. This is akin to the [statements] of the Predecessors [Abū Saʿīd al-Khudrī, Isḥāq and others] who said that the verse [Q.XI.107] qualifies every warning in the Qur'ān. The correct viewpoint regarding these verses is that, although they are both general and absolute, there is nothing in them that definitively proves that Hellfire itself is permanent and unending just as God is Eternal. There is no definite evidence in the Qur'ān or the Sunna for that. There is a difference between the punishment of its denizens being permanent while Hellfire lasts, and between Hellfire being everlasting and never ending such that it never transforms or fades away.

Nonetheless, it should not be said that in this case there exists no difference between the worldly punishment and that of the Hereafter, since [in this thinking] each of them will [ultimately] fade away and end. We respond that the differences between the two are clearly evident. The worldly punishment ends with the death of the one being punished. As for the punishment of the Hereafter, the one deserving of it remains alive and does not die, and the punishment never leaves him. In addition, no one can ward it off from oneself. The Exalted said, *The doom of thy Lord will surely come to pass; there is none that can ward it off.*[62] It is obligatory and will never depart away. The Exalted said, *The doom thereof is [an obligatory] anguish (gharāman),*[63] as *gharāman* means 'obligatory'.

As for the traditions regarding this issue: Abū Umāma[64] narrated that the Prophet (may God bless him and grant him peace) said, 'There will come upon Hellfire a day when it will be like a paper that is kindled and ignited. Its gates will be flapping open.'[65]

Ḥarb[66] said in his book *Masā'il*[67] that he asked Isḥāq[68] about the verse of God (Almighty and Most Glorious is He), *Abiding there so long as the heavens and the earth endure save for that which thy Lord willeth.*[69] He answered that this verse qualifies every warning in the Qur'ān. Jābir[70] and Abū Saʿīd, as well some of the other Companions of the Prophet (may God bless him and grant him peace), opined similarly. Al-Muʿtamir b. Sulaymān[71] said the same. Ḥarb then said, 'The meaning in my view, and God knows best, is that it qualifies every warning in the Qur'ān for those who worshipped Him alone.' But [those who contend that Hellfire may end for the disbelievers maintain that] interpreting it in the aforementioned fashion is incorrect since the exception [of His will] follows the warning to the disbelievers, as previously discussed.

Ḥarb also narrated that ʿAbd Allāh b. ʿAmr[72] said, 'There will come upon Hellfire a day when its gates will be slammed shut, and there will be no one left in it. That will occur after they have remained in it for a long period of time.'[73] Finally, Abū Hurayra said, 'My statement that there will come upon Hellfire a day when no one will remain in it is based on [the verse], *As for those who will be wretched (on that day) they will be in the Fire; sighing and wailing will be their portion therein, Abiding there so long as the heavens and the earth endure save for that which thy Lord willeth. Lo! thy Lord is doer of what He will.*'[74]

ʿAbd b. Ḥumayd [al-Kashshī][75] mentioned in his *Tafsīr* that Ḥammād b. Salama[76] relayed from Thābit[77] that al-Ḥasan [al-Baṣrī] narrated that ʿUmar [b. al-Khaṭṭāb] said, 'Even if the denizens of Hellfire remained in it for the same number [of years] as the [number of] sands in ʿĀlij, there would still be a day in which they will exit it.'[78] The narrators of this tradition are all trustworthy. Al-Ḥasan [al-Baṣrī] also heard this from some other Successors, and he narrated it without challenging it. The existence of this tradition indicates that it was circulating amongst these imams and they did not dispute it. [And remember] that they used to debate those who would stray from the Sunna to the slightest degree, and they would respond with *ḥadīth*s that would refute [innovative] practices. Imam Aḥmad used to say, 'The traditions narrated by Ḥammād b. Salama are lodged in the throats of the innovators [and these prevent them from spreading their innovations].' Had this tradition been an innovation that was contrary to the Sunna and the consensus [of the scholars], they would have rushed to repudiate and refute it.

In the *Tafsīr* of ʿAlī b. Abī Ṭalḥa,[79] Ibn ʿAbbās said regarding His statement, *He will say, Fire is your home. Abide therein for ever, save him whom God willeth. Thy Lord is wise, aware,*[80] 'It is not proper for anyone to render a judgement above God's in regards to His creatures, or to say who is deserving of Paradise or Hellfire.'[81] Ṭabarī also mentioned a narration from Ibn ʿAbbās [that is relevant to this discussion]: 'This exception indicates that God made the length of His punishment of them predicated upon His will.'[82]

Some claim that the exception of God's will applies to: [1] those types of punishment which God has [not] willed; or [2] the timespan before they entered [Hellfire], i.e. from the time of their resurrection to their entrance into it; or [3] that it pertains to the [sinful believers] who prayed to Him, since *mā* can actually mean 'those' (*man*); or [4] that *mā* means 'and', i.e. '*and* that which God wills'.

All of these interpretations are weak and feeble—they are repudiated by the statement of Ibn ʿAbbās, and are not suitable to this verse. Whoever deeply reflects on them is certain of their invalidity.

Suddī[83] interpreted the Exalted's statement, *They will abide therein for ages* (*aḥqāban*),[84] as meaning 700 periods of time wherein every period is seventy years, every year is 360 days, and every day is 1000 years of [our worldly] length. Therefore, their stay within it is finite and measurable. The majority [of exegetes] interpret *aḥqāban* ('for ages') to be finite.

Another group stated that the aforementioned verse is abrogated by His statements, *Nor will they be expelled from thence*;[85] *they will abide therein*.[86] Those who argue [that the punishment will end] state that these two verses instead indicate that the punishment [of the disbelievers] is permanent and continuous while Hellfire remains—they are in it forever and will never exit it [while it exists]. Now this is true and known by the proofs within the Qur'ān and the Sunna. But the matter [being debated] concerns something else, and that is whether Hellfire is everlasting and permanent along with the Lord's eternity. Where is there any proof for that in the Qur'ān or the Sunna?

Another group said that this verse [i.e. Q.LXXVIII.23] only concerns the [sinful believers] who worshipped Him alone. This [interpretation] is worse than saying [Q.LXXVIII.23 abrogated the others] as the context of these verses explicitly repudiates that.

Others said that the verse is intended to indicate that after one period of time passes another period follows ad infinitum. But what they have said is not indicated by the verse in any manner whatsoever. Had this verse affirmed the endless nature of the punishment, it would not have been mentioned as periods of time. It is not said that something is for long periods of time, ages or generations if it is never ending. For this reason, the bliss of the people in Paradise is not said to be [for a long period (*aḥqāban*)]. It is also not said that something eternal, which never vanishes, remains for many periods of time or for thousands of years. The Companions understood the meanings of the Qur'ān better than the rest of this Community. ʿUmar b. al-Khaṭṭāb understood it differently than those groups, just as Ibn ʿAbbās understood the verse of the exception [of God's will] differently than they did.

The understanding of the Companions of the Qur'ān is the ultimate goal, and one should depend on their [interpretations]. Ibn Masʿūd said, 'There will come a time when the gates of Hellfire will flap and there will be no one in it. This will occur after having remained in it for a long period of time.'[87] Ibn Jarīr [al-Ṭabarī] narrated a tradition from [Saʿīd b.] al-Musayyab[88] based on [what he heard from] Ibn ʿAbbās regarding, *Abiding there so long as the heavens and the earth endure save for that which thy Lord willeth*,[89] that 'God will command Hellfire to consume [or annihilate] them (*ta'kulahum*).'[90]

[Ibn Jarīr] also mentioned a statement of al-Shaʿbī [in this regard]:[91] 'Hellfire is the faster of the two abodes to be populated, and it will be destroyed more quickly also.'[92] He [Ibn al-Qayyim] states that this statement does not indicate that the other abode [i.e. Paradise] will be destroyed. His statement, 'The faster of the two abodes to be populated', may indicate: firstly, that people are quicker to [perpetrate the evil] deeds by which they will be entered into Hellfire, and will be slower to [carry out the righteous] deeds [required to enter] the abode [of Paradise]. Secondly, that the denizens [of Hellfire] will enter it before the pious will be entered into Paradise. The pious believers will only enter Paradise after they traverse the pathway [over Hellfire] and after being held up at the bridge beyond it; and [by this time] the denizens of Hellfire will have already taken their places therein, since they never make it past that pathway.

In addition, [we read] in the authentic *ḥadīth*, 'A caller will exclaim, "Every nation must follow what they used to worship." The polytheists will therefore follow their idols and deities, and fall into Hellfire. This nation will remain standing until our Lord (Almighty and Most Glorious is He) will come and say, "Will you not proceed as others have gone?" [So they will follow Him].'[93]

Now, those who opined that Hellfire is definitely eternal and that it will never become annihilated employ the following ways:

1. The verses and traditions that prove they will remain in it forever (*khulūd*), that they do not die in it,[94] that they will never exit it,[95] that death will be [symbolically] slaughtered [after everyone takes their place] in Paradise or Hellfire,[96] and that the disbelievers will never enter Paradise until a camel can enter a needle point.[97]

But these do not prove that Hellfire will never be annihilated. Instead, they only prove that while [Hellfire] remains the [disbelievers] will be within it.

2. They contend that it represents the consensus [of this Community].

But we have mentioned many sayings of the Companions and Successors, which contradict their opinion. It has even been contended that the consensus of the Companions is on our side based on these transmissions, since no other known ones contradict them.

3. [They maintain] that it is well known by necessity in the Islamic religion that Paradise and Hellfire will never become annihilated; rather, they will remain forever. It is for this reason that all of the Sunnis rejected Abū Hudhayl, Jahm [b. Ṣafwān] and others like them who claimed that both Paradise and Hellfire will become nonexistent [or that their inhabitants will become motionless]. They were considered to be innovators who opposed the Sunna.

There is no doubt that this opinion was only advanced by heretics, and that they are outside the fold of Islam due to it. But where is the religious proof or rational reason that dictates that Hellfire will remain forever just as God remains eternally, much less than [to claim] that this is known by necessity?

4. The authentic Sunna has notified us that those who worshipped Him alone will be taken out of Hellfire, but not the disbelievers; and this is well known from the Sunna and it is definitive.

Now what they have said is true and there is no doubt about it. But the [sinful believers] who worshipped Him alone will exit [Hellfire] while it remains existent. One the other hand, the disbelievers will not [be removed from it] while it exists.

5. Rational thought points to the disbelievers remaining [in

Hellfire] forever and not being taken out of it. That is because their souls will never be receptive to any goodness. Had they been taken out of it, they would have returned to being disbelievers as they were before. The Exalted has indicated that in His statement, *And if they were sent back they would return unto that which they are forbidden.*[98] This proves that due to their haughtiness, stubbornness and lack of receptivity to any goodness whatsoever, their evil and wicked souls are not suitable for anything but punishment. Had they been [receptive], they would have become suitable [for Paradise] after a lengthy punishment. But because the punishment did not have an impact on their souls, even after the long periods of time, nor did it make them pure, it becomes known that they have no receptivity to good, fundamentally. Therefore, the reasons which lead to their punishment were not extinguished; and therefore, their torment [in Hellfire] will also not cease.

This is a strong argument as it is based on [upholding His] wisdom, and that [His] wisdom, which dictated their entrance into Hellfire, dictated that they be in there forever. But this line of thinking cannot be employed by the Muᶜtazila and Qadariyya since [most of them] denied [His] wisdom. As for a [subgroup of the Muᶜtazila] who affirmed [His wisdom], they view that if the punishment [of the denizens] is to their advantage then that would be concordant with His wisdom [since they view that God is obligated to do what is advantageous]. But how can the denizens derive any advantage if the punishment is never ending and everlasting?

As for those who affirm the Exalted Lord's wisdom [and are not Muᶜtazila] they can adopt this thinking. But wisdom does not [necessarily] dictate that their punishment must remain along with the Sublime's Eternal [Essence]. In addition, God did not inform us that He created them for that [purpose]. Instead, they are punished for a praiseworthy objective—once that occurs, then the purpose of their punishment is attained. God (Glory be to Him) does not punish His creation in vain.

In fact, He is capable of creating them in another form that is devoid of any of their souls' prior evil and wickedness after expunging them of those through that long punishment. They were created [initially in a form] that was receptive to goodness [by virtue of] their innate disposition. This receptivity is a necessary concomitant of their character, and it is through [this innate disposition] that they affirmed their Creator and Originator. But they were overtaken by [evil] such that the requisites [of their innate disposition] were negated. But after that extraneous incident (*ṭāri'*) is removed through the long punishment, all what remains is the basis of their receptivity [i.e. their innate disposition], which can then manifest itself fully.

As for the Exalted's statement, *And if they were sent back they would return unto that which they are forbidden,*[99] that is applicable before they encounter the punishment. The Exalted said, *If thou couldst see when they are set before the Fire and say, Oh, would that we might return! Then would we not deny the revelations of our Lord but we would be of the believers! Nay, but that hath become clear unto them which before they used to hide. And if they were sent back they would return unto that which they are forbidden. Lo! they are liars.*[100] Those wicked deeds and evils were still entrenched in their souls—since it was before Hellfire had expunged them. Had they been sent back [before being punished] they would have returned [to their evil ways] because the requisite [i.e. their evil] still exists and will lead them to repeat their [sins]. But where did God (Glory be to Him) inform us that had they been sent back after a long or endless punishment then they would have returned to what they were forbidden.

The secret of this question is that the original innate disposition must inevitably manifest itself, just as the extraneous incident did its work. This innate disposition is universal to all of Adam's offspring. Abū Hurayra narrated that the Prophet (may God bless him and grant him peace) said, 'No baby is born except that it is upon the innate disposition'[101] or 'upon this religion'.

ʿIyāḍ b. Ḥimār al-Mujāshiʿī[102] narrated that the Prophet (may God bless him and grant him peace) related from his Lord, 'I have created all of My servants on the true belief (*ḥunafā'*), but the devils came upon them and preoccupied them away from My religion, and commanded them—without authority—to worship others along with Me.'[103] Therefore, God informed us that the true religion (*al-dīn al-ḥanīf*) is fundamentally instilled within [humanity] and they were created upon it. But [humankind] was barred from it due to the devils cutting them off. It is impossible that the effect of the devils occurs while the manifestation [of the innate disposition] by the Beneficent and Glorious does not. Everything is His creation (Glory be to Him) and there is no Creator besides Him. Some of the creatures are beloved and pleasing to Him, and their manifestations are attributable to Him, while other creatures are disliked and hated by Him, and their effects are not attributable to Him. Evil is not attributable to Him, while all goodness is in His Hands.

Now some counter that God's statement, *Had God known of any good in them He would have made them hear*,[104] indicates that the [disbelievers] lack receptivity [to any good or fail to possess] any goodness itself. God (Glory be to Him) will take out from Hellfire those [believers] who have even an atom's weight of goodness in their hearts[105]—the goodness being faith in God and His messengers, and obeying them both with heart and body. Thus, it becomes known that those denizens do not even have this slightest amount of good in them. [They add that] the denizens are no longer receptive because of their disbelief and obstinate rejection; and they were not able to derive benefit from their innate disposition.

Now if it is maintained that the youth who was killed by al-Khiḍr was stamped as a disbeliever early on;[106] that Noah said about his people, *And will beget none save lewd ingrates*;[107] and that a *ḥadīth* traceable [to the Prophet] states, 'Indeed the children of Adam were created in various classes. Among them are those who are born as believers, live as believers and die as believers. And among them are those who are born as disbelievers, live as disbelievers and die as disbelievers...'[108]—we respond that the aforementioned [proofs] do not contradict the fact that [the offspring of Adam who disbelieve] are born with an innate disposition. The [youth] was stamped and was born being predestined to disbelieve had he reached maturity. However, at the time of his birth he was unaware of either disbelief or belief. The innate disposition is therefore a predestined state that is not associated with the [actions of an] agent. The disbeliever is considered to be born both with the innate disposition and born as a disbeliever; these two considerations are correct and well established. The first [i.e. innate disposition] declares his receptivity and preference of Islam/submission [to God]. But the latter [i.e. disbelief] occurs if [the individual is allowed to reach] maturity due to his actions and will.

Now, if [God's] original creation of the innate disposition, the overwhelming [nature of His] mercy (which precedes [His wrath]), [His] far-reaching wisdom and [His] complete self-sufficiency are considered, then the matter becomes obvious to you [i.e. that the punishment of the disbelievers in Hellfire will end].

6. The abode of justice [i.e. Hellfire] and the abode of grace [i.e. Paradise] are analogous in that they are both eternal. They are manifestations of His mercy and His justice; and His justice and mercy are necessary concomitants of His Essence.

This [argument], though, is not cogent. Justice is His right (Glory be to Him), but it is not obligatory upon Him to carry it out. Yet no deficiency or blame accrues to Him, in any respect, if He does not. Nonetheless, God has promised His grace to His servants, and He has made it obligatory upon Himself. There are many differences between the two abodes from many aspects, both religious and rational:

[I] God (Glory be to Him) notified us that the bliss of Paradise is never ending, that His favours upon its inhabitants will never be cut-off and are unfailing. Yet this was never said about the punishment of the denizens of Hellfire.

[II] He informed us that the punishment of the denizens of Hellfire will end in many verses, as has preceded [in our discussion], but He did not inform us of anything that would indicate that the bliss of the inhabitants of Paradise will end. It is for this reason that those who support the view that Hellfire is everlasting and never ending have to re-interpret those verses about Hellfire. On the other hand, they do not need to qualify those verses regarding the bliss of the inhabitants of Paradise.

[III] The *ḥadīth*s that mention the ending of the punishment of Hellfire did not mention anything about the bliss of Paradise ceasing.

[IV] The Companions and the Successors only mentioned that the punishment will end; none of them ever mentioned that the bliss will end.

[v] It is established that God (Glory be to Him) will enter some who have done no [good] deeds at all into Paradise. In contrast, [none will enter] Hellfire [except due to their evil deeds].

vi) The Sublime will originate creatures for Paradise whom He will allow to enjoy themselves therein, whereas He will not originate any creatures solely to punish them in Hellfire.

vii) Paradise is a requisite of His mercy, whereas Hellfire is a requisite of His wrath. Those who enter Hellfire are many times greater than those who enter Paradise; therefore, had the punishment of those denizens been eternal, like the eternal bliss of the inhabitants [of Paradise], then His wrath would have prevailed over and surpassed His mercy—but that is impossible.

viii) Paradise is the abode of His grace, whereas Hellfire is the abode of His justice, but His grace triumphs over His justice.

ix) Hellfire represents the fulfilment of His rights, whereas Paradise represents the fulfilment of His promise that He obligated upon Himself. God (Glory be to Him) may abandon His rights, but He will never abandon His true promise that He obligated upon Himself.

x) Paradise is the ultimate objective for which they were created in the Hereafter, and the deeds necessary to achieve that are the objective for which they were created in this world. This is in contrast to Hellfire, for God (Glory be to Him) did not originate His creation to disbelieve in Him or to worship others besides Him; rather, God created them to worship Him, so that He may have mercy upon them.

xi) The [mercy that leads to] bliss is a requisite of His Names and Attributes, whereas the punishment is an act of His. The Exalted said, *Announce, (O Muḥammad), unto My servants that verily I am the All-Forgiving, the Merciful, and that My doom is the dolorous doom;*[109] *Verily thy Lord is swift in prosecution and verily He is forgiving, merciful;*[110] *Know that God is severe in punishment, but that God (also) is forgiving, merciful.*[111] Whatever is a requisite of His Names and Attributes will be eternal alongside His eternality.

Now if it is maintained that the punishment proceeds from His majesty, wisdom and justice—and these are also eternal Beautiful

Names and perfect Attributes of His—therefore the [punishment] will also be eternal, we would respond: By God, the punishment proceeds from [His] majesty, wisdom and justice, but they will end once [His] majesty, wisdom and justice dictate that the intended objective has been attained. Neither the punishment nor its ending can be disassociated from His majesty, wisdom or justice. But once [the punishment ends His] majesty will be balanced by [His] mercy, and [His] wisdom will be juxtaposed with [His] magnanimity, beneficence, pardoning and forgiveness. His majesty and wisdom are eternal and perfect. Everything that He has originated, will create, has commanded and will command proceed from His majesty and wisdom.

XII) The punishment is intended for another [reason], not for itself. On the other hand, [His] mercy, beneficence and blessings are all intended for themselves. Beneficence and blessing are objectives, whereas punishment and pain are [solely] a means. Therefore, how can one of them be compared to the other?

XIII) God (Glory be to Him) informed us that His mercy encompasses everything,[112] that His mercy prevails over His wrath,[113] and that He has prescribed mercy upon Himself. Therefore, it is inevitable that His mercy encompass [even] those being punished. Had those [disbelievers] remained in the punishment for an unlimited [duration], then His mercy would never encompass them. This is patently obvious.

Now if it is maintained that since the Sublime [specified His mercy for only some in His statement], [*My mercy embraceth all things*]; *therefore, I shall ordain it for those who ward off (evil)*,[114] it follows that others will not [be shown mercy] since they do not possess the characteristics that would allow them to be suitable [for His mercy], then we respond that [His] mercy, which He prescribed, is different than [His] *vast* mercy, which encompasses all of creation. Instead, it is merely a special mercy that only they are selected for. He ordained it only for them as they are the fortunate ones, who will not be punished. They are appropriate for [His] mercy, triumph and bliss. He mentioned the specific [mercy] after the general one in order to distinguish them. That which is written for those who are pious is a special type of God's vast mercy.

The point is that [ultimately His] mercy will necessarily encompass the denizens of Hellfire. His mercy inevitably extends [to everything] just as [His] knowledge does. The angels said, *Thou comprehendest all things in mercy and knowledge.*[115]

xiv) The *ḥadīth* which describes the intercession has been authentically narrated from the Prophet (may God bless him and grant him peace) [and includes]: 'My Lord is angry today in a way that He has never been before. He will never be as angry as that again.'[116] This explicitly states that this [His] wrath [on the Day of Judgment] will be great, but that it will not remain as such. It is well known that the denizens of Hellfire will enter it due to that wrath. Had that wrath perpetuated, then their punishment would have been eternal likewise as it is a consequence of that wrath. But when the Lord (Most Blessed and Exalted is He) becomes content and that wrath wanes, then its consequences also dissipate. In addition, the general punishments and afflictions of this world are consequences of His wrath. If His wrath continued, then those afflictions would so also. Yet, once He is content and His wrath wanes, those afflictions also dissipate, and are replaced by [the requisites of His] mercy.

xv) God's pleasure is more beloved to Him than His wrath, His pardoning is more beloved to Him than His penalty, His mercy is more beloved to Him than His punishment, and His bestowal of favours is more beloved to Him than His withholding. Wrath, penalty and withholding only occur because of causes that contravene the requisites of the former Attributes and Names. Just as God (Glory be to Him) loves His Names and Attributes, He loves their consequences and requisites. In [a number of] *ḥadīth*s [it is reported] that 'He is One and loves those who are first-rate';[117] 'He is beautiful and loves beauty';[118] 'He is pure and loves purity';[119] and 'He is the One Who pardons and loves those who pardon [others].'[120] He is also the One Who is thankful and loves those who are thankful, omniscient and loves those who are knowledgeable, magnanimous and loves those who are magnanimous, modest and veiled [by light] and loves those who are modest and cover themselves,[121] most patient and loves those who are patiently steadfast,[122] and merciful and loves those who are merciful. God dislikes everything that opposes those [characteristics].

Therefore, He dislikes disbelief, wickedness, disobedience, injustice and ignorance. God (Glory be to Him) only [ontologically] wills those [evil characteristics] because they [indirectly] result in what He loves and is pleased with. But once what He loves and His intended ultimate objectives are attained then there no longer remains any purpose for these [things which are disliked by Him], neither in and of themselves nor for other [reasons]. Thus, they vanish and are replaced by their opposites, which are beloved to the Sublime, and are the consequences of His Names and Attributes. One must understand the secret of this aspect. Otherwise, read again [points XIII through XV]. Do not be quick to dismiss this.

The secret of this matter is that God's being most wise and merciful—Glory be to Him—entails that He only creates for wise purposes and mercy. So those whom He punishes are punished for a wise purpose, and this proceeds as a requisite [of their sins]. This also occurs in this world's divinely-prescribed and determined punishments, which result [initially] in chastisement, correction and restraint; but then lead to mercy and kindness, which ultimately result in their souls becoming purified, righteous and freed from evil and wickedness.

Had the evil and unjust souls been returned to this world before being punished, they would have returned to what they were forbidden. They are not suitable to live in the abode of peace [i.e. Paradise] as it is incompatible with lies, denial, evils and injustices. But if these souls are punished in Hellfire such that they are expunged from their evils and wickedness, the wisdom of that would be considered reasonable. The creation of souls whose evilness never vanishes whatsoever, as they are pure evil and deserving of eternal and everlasting punishment, is not consistent with [His] wisdom and mercy, even if He is capable [of punishing the denizens eternally].

They [contend] that these are the conclusions derived from deep reflection. Many sages have thought hard about this [and now this group's arguments end].

I had asked the Shaykh of Islam [Ibn Taymiyya] (may God sanctify his spirit) [about this issue] and he responded, 'This is a great and major question,' but he did not elaborate any further. A period of time passed by until I read the exegesis of ʿAbd b. Ḥumayd al-Kashshī and found some of these traditions [of the Companions and Successors] that I have already mentioned. So I sent that book to him while he was in one of his last gatherings. I marked those places [in the book] and I told my messenger, 'Say to him, "There is some ambiguity and uncertainty herein."' So Ibn Taymiyya wrote his well-known work[123] on it (may God have mercy on him). Now, whoever possesses any further knowledge in this matter, let him provide it. Above every scholar is one who is more knowledgeable.

My position in this matter is the same as that of the Emir of the Believers ʿAlī b. Abī Ṭālib[124] (may God be pleased with him). He mentioned the entrance of the inhabitants of Paradise into Paradise and the denizens of Hellfire into Hellfire, and he described that in the best manner. Then he said, 'Thereafter God will do what He wills with His creation.'[125]

I also agree with the view of ʿAbd Allāh b. ʿAbbās (may God be pleased with him [and his father]) as he said, 'It is not proper for anyone to render a judgment in regards to God's creatures, and say who is deserving of Paradise or Hellfire.' He mentioned this when interpreting His statement, *He will say, Fire is your home. Abide therein for ever, save him whom God willeth.*[126]

I also agree with the view of Abū Saʿīd al-Khudrī as he said, 'All of the Qur'ān is qualified by this verse: *Thy Lord is doer of what He will.*'[127] I likewise agree with the view of Qatāda as he said, regarding His statement, *Save for that which thy Lord willeth,*[128] 'God is more knowledgeable about the interpretation of this.' I similarly agree with the view of [ʿAbd al-Raḥmān] ibn Zayd [b. Aslam] as he said, 'God informed us about what He wills for the inhabitants of Paradise when He said *a gift unfailing*;[129] but He did not inform us regarding His [ultimate] will for the denizens of Hellfire.'

The viewpoint that Hellfire and its punishment are eternal just as God is eternal represents a notification about what God (Almighty and Most Glorious is He) will do. If something is not concordant with what He has informed us, then it represents something that is said about Him without knowledge. The texts do not substantiate [the punishment of Hellfire being eternal], and God knows best.

Now, we will [briefly] consider some invalid views.[130] One [viewpoint according to some Israelites] is that [the disbelivers] will be punished in Hellfire for only as long as they remained in this world. [Ibn ʿArabī] claims that the Fire will subsequently be transformed; thus, the [disbelievers] will experience some type of pleasure therein just as one who has scabies takes comfort in scratching it. The position [of Jahm b. Ṣafwān] is that both [Hellfire] and Paradise will become annihilated. The doctrine [of Abū Hudhayl al-ʿAllāf] holds that movements within [Hellfire] will cease, and its denizens will remain there motionless for eternity.

Only the Companions (may God be pleased with them) and those who followed their path were guided to the truth. We ask God to grant us success.

If it is said, 'What is the wisdom in the disbelievers being more numerous than the believers, and the denizens of Hellfire being many times greater than the inhabitants of Paradise? The Exalted has said, *And though thou try much, most men will not believe*;[131] *few of My bondmen are thankful*;[132] *save such as believe and do good works, and they are few*;[133] and *if thou obeyedst most of those on earth they would mislead thee far from God's way*.[134] Those banished to Hellfire are 999 out of every 1000; only one will go to Paradise.[135] How can this arise from [One Whose] mercy is vast and supreme, and One Whose wisdom is far-reaching? Should not the matter have been the opposite?'

We respond that this question corroborates the viewpoint of the Companions and Successors regarding this issue [i.e. that the punishment of Hellfire will end], and that it all goes back to [His] mercy, which has encompassed everything, has preceded [His] anger, and will prevail over it[136]. In this regard, we can repudiate that question completely.

Had those who were faithful and righteous been the overwhelming majority, then the possibility of waging battle [in His path]—which is one of the most eminent types of worship—would have eluded us. The consequences and perfections that [the believers] accrue [from fighting] would also have been forgone. Therefore, there is nothing better than what the wisdom of the Most Wise has dictated.

CHAPTER EIGHT

A Response to Those Who Question God's Wisdom in Allowing His Enemies to Overpower His Saints

[POINTS 37–40]

POINT 37: Regarding their question, 'What is the wisdom in allowing His enemies to overpower over His saints, whereby they severely injure and torment them?' [we respond] that God possesses many dazzling wisdoms in that. Many things which are beloved to Him occur, whether it is worshipping [Him] through patience and fighting, bearing harm for His sake, being content with Him in ease and hardship, as well as remaining firm in worshipping and obeying Him despite the overwhelming strength and injurious nature of the opposition. By requiring them to sacrifice themselves for His sake [and endure] the harm that His enemies inflict upon them, His saints will be purified of the usual customs and natural dispositions characteristic of human beings. It will also differentiate the truthful one from the liar, and those who desire His [pleasure] and worship Him in all states from those who only worship Him in a corrupted fashion [i.e. only in good times].[1] It is also so that some may attain the level of martyrdom, which is one of the highest levels. Those who love Him consider nothing to be greater than sacrificing themselves out of love for Him in order to attain His pleasure, and to fight against His enemies.

Therefore, there are many blessings, mercies and wisdoms that God has in allowing this overpowering. If you want to understand this further, then deeply reflect on the verses towards the end of [Sūrat] Āl ʿImrān, beginning where He says, *Many were the ways of life that have passed away before you*;[2] and *It is only the Devil who would make (men) fear his partisans. Fear them not; fear Me, if ye are true believers;*[3] to finally *It is not (the purpose) of God to leave you in your present state till He shall separate the wicked from the good.*[4]

Had it not been for such overpowering, the virtue of patience, forgiveness, forbearing and suppressing one's anger would not have been manifested, nor would the sweetness of victory, triumph and conquering [been so enjoyable]. The beauty of things becomes manifest [when compared] to their opposites. Had it not been for that overpowering it would not have been necessary to vanquish, humiliate and subdue their enemies. Therefore, that overpowering [indirectly] brought about strength from His saints, which then resulted in them taking action. Due to that [strength and action] He deemed that they deserved to be honoured. As for His enemies, God deemed that they were deserving of His punishment [due to their injustice]. Thus, the [enemies'] overpowering allowed Him to manifest His wisdom, might, mercy and blessings upon both groups [respectively]. He is the Almighty, the Most Wise.

POINT 38: Regarding their statement, 'What is the wisdom in obligating humankind and jinn, and subjecting them to [the possibility] of punishment and various types of hardships?' [we respond]: Know that had it not been for obligations, the creation of humankind would have been in vain and aimless; God is exalted above doing that. He has declared Himself infallible from that, just as He has declared Himself infallible above any faults or deficiencies.

The Exalted said, *Deemed ye then that We had created you for naught, and that ye would not be returned unto Us?*[5] He also said, *Thinketh man that he is to be left aimless?*[6] Shāfiʿī[7] interpreted this as 'not being commanded nor forbidden'. It is obvious that abandoning humankind, such that they are not obligated [and will thus act] like animals, is contradictory to [His] wisdom. They were created for the purpose of [attaining] their perfection, which involves them acknowledging their Lord, loving Him and carrying out their duties to Him by worshipping Him [alone]. The Exalted said, *I created the jinn and humankind only that they might worship Me;*[8] *that ye may know that God is able to do all things, and that God surroundeth all things in knowledge;*[9] *that is so that ye may know that God knoweth whatsoever is in the heavens and whatsoever is in the earth, and that God is knower of all things.*[10]

This recognition and worship are the two ultimate objectives of His creation and commandments. They represent the ultimate perfection of humanity. God's divine providence and mercy for them (Exalted is He) gave them the opportunity [to achieve] this perfection, arranged for them these respective causes—whether apparent or hidden—and enabled them [to reach it].

Obligations revolve around Islam, faith (*īmān*) and devotion [to Him] (*iḥsān*). They all go back to being thankful for all [His] blessings both small and large, extolling Him and glorifying Him. We should conduct ourselves towards Him in a manner that befits Him: mentioning His blessings, showing gratitude to Him and not being ungrateful, obeying Him and not disobeying Him, and remembering Him and not being forgetful. The servant should also be characterized by every beautiful moral trait, which is affirmed with every beautiful action and right statement; and one should avoid every evil characteristic, and abandon every repugnant action or slanderous statement.

Our obligations to Him, therefore, encompass all of the noble characteristics, righteous actions and truthful statements, as well as being benevolent to the creation, perfecting oneself with all of these perfect traits, renouncing all that is in opposition to the above and being free [of evil]. He granted us through these obligations the opportunity to attain an eternal reward and proximity to the Lord in the everlasting abode.

Which of the two matters is more befitting to [His] wisdom: the aforementioned or leaving [humanity] neglected like horses, mules and donkeys only to eat, drink and reproduce? Has His perfect Holiness decreed that? *Now God be Exalted, the True King! There is no deity save Him, the Lord of the Throne of Grace.*[11] How is it fitting with His perfection that He end all commandments or prohibitions, rewards or punishments, forgo sending the messengers, revealing the Books, prescribing the Divine Law and establishing His rulings? Can those who permit what is contradictory to [His wisdom truly] know God? Does not that only indicate their false assumptions about Him? The Exalted said, *And they measure not the power of God its true measure when they say, God hath naught revealed unto a human being.*[12]

Deeming the goodness of obligations through rational thought is akin to declaring benevolence, granting blessings, favouring others and generosity to be good. Moreover, [obligations are] some of the greatest types of benevolence and blessings. It is for this reason that God (Glory be to Him) named [obligations] to be a *blessing*, *favour*, *grace* and *mercy*. He also informed us that the joy associated with [obligations] is better than any happiness resulting from a [material] blessing (which can be bestowed upon either those who are righteous or wicked). The Exalted said, *Hast thou not seen those who gave the grace of God in exchange for thanklessness.*[13]

God verily hath shown grace to the believers by sending unto them a messenger of their own who reciteth unto them His revelations, and causeth them to grow, and teacheth them the Book and wisdom; although before (he came to them) they were in flagrant error.[14] The Exalted also said, *He it is Who hath sent among the unlettered ones a messenger of their own, to recite unto them His revelations and to make them grow, and to teach them the Book and wisdom, though heretofore they were indeed in error manifest, along with others of them who have not yet joined them. He is the Almighty, the Most Wise. That is the bounty of God; which He giveth unto whom He will. God is of infinite bounty.*[15]

God also said, *We sent thee not save as a mercy for the peoples;*[16] *Say: In the bounty of God and in His mercy: therein let them rejoice. It is better than what they hoard;*[17] *This day have I perfected your religion for you and completed My favour unto you, and have chosen for you as religion—Islam;*[18] *Remember God's grace upon you and that which He hath revealed unto you of the Book and of wisdom, whereby He doth exhort you.*[19]

He also said, *And know that among you is God's Messenger: were he, in many matters, to follow your (wishes), ye would certainly fall into misfortune: But God has endeared the faith to you, and has made it beautiful in your hearts, and He has made hateful to you Unbelief, wickedness, and rebellion: such indeed are those who walk in righteousness. A grace and favour from God; and God is full of knowledge and wisdom.*[20] He said to His Messenger, *But for the grace of God upon thee (Muḥammad), and His mercy, a party of them had resolved to mislead thee, but they will mislead only themselves and they will hurt thee not at all. God revealeth unto thee the Book and wisdom, and teacheth thee that which thou knewest not. The grace of God towards thee hath been infinite.*[21]

Do not the obligations, their consequences and fruits—whether in the heart or the body both in this world and the Hereafter—represent the true blessings and grace? Do not sound rational thoughts and proper innate dispositions deem that to be consistent and fitting with the perfection of the Lord, His Names and Attributes?

POINT 39: The [Ashᶜariyya] contend that the debate between Ashᶜarī and Jubbā'ī regarding three [hypothetical] brothers—one of whom died as a child, the other grew up to be a disbeliever, while the third was a believer—sufficiently invalidates [the Muᶜtazilī notion that events occur in accordance with His] wisdom and causality, [only] so as to take care to provide what is most advantageous [for His servants by way of necessity for God].

By God, it only invalidates the ways of the heretics (*ahl al-bidᶜa*) from the Muᶜtazila and the Qadariyya, as they obligate their Lord to take care of what is most advantageous for every servant—however, it is more correct [to say] that it is only what they consider to be advantageous. They prescribe their own canonical laws based on their own reasoning, deny and forbid Him from [prescribing] anything outside of [their desires], and then they obligate Him to carry these out. They are the most foolish, as they denied Him His Attributes of perfection and His ability to act. They maintained that their man-made canonical laws were just and affirmed His Oneness, yet [in reality] their [doctrine] only represents slander and calumny [against God].

The [reality of ascribing] justice to God instead means that He carries out His actions righteously and equitably (*bi'l-qisṭ*), while [the reality of affirming] His Oneness should be to [characterize Him] with His perfect Attributes. *There is no deity save Him: That is the witness of God, His angels, and those endued with knowledge, standing firm on justice. There is no deity save Him, the Exalted in power, the Most Wise. The religion before God is Islam (submission to His will).*[22] This is the [true] meaning of His Oneness and justice, and it is what the messengers conveyed. On the other hand, those who stripped away [His Attributes misinterpreted] His Oneness and justice.

The point is that this debate [between Ashᶜarī and Jubbā'ī]—even if it invalidated the viewpoint of [the Muᶜtazila] and shook their fundamentals—does not negate God's wisdom. He possesses [the ultimate] wisdom and He has hidden it so that His creatures cannot encompass it [fully]. He has only made them privy to what is like a drop of water in an ocean.

God (Glory be to Him) has many wise purposes [in the case that this hypothetical example is true] for the one who died as a child, for the other whose lifespan was extended past puberty and was a Muslim, as well as for the last who remained alive past puberty but subsequently became a disbeliever. If everyone whom God knew was going to become a disbeliever after reaching puberty instead died as a child, then waging battle [in His path] and other types of worship that God loves and is pleased with would have become null. His signs and wonders would not have become manifest to all nations, nor would His events and days [of triumph] over His enemies. In addition, the evidences and arguments against the people of falsehood (*ahl al-bāṭil*) would not have become established so as to refute their ambiguous claims, or grant victory to the truth over falsehood, as well as the many other reasons and wisdoms that only God can recount.

God (Glory be to Him) loves to manifest His Names and Attributes amongst the creation. Had He brought about the death of everyone whom He knew would become a disbeliever after puberty then all of those [manifestations] would not have occurred. Forgoing them contradicts the perfect manifestation of those Names and Attributes as well as their requisite consequences. This was previously discussed in detail.

POINT 40: The [Ashᶜariyya and others] contend that the Sublime attributed all matters solely to His will. For example, [they refer to] His statements: *He punisheth whom He will and showeth mercy unto whom He will;*[23] *He will forgive whom He will and He will punish whom He will;*[24] *God verily sendeth whom He will astray, and guideth whom He will;*[25] and *He will not be questioned as to that which He doeth.*[26] Although all of these [verses] are true, is there contained therein any negation of His wisdom, His praiseworthiness and praiseworthy objectives that He intends through His actions? Furthermore, [where does it negate] that He does not carry out actions to result [either directly or indirectly] in others, that He does not command things for reasons, or that there are no reasons or ultimate objectives for His actions?

Do they think that those who affirm His wisdom and causality hold the view that He does not act through His will or that He can be questioned about that which He carries out? Instead, those [who affirm His wisdom and causality] state that He acts through His will in accordance with [His] wisdom and what is beneficial, and that He puts things in their proper places. The sovereignty is His alone, the Exalted Lord is the True King, and He alone is deserving of perfect praise. The fact that God does what He wills does not contradict that He acts utilizing causes for wise purposes, ultimate objectives and praiseworthy outcomes; but it also does not mean that He only wills through those means.

As for His statement, *He will not be questioned as to that which He doeth, but they will be questioned,*[27] this is due to the perfect nature of His knowledge and wisdom, not because they are not so. In addition, the context of the verse has another meaning, and that is negating divinity for all others besides God, while affirming divinity for Him alone. The Sublime said, *Or have they chosen gods from the earth who raise the dead? If there were therein gods beside God, then verily both (the heavens and the earth) had been disordered. Glorified be God, the Lord of the Throne, from all that they ascribe (unto Him). He will not be questioned as to that which He doeth, but they will be questioned.*[28] Where in this [verse] is causality negated in any aspect? But those who follow falsehood are fixated on substantiating their interpretations and false [doctrines] using allegorical phrases and meanings where the truth may bear a resemblance to falsity. But if one expounds on these in a detailed fashion and clarifies them, it becomes clear that they have no proof. It may even prove the opposite of what they intend. We depend on God for success.

CHAPTER NINE

An Exposition of the Statement of the Predecessors that One of the Principles of Faith is Contentment with Predestination, Whether Good or Evil, Pleasing or Painful

It was previously mentioned that [God's] determination involves no evil whatsoever from any aspect, since it involves God's knowledge, power, words and will, whereby all these are pure good and perfect from every aspect. Evil is not attributable to the Exalted Lord in any aspect—neither in His Essence, Names, Attributes nor actions. Relative evil is present in what is [ontologically] decreed and determined only in so far as its attachment and association is evil from one aspect, but good from another [preponderant aspect].

Examples of this include the retaliation and punishments for transgressions of legal limits or the killing of disbelievers. They are evil relative to them in some aspects but good in other ways, since they result in advantages such as deterring [the disbelievers], being an exemplary punishment, and [allowing the believers] to defend themselves against [the disbelievers].[1] Similarly, pains and diseases are harmful from some aspects but good from others. This was also discussed previously.

Good and evil are the same species as pleasure and benefit or pain and harm, respectively, but this only applies to what [He has] decreed and determined. It does not apply to the Attributes of the Lord Himself or His actions that He carries out. For example, cutting the hand of the thief is painful and harmful relative to him, but the Lord's [religious] decree and determination of that [punishment] is just, good, most wise and advantageous [in the larger context]. This will be discussed further in the next chapter, God willing.

If it is asked, 'What is the difference between the determination being good or evil or it being pleasing (*ḥilw*) or painful (*murr*)?' we reply that pleasure and pain involve our experiences due to causes in this immediate life, while good and evil describe the ultimate outcome [in the Hereafter]. It is either pleasing or painful initially and immediately, and either good or evil in the end as an ultimate outcome.

God's custom and methodology (Glory be to Him) is that those causes which are pleasing in this immediate [worldly life often] ultimately lead to painful [evil] outcomes in the Hereafter. On the other hand, those which are painful [in this life often] lead to pleasing [good] ends [in the Hereafter]. His decree and predestination are ordered in such a manner that nothing whatsoever occurs outside them.

The good that should be sought is the eternal pleasure, whereas the evil that should be feared is the enduring pain. The causes which lead to evil may involve some pleasure, and the causes which result in good may involve some pain. Pain followed by eternal pleasure is worthier to be preferred and faced than a pleasure which will be followed by enduring pain. The pleasure of one hour if compared to longstanding pain becomes as if it never existed. Likewise, the pain of one hour if compared to perpetual pleasure becomes as if that pain never occurred.

CHAPTER TEN

The Impermissibility of Stating that the Lord (Exalted is He) Intends Evil or Performs it

This is a point of disagreement between those who have affirmed His determination and those who have denied it [i.e. the Qadariyya]. The [Qadariyya] state [correctly] that it is not permissible to say that God (Glory be to Him) wills evil or performs it. They state, 'He does not intend or carry out evil, because the one who does so is evil. This is well known linguistically, rationally and in religious discourse. This is just like the oppressor is the one who carries out oppression, and the wicked one carries out wickedness and desires it. The Exalted Lord is infallible above all that, and His Names are free from any evil being attributable to them. All of His Names are good and all of His actions are good. It is impossible that He would will evil or carry it out. Evil does not occur by His will or action.' But the [Qadariyya] also claimed that the Sublime's actions are the same as what He enacts, and since His acts are not evil, then evil also cannot be enacted by Him; therefore, [in their opinion], evil is created by humans.

The Jabriyya countered by claiming, 'The Lord (Glory be to Him) wills evil and carries it out.' The [Jabriyya] stated that 'since evil exists, it is inevitable that there be someone to create it, and there is no Creator except God. God creates through His will, therefore every creature is willed by Him and is an act of His.' They agreed with the [claim of the Qadariyya] that an act is the same as what is enacted, and creating is the same as the creation. They claimed that since evil is a creation and an enactment of His, it therefore occurs by His acting, creating and willing. The [Jabriyya] also claimed that the only reason that it is not said explicitly that He wills or enacts evil is out of linguistic deference to Him. They consider this akin to not saying explicitly that 'He is the Lord of the dogs and pigs,' but instead stating that 'He is the Lord and Creator of everything.' The [Jabriyya finally] stated that evil actions do not subsist within the Lord's Essence. [In other words, according to them], His actions do not subsist within Him as they are the same as what He enacts; instead, they subsist within creatures.

Now, the correct viewpoint is that it is impermissible to generalize that He wills or performs evil, i.e. one should neither deny nor affirm that, because using the term 'wills' and 'performs' may either convey a false meaning or negate the correct meaning. That is because God's will (*irāda*) can be generalized to indicate the ontological will (*mashī'a*), or to mean love of (*maḥabba*) and pleasure with (*riḍā*) something. The former [i.e. ontological will] is exemplified by His statements: *If God's will is to keep you astray;*[1] *and whomsoever it is His will to send astray;*[2] *And when We would [will to] destroy a township.*[3] The second [religious meaning] is exemplified by His statements: *And God would [will to] turn to you in mercy;*[4] *God desireth for you ease;* and *He desireth not hardship for you.*[5] His [ontological] will results in the occurrence of what is willed, but it does not necessitate that He loves or is pleased with it. Whereas in the case [of the religious will], the occurrence of what He wishes may not necessarily occur even though He loves and is pleased with it [due to His wisdom and reasons elucidated previously].

Now, God's actions themselves (Glory be to Him) are not divided [into beloved or not], since all of His actions are beloved and pleasing to Him. Therefore, one must differentiate between His actions and what He enacts. His actions are all pure good, just, advantageous and wise—there is no evil within them from any aspect whatsoever. As for what He enacts, it is subject to division [into good or not]. Only Ahl al-Sunna confirms this viewpoint, i.e. an action is different than what is enacted, and creating is different than the creature. This is concordant with rational thought, the innate disposition, linguistics, the proofs of the Qur'ān and *Ḥadīth*, and the consensus of Ahl al-Sunna. Baghawī[6] mentioned this in [his book] *Sharḥ al-Sunna.*

Now we can see that there are two wills and two intents. There is [His] will to act, which results in His act that subsists in Him. The other is His will that His servant acts, and it represents what He enacts—this is detached from Him. These two are not necessary concomitants. God may wish that His servant acts [in accordance with His religious commandments], but not will that [1] He assist him and grant him success to accomplish that action or [2] that [He] dissipate the barriers which prevent [the servant] from doing so. God commanded Iblīs to prostrate to Adam, but He did not will that He assist [Iblīs], grant him success to accomplish that prostration, or strengthen his heart and turn him towards it. Had God willed these things, Iblīs would have inevitably prostrated [to Adam]. His statement, *Thy Lord is doer of what He will,*[7] notifies us of His will regarding His actions, and not the actions of His servants. This action and will of His cannot be subdivided into good and evil, as was mentioned above.

Now if it is said, 'He intends evil,' this may lead some to think that He loves it or is pleased with it. And if it is said, 'He does not intend [evil],' this may lead some to think that He did not create or originate it. Both of these interpretations are false. Likewise, if it is said, 'Evil is an action of His,' or that 'He performs evil,' this may lead some to think that evil is an action of His that subsists within Him—this is impossible. Or if it is said that 'He did not perform [evil]' or 'that [evil] is not an action of His,' this may lead some to think that He did not create or originate it, and this again is impossible.

Therefore, reflect on how, if these expressions are generalized, whether by one denying or affirming them they imply both truth and falsehood. This only becomes apparent after thorough examination and detailed inquiry. The truth in this matter is what has been pointed out in the Qur'ān and the Sunna: evil is not attributable to the Lord (Exalted is He)—neither as an attribute nor as an action [of His]. None of His Names are named in accordance with them in any aspect. Evil only pertains to what He enacts in a general manner (*bi-ṭarīq al-ʿumūm*). The Exalted said, *Say: I seek refuge in the Lord of the Daybreak. From the evil of that which He created.*[8] The word *mā* [translated as *which*] is either a conjunction or a relative pronoun. If it is a relative pronoun then it pertains to what He has enacted. The meaning is either: from the evil of what He has enacted or from the evil of what His creatures do.

Now the agent [of an action] can be omitted, as in His statement that relates what the jinn believers say: *And we know not whether harm is boded unto all who are in the earth, or whether their Lord intendeth guidance for them.*[9] Or evil may be ascribed to the place wherein it subsists. For example, God's friend Abraham said, *Who created me, and He doth guide me, and Who feedeth me and watereth me, and when I sicken, then He healeth me.*[10] Also, consider the statement of al-Khiḍr, *As for the ship, it belonged to poor people working on the river, and I wished to mar it.*[11] On the other hand, he said regarding the two young adults, *Thy Lord intended that they should come to their full strength.*[12]

All three types [i.e. omission of the agent's mention, and ascription of evil to the creature's actions or to the creature itself] were combined in Sūrat al-Fātiḥa when God said, *Show us the Straight Path, the path of those whom Thou hast favoured; Not the (path) of those who earn Thine anger nor of those who go astray.*[13]

God (Exalted is He) only attributes good to Himself—never evil. The Exalted said, *Say: O God! Owner of Sovereignty! Thou givest sovereignty unto whom Thou wilt, and Thou withdrawest sovereignty from whom Thou wilt. Thou exaltest whom Thou wilt, and Thou abasest whom Thou wilt. In Thy Hand is the good. Thou art able to do all things.*[14] Those who claim that both good and evil are in His Hand have erred for three reasons. Firstly, there is nothing in the expression that indicates that He wished [evil]. Instead, God intentionally left out mentioning it in order to make it clear that [evil] is not wished for. Secondly, only grace or justice are within God's Hand. This is shown in the authentic *ḥadīth* that the Prophet (may God bless him and grant him peace) said, 'The Right Hand of God is full, and its fullness is not affected by continuous expenditure night and day. Do you see what He has granted since He created the heavens and the earth? Yet all that bestowal has not decreased what is in His Right Hand... And in His other Hand is the balance—He lowers some and elevates others.'[15] Therefore, His grace is within His [Right] Hand, while justice is within the other. Both of them are good and there is no evil in them from any aspect. Thirdly, the Prophet said, 'Here I am at Your service, all goodness is in Your Hands. Evil cannot be attributed to you.'[16] This [*ḥadīth*] interprets the previous verse. The Prophet differentiated between good and evil, and made [good to be] within the Hand of the Lord (Glory be to Him). Conversely, the Prophet dissociated the attribution [of evil] to Him, despite affirming in general that His [enacted] creation includes both.

Now, the Exalted Lord's Names are derived from His Attributes and actions—they are not derived from what He has created. Every Name of His is derived from one of His Attributes or an action that He performs. Had a Name of His been derived by taking into consideration His creation, who are distinct from Him, then He would have been deemed to be a created thing: moving, motionless, tall, white or otherwise, just because He is the Creator of these characteristics. Since He is not named with any of those—despite the fact that He created them—it becomes known that His Names are derived from His actions and Attributes that subsist within Him. God (Glory be to Him) is not characterized by anything which is created and distinct from Him, nor is He named with any of the characteristics [of the creatures].

Some of those who derive His Names, actions or Attributes from those of His creatures claim, in essence, that nothing subsists within Him, whether it be justice, beneficence, words, will or any action whatsoever. Those who [adopted the doctrine of the Jahmiyya] have denied the essence of His Attributes saying, 'No real Attributes subsist within Him.' Therefore, they have denied and stripped away His Attributes or derived them [from His creatures]; and they have denied His actions and attributed them instead to [His] works and creatures. The reality of their doctrine is that the Exalted's Names become expressions that are devoid of any meaning or reality. This is blasphemy. Furthermore, [this doctrine] denies that [His Names] are the most beautiful.

The Exalted has said, *The most Beautiful Names belong to God: so call on Him by them; but shun such men as use profanity in his Names: for what they do, they will soon be requited.*[17] The Qur'ān and the Sunna have established that the origin (*maṣdar*) of His Names is found in

His Attributes; and examples establishing them include the Exalted's [following] statements: *Power belongeth wholly to God;*[18] *God! He it is that giveth livelihood, the Lord of unbreakable might;*[19] and *Then know that it is revealed only in the knowledge of God.*[20]

The Prophet (may God bless him and grant him peace) said, 'The splendour of His Countenance would burn all of His creation as far as His sight reaches.'[21] ʿĀ'isha said, 'Praise be to God Whose hearing encompasses all sounds.'[22] The Prophet also said, 'O God, I seek refuge in Your pleasure from Your wrath';[23] 'I ask You by virtue of Your knowledge of the Unseen, Your [vanquishing] power over all Your creation [and Your ability to create]';[24] and 'O God, I seek refuge in Your glory (*ʿizza*) from You sending me astray.'[25]

Had it not been for these origins [and manifestations] then His Names, Attributes and actions would have become dissociated from any real meaning. It [should be recognized that] His actions are distinguished from His Attributes, and His Names are distinguished from His actions or Attributes. However, if actions or attributes do not subsist in Him, then there is no meaning to the Name itself. Claiming so [as the Jahmiyya do] is the ultimate form of blasphemy (*ghāyat al-ilḥād*).

CHAPTER ELEVEN

An Exposition of the Secrets within the *Ḥadīth* of the Prophet, 'O God, I Seek Refuge in Your Pleasure from Your Wrath, and in Your Forgiveness from Your Punishment. I Seek Refuge in You from Yourself. I Cannot Praise You Enough; You are as You Have Praised Yourself'

This eminent and great *ḥadīth*[1] indicates many things. To begin with, one should seek refuge in and assistance through the Attributes of the Lord (Exalted is He) just as one does with His Essence. This is also indicated by another *ḥadīth*: 'O Ever-Living; O Self-Subsisting (*Qayyūm*); O Originator of the heavens and the earth; O Almighty and Most Generous (*dhā al-Jalāl wa'l-Ikrām*), there is no deity worthy of worship but You, through Your mercy I seek Your assistance, [so please] make all of my affairs good. Never forsake me to myself or to any of Your creation—not even for a moment.'[2]

A further *ḥadīth* [of the Prophet] is similar: 'I seek refuge with Your glory from You sending me astray.'[3] The Prophet also sought refuge with the perfect words of God[4], with His beneficent Countenance, and with His Exalted [Essence]. The aforementioned are proof that [His] Attributes are eternally existent, since one cannot seek refuge with something that is non-existent [or created]. [His Attributes] subsist within Him and are not created, since one cannot [in a religious sense] seek refuge with a creature. This is valid as the Messenger of God (may God bless him and grant him peace) never sought refuge with or assistance from a creature [in religious matters], nor did he ever advise his Community to do so.

The first *ḥadīth* also indicates that forgiveness is an action and

Attribute of His that subsists within Him. Therein is another response to those who claim that His actions are the same as what He enacts. Yet what is enacted is created, and it is not permissible to seek refuge in [something created].

It also indicates that some of the Sublime's Attributes and actions are superior (*afḍal*) to others. The Attribute that we seek refuge in is superior to the Attribute of His which we seek refuge from. Therefore, His Attribute of mercy is superior to wrath, and it is for that reason that the former prevails over and overcomes the latter. In addition, God's words (Glory be to Him) are Attributes of His. It is well known that His words by which He praises Himself and mentions His Attributes and Oneness are superior to His words by which He criticizes His enemies or mentions their characteristics. For this reason, Sūrat al-Ikhlās [CXII] is superior to Sūrat Tabbat [CXI], and the former is equivalent to one third of the Qur'ān.[5] Also, the Verse of the Throne (*āyat al-kursī*)[6] is the greatest one in the Qur'ān. Do not listen to those who [have little understanding] and are veiled away [from the truth] who state that because all of His Attributes are eternal one cannot be deemed to be superior to another. The transmitted and rational proofs all invalidate that claim.

God (Glory be to Him) has [created] those who are virtuous, those whom He has graced and bestowed goodness unto, and those who are blissful [through the grace of] what is within His Right Hand. Conversely, He [created] those whom He will manifest His justice and deprive through His other Hand. He has placed those who are blissful within the grasp of His Right Hand, whereas those who are wretched are in the grasp of His other Hand. Furthermore, the righteous and just are on pillars of light to His right. The heavens are folded up in His Right [Hand], and the earth is in His other Hand.[7]

In addition, the first *ḥadīth* indicates that since His pleasure and wrath, as well as forgiveness and punishment, are paired [Attributes], one should seek refuge with the former [Attribute] from the latter. But when it came to His Holy Essence, which is not paired or associated with another, the Prophet said, 'I seek refuge in You from Yourself.' This perfectly affirms His Oneness and determination with the shortest and most succinct expression.

Evil and its causes, which one seeks refuge from, all occur by the Exalted Lord's [ontologic] decree and determination. God alone creates, determines and originates. Whatever He wills exists, and whatever He does not will does not exist. What one seeks refuge from is either [1] an Attribute of His [associated with His justice], [2] an action of His [due to His justice], or [3] what He has enacted, as it is a consequence of His action. What [He] has enacted possesses no benefit or harm except by His permission, as He is its Creator. The Exalted has confirmed this regarding the most harmful thing to a person—namely magic: *They injure thereby no-one save by God's leave.*[8]

What one seeks refuge from can only occur by [the permission of] His will, His [ontologic] decree and determination. God's protection of a person and riddance of [evil] away from him also occurs by His will, decree and determination. Therefore, God grants refuge from His decree by His decree, [and refuge] from the manifestation of His will and wish by the dictate of His will and wish. Everything occurs by virtue of His ontological and determined will. Ultimately, everything is created, determined and decreed by Him. In addition, God is the One Who gives refuge to His servant from Himself by Himself.

A person also seeks refuge from sins and their punishment or pain, as well as their causes. Causes occur by His decree, effects occur by His decree, and seeking refuge from them is by His decree. Therefore, God is the One Who gives refuge from His decree by His decree. God predestined that [the sinner fated to repent] would seek refuge in Him, and [He] willed it. He also predestined that He would grant [that individual] protection and willed it. Everything necessarily occurs by His decree, predestination and will.

Had any other person besides the Messenger stated this [*ḥadīth*] then one who is ignorant would have denied and rejected [its realities]. God alone possesses benefit or harm, the ability to create and command, as well as the [power to] grant refuge. Whatever is being-sought-refuge-from is in His Hands, under His disposal, and something created.

This is similar to the Prophet's saying in another *ḥadīth*, 'There is no refuge or safe haven from You except with You.'[9] God is the

One Who grants safe haven from Himself by Himself. He is the One Who gives refuge from Himself by Himself. Likewise, His servant flees away from Him to Him.

This all represents an affirmation of His Oneness and determination, and that there is no other lord or creator besides Him. Moreover, creatures do not possess any [ability to independently bring about] harm or benefit, or any such ability to bring about death, life or resurrection. Instead, all matters return back to God alone, and no else has any part in them whatsoever. The Exalted said to the most distinguished and beloved to Him of His creation, *It is no concern at all of thee (Muḥammad).*[10] He also responded to those who asked, *Have we any part in the cause*, by saying, *The cause belongeth wholly to God.*[11] All sovereignty is His, all matters return back to Him, all praise is due to Him, all intercession is His, and all goodness is in His Hands. This represents affirmation of the fact that He alone is the Lord and God; there is no other deity or lord besides Him.

Say: Bethink you then of those ye worship beside God, if God willed some hurt for me, could they remove from me His hurt; or if He willed some mercy for me, could they restrain His mercy? Say: God is my all. In Him do (all) the trusting put their trust;[12] *If God touch thee with affliction, there is none that can relieve therefrom save Him, and if He touch thee with good fortune (there is none that can impair it); for He is able to do all things;*[13] *That which God openeth unto humankind of mercy none can withhold it; and that which He withholdeth none can release thereafter. He is the Almighty, the Most Wise.*[14]

No one can bring about righteous deeds but Him, and no one can absolve sins but Him. The movement of anything the size of an atom or greater cannot occur except by His permission. Furthermore, poison or magic, a demon or an animal cannot cause harm except by His permission and will. He allows it to afflict those whom He wills, and averts it away from those whom He wills.

Finally, the Prophet concluded the supplication by saying, 'I cannot praise You enough; You are as You have praised Yourself.' This represents an acknowledgement that His Essence, exaltedness and perfect Attributes are greater and more glorious than can be recounted by any [of His] creatures. Nor can anyone truly praise God as He can (Glory be to Him). This [section of the *ḥadīth*] represents the Oneness of His Names, Attributes and Characteristics (*nuʿūt*). The prior [section] establishes the Oneness of God, Whom we must worship and deify. It also establishes that only the Exalted should be feared and sought hope from or refuge in. The opposite [of His Oneness] is polytheism and the opposite of [His Beautiful Names and exalted Attributes] is stripping Him of them. We ask God for success.

CHAPTER TWELVE

Faith in the Divine Determination and Decree, His Justice, Monotheism and His Wisdom are All Included in the Prophet's *Ḥadīth*, 'Your Judgment upon me Will be Carried Out, and Your Decree for me is Just'

It has been reported that the Prophet (may God bless him and grant him peace) said, 'If a servant is afflicted with any type of distress (*hamm*), sorrow (*ghamm*) or grief (*ḥuzn*) but then says, "O God, I am Your servant, the son of Your two servants. My forelock is in Your Hand, Your judgment upon me will be carried out, and Your decree for me is just. I ask You by every Name that You have named Yourself with, or have revealed in Your Book, or have taught any of Your creation, or have kept hidden within Your knowledge of the Unseen, that You make the Qur'ān the life of my heart, the light of my chest, relief from my grief, and deliverance from my distress and sorrow." At that point, God will deliver him from his distress and sorrow, and replace them with happiness.'[1]

This authentic *ḥadīth* proves many things. Firstly, it includes the types of hardships encountered by the heart. Distress occurs in anticipation of a hardship that may occur in the future, and it preoccupies the heart. Grief occurs as a result of a past hardship, whether the loss of a beloved or the occurrence of a disliked entity. Sorrow occurs as a result of some hardship that is occurring in the present. These three represent some of the greatest diseases and ailments of the heart.

Every individual attempts to rid himself of the aforementioned by using whatever [means] he assumes or imagines will work. Most of the ways and treatments which people use to rid themselves of them instead only make those diseases stronger. For example, a person who tries to cure himself with a variety of sins, whether they are major or minor; or like a person who uses distractions, games, singing, listening to music, etc. as a cure. Most people—if not all—use these methods to rid themselves of those [diseases]. But they have tried the wrong methods.

Only those who try to remove them with the medicine which God has prescribed [are successful]. This medicine is composed of many components; whenever one of those parts is deficient then the cure is deficient to a similar degree. The greatest component of that medicine is worshipping God alone and asking for [His] forgiveness. The Exalted said, *So know (O Muḥammad) that there is no deity save God, and ask forgiveness for thy sin and for believing men and believing women.*[2] Then within the text of one tradition, Satan says, 'I have destroyed the progeny of Adam by [whispering to] them to sin, but they have ruined my [plans] by asking for forgiveness and by [saying] there is no deity [worthy of worship] but God. Once I saw that, I spread amongst them whims [and blameworthy innovations] such that they sin but do not ask for forgiveness, because they think that they are doing good deeds.'[3] Therefore, such people [are in a state of] sin yet do not repent as they think that they are doing good deeds [with that behaviour].

For that reason, the supplication that relieves one of calamities includes pure monotheism, namely 'There is no deity except God, the Great (*al-ʿAẓīm*), the Forbearing. There is no deity except God, the Lord of the great Throne. There is no deity except God, the Lord of the seven heavens, the Lord of the earth, the Lord of the mighty Throne.'[4] The Prophet (may God bless him and grant him peace) referred to the supplication of his brother Dhū al-Nūn [i.e. Jonah], saying, 'There is no one who is afflicted by a calamity and supplicates with [the following verse] except that God delivers him from that calamity: *There is no deity save Thee. Be Thou Glorified! Lo! I have been a wrongdoer.*'[5] Therefore, the servant's declaration of God's Oneness endears him to God. Seeking forgiveness and repenting removes impediments and unveils one's heart; thus, allowing one to become proximate to God. Once that occurs, the heart's distress, sorrow and grief vanish. But if the heart is cut-off from Him then it is barraged from all directions by distress, sorrow and grief. For this reason, truly recognizing one's servitude to Him, acknowledging His signs, and using the supplication [within the *ḥadīth*] all lead to deliverance from distress, sorrow and grief.

The Prophet included within this [supplication] his recognition that he is under God's power, kingdom and administration [when he said], 'My forelock is in Your Hand.' An individual who is led by a very strong being holding onto his forelock is unable to do anything but follow.

Then the Prophet followed that by affirming that God's judgments will occur and be carried out whether one agrees with them or not. If He [ontologically] rules something to be then no one can repel [that judgment] whatsoever. This, then, represents one's recognition of the Lord's omnipotence, as well as one's utter incapacity and weakness.

After that the Prophet followed on with his recognition that every judgment and decree of the Judge's will is purely just—it is absolutely devoid of oppression or injustice. He said, 'Your judgment upon me will be carried out, and Your decree for me is just.' This is general to every decree of the Sublime upon His servant, whether before his existence, during his life, after his death, or on the Day of Judgment. It also includes God's [ontological] decree for one's sins, and His recompense for them. Whoever's heart experiences unease in this regard—as in [failing to] recognize this as a necessary type of knowledge (*al-ʿilm al-ḍarūrī*)—then he does not [truly] understand his Lord and His perfection, the justice of His rulings, nor himself and his deficiencies. Instead, this person remains ignorant and unjust, lacking in [both] knowledge and balance.

In addition, the [Prophet's] statement, 'Your judgment upon me will be carried out, and Your decree for me is just,' represents a rebuttal to both the Qadariyya and Jabriyya. Even if they pay lip service to these principles, their doctrines contradict them. The Qadariyya deny the Sublime's ability to create that which allows the servant to become guided, except for that which He had initially endowed him with. Therefore, their doctrine does not acknowledge God's power over His servant beyond the Divine Law.

It is well known that it is incorrect to interpret this *ḥadīth* [in the manner of the Qadariyya]. Sometimes the servant obeys Him and sometimes disobeys Him [from a religious standpoint]. On the other hand, an ontologically-decreed ruling will be carried out inevitably; it is established upon the servant via His perfect (*tāmmāt*) words, which neither a righteous nor wicked person can escape.

His statement thereafter, 'Your decree upon me is just,' is proof that God (Glory be to Him) is just in all His [ontological] decrees for His servants, whether good or harmful, pleasurable or painful, as well as His recompense for them. The *ḥadīth* proves that [it is necessary] to have faith in His determination, and that God's decree is just. The first represents His Oneness and the second represents [His] justice.

The Qadariyya deniers claim that He would be unjust in allowing people to go astray and to consequently punish them had His judgments been predestined. As for the Jabriyya who espouse divine compulsion, they do not consider injustice to be real. Instead, [they consider] it to be essentially impossible and not within His power. They do not believe that the Exalted Lord is capable of carrying out anything called injustice. Therefore, they claim that it cannot be said that He refrained from injustice or acted with justice. According to their doctrine, there is no benefit to [the Prophet's] saying, 'Your decree upon me is just.' Instead, [they claim] it is like one saying, 'Your decree will occur without a doubt.' This [statement] is, however, the same as [what has preceded] in the [*ḥadīth*]: 'Your judgment upon me will be carried out.' Hence, [in their estimation] the latter represents a repetition of the former and has no benefit.

Likewise, according to the doctrine [of the Jabriyya] God is not praiseworthy for abandoning injustice, since one is not laudable for abandoning something that is essentially impossible for one to do in the first place. Moreover, there is no meaning [in their doctrine] to the [*ḥadīth qudsī* that says] 'I have forbidden Myself from carrying out injustice.'[6] The [Jabriyya] consider the meaning of it to be that He has forbidden Himself from doing something impossible and outside of His power.

There is also no benefit [in their doctrine] to His statement [that the servant] *feareth not injustice nor begrudging (of his wage)*,[7] since [they contend that] he should not be fearful of [being treated] unjustly because it is essentially impossible [for God] to do so. There is also no benefit [in their doctrine] to His [following] statements: *God willeth no injustice for (His) servants*;[8] and *I am in no wise a tyrant unto the servants*.[9]

[The correct viewpoint] is that the administration of His judgments upon His servants is within His power; and His justice occurs in a manner concordant to His praiseworthiness. God (Glory be to Him) is the King, and He is praiseworthy and omnipotent.

A similar statement [to the *ḥadīth*] is the statement which the Sublime relays from His Prophet Hūd (may God grant him peace), *I have put my trust in God, my Lord and your Lord. Not an animal but He doth grasp it by the forelock! My Lord is on a straight path.*[10] When Hūd says, *Not an animal but He doth grasp it by the forelock*, it is like the [Prophet Muḥammad's] statement, 'My forelock is in Your Hand, Your judgment upon me will be carried out.' Whereas when Hūd says, *My Lord is on a straight path*, it is like the [Prophet Muḥammad's] statement, 'Your decree for me is just.' This indicates that God does not treat us except in a manner which is just, most wise, beneficial and merciful. He is never unjust to anyone, nor does He punish anyone for something that they have not done, nor does He withhold [the reward] for any of one's righteous deeds.[11]

God (Glory be to Him) is on the Straight Path both in His statements and in His actions. He states the truth and acts in accordance with what is good and righteous. The Sublime has notified us that He is on the Straight Path in both Sūrat Hūd and Sūrat al-Naḥl. He informed us in the former[12] that He is on the Straight Path in regards to His administration, while in the latter[13] He notified us that He commands that which is just and that His actions are also [just].

The Jabriyya have claimed that all that is predestined [including the sins of humanity] is just, while the Qadariyya claimed that only if the angels, jinn and humans are allowed to act outside [the constraints of] His determination and creation is it just. Both groups are wrong. The correct viewpoint is that justice refers to treating things appropriately, and injustice is treating something inappropriately. God (Glory be to Him) named Himself the Just Ruler (*al-Ḥakam al-ʿadl*).

The Qadariyya deny the reality of the His Name, the Ruler. They claim it only concerns judgments in His Divine Law. They think that they are affirming the true meaning of [His] justice, but this leads them to deny His determination. Moreover, they have attributed to Him the ultimate in injustice, as they claim that He will eternally punish in Hellfire [Muslim believers] who spent all of their lives obeying Him but then perpetrated one major sin and died.

Should it be asked, 'If His decree of recompense is just—since it represents punishment for the sin—then how can the [ontological] decree for that sin be just according to the doctrine of Ahl al-Sunna?' [Then know that] this question does not pertain to the Qadariyya or Jabriyya, since the former's view is that He never decrees a sin, while the latter hold that everything that is decreed is just. Therefore, this question only pertains to us [the Ahl al-Sunna].

The response is: Yes, all of His decrees regarding His servants are just. He has treated them appropriately—any other way would not be deemed to be appropriate. He has punished appropriately and placed the [ontological] decree [of the sin] concordantly. Therefore, the cause and effect are put in their appropriate places. Just as the Sublime recompenses one with punishment, He punishes one with the [ontological] decree of a sin. His judgment of that sin [as being appropriate to a person] represents a punishment for a prior sin [that the individual has done]: sins amass more sins. The prior sin represents a punishment for one's heedlessness and turning away from his Lord. This heedlessness and turning away is a result of one's nature (*jibilla*) and upbringing (*nash'a*).

If God wishes to perfect someone He will bring his heart closer to Him, endear him to Him, inspire him with righteous conduct, and imbue him with the causes leading to goodness. On the other hand, He will forsake those whom He does not want to perfect, will stamp [their hearts], and leave them to themselves [and their temptations], because they are not suitable or appropriate for perfection nor will they even accept goodness. Here ends people's [ability] to understand His predestination.

As for the fact that God (Exalted is He) has made some suitable and has given them what is good for them, whereas [He has deemed] others not suitable, and therefore has withheld from them what is not appropriate for them, this is all a consequence of His lordship and divinity, knowledge and wisdom. God (Glory be to Him) is the Creator of all things and their opposites; [His creating] is a requisite of His perfection and a manifestation of His Names and Attributes. This was previously discussed.

The point is that God is the Most Just in what He decreed, whether it is causes or effects. His decree upon His servants only occurs appropriately—any other decree would not be appropriate. He is the Ruler Who is Just, Self-Sufficient and Most Praiseworthy.

The [Prophet's statement], 'I ask You by every Name of Yours that You have named Yourself with, or have revealed in Your Book, or have taught any of Your creation, or have kept hidden within Your knowledge of the Unseen'—if this narration is recorded [correctly] as such then there is an obscurity (*ishkāl*). God has made [the Names] which He revealed in His Book, taught some of His creation or kept hidden within His knowledge of the Unseen as subsets to the Names He has named Himself with.

Nonetheless, this *ḥadīth* proves that the Names of God are not created, as He has spoken them and named Himself with them. For this reason, the Prophet did not say, 'Every Name that You have created for Yourself.' In addition, had His Names been created the Prophet would not have supplicated Him using them, since it is not permissible for a person to supplicate [in the name of] something created. Thus, this *ḥadīth* clearly proves that His Names are not derived from human attempts to name them as such. Instead, His Names are derived from His Attributes; and since His Attributes are eternal and self-subsisting, His Names are not created.

Now some claim that although God (Glory be to Him) is eternal, He was without some Name until He created for Himself that Name, or until His creation named Him with that Name—this is one of the greatest blasphemies and heresies. The Prophet did not say [regarding His Names], 'That You have created for Yourself,' nor 'that which Your creation have named You with'. Instead, the

Prophet said, 'That You have named Yourself with.' This is proof that the Sublime spoke that Name and named Himself with it, just as He has named Himself in His Books, which He spoke [to the messengers].

The [Prophet's] statement, 'Or have kept hidden within Your knowledge of the Unseen,' is a proof that the number of His Names is greater than ninety-nine, and that God has Names and Attributes that He has hidden in the knowledge of the Unseen—no one else but Him knows these. The *ḥadīth* [that says], 'God has ninety-nine Names—whoever memorizes them will enter Paradise,'[14] does not negate that He has other [Names]. This is the opinion of the consensus. Only Ibn Ḥazm[15] disputed this by claiming that His Names are limited [to ninety-nine].

The *ḥadīth* also proves that supplicating to God (Glory be to Him) by using His Names and Attributes is more beloved to Him and more beneficial to the servant than supplicating to Him by using what He has created; and there are many other *ḥadīth*s which indicate the same. For example, consider the *ḥadīth* which refers to His greatest Name (*ism Allāh al-aʿẓam*): 'O God, I ask You because You are the One worthy of praise. There is no deity besides You, the Benefactor, the Originator of the heavens and the earth. O Almighty and Most Generous! O Ever-Living! O Self-Subsisting!'[16]

In another *ḥadīth* [we read], 'O God, I ask You by virtue of Your being God, the One (*al-Aḥad*), the Self-Sufficient Master (*al-Ṣamad*), Who begets not nor was begotten, and there is none co-equal or comparable to Him.'[17] Then in another *ḥadīth*, 'I ask You by virtue of Your knowledge of the Unseen, Your [vanquishing] power over all Your creation [and Your ability to create].'[18] All of the aforementioned are in accordance with the Exalted's statement, *The most Beautiful Names belong to God: so call on Him by them.*[19]

The [Prophet's] statement, 'That You make the Qur'ān the life (*rabīʿ*) of my heart and the light of my chest', combines two principles: life and light. The [literal meaning] of *rabīʿ* is 'the rain that brings the earth back to life and makes plants grow forth'. Therefore, the Prophet is supplicating to God by recognizing: [1] his servitude to Him; [2] his worship of Him alone; and [3] His Names and

Attributes. The Prophet is [requesting God] to allow His Book—which He rendered a spiritual guide to all of humankind—to result in a [spiritual] life for his heart. This is akin to how God has made water bring the earth back to life, and made the sun light up the earth. Life and light are the sum total of all that is good.

The Exalted said, *Is he who was dead and We have raised him unto life, and set for him a light wherein he walketh among men, as him whose similitude is in utter darkness whence he cannot emerge?*[20] The Exalted also said, *And thus have We inspired in thee (Muḥammad) a spirit of Our command. Thou knewest not what the Book was, nor the Faith. But We have made it a light whereby We guide whom We will of Our bondmen.*[21] Thus, God informed us that [His Book] is a *spirit* resulting in a [religious] life and a [spiritual] light leading to guidance. On the other hand, those who reject it are [spiritually] dead and astray.

God has made a similitude for both His saints and His enemies through these two principles in the beginning of Sūrat al-Baqara,[22] in the middle of Sūrat al-Nūr[23] and in Sūrat Hūd.[24] This includes the similitudes of water and fire.

The [Prophet's] statement, 'Relief from my grief, and deliverance from my distress and sorrow,' [calls for a] deliverance that encompasses the removal of that which is harmful, thus leading to that which is beneficial and joyful. In conclusion, this *ḥadīth* includes supplicating for all sources of good, and repelling all that is evil. We ask God for success.

CHAPTER THIRTEEN

The Rulings Regarding Contentment with His Decree and the Correct Position

This chapter concerns attainment of complete faith in His decree and predestination. Scholars have differed on whether it is obligatory or preferable. Some Ḥanbalīs feel that it is obligatory, arguing that it is a necessary concomitant of being content with God as their Lord, which itself is obligatory. They used an Israelite tradition as evidence: 'Whoever is not content with My decree and is not patient after My afflictions should follow another lord besides Me.'[1]

Others have felt that it is preferable since deeming something to be obligatory requires evidence from the Divine Law, and there is no proof in this case that renders it so. This latter opinion is preponderant, since being content is part of devotion (*iḥsān*), which itself is one of the highest levels [of faith].

Two groups, though, have rendered repugnant viewpoints in this matter. The Qadariyya deniers have claimed that since sins are not included within His decree and predestination [not even ontologically] it is not permissible to be content (*riḍā*) with them. On the other hand, the Jabriyya heretics, [who espouse divine compulsion] and have denied His commandments and prohibitions, have claimed that because sins are within God's decree and predestination, and since being content with His decree is a form of proximity and obedience to Him, one should be content with [sins] and not be displeased by them.

Those who affirm [His decree and predestination] have differed in their response to the [Qadariyya and Jabriyya]. One group said that there are two aspects [to any sin]. First is the aspect that one must be content with, which is the fact that God (Glory be to Him) has created and willed it. The other aspect should be detested, which is the servant's action and acquisition. This would have been a good response had they followed through appropriately. But acquisition, as affirmed by many of them, has no basis in reality. They consider it to be the association of the action with one's will and power, despite the fact that the latter are not effective.

Another group has responded to the [Qadariyya and Jabriyya] saying that they accept the decree, since it is an action of the Lord, but they detest what is decreed as regards the action of the servant. This is also a good response, but they followed it with inconsistencies and invalidities. They claimed that an action (*fiʿl*) is the same as what is enacted (*mafʿūl*) and that the decree is the same as what is decreed. Had the first group maintained that acquisition has an effect and is a cause for the existence of an action, and had the latter group maintained that [the Lord's] action is different than what is enacted, then both groups would have responded correctly.

A [third] group responded that we are commanded to be content with some decrees, but are prohibited from being content with others. In other words, we should be content with decrees which God loves and is pleased with, but not content with those which He hates and is angered by. This is similar to the fact that He hates and is angered by some creatures even though He is their Creator. This can be extrapolated to actions and statements also. While it is also a good response, it needs more [clarification] in order to become complete.

We say that there are two types of [God's] decrees: religious (*dīnī*) and ontological (*kawnī*). We are obligated to be content with the religious [decrees], and one can only be considered to be a Muslim if one does so. As for the ontological [decree], we should be content with and thankful for some of them, like blessings. In fact, being completely thankful for one's [blessings] requires contentment. On the other hand, it is impermissible to be content with some [ontological decrees], such as sins or faults, which God is angered by—even if they occur by His decree and predestination. Finally, it is preferable to be content with some [ontological decrees] like hardships.

The above concerns contentment with His decree, and what is decreed. Since [His] decree is a [manifestation of His] Attributes or actions—like His knowledge, Book, determination or will—contentment with them represents one's perfect contentment with God as one's Lord (*Rabb*), Deity (*Ilāh*), Sovereign Owner (*Mālik*) and Administrator (*Mudabbir*). Through this explanation the truth becomes clear and the ambiguity is resolved in this great topic.

If it is asked, 'How can contentment with His decree of hardships be reconciled with our intense hatred of them and [desire] to flee away from them? And how can the servant be obligated to be content with something that is painful and disliked to him? Indeed, experiencing pain denotes our dislike and hatred of that entity by necessity, and these two are the opposites of contentment. It is impossible to reconcile two opposites.'

The response is that something can be beloved and pleasing from one aspect, yet disliked from another. An example is taking a bitter yet beneficial medicine—the patient is content with it even though he has an intense dislike for it. Another example is fasting on a day that is extremely hot—the one who fasts is content with it even though he dislikes it. Or consider the waging of battle against the enemies [of God], about which the Exalted said, *Warfare is ordained for you, though it is hateful unto you; but it may happen that ye hate a thing which is good for you, and it may happen that ye love a thing which is bad for you.*[2] The person who sincerely engages in waging battle knows that it is better for him, and therefore he is content with it. At the same time, he dislikes it since it exposes him to [the possibility] of death, pain and being separated from those who are beloved to him. But once his contentment with something is strengthened and firmly rooted, then his dislike morphs into love even though [the possibility of] encountering pain remains. Experiencing pain does not contradict being content with such [trials]. In addition, experiencing dislike does not contradict love, from one aspect; and from another aspect, it does not contradict contentment.

If it is said that the aforementioned concerns the contentment of the servant with the decree of the Lord, [some ask], 'Can it be said that God (Glory be to Him) is content with what He has decreed of disbelief, wickedness and sinfulness from any aspect?' We respond: This topic is more controversial than what has preceded. Most, if not all, of the Ashᶜariyya have said that the Lord's pleasure, love and will are congruent, i.e. everything that He has willed and intended are beloved and pleasing to Him. They said, 'It is not impermissible to say that He is pleased with them [disbelief, etc.], but one should not single them out specifically.' Instead, [the Ashᶜariyya claim] that it should be said, 'He is content with everything that He has created, decreed and determined, but [specific] matters, which are blameworthy, should not be mentioned.' It is similar to when others say, 'He is the Lord of everything,' but never say [in particular] that 'He is the Lord of such-and-such despicable or vile things.' Therefore, they explicitly state that He is content with those specific things, yet it is impermissible to mention such out of respect and in deference to Him.

If [some of the Ashᶜariyya] are asked about God's statement, *He is not pleased with thanklessness for His bondmen,*[3] they respond: firstly, God is not pleased with the non-occurrence [of disbelief], but He is content with those who are thankless/have disbelieved because this has only occurred by His will and wish. Secondly, He is not pleased with it from a religious standpoint, i.e. He has not prescribed it nor has He commanded it, but He is content with it ontologically. Based upon their viewpoint, then, the meaning of the verse is that He is not pleased with the non-occurrence of disbelief from His servants, but if it does occur then He loves it and is pleased with it. This is obviously invalid and corrupt, as you can see.

God (Glory be to Him) has informed us that He is not pleased with whatever [disbelief] exists, although it does occur by His will. The Exalted has said, *He is with them when by night they hold discourse displeasing unto Him.*[4] Their discourse has occurred by His [ontological] will and decree, yet the Sublime has informed us that He is not pleased with it. Likewise, there is the Sublime's statement, *God loveth not mischief.*[5] Therefore, the Sublime does not love it in a religious sense even if it has occurred by His [ontological] decree. Likewise, He does not love Iblīs and his army, nor Pharaoh and his followers, even though He is their Lord and Creator.

Whoever deems that [His] love and pleasure are congruent with [His] intention and will must, then, necessarily regard that God

(Glory be to Him) loves Iblīs and his army or Pharaoh, Hāmān and Korah, as well as all of the disbelievers and oppressors, and their actions. In addition to the fact that this is necessarily [understood to be] contrary to the Qur'ān, the Sunna and the consensus [of the scholars], it also conflicts with what people have been innately disposed to. The [transmitted evidence and sound innate disposition] can never be altered by these subversive and false ideas.

God (Glory be to Him) has notified us that He detests, dislikes, hates and is angered by many actions when He said: *And marry not those women whom your fathers married, except what hath already happened (of that nature) in the past. Lo! it was ever lewdness and abomination, and an evil way;*[6] *That will be because they followed that which angereth God;*[7] *It is most hateful in the sight of God that ye say that which ye do not;*[8] and *God was averse to their being sent forth and held them back.*[9]

It is not permissible to interpret [His] dislike as only applying to religious commandments. God commanded the [believers] to strive [against evil] and then said, *The evil of all that is hateful in the sight of thy Lord.*[10] He notified us that He dislikes, hates, detests, opposes and is angered by [evil], while He criticizes and damns [the evildoers amongst the disbelievers]. It is impossible that God would love [evil], or be pleased with it, when He (Glory be to Him) is infallible and sanctified above doing so.

It is not even appropriate for His servants to love or be content with corruption, evil, injustice, transgression or disbelief, as it would represent a fault and blameworthy characteristic. Therefore, how can it be permissible to attribute that to God (Most Blessed and Exalted is He)? Many of those who affirmed [His] determination have erred greatly regarding this principle. Their misbelief is on the same level as that of those who deny [His] determination; indeed, it can be even more repugnant.

Those who denied [His determination] used [this erroneous belief of some of those who affirmed His determination] to gain an upper hand and rebuke the latter due to the repugnance and disgraceful nature of it. Some [of those who affirm His determination, i.e. the Ashʿariyya] erroneously believe that [God] loves disbelief, wickedness, sinfulness, injustice, transgression and corruption, while the [deniers of His determination] claim that these are not within His will, power and creation [and that is the only reason they exist in the first place]. The former maintained that nothing exists in His kingdom except that it is beloved and pleasing to Him. The deniers [i.e. the Qadariyya] claim that some things may exist in His kingdom which He has not willed, and He may will something yet it does not exist.

Glorious and Exalted is God above what both of these groups say. Praise be to God Who has guided us to what He has sent His messengers with, what He has revealed in His Book [the Qur'ān], and the [sound] innate disposition He has endowed His servants with. He has delivered us from the innovations of each of those two groups. All praise, gratitude and good commendations are for Him, and all grace and blessings [are from Him]. We ask Him to grant us success [in attaining] that which He loves and is pleased with, and that He protect us from going astray due to innovations and seductions.

CHAPTER FOURTEEN

The Division of Matters into the Ontological Pertaining to God's Creating and to the Religious Pertaining to God's Commandments

This chapter is connected to the one preceding it, and each one corroborates the other. Now, that which is ontological is attached to His lordship and His creating, whereas that which is religious is connected to His divinity and Divine Law. God (Glory be to Him) has notified us that He creates and commands. His creating includes His decree, determination and action, while His commandments include His Divine Law and religion. God is the One Who has created, prescribed and commanded.

His rulings are established amongst His creation both through His determination and Divine Law. There is no way for anyone to escape His ontological and determined rulings. As for His religious and divine rulings, those who are wicked and corrupt may disobey Him. Therefore, these two [i.e. His ontological and religious decrees] are not necessary concomitants. He may decree and determine something which He has not commanded nor prescribed. Conversely, He may prescribe and divinely command something which He does not decree nor determine to occur.

These two [ontological and religious] decrees only unite in the case of His servants who obey Him and have faith. On the other hand, His religious decrees and divine rulings stand alone when what He has commanded and prescribed is not carried out by those who are charged to do so. Ontological rulings stand-alone when only sins are carried out.

If the above is known then there are two types of decrees (*qaḍā'*) in the Book of God: [first], the determined and ontological type, like His statement, *And when We decreed death for him;*[1] *And it is judged (quḍiya) between them with truth.*[2]

As for the [second type], the religious and prescribed [decree], it is represented by His statement, *Thy Lord hath decreed, that ye worship none save Him.*[3] This indicates that He commanded and prescribed it. Had it been an ontological decree, then only God alone would have ever been worshipped.

There are also two types of rulings (*ḥukm*): the ontological [type] is represented by His statement, *He saith, My Lord! Judge Thou with truth.*[4] This means that [the Prophet] is [supplicating to God] to grant victory to His [devout] servants and humiliate His enemies.

The religious one is represented by His statement, *That is the judgment of God. He judgeth between you;*[5] and *God ordaineth that which pleaseth Him.*[6] Furthermore, [such rulings] can encompass both the ontological and religious meanings, as in His statement, *He allots to no one a share in His rule.*[7]

There are also two types of [His] will (*irāda*): the ontological one is represented by His statement, *Thy Lord is doer of what He will;*[8] *And when We would destroy a township;*[9] *If God's will is to keep you astray;*[10] *And We desired to show favour unto those who were oppressed in the earth.*[11]

As for [His] religious [will] it is represented by His statements: *God desireth (yurīd) for you ease; He desireth not hardship for you;*[12] *And God would turn (yurīd) to you in mercy.*[13] Had the [desired] will [mentioned in the first verse] been of the ontological type, then none of us would have ever encountered hardship; [and had the desired will been of the ontological type mentioned in the second verse], then repentance would have been sought by all those who are charged [i.e. all of humanity].

Through this detailed exposition the ambiguity regarding the question whether the divine command and will are necessary concomitants of each other or not ceases. But the Qadariyya opined that His divine command is accompanied by His will, thereby manifesting [those commandments]. On the other hand, those who affirm [His wisdom] maintain that His divine command may not be accompanied by His will, thereby manifesting [those commandments].

The truth of the matter is that [His divine] command is a necessary concomitant of His religious will, but may not be accompanied by His ontological will. He only commands that which He wills religiously to be a Divine Law. But He may command something that He does not will nor determine to occur ontologically. For example, He commanded all to believe, but He does not grant success to most to achieve that faith. Therefore, this is a religious will rather than an ontological will. Another example is His command to His friend [Abraham] to sacrifice his son, but He did not will its occurrence ontologically nor determine it.[14] Another example is His command of fifty prayers to His Messenger [Muḥammad], but He did not will its occurrence ontologically nor determine it.

Now, there is a difference between these last two examples and the example of the [disbeliever] who does not become faithful. God (Glory be to Him) did not love that Abraham sacrifice his son, but rather loved to see [Abraham's] firm resolve in following [His commandment] and settling himself upon it. His commandment to Muḥammad (may God bless him and grant him peace) during the Night Journey with fifty prayers is similar. As for the commandment to those whom He knew would not believe, God loves His servants to believe in Him and His messengers, yet His wisdom dictated that He would assist and grant success to some to carry out what He has commanded, and that He would forsake others by not doing so—thus, the latter did not benefit from His commandment. On the other hand, [the benefit of the Lord's] commandment [to Abraham] to sacrifice [Ishmael] did occur.

As for prescribing (*kitāba*), it is represented from an ontological perspective by His statements: *God hath decreed (kataba): Lo! I verily shall conquer, I and My messengers;*[15] *And verily We have written in the Book, after the Reminder: My righteous servants will inherit the earth;*[16] and *For him it is decreed (kutiba) that whoso taketh [a devil] for friend, he verily will mislead him and will guide him to the punishment of the Flame.*[17]

As for the divine commandments [of prescribing or ordaining], they are represented by His statements: *O ye who believe, fasting is prescribed (kutiba) for you;*[18] *Forbidden unto you are your mothers*[19]... to His statement *This is God's ordinance, binding upon you;*[20] *And We prescribed for them therein: The life for the life.*[21]

As for the ontological command (*amr*), it is represented by His statements: *But His command, when He intendeth a thing, is only that He saith unto it, Be! And it is;*[22] *And Our commandment is but one (commandment), as the twinkling of an eye;*[23] *The commandment of God is always executed;*[24] *And it is a thing ordained.*[25]

[Then there is], *And when We would destroy a township We send commandment to its folk who live at ease, and afterward they commit abomination therein, [and so the Word (of doom) hath effect for it, and we annihilate it with complete annihilation].*[26] This [verse reflects] an ontological and determined commandment, not a religiously-prescribed command. God does not command any abomination. Instead, the meaning is that He [ontologically] decreed and determined its occurrence. One group said that it was a religious commandment—meaning that God had commanded them to do good, but they refused and committed abominations.

The first viewpoint is more correct from many aspects:

1. The latent meaning (*iḍmār*) contradicts the original script, and one cannot accept that unless one cannot reach the correct meaning without it.

2. It would necessitate two latent meanings: the first is that God commanded them to obey, and second that they refused such or disobeyed.

3. What follows the letter *fā'* [i.e. *after they commit abomination therein*] is what has been commanded. It is like saying, 'I commanded him so he did such-and-such.' The one being spoken to does not understand otherwise, so [this commandment is an ontological one].

4. God (Glory be to Him) made His mentioned commandment the cause for that town's destruction. It is well known that His [religious] commandment to obey and worship Him alone is not an appropriate reason for their destruction; rather, it would have been a cause for their salvation and victory. If it is said that His commandment for obedience was [rejected and they instead perpetrated] abominations, and so that was the cause for their destruction, then it is replied that this is incorrect (as will be shown next).

5. This commandment is not reserved solely for those who live in luxury. Instead, God (Glory be to Him) commands both—those

who are living in luxury and those not—to obey Him and follow His messengers. Thus, it is not correct to specify that only those who live in luxury are subject to His commandment to obey Him.

6. If the commandment had been to obey [God's Divine Law], then it would have been the same as sending His messengers to them. It is well known that it is not appropriate to say, 'We sent Our messengers to those who live in luxury, and thereafter they committed abominations.' If the [messengers] would have only been sent to those living in luxury, then the rest of the people would have contended that no one was sent to them.

7. God's will (Glory be to Him) to destroy that town only came after sending the messenger to them and their rejection. Before [sending the messenger] He did not wish their destruction—they were excused because they were unaware and the message had not yet reached them. The Exalted has said, *In truth thy Lord destroyed not the townships tyrannously while their folk were doing right.*[27]

Thus, His will that they would commit abominations in that town was an ontological and determined one, not a prescribed and religious one. The people of that town collectively disbelieved, while their leaders committed abominations. At that point, God's [ontological] command declared that they were deserving of destruction.

To return to mentioning both the ontological and religious commandments, the religious [commandment] is represented by His statements: *God enjoineth justice and kindness*;[28] and *God commandeth you that ye restore deposits to their owners.*[29] There are, in fact, many more examples of these.

As for the ontological allowance (*idhn*), it is represented by the Exalted's statement, *They injure thereby no-one save by God's leave.*[30] This indicates that His will and determination allows it to occur.

As for the religious one, it is within His statement, *Whatsoever palm-trees ye cut down or left standing on their roots, it was by God's leave.*[31] This indicates that it occurred by His [religious] commandment and consent. Further examples include: *Say: Have ye considered what provision God hath sent down for you, how ye have made of it lawful and unlawful? Hath God permitted you, or do ye invent a lie concerning*

God?[32] *Or have they partners (of God) who have made lawful for them in religion that which God allowed not?*[33]

As for the ontological appointment (*jaʿl*), it is represented by His statements: *We have put on their necks shackles reaching unto the chins, so that they are made stiff-necked. And We have set a bar before them and a bar behind them, and (thus) have covered them so that they see not;*[34] *He hath set uncleanness upon those who have no sense;*[35] *And God hath given you wives of your own kind.*[36] There are many more examples of this.

As for the religious appointment, it is represented by His statement, *It is not of God's ordaining that certain kinds of cattle should be marked out by superstition and set aside from the use of man; yet those who are bent on denying the truth attribute their own lying inventions to God.*[37] This means that He did not prescribe (*sharaʿa*) [this practice] nor command it, but they were created by Him. This [false worship] was allowed by His [ontological] determination and will. As for His statement, *God hath appointed the Kaʿba, the Sacred House, a standard for humankind,*[38] this encompasses both appointments: the [ontologically] determined one and His religious one. This is not because both types are the same, but instead because the wording is generalized to encompass both. Reflect on that.

[His] ontological words (*kalimāt*) are represented by His statements: *Thus is the Word of thy Lord justified concerning those who do wrong: that they believe not;*[39] *And the fair Word of thy Lord was fulfilled for the Children of Israel because of their endurance.*[40] Also included is the *ḥadīth* of the Prophet (may God bless him and grant him peace), 'I seek refuge in God's perfect words—which neither a pious nor wicked one can escape—from the evilness of what He has created.'[41] These are His ontological words through which He has created and originated all things. They are not His religious words, which He uses to command and forbid, since wicked disbelievers have not obeyed [His commandments].

As for [His] religious [words], there is, *And if anyone of the idolaters seeketh thy protection (O Muḥammad), then protect him so that he may hear the Word of God.*[42] Moreover, the Prophet (may God bless him and grant him peace) said about [marriage], 'You have been allowed intimacy with [your wives] by God's words,'[43] indicating that this has occurred by His religious permission. His [religious] statement [or word on the matter] is *Marry of the women, who seem good to you.*[44]

The two types have been juxtaposed in the verse, *And she put faith in the words of her Lord and His Books.*[45] Here His Books are His words with which He commands, forbids, deems good or prohibits, while His words (*kalimātihi*)—[in general]—are those with which He creates and originates things. Thus, God informed us that [Mary] was not one of the Jahmiyya, who deny His religious and ontological words, and consider them to be created just like His other creations.

As for the ontological sending (*baʿth*), it is represented by His statements: *Hence, when the prediction of the first of those two [periods of iniquity] came true, We sent against you some of Our bondmen of terrible prowess in war*;[46] and *Then God sent a raven scratching up the ground.*[47]

Whereas His religious sending is exemplified by His statements: *He it is Who hath sent among the unlettered ones a messenger of their own*;[48] *Humankind were one community, and God sent (unto them) prophets as bearers of good tidings and as warners.*[49]

As for His ontological sending (*irsāl*), it is represented by His statements: *Seest thou not that We have set the devils on the disbelievers to confound them with confusion?*[50] *And He it is Who sendeth the winds.*[51]

His religious dispatching is exemplified by His statements: *He it is Who hath sent His messenger with the guidance and the Religion of Truth*;[52] *We have sent unto you a messenger as witness against you, even as We sent unto Pharaoh a messenger.*[53]

As for what is ontologically forbidden (*taḥrīm*), it is represented by His statements: *And We had before forbidden foster mothers for him*;[54] *(Their Lord) said, For this the land will surely be forbidden them for forty years*;[55] *And there is a ban upon any community which We have destroyed: that they shall not return.*[56]

As for the religious prohibitions, they are exemplified by His statements: *Forbidden unto you are your mothers*;[57] *Forbidden unto you (for food) are carrion*;[58] *To hunt on land is forbidden you so long as ye are on the pilgrimage*;[59] *God permitteth trading and forbiddeth usury.*[60]

As for the ontological bestowal (*ītā'*), it is exemplified by His statements: *God bestoweth His sovereignty on whom He will;*[61] *Say: O God! Owner of Sovereignty! Thou givest sovereignty unto whom Thou wilt;*[62] and *We bestowed on them a mighty kingdom.*[63]

As for the religious bestowal, it is represented by His statements: *And whatsoever the Messenger giveth you, take it;*[64] and *Hold fast that which We have given you.*[65] As for His statement, *He giveth wisdom unto whom He will, and he unto whom wisdom is given, he truly hath received abundant good,*[66] it includes both [the religious and ontological types]. God bestows [understanding of wisdom] upon whom He wills by [His ontological] command, and by religiously granting success and inspiring one [to seek it out].

The good fortune of His prophets, messengers and their followers is of the religious type. On the other hand, His enemies' share is the ontological fate, and they follow it wherever it leads them. The religion [of the disbelievers] is one of fate, while the religion of the messengers and their followers is that which is associated with [God's] prescribed commandments. The [believers] worship [God] according to His commandments and believe in His determination. Those who dispute with God and disobey His commandments use the excuse of His predestination, and then say that they are acting in accordance with the will of God. Although that [statement] is true, it is only in accordance with His ontological will, not the religious one. But they cannot use this as an excuse [on the Day of Judgment] nor will it benefit them. If everyone was exempt because of [His ontological decree and determination], then none of His creation would be blameworthy or due punishment, and none would be considered to be disobedient or a disbeliever. Whoever claims that [His ontological and religious wills are the same] has disbelieved in God, His Books and all of His messengers. We depend on God for success.

CHAPTER FIFTEEN

An Exposition of God's Wisdom in Allowing People to Sin

We have recounted in another book of ours, *al-Futūḥāt al-qudsiyya*,[1] eight viewpoints by which to consider sins:

1. THE ANIMALISTIC VIEWPOINT: Here one only sees the temptations and pleasures one desires to experience. Both humans and animals may view it in this fashion. It may be even that a human may enjoy the pleasure therein with greater intensity.

2. THE DETERMINISTIC VIEWPOINT: Here one views that the agent and mover is another being; and thus, he considers himself to be sinless. This is the viewpoint of the polytheists and the enemies of the prophets [for example, the Jabriyya].

3. THE [FREE-WILL] VIEWPOINT: Here one asserts that he is the creator and originator of his own actions without the will of God or His creative power. This is the viewpoint of the Qadariyya, who are the Zoroastrians [of this Community].

4. THE VIEWPOINT OF THOSE WHO ARE KNOWLEDGEABLE AND FAITHFUL: They affirm God's determination and Divine Law, whereby they witness that their actions are encompassed within God's decree and determination.

5. THE VIEWPOINT OF NEED, POVERTY, INABILITY AND WEAKNESS: Here a person perceives that if God does not assist, strengthen and grant him success, then he will be ruined. The difference between this viewpoint and the deterministic one is obvious.

6. THE MONOTHEISTIC VIEWPOINT: Here one witnesses that God (Almighty and Most Glorious is He) is the Creator and Originator, His will is overpowering, and that humans are too weak to be able to disobey Him without Him allowing them. The difference between

this and the fifth viewpoint is that the person recognizes to a greater degree his absolute weakness, poverty and neediness. Again, this aspect illustrates that God alone is the Creator, and that there is no power or strength save in Him.

7. THE VIEWPOINT OF WISE PURPOSES: Here one views the wisdom of God (Almighty and Most Glorious is He) in His decreeing and allowing the servant to sin. God has many wise purposes that our intelligence cannot fully comprehend or understand. We have recounted in that book about forty wisdoms and we [will mention below] many of them.

8. THE VIEWPOINT OF HIS NAMES AND ATTRIBUTES: Here one views that His creating, commandments, decree and determination are all connected to His Names and Attributes (Exalted is He), and that the former are requisites and consequences of the latter.

For example, His Beautiful Names allow a servant to sin, since He is the One full of Forgiveness, the Relenting (*al-Tawwāb*), the Effacer [of sins] and the Forbearing. Thus, all of His Names will inevitably manifest themselves and have consequences. If people did not commit sins, God would dispense with them and create others who would sin [but thereafter would seek forgiveness], whereupon He would forgive them.[2]

This latter viewpoint [number 8] and the one that preceded it [number 7] are the most dignified and eminent ones. Indeed, only the elite have knowledge and a profound understanding of them. In fact, there is a vast difference between all of these viewpoints, but especially between the first one and the last two, as the latter result in the servant loving [his Lord]. They also open many doors of knowledge and understanding, which cannot even be described; but only a few can open them. They entail [His] far-reaching wisdom in [ontologically] decreeing and determining sins and lapses. The [scholars] have only pursued and understood a few of the wise purposes behind [His] commandments and prohibitions, as well His creating. It is rare for you to see a [scholar] adequately comprehending this matter in his writings. How can a person see [God's] wisdom in this matter if he does not believe that his actions are created by Him and allowed by His will? How can someone have [a correct] understanding here if he believes that God's actions are done without consideration of wise purposes; or that there are no such things as reasons or final objectives (*lām al-taʿlīl*, *ʿilla* or *ghāya*), but only *lām al-ʿāqiba*?[3]

The point is that witnessing God's wisdom in His decree and determination of the conduct of His servants—whilst also upholding [the reality that] they possess free choice and a will—is one of the finer, more subtle and mysterious issues that people have discussed. Only God, the Most Wise and Omniscient (Glory be to Him), knows these wise purposes [in detail], but we will allude to some of them:

[1] God (Glory be to Him) loves the repentant believers. His love of their repentance is such that He is happier with that than [the joy] a person who finds his ride, food and drink in a deadly desert feels after having lost them and given up hope.[4] There is no greater or more complete joy than this. We will elucidate and expand upon this shortly, God willing. Had God not completely loved repentance and those seeking repentance, His happiness would not have occurred [to such a great degree]. It is well known that the presence of an effect without its causative factor is impossible; something cannot exist without its requisite concomitant. Similarly, an end without its means cannot occur.

This explains the statement by some gnostics, 'If it had not been for the fact that repentance is one of the most beloved things to Him, God would have never allowed the lapse of the most noble of humanity to Him [i.e. Adam] to occur.' Thus, repentance is the perfect and ultimate objective of all of humanity; and the perfection of their father [Adam] occurred through it. Note the difference between [Adam's] initial state when it was said to him, *It is (vouchsafed) unto thee that thou hungerest not therein nor art naked, And that thou thirstest not therein nor art exposed to the sun's heat*,[5] and then after [his repentance] God said, *Then his Lord chose him, and relented toward him, and guided him*.[6] The initial state is one of eating, drinking and enjoyment, whereas the latter is one of being chosen, selected and guided. The difference between the two is immensely vast.

Since Adam's perfection was only achieved through repentance, the perfection of his offspring can only occur likewise. The Exalted said, *So God punisheth hypocritical men and hypocritical women, and idol-*

atrous men and idolatrous women. But God pardoneth believing men and believing women, and God is all-forgiving, merciful.[7] Again, the perfection of the offspring of Adam is achieved in this world through sincere repentance, whereas in the Hereafter it is by being rescued from Hellfire and entered into Paradise. The latter perfection is dependent upon the former. The point is that because God (Glory be to Him) loves and is happy with repentance, He [ontologically] decreed that His servants will sin, but if they are forthcoming with righteousness then He will [ontologically and religiously] decree their seeking of repentance. Furthermore, [He decreed] that if their wretchedness/evil overwhelms them, He will implement His justice and punishment for these sins.

[2] God (Glory be to Him) loves to bestow His grace, complete His blessings, and reveal His benevolence and magnanimity to His servants. Due to His great love of all of this, He has done the aforementioned in a great number of ways, both manifest and hidden. Some of the greatest types of [His] beneficence and kindness include showing benevolence to those who have done evil, overlooking those who have perpetrated injustice, forgiving those who have done wrong or sinned, pardoning those who repent, and accepting the apology of those who make amends.

God has advised His servants to possess these virtuous characteristics and praiseworthy actions [of benevolence and forgiveness]. Yet, He is more worthy and is more deserving of [displaying] these than [humans]. Finally, God's [ontological] determination of causes for these matters does, indeed, contain many wisdoms and praiseworthy end results that dazzle the mind. Glory and praise be to Him!

Had God (Almighty and Most Glorious is He) willed that no one on this earth would disobey Him, then no disobedience would have occurred. Rather, His will has dictated that which is concordant with His wisdom. The most ignorant are those who claim that God is disobeyed against His will or allowance. Glorious and Exalted is God above what they claim.

[3] God (Glory be to Him) possesses Beautiful Names and each Name of His has an effect upon His creation and commandments. Examples of these consequences include that there must be some-

one to be given provision by the Provider (*al-Rāziq*), someone to be forgiven by the All-Merciful (*al-Rāḥim*), entities to be seen or heard by the One Who is the All-Hearing and the All-Seeing, in addition to His many other Names.

Thus, had there not been anyone amongst His servants who would err or sin such that He would accept his repentance, forgive and overlook, then the manifestation of various Names of His—such as the All-Forgiving, the Effacer [of sins], the Forbearing and the Relenting—would not occur. The manifestation of the effects of the Names and what they are attached to of the creation is like the manifestation of the effects of all His other Beautiful Names. For example, His Name of the Creator (*al-Khāliq*) dictates that there must be creatures. The same is dictated by [His Names] the Originator (*al-Bāri'*) and the Fashioner (*al-Muṣawwir*).

Deeply reflect on His Names the Provider and One full of Forgiveness and their dazzling consequences amongst the creation. If it was not for His provisions and His forgiveness, the creation would not have even existed originally. Everyone has a share in His provisions and forgiveness—they may be included in one's second life [i.e. Paradise] or only within this [worldly] life.

[4] God (Glory be to Him) makes His glory known to His servants through His decree and determination, as well as by the administration of His will and rulings. Thus, it becomes clear to them that there is no escaping His [ontological] decree. Rather, they recognize that they are within the grasp of their King and Sovereign Owner, that they are His servants, and that His judgments are just.

[5] [Such matters] allow the servant to recognize his need for God's protection, help and preservation, similar to how an infant or child needs someone to protect and preserve him. If the True Lord does not do so, then he will inevitably become destroyed [spiritually], since there are many devils surrounding him who want to ruin him and bring evil to all of his affairs and states. If his Guardian and Owner abandons him, he will become lost and incapable, and will commit sins, errors and lapses. The scholars who know God agree that the servant's salvation only occurs if

God does not leave him to rely on himself, and they agree that being forsaken occurs if God abandons a person to himself.

[6] God (Glory be to Him) induces His servant to seek refuge in Him and ask for God's protection from his evil self and the plotting of his enemies. This demand represents one of the greatest causes leading to a servant's bliss.

Accordingly, the servant will begin praying and supplicating, beseeching and imploring, as well as being humble, repenting, and having love, hope, fear and other perfections that approach one hundred types. Some of these cannot be expressed verbally, but can only be experienced spiritually.

The servant's spirit is, consequently, able to reach a special proximity [to the Lord] that would not have otherwise been achieved in the absence of these causes. Then the servant will find himself at the doorstep of his Lord after being distant. This is all due to the fact that God loves and rejoices with those who repent.

There is a vast difference between one who is haughty and proud and the one who is humble. Every time the former is asked to do something concordant with his status as [His] servant, he only thinks [himself to be great due to] his deeds, and that [pride] prevents him from worshipping his Lord and God appropriately [with humility and sincerity]. The latter's heart, though, is completely humble [before the Lord]. He has no frivolities, idiocies or false images of himself. He only sees himself as sinful, and views his Lord as beneficent. He worships God with all his heart, feels himself to be completely inadequate, lowers his head, gaze and voice before his Lord with humility and submission. He moves with tranquillity and prostrates before Him as if it was his last before his death. Had there been no other fruit and wise purpose to His [ontological] decree and determination [of sins] than this, it would be sufficient. We rely on God.

[7] God (Glory be to Him) brings about perfect worship (*ʿubūdiyya*) from the servant [through the aforementioned deeds]. Yet, this can only occur if it is characterized by complete submission and humility. The one whose servitude [to the Lord] is most perfect is the one who is most perfect in his humility, submission and

obedience to God. The [sincere] servant is humble before his True Lord in every respect: he is submissive to His might, His vanquishing power, His lordship, His administration, and also submits himself [and acknowledges] His benevolence and blessings upon him.

Now, there are two types of submissiveness and worship that result [from the aforementioned]. They have an amazing effect on the servant by allowing him to achieve [higher levels of] obedience and success. The first is submissiveness due to love. This is different than what was discussed previously for it represents the true essence and spirit of love. In reality, if a person really possesses understanding, he will realize that it is this quality [i.e. love of God] that is what is ultimately desired from the servant.

The loving heart displays many ways of attempting to become proximate [to the Lord]: affection (*tawaddud*), flattery (*tamalluq*), altruism (*īthār*), contentment (*riḍā*), praise (*ḥamd*), gratitude (*shukr*), patience (*ṣabr*), dedication (*taqaddum*), and enduring great hardships (*taḥammul al-ʿaẓā'im*). None of these would have occurred if one only had fear or hope [of the Lord]. Some of the Companions said, 'My heart's love for God brings about obedience to Him in such a manner that would not have occurred if only fear of Him existed.'[8]

The second is the submissiveness which results [indirectly] from disobedience. If both of these types of submissiveness are aggregated together then this results in the vanishing of forms, souls and powers.[9] One then ceases to claim [greatness], imagine [false] things or have mystical outbursts. One's ego becomes erased from his heart and tongue, and this impoverished person no longer complains [to God] or turns away from [Him].

One now only witnesses two testimonies. Firstly, one witnesses that only the Beloved [Lord] is Majestic, Glorious, Almighty and Most Generous, and that no other creature can have even an atom's share in those characteristics. Secondly, one witnesses his complete humility, absolute poverty (*faqr*) and brokenness in every manner. Once one witnesses these two testimonies in actuality, his heart will have reached a lofty level, whereby one will become proximate [to God] and will enjoy great bliss and spirituality.

It also necessitates such a person to be embarrassed and discount any righteous deeds he may have done, even if they are akin to the mountains, since he will require many more good deeds than even those to expiate and atone for his sins and evil deeds. He will thus deem great any little [blessing] that the Lord bestows upon him since he is not worthy or deserving of even that. He will continue to do righteous deeds and yet consider himself to be sinful. This humility and brokenness all [indirectly] result from a sin; and thus, there is nothing more beneficial for this person than this medication.

Again, the servant may sometimes, when seeing his good deeds and upright nature, become haughty and think himself to be exceptional. But once he incurs a sin he realizes that he is ordinary, becomes humble and submissive, and attains certainty that he is a [servant of God].

[8] The servant will realize his true nature, and that he is unjust. He will also recognize that every evil that arises from his self is from his essence, and that his ignorance and injustice are the source of that evil. On the other hand, [he realizes that] all good, knowledge, guidance, repentance and piety are due to the grace of the Lord (Exalted is He) and that God alone is the only One Who can purify him. Had God not willed the purification of the servant, He would have forsaken him to be overcome by his injustice and ignorance. Thus, the Exalted is the One Who purifies those whom He pleases such that they can thereafter bring forth a variety of good and pious deeds. Conversely, those whom He forsakes will instead perform all types of evil and wicked deeds. One of the supplications of the Prophet was, 'O God, bestow upon myself piety, and purify [my soul] as You are the best to purify it. You are the Benefactor (*al-Walī*) and the Guardian.'[10]

Furthermore, one's recognition of personal deficiencies leads to many wisdoms and benefits. One of them is that he refuses to be characterized by deficiency, and therefore will strive for perfection. In addition, he recognizes his abject need for [his Lord] to support and guard him. Also [by recognizing his faultiness], the believer relieves himself and others from all the frivolities and idiocies that are claimed by those who are ignorant, such as their claims that they are pre-eternal or attached to pre-eternity, that they are united with

God [i.e. monism], or incarnated in Him, or other impossibilities. Had such people witnessed their deficiencies and true natures, they would not have fallen into these ideologies.

[9] God (Glory be to Him) manifests to His servants the vast expanse of His clemency and generosity in that He conceals their sins. Had God willed He could have punished the sinner immediately and exposed him amongst his people. In that case, it would be very difficult for [the sinner] to live happily amongst them. Instead, though, He allowed him to remain esteemed [by his people] by concealing [his sins]—this is all due to His clemency. God continues to preserve him despite his sins and iniquities.

In some traditions, it is related that God (Exalted is He) says, 'I am the Magnanimous and Most Generous. Who is greater than Me in magnanimity or generosity? Although My servants oppose Me by perpetrating major sins, I preserve them in their homes.'[11] Thus, there is no greater clemency and no greater generosity than this. Had it not been for His clemency, generosity and forgiveness, the heavens and earth would not remain in their place: *God graspeth the heavens and the earth that they deviate not, and if they were to deviate there is not one that could grasp them after Him. Lo! He is ever forbearing, all-forgiving.*[12] God also said, *Whereby almost the heavens are torn, and the earth is split asunder and the mountains fall in ruins, That ye ascribe unto the Beneficent a son.*[13]

[10] God makes it known to His servants that there is no salvation except through His forgiveness and mercy, and that the servant is justly held hostage by his sins. If God does not encompass him in His grace and mercy, he will inevitably be punished. None of His creation is exempt from being in need of His mercy and forgiveness, just as none is exempt from being in need of His blessings and grace.

[11] God (Glory be to Him) also makes known to His servant His generosity in accepting his repentance, and His mercy despite his injustice and transgression. He is the One Who generously granted him [His] guidance and inspired him to seek repentance. Thereafter, He accepted it and absolved him. Thus, God forgave the servant both [before he actually sought repentance] and after doing so. The repentance of the servant is encompassed by forgiveness beforehand from God as He has granted him the permission to seek repent-

ance and enabled him to do so, and then afterwards God accepts his repentance and is pleased with it.

[12] It also justifies the manifestation of God's justice upon His servant. One will recognize that God is justified to the highest degree when He allows His servant to undergo hardships. The servant will not say, 'Where did this come from?' Instead, one is not afflicted with any hardship, whether limited or great, except due to his sins. Furthermore, God has forgiven him for much more than what has befallen him.

In addition, one is only released from a hardship after his repentance. Thus, God has made hardships, tribulations and tests a mercy for His servants [and as a means] to pardon them. These [hardships] are some of His greatest blessings upon them even though they may dislike them. On most occasions, the servant does not know which of the two blessings is better for him—the one that he dislikes or the one that he likes. The believer does not encounter any grief, hardship or harm, even a thorn, except that God will pardon him for some of his sins.[14] Since some sins inevitably incur punishment, it is better and much easier for the servant if he is punished for them before his death, rather than [in the grave or the Hereafter].

[13] Another [benefit] is that the servant will deal with other human beings, if they harm or make mistakes with him, in a manner similar to how he asks God to treat him for his errors, mistakes and sins. Since the reward is concordant with the deed, whoever forgives others will find that God will forgive him; whoever indulges his brother if the latter harms him will find God to be merciful with him for his sins; and whoever is lenient and overlooks [others] will find that God will overlook [his errors]. But whoever probes [into the faults of others] will be dealt with likewise.

Do not forget about the one whom the Prophet alluded to in the *ḥadīth* [that says], 'The angels took his spirit at death and said, "Did you do any good?" He replied, "I do not know." They then said, "Try to remember." He said, "I used to sell goods to people. I would give those who were able [to pay] more time, and I would forgo [the debt] of those who were in [financial] hardship." God said, "We have more right to that than him," and thus God forgave him.'[15] Thus God (Almighty and Most Glorious is He) deals with the servant and his sins in a fashion, which is similar to how the servant treats other people if they harm him [and God is the Greatest]. If a servant knows this, then he realizes that his sins [indirectly] lead to many wisdoms and morals that are very beneficial to him.

[14] If one treats well others who harm him, and does not take vengeance on them, then God (Glory be to Him) will counter one's sins and errors with forgiveness and grace. Of course, God's benevolence, generosity and reward are far greater. Therefore, whoever loves for God to counter his sins with beneficence, he should treat others benevolently despite their harm to him.

In addition, he who recognizes that sinning and erring are necessary concomitants of being a human will not deem the harm that others inflict upon him to be great. A person should also deeply reflect on his status with God, His great benevolence upon him, as well as his great need for his Lord—other people are not dependent on him similarly.

Also, one [who recognizes that sins and perpetrating evil are intrinsic to human beings] will give others excuses, become more merciful and accommodating of them, avoid becoming annoyed with them or seething with anger. He will desist from supplicating against them or asking God to make the earth swallow them up or send calamities upon them. He will instead ask God to bestow upon them good, repentance and forgiveness, just as he would ask for himself, since he considers himself to be [sinful] just like them. He may even supplicate for their forgiveness and being pardoned more than he would do so for himself.

How different is this from his initial state when he looked down upon them with hatred and contempt, had no mercy in his heart, nor hoped or supplicated for their salvation? Thus, this person's sins may [paradoxically] be one of the greatest causes for him being forgiven [by God]. Despite them having harmed him, he now upholds the commandments of God—in order to serve Him—and has mercy upon them, treats them well and benefits them, instead of being harsh, blunt or overpowering.

[15] Another reason is that [sinning may indirectly] remove

arrogance and pride from one's heart, which would otherwise result from one being impressed with personal acts of worship. It instead replaces them with humility, brokenness, poverty and need. The Prophet (may God bless him and grant him peace) said in a *ḥadīth*, 'If you did not sin I would be afraid of something worse for you than that—pride.'[16]

Ultimately, there is no better clothing for the servant to wear, nor anything more perfect or beautiful, than the cloth of servitude and submissiveness [to the Lord]. It is only in this manner that one achieves an honourable status.

[16] God (Almighty and Most Glorious is He) created many ways for our hearts to serve Him, including fear, awe, reverence and what results from them, such as love for Him, returning to Him and imploring Him to guide us. All of these types of worship are stirred up and brought about by causes. Whatever causes the Lord (Exalted is He) has [ontologically] decreed to result in the above ultimately become a source of His mercy for us.

It may also be that a sin will lead a person to subsequently have fear, awe and reverence of God, while also returning to Him, loving Him, preferring matters in accordance with His [pleasure], and taking refuge with God in a greater fashion than any of his pious deeds. In addition, many times a sin ultimately [indirectly] leads a servant to become upright, flee to God and be distanced from his evil ways.

[17] Also, the servant will appreciate the value of his well-being [away from sins], and God's grace in guarding him and allowing him [to worship Him]. In general, one who has only grown up in well-being does not know the hardships that others endure or the value of his blessings. Thus, those who are obedient to God will realize that they are the blessed ones in reality, and that they must thank God many times what others would—even if they were only able to lay on bare ground [to sleep] and eat only pebbles. On the other hand, those whom God allows to pursue only evil are the ones that He has forsaken and deemed unworthy [of His mercy]. Even if God has given the latter much of this [material] world, they are in reality the afflicted ones.

Thus, if God, due to His mercy, tests a servant—who initially desired fortunes and a share of this world, and who thought that he suffered much due to being in financial straits—with some sins, the servant may thereafter realize that being blessed [with obedience to God] is much greater than any fortune that he may have previously desired. Consequently, his hopes and aspirations will only be to return to that state of [righteousness], and that God grants him His pardon.

[18] In addition, the act of repentance leads to many great benefits that would not have otherwise occurred—these include love, gentleness, kindness, thankfulness to God and praise of Him, as well as contentedness, amongst other forms of worship.

Thus, if a person repents to God and God accepts his repentance, he will realize many types of blessings that he did not initially know in detail. He will continue to enjoy them and their consequences, unless he limits or ruins them.

[19] God (Glory be to Him) loves and is greatly pleased with His servant when he repents. It has already been established that reward is concordant with the deed. One should not forget the happiness that one feels with sincere repentance. Deeply reflect on how your heart dances with joy [on such occasions], even though you may not know the exact reason for that happiness.

Only those whose hearts are [spiritually] alive feel joy when they repent. As for those whose hearts are [spiritually] dead, they only feel happiness when they fulfil their desires—they know of no other type of joy. One should weigh, therefore, between these two types of joy—the happiness that results from fulfilling one's desires is followed by a variety of emotions, including sadness, anxiety, worry and other afflictions. These people have only bought a moment's happiness, but it ultimately leads to eternal grief.

On the other hand, happiness that occurs due to obedience and after sincere repentance results in perpetual joy, bliss and a good life. Thus, you should compare the two and then select which is more appropriate for you. Ultimately, every person acts in a manner concordant with his nature.

[20] In addition, once a person sees his sins, errors and negligence in fulfilling the rights of his Lord, he then appreciates his

Lord's blessings more and considers them to be great, not few. He will also deem the many pious deeds that he has performed to be insufficient, because he is aware that the amount of good needed to cleanse himself of his inordinate number of filthy deeds[17] are many times greater. Thus, he always deems his good deeds to be insignificant, regardless [of their noble status], and considers the blessings of God to be great, even if limited [in terms of seeming importance]. This has already been alluded to, and it is one of the most subtle issues. One should take care to do the above, as it will have an amazing effect on one. Had there been no other wisdom for allowing sins, except this, it would have sufficed.

There is such a vast difference between the state of the aforementioned person and the state of those who do not acknowledge the blessings of God, and feel that they should be given much more in line with their status, or feel that their Lord has not been fair with them. The latter stubbornly reject their lot due to what they feel is their perfect and virtuous nature. They feel they should have been given riches and should have been able to overpower their competition. These types are amongst those people most detested and hated by God. The wisdom of God has dictated that these people remain abased, since they criticize the Creator and complain to Him, yet submit themselves to other creatures, serve them, and want more and more from them. Their hearts are preoccupied with serving rulers and people in powerful positions—they wait for the scraps and cast-offs thrown to them. Absent from their hearts is service to God, devotion to Him, delight in supplicating to Him, tranquillity in remembering Him, finding consolation in fearing Him, and contentedness with Him. May God protect us from becoming bereft of His blessings and having our well-being removed away, from His retribution taking us suddenly, and from all types of His wrath.

[21] The occurrence of a sin makes a servant wake up. It prods him to take precautions against his enemies, to know their hideouts and inroads, and [to anticipate] their strike. Thus, he is readied for the next time, prepared for them and knows how to deflect their evil and plots. Had he, on the other hand, been naive and resting

still, he could not be sure that they would not overwhelm and conquer him all at once.

It may be that a person's heart is sometimes preoccupied with some distractions and not paying attention to his enemy, but once he is struck by his enemy and sins, he then [awakens], becomes rejuvenated, collects his strength and fervour, re-establishes his defences and pursues his reprisal—that is, if he has a noble and free heart. This is akin to a courageous warrior who, after being wounded, will act as if nothing struck him, and instead becomes more stirred up and enraged in pursuit of his enemy.

However, if one's heart is weak and cowardly, he will be like a cowardly and feeble man who flees in retreat after being wounded. There is no good in a person who lacks chivalry or honour, and does not exact revenge from his worst enemies. One of the most beneficial things for the heart is to avenge itself against an enemy, and there is no greater enemy than Satan. Thus, if one's heart pursues its honour, it will take strong action to exact revenge and infuriate the enemy to the utmost. Some of the Predecessors said, 'A believer will wear out the Devil just like one of you would exhaust his camel on a long journey.'[18]

[22] Moreover, a person who experiences everything [i.e. sins but repents] will become like a physician whom patients benefit from in their treatments and medications. A physician who has encountered a disease directly and treated it is more experienced than one who has only read about it. This is well known for the body and it is the same for diseases of the heart and their remedies.

Some of the Sufis have said, 'The most knowledgeable people about evil are those who have experienced the most [hardships] and evil.'[19] ʿUmar b. al-Khaṭṭāb said, 'The laws of Islam will be stripped away layer by layer. People will grow up in Islam not knowing what it was like to live in the Time of Ignorance (*jāhiliyya*).'[20] Thus, the Companions of the Prophet were the most knowledgeable of this Community about Islam, its particulars, and the detailed arrangements of its gateways and pathways. They were the most devoted to Islam, loved it the most, and strived against the enemies of Islam the best. They were the best to communicate its defining characteristics and the need to avoid disobedience because they completely knew what the alternative life was like.

It is like a person who used to live in a state of poverty, illness, fear or isolation, but then God brings about for him wealth, health, security, delight and joy. This person will appreciate, love and enjoy this newly-found state more because of his prior condition.

On the other hand, those who grew up secure with health, wealth and joy, and who know nothing else, may be unaware of the causes that will remove them from [that state] to its opposite. They may even think mistakenly that the means to their destruction and ruin will instead lead them to further goodness and security. Thus, their ruin occurs as a result of their actions without them even realizing it. The aforementioned describes the predicament of many people. But, on the other hand, if a person has experienced the two opposing [states] and knows their differences and the reasons for ruin in detail, he will strive to maintain his blessings.

A poet said,

> I learned about evil—not to do it, but to avoid it
> Whoever does not understand evil will fall into it.

This is the state of the believer: he is aware and has a deep understanding of evil. He is the most knowledgeable of people about evil, but also the furthest away. If he speaks about evil and its causes, another person would think that he was the most evil person; but if he would mingle with him, he would find him to be the most righteous. The point is that those who are afflicted with evil become very knowledgeable about the pathways through which it occurs. This allows them not only to prevent it in the future from themselves, but also from others, whether the latter ask for advice or not.

[23] God (Glory be to Him) tests His servant with the pain of being barred and distant from Him, along with being removed from the comfort of proximity to Him. Thus, if the servant is content with this [spiritual distance] and does not miss proximity to God, but rather is content and at ease with other than God, then God will place him in a lower rank concordant with his actions as he is not worthy [of a more lofty one]. But if the servant implores and

beseeches Him; seeks His aid like one who is anxious about [how he is going to get out of some calamity]; supplicates the prayer of one who is in dire need of his Lord; affirms that he has truly lost his [spiritual] life; and calls out to his Lord to return him to it; at that point he confirms that he is worthy of [a more lofty] rank, and is thus able to return to his [spiritual life], which he is in dire need of. His happiness and joy now intensify, and his pleasure and bliss become more complete. He now knows the importance [of proximity to God]; and thus, he holds fast and hard on to what he has.

Again, it is like the person in a desolate desert who loses his ride which carries his food and drink; so when he finds it after being certain of death, he appreciates what he has found to a much greater degree. God has many other secrets, wisdoms and signs that the human intellect cannot attain or comprehend.

If the servant is afflicted with loneliness after companionship, or with the emotions associated with being distant after being proximate, then he will long for the pleasure of the previous state—especially if he remembers the benevolence, kindness, compassion and proximity of God.

But if a person continues to sin and does not long for his initial good state, and does not feel his great loss and need to return to the proximity of the Lord, then such types of people are not ready [for an elevated rank]. Indeed, this is a sufficient punishment for his sins.

[24] The Divine wisdom dictated that humans are endowed with both temptations and anger. These two forces are essential characteristics that are inherent to humankind. It is through them that tribulation and testing occur. One is then either able to reach the higher levels in Paradise and meet God (Exalted is He) or alternatively descend into the lowest levels of Hellfire. God will differentiate between those who only desire to strive for Paradise, who use their anger for God's sake and to follow His Book, Messenger and religion, and between others who desire only to pursue their whims and worldly temptations, and use their anger in a [selfish] manner limited only to attaining good fortunes for themselves (even if they see the prohibition and legal limits of God being transgressed). God will not place these two types of people in the same abode [in the Hereafter].

The point is that creating humans in this fashion entails the utmost degree of wisdom, and it is incumbent upon each of these two forces to manifest their consequences. Thus, sins, infringements and disobediences will occur; and had these wrong conducts not occurred, we would not be human beings but rather angels. The Prophet said in a *ḥadīth*, 'Every child of Adam sins, and the best of the sinners are the repentant.'[21] Those human beings who are able to guard their virtue and entrench themselves within the pavilion of chastity are the least in number, but are the elite and most superior [in rank].

[25] One of the indicators that God (Glory be to Him) desires goodness for a servant is that He makes the servant forget his good deeds and He lifts it away from his heart and speech. On the other hand, if this person sins, then he will always remember it and concentrate all of his efforts in all of his states on absolving himself of it—this is the essence of mercy in this matter.

Some of the Predecessors said, 'A servant may do a sin but be entered into Paradise because of it, whereas he may do a good deed but be entered into Hellfire due to it.' It was asked, 'How can that be?' They responded, 'Such a person would sin but he would always remember it, cry, feel remorse, seek repentance and forgiveness, implore and return back to God, humble himself and feel broken. He will thereafter work hard to do many good deeds. Thus, it becomes [paradoxically] a mercy and means to his salvation. On the other hand, a person may do a good deed and deem it to be a favour upon the Lord and creation. He feels pride and deems himself superior to others. He is even surprised if people do not aggrandize, honour or praise him. These feelings will increase until they lead him to Hellfire.'[22] Therefore, one of the signs of being blessed is that the servant discounts his good deeds, whereas he always remembers his sins. On the other hand, those who are wretched are marked by the fact that they always recall their good deeds, whereas they belittle their sins. We rely upon God.

[26] Furthermore, once the servant sees his sins, errors and inadequacies, it becomes obvious to him that he should not view himself as better than others. He will not think of himself as being better

than any other Muslim who believes in God and His Messenger and avoids what God and His Messenger have prohibited. Also, he ceases to think that he deserves great respect or more rights than others, and he desists from criticizing others if they do not deal with him in that manner. He therefore views himself as having too low a status than to have rights upon the servants of God, or that they must take care of him, or that he is superior and therefore they must honour and aggrandize him. As a result, he now feels that those who simply greet him or smile when they see him have been good to him and done even more than what he deserves.

This believer is at ease with himself and gives other people a peace of mind by not complaining or being angry with them. He is not angry with existence in general; and thus, he enjoys a good life and peace of mind. There is a vast difference between a [believer] like this and one who continuously criticizes others and complains resentfully that they do not carry out their obligations towards him. People resent the latter to an even greater degree. Glory be to God Whose wisdom has inspired and awed the minds of humanity.

[27] In addition, it becomes incumbent upon [this believer] to desist from mentioning the inadequacies of others or even thinking about them since he is preoccupied with his own faults. Blessed are those whose own faults preoccupy them from involving themselves with the inadequacies of others, and woe unto those who forget their faults and preoccupy themselves with the shortcomings of others. The latter is a sign of wretchedness while the former is one of the signs of bliss.

[28] Furthermore, if a person falls into sin, he recognizes that he is no different from his sinful brothers. He also realizes that everyone is afflicted and necessarily dependent upon God's mercy and forgiveness. Thus, just as he wants his Muslim brothers to ask forgiveness for him, he should ask forgiveness for his Muslim brothers. He should supplicate, 'O my Lord, forgive myself, my parents, the Muslim men and women, and the believers both men and women.' Some of the Predecessors used to love to recite this supplication seventy times a day. Our Shaykh [Ibn Taymiyya] mentioned many great benefits of this supplication, much of which I do not recall—it

may have even been an invocation of his that he would always say—but he said it was permissible (*jāza*), in general, to say it between the two prostrations [in one cycle of prayer].

Thus, if a person sees that his brethren are afflicted just as he is, and are in need of [God's mercy] just like him, he will not avoid helping them except if he is completely ignorant of the forgiveness of God and His grace. A person who desists from assisting others should know that [expecting others to thereafter] help him is not justified, as the recompense is concordant with the deed.

Some of the Predecessors said, 'God reprimanded the angels due to their statement, *Wilt thou place therein one who will do harm therein and will shed blood.*[23] God thereafter tested Hārūt and Mārūt.[24] It was only then that the angels began to ask forgiveness for the offspring of Adam and supplicate for them.'[25]

[29] In addition, if a person sees himself as being disobedient, sinful and neglectful of the Lord's [commandments]—in the face of the excessive bounties of God in every moment, His kindness and protection, one's great need for the Lord, and the fact that he cannot exist for even a single breath without Him—then how can he desire that people treat him well according to his desire, while he does not even obey his Lord appropriately?

This knowledge makes it incumbent upon one to ask for forgiveness for other sinners, to overlook and indulge them, and to pass up on pursuing what may even be rightly his. Once the servant attains these fruits, it becomes a sign that he is a mercy in his own right.

On the other hand, in relation to those who do the opposite [i.e. act arrogantly and are proud, as mentioned in Points 15, 20 and 26], it is—by God—a sign of their wretchedness. They will incur the opposite [of mercy, i.e. God's punishment]. Due to the fact that they are insignificant and disgraceful in God's sight, He removes any obstacles between them and sins so as to justly and rightly punish them. Furthermore, those people's sins will multiply leading to second and then third ones and so on—what a great affliction! They will therefore be ruined in ways that they do not even realize, and shall be punished by the will of God in the lowest levels of Hellfire. Whoever does not have a profound understanding of this matter will become ruined in ways he could never have anticipated. Good deeds aggregate together and the same applies to evil sins: each leads to its like.

Some of the Predecessors have said, 'One of the rewards for a good deed is that it is followed by another pious deed, whereas one of the punishments of a sin is that another sin [is subsequently perpetrated].'[26] This is more evident than needing any maxim or proof. We rely on God.

[30] If one contemplates the wisdom of God (Glory be to Him) it becomes clear that He has tested His servants and elite to allow them to reach the loftiest objectives and most perfect ends. They could not have reached these except by traversing a bridge composed of trials and tribulations. This bridge is so integral that they cannot reach Paradise except over it. Outwardly, this bridge involves suffering and hardship, but in reality it is a mercy, honour and blessing for us. God has bestowed upon us many great blessings and mercies as a result of these trials and tribulations.

Deeply reflect on the case of our father Adam and how his tribulation resulted in him repenting and then being selected, chosen, guided and granted an elevated status. Had it not been for this tribulation—which was being exited from the Garden and what followed thereafter—he would have not achieved all of that. There is a vast difference between his initial state and his latter one.

Next, deeply reflect on the case of our second father, Noah, and how his tribulation and patience [in the face of] his people's [disbelief] for many centuries ultimately resulted in God satisfying him and drowning all of the disbelievers due to his supplication. Furthermore, God made the people thereafter descendants of his, and made him one of the top five messengers who were described as having firm resolve. In addition, God commanded Muḥammad, His Messenger and Prophet (may God bless him and grant him peace), to be patient like Noah. He also praised Noah because he was thankful: *He was a grateful servant*.[27] Thus, God described Noah's patience and thankfulness as being perfect.

Then deeply reflect on our third father, Abraham (may God bless him and grant him peace), for he is the leader of the true believers, the master of the prophets, the basis for the current world, and a friend of the Lord of the Worlds from amongst the offspring of Adam. Reflect on how his patience in the face of his trials, self-sacrifice for God's sake, and championing His religion resulted in God taking him as a friend. God also commanded His Messenger and friend Muḥammad (may God bless him and grant him peace) to follow Abraham's religious creed.[28]

I will just mention here one aspect regarding Abraham's trial: his being asked to sacrifice his son. God honoured and rewarded Abraham for his submission to the commandment of God in this regard, and He blessed his offspring and made them immensely numerous, filling all corners of the earth. There is no one more generous than God (Most Blessed and Exalted is He), and He is the Beneficent. Thus, God will grant whoever leaves something for His sake, or does something for His sake, many times more than what he has forgone and reward him manifold for what he has done.

A person's fear is especially heightened to the utmost degree when asked to sacrifice his son due to the concern that his lineage will become cut-off. But when Abraham offered his son up to God and Ishmael likewise offered himself up, God multiplied his lineage and blessed them until they filled this earth. Furthermore, God brought forth the prophets, including Muḥammad (may God bless him and grant him peace), from amongst Abraham's lineage specifically.

It has been mentioned that David (may God bless him and grant him peace) wanted to take a census of the number of Israelites and, although they remained doing so for some time, they could not accomplish it. God then inspired to David, 'You know that I promised your father Abraham—after I commanded him to sacrifice his son whereupon he fulfilled and obeyed My command—that I would bless his offspring until they became like the number of the stars, which cannot be enumerated. Yet you wanted to count them despite the fact that I willed that they could not be enumerated [by humanity]...'[29] Thus, God made these two great nations—the offspring of Israel and Ishmael—descendants of Abraham; and they cannot be enumerated except by God, Who created and provided for them.

In addition to all of the above, God bestowed much honour upon Abraham, and made all of the nations, as well as the angels in the heavens, venerate and praise him highly. These are some of the fruits of his pious deed. Thus, may destruction come upon those who know [God's command], but chose to follow otherwise! They have lost everything and their regret will be even more immense.

Moreover, deeply reflect on the case of Moses (peace be upon him). His trials and tribulations began from the time of his birth, but ultimately God spoke to him, brought him near to Him, wrote the Torah with His Hand for him, and raised him to the highest ranks [in Paradise]. Furthermore, God tolerated more from him more than from any other prophet as he threw the Tablets on the ground, causing them to break; he grabbed the beard of Aaron, a prophet of God, and dragged him by it; he hit the face of the Angel of Death and knocked out his eye; and he argued with his Lord on the Night Journey concerning the matter of the [number of prayers obligated upon the] Messenger of God [Muḥammad] (may God bless him and grant him peace). But his Lord loves him, regardless, and his status was not lowered whatsoever [by such events]. Rather, Moses is one of the most distinguished in the sight of the Lord and is proximate to Him. Had it not been for what Moses had previously undergone, his patience in the face of hardships and great tribulations for God's sake, his withstanding for God's sake the difficult circumstances under the nation of Pharaoh and his people and then with the nation of Israelites and their harm, then [his rank] would have not been so [eminently lofty].

Then, deeply reflect on the case of the Messiah (may God bless him and grant him peace) and how he was patient with his people and endured for the sake of God, until God raised him up to Him and cleansed him from presence of the disbelievers. God then took revenge against his enemies whom He sundered and dispersed on this earth, and stripped them of their kingdom and honour until the Day of Judgment.

If you subsequently reflect deeply upon the Prophet Muḥammad (may God bless him and grant him peace), his patience for God's sake, and how he endured what no other prophet had to with his people, [you will find that] he encountered many different circumstances, including peace and war, wealth and poverty, security and fear, as well as having to emigrate after living in his hometown. He had to forgo much for God's sake, withstand the death of many of those whom he loved and who were loyal, in addition to numerous other types of harm that the disbelievers inflicted upon him, whether it was their statements, actions, magic, lies, slandering him or blasphemy. Yet, he was patient throughout and followed the commandment of God to call others to God and Islam. No prior prophet was harmed or had to endure as much as him for God's sake. Nor was any prophet given what he was given as God honoured him with people's praise of him, made him the master of all people, and made him the most proximate and distinguished of all people to Him. Indeed, God granted Muḥammad the compelling intercession on the Day of Judgment. These [distinctions] were all due to the trials and tribulations he encountered. God thus made him more noble, esteemed and blessed, and He elevated him to the loftiest rank.

This is also the state of those who follow the Prophet [Muḥammad] and have inherited his [knowledge]. Everyone has their share of these tribulations—God drives them to their perfection depending on the extent to which they follow [the Prophet's message]. As for those who do not [adhere to the message], they have only a share of this world whereby they eat, live a carefree life, and enjoy themselves to attain what has been [ontologically] determined for them. Yet, God's saints (*awliyā'*) endure tribulations while others are indifferent and live a base life. The saints live [intermittently] in a state of fear [for their safety] while others are secure. Sometimes the saints are grieved while others live happily amongst their families. Those [living a carefree life] are anxious to maintain other peoples' respect and deference, as well as to preserve their wealth—regardless of what it takes—while the saints are concerned with establishing the religion of God, promoting His words and strengthening His other saints. They strive to call others to Islam for His sake alone so that they will worship God alone (not other [false deities]) and obey His Messenger (not others).

Thus, God (Glory be to Him) possesses many wise purposes in

His tribulations of the prophets, messengers and believing servants which are not [totally] comprehensible to people's minds. Again, one cannot attain the highest and most praiseworthy stations except by traversing a bridge of hardships and tribulations. All praise is due to God alone, and may God bestow His blessings and peace upon Muḥammad, his family and his Companions until the Day of Judgment.

Now, deeply reflect upon the dazzling wisdoms and perfection of this straight and true religion that was conveyed by Muḥammad (may God bless him and grant him peace). Had the Prophet not brought forth any other sign, the Divine Law would suffice as proof that [his message was revealed] by God. It also represents evidence of God's perfect knowledge and wisdom, vast mercy and benevolence, as well as His knowledge of the Unseen and material world, and fundamentals and consequences of matters. It is one of the greatest blessings that God has bestowed upon His servants. The Exalted has said, *God verily hath shown grace to the believers by sending unto them a messenger of their own who reciteth unto them His revelations, and causeth them to grow, and teacheth them the Book and wisdom; although before (he came to them) they were in flagrant error.*[30]

God has also reminded us of His great blessings, and that we should thank Him for allowing us to follow it: *This day have I perfected your religion for you [and completed My favour unto you, and have chosen for you Islam as your religion]*.[31] One should, likewise, deeply reflect upon how He has described this religion, which He selected for them, as being perfect and a blessing. There is no inadequacy, flaw or gap in it. Nothing within it is inconsistent with wisdom, but rather it is complete in its righteousness and magnificence. In addition, He described His favour as being complete, which signifies that He will never take it away after having bestowed it upon them, and that it will remain perpetuated in this world and in the Hereafter.

Furthermore, deeply reflect upon the beauty in juxtaposing *completed* with *My favour* and *perfected* with *your religion*. The religion is a characteristic of theirs as they are the ones uprightly establishing it, whereas the blessing is His. God is the One Who arranges, confers and bestows it upon them—it is truly His blessing. The followers of Muḥammad were selected for this perfection, which was not bestowed upon any other nation. Thereafter, He reiterated His favour and certified that it is perfect and complete by saying *have chosen for you Islam as your religion.*[32] Some of the pious Predecessors would say, 'Oh, what a great religion! Even if there were only [a few] men [upholding it, the religion would remain triumphant].'

Now, God has accepted His servants' praise of Him and remembrance of His favours, Names, Attributes, wisdom and exaltedness—even though they cannot do so in a manner consistent with what He is deserving, or similar to how He has praised Himself. A creature cannot praise Him in a manner befitting Him (Most Blessed and Exalted is He) or acknowledge [the blessings of] His Book and religion as they deserve. Moreover, none of this Community can even praise His Messenger as he deserves—the Prophet is more eminent than what their praise of him could entail. Despite this, God (Exalted is He) loves to be praised and extolled, and loves that His Book, religion and Messenger [be also praised].

The innate disposition and reason have witnessed that this universe has a Lord who is omnipotent, most wise, omniscient, merciful and perfect in His Essence and Attributes. God only wishes wellbeing for His [believing] servants through His Divine Law and the eminent Sunna [of the Prophet Muḥammad]. In fact, both of these are concordant with people's endowed intellect. Thus, the Divine Law and the Sunna affirm what is good as good and what is evil as evil. In addition, they both seek to attain what people's nature acknowledges to be beneficial in regards to their affairs, and repel what is harmful and evil to them.

Now, one should recognize that not even the kings of this earth deem it necessary or wise to notify everyone under their authority of all that they know; or reveal to them everything that they are doing, the politics of it, the reasons for it and the meaning behind it all. They do not even inform their subjects of those things every time they command them to do something, send them out on a mission, or draw up their political agendas. There is no doubt that to do so would be unwise and not advantageous.

Thus, in light of the right of the Lord of the Worlds, Who is

Most Wise and Whose knowledge and wisdom are infinite compared to ours, those who are reasonable should use what they know of His wise purposes as proof that there is a wisdom for that which they do not understand. Furthermore, they should realize that there is a wise purpose for everything that God has created, commanded and prescribed.

Does wisdom necessitate that God (Exalted is He) reveal to each of His servants everything that He does, the reasons for all that He administers or wills, or His wise purpose for originating and creating every small entity? Are creatures even able to [comprehend all of that]? Instead, God has concealed much of His design and imperative from His creation, whereby He has not even revealed them to the proximate angels or prophets He sent.

The Lord's actions and commandments proceed entirely from His wisdom, mercy and beneficence.[33] It is sufficient we understand in general that His wise purposes for what He created, commanded and prescribed are far-reaching and absolutely wise, even if we cannot comprehend their particulars. God (Glorious and Exalted is He) has established the affairs of His servants by informing them of the grand meanings of His creation and commandments whilst leaving aside, in many cases, their details and particulars. This is a general principle regarding this matter.

One should suffice with knowing the universal wisdoms and general reasons for them. We should recognize that everything that He has commanded encompasses far-reaching wisdoms. As for the detailed secrets of these wise purposes, they are not attainable for all of humanity. Rather, God provides insight to those whom He wishes of His creation to what He wills. Ultimately, you should adhere to this principle and safeguard it.

NOTES

Translator's Introduction

1 For biographical details, see Tallal Zeni (tr.), *Ibn Qayyim al-Jawziyya on Knowledge* (Cambridge: Islamic Texts Society, 2016), pp. ix–xvi.

2 Bakr Abū Zayd calculates Ibn al-Qayyim's works to be ninety-eight, of which thirty are extant. See Bakr Abū Zayd, *Ibn Qayyim al-Jawziyya: ḥayātuhu āthāruhu mawāriduhu* (Riyadh: Dār al-ʿĀṣima, 1995), pp. 200–309.

3 *Miftāḥ dār al-saʿāda* is considered to be a middle work, while *Shifā al-ʿalīl* is a late one, according to the division of Ibn al-Qayyim's oeuvre into early, middle and late by Holtzman. See Livnat Holtzman, 'Ibn Qayyim al-Jawziyyah', in Joseph E. Lowery and Devin Stewart (eds), *Essays in Arabic Literary Biography II: 1350–1850* (Wiesbaden: Harrassowitz Verlag, 2009), pp. 202–203.

4 Jon Hoover, 'God's Wise Purposes in Creating Iblīs: Ibn Qayyim al-Ǧawziyyah's Theodicy of God's Names and Attributes', in Caterina Bori and Livnat Holtzman (eds), *A Scholar in the Shadow: Essays in the Legal and Theological Thought of Ibn al-Qayyim al-Ǧawziyyah* (Rome: Istituto per l'Oriente C. A. Nallino, 2010), p. 116.

5 Jon Hoover, *Ibn Taymiyya's Theodicy of Perpetual Optimism* (Leiden: Brill, 2007), p. 5.

6 See below, p. 23.

7 See below, p. 103.

8 The 'religious' or 'deontological' refers to that which has been given a legal status according to the Divine Law; hence it is *sharʿan*, *sharʿī* or *dīnī*, or 'by the Law'. The 'ontological' refers to that which has simply been created and allowed to exist by the Divine Himself, without that necessarily implying that His pleasure is attached to it; hence it is merely 'decreed' (*qadaran*) or 'existent in the cosmos' (*kawnī*) by the divine will. The nuance at work here in Ibn al-Qayyim's thought will become more apparent as he develops this distinction throughout the book. For example, see the discussions in Chapter Thirteen and Chapter Fourteen on the topic.

9 See below, p. 39.

10 See below, p. 88.

11 See Chapters 4–6 and 8 below.

12 Rāzī states, 'The acts of men occur by compulsion' and 'affirming determinism is inescapable'. Shihadeh notes that 'al-Rāzī concludes that man, though a

voluntary agent in the sense of acting with awareness, is ultimately compelled... It was almost unprecedented in Sunni theology that such an uncompromisingly bold and systematic determinism (*jabr*) be affirmed.' See Ayman Shihadeh, *The Teleological Ethics of Fakhr al-Dīn al-Rāzī* (Leiden: Brill, 2006), p. 37.

13 See below, pp. 34–35. Also, see Fakhr al-Dīn al-Rāzī, *al-Mubāḥith al-mashriqiyya* (Qom: Intishārāt Bīdār, 1950), p. 523.

14 Hoover, *Ibn Taymiyya's Theodicy*, p. 73. See also below, Chapter 10.

15 Ovamir Anjum, *Politics, Law, and Community in Islamic Thought: The Taymiyyan Moment* (New York: Cambridge University Press, 2012), p. 204. I would like to thank Ovamir Anjum for personally providing insights on Ibn al-Qayyim and his works.

16 Sherman A. Jackson, *Islam and the Problem of Black Suffering* (Oxford: Oxford University Press, 2009), p. 137.

17 For the statements of Bājūrī and Mārghanī, see Suraqah Abdul Aziz (tr.), *A Refined Explanation of the Sanusi Creed [entitled] The Foundational Proofs* (Rotterdam: Sunni Publications, 2013), p. 111.

18 See below, p. 98.

19 See David B. Burrell and Nazih Daher (tr.), *The Ninety-Nine Beautiful Names of God* (Cambridge: Islamic Texts Society, 1995), p. 55–6.

20 See below, p. 132.

21 See below, p. 193.

22 See below, p. 261.

23 See below, p. 263.

24 See below, p. 96.

25 See below, p. 203.

26 See below, p. 203.

27 Hoover, *Ibn Taymiyya's Theodicy*, pp. 1–2.

28 See below, p. 95.

29 See Jackson, *Islam and the Problem of Black Suffering*, pp. 76, 81, 84–6, 90–1.

30 Shihadeh explains that the 'definition of "good" and "bad" works at two levels. In the sphere of human action, it underpins a theory of divine command ethics by establishing that revelation is the sole legitimate source for norms that govern human action and behavior. At the same time it supports a broader theological voluntarism: since God's command applies only to His creatures, His own will and acts are unconstrained by any duties or prohibitions.' See Ayman Shihadeh, 'Theories of Ethical Value in Kalām: A New Interpretation', in Sabine Schmidtke (ed.), *The Oxford Handbook of Islamic Theology* (Oxford: Oxford University Press, 2016), p. 402.

31 This Ashʿarī doctrine was the 'antithesis of Muʿtazilī realism... [It represents a] refutation of Muʿtazilī claims that ethical value is a real attribute of acts and consequently cognizable to the mind... [T]he mind therefore has no moral objects of knowledge in the external world'. See ibid., p. 397. Shihadeh affirms

that the neo-Ashʿarī Rāzī's 'ethical rationalism is antithetical to the realism propounded by the Muʿtazila', much like classical Ashʿariyya. Ibid., p. 402.

32 Shihadeh states that Rāzī 'implements consequentialism not only as the background on which the revealed law is superimposed, but also as the chief rational normative principle in jurisprudence through which the law is refined and extended. Although God's commands are not motivated, al-Rāzī nevertheless contends that they generally serve the interest of humans. So, in discussing the problem of the religious states of advantageous acts on which revelation is silent (*maṣlaḥa mursala*), he argues that the agent ought to seek such advantages and to avoid harms, since these principles 'are known almost immediately (*bi-l-ḍarūra*) to be at the heart of the teachings of the prophets (*dīn al-anbiyā'*) and the objective of revealed laws (*al-maqṣūd mina l-sharā'iʿ*)'. Ibid., p. 404.

33 Ibid., p. 384.

34 Hoover, *Ibn Taymiyya's Theodicy*, pp. 1–2.

35 The late-Ashʿarī doctrine on the matter can be seen in the following words of Aḥmad b. ʿĪsā al-Anṣārī, in his commentary on Sanūsī's *Umm al-barāhīn*: 'It is impossible for Allah, the Exalted to be described with motives in His actions or judgments. The word "motives" [*aghrāḍ*] is the plural of motive [*gharaḍ*] and it is the incentive to look after benefits and repel harms. This is impossible with regards to His Divine Entity because He is in no need of obtaining benefits or repelling harms; He is Free of all needs [*al-Ghanī*] and independent from everything.' Abdul Aziz (tr.), *A Refined Explanation of the Sanusi Creed*, p. 111.

36 Rodrigo Adem (tr.), *Al-Māturīdī and the Development of Sunnī Theology in Samarqand* (Leiden: Brill, 2015), p. 299. Ibn Taymiyya states, 'Injustice is to put something into an improper place, while justice is to put everything into its proper place. God (Glory be to Him) is Most Wise and Just, and He puts all things into their proper places… [This is in agreement with the definition put forth by the grammarian] Abū Bakr b. al-Anbārī [d. 328/940].' Ibn Taymiyya, *Risāla fī maʿnā kawn al-Rabb ʿādilan wa-fī tanzīhihi ʿan al-ẓulm*, in *Jāmiʿ al-rasā'il li-Ibn Taymiyya* (Riyadh: Dār al-ʿAṭā', 2001), pp. 123–124.

37 Aron Zysow, 'Karrāmiyya', in *The Oxford Handbook of Islamic Theology*, pp. 258–259.

38 Jackson, *Islam and the Problem of Black Suffering*, pp. 110–111.

39 Adem (tr.), *Al-Māturīdī*, pp. 263 and 296–300.

40 Michael E. Marmura (tr.), *The Metaphysics of the Healing* (Provo: Brigham Young University Press, 2005), p. xxi.

41 See Shams Inati, *The Problem of Evil: Ibn Sīnā's Theodicy* (Binghamton: Global Publications, 2000), pp. 169–173.

42 Inati, *The Problem of Evil*, p. 172.

43 Ibn al-Qayyim, *Shifā' al-ʿalīl* (Riyadh: Dār al-Ṣamayʿī, 2013), p. 213.

44 Abū Ḥāmid Muḥammad b. Muḥammad al-Ghazālī (d. 504/1111) is considered by many to be the 'Renewer' (*mujaddid*) of his century and 'the Proof (*ḥujja*)

of Islam'. He wrote many significant books, including the *Iḥyā' ʿulūm al-dīn* [The Revival of the Religious Sciences], which bridged the gap between orthopraxy and Sufism, and is considered to be his greatest work. He also wrote *Tahāfut al-falāsifa* [The Incoherence of the Philosophers], which successfully refuted Greek philosophy and its supporters amongst the Arab philosophers, such as Fārābī and Ibn Sīnā. One of his books in the field of logic was *Miʿyār al-ʿilm fī fann al-manṭiq*. His theology was essentially Ashʿarī, while his jurisprudence was Shāfiʿī. He also provided the Islamic creed for the schools built by Niẓām al-Mulk, which led to a 'Sunni revival'. See Abdul Rahman Azzam, *Saladin: The Triumph of the Sunni Revival* (Cambridge: Islamic Texts Society, 2014), pp. 8 and 12.

45 See Michael E. Marmura (tr.), *The Incoherence of the Philosophers* (Provo: Brigham Young University Press, 2000), and the first, thirteenth and twentieth discussions, respectively. See also Alladin Yaqub (tr.), *Al-Ghazālī's Moderation in Belief* (Chicago: The University of Chicago Press, 2013), p. 244.

46 Eric Ormsby, *Theodicy in Islamic Thought: The Dispute over al-Ghazālī's "Best of All Possible Worlds"* (Princeton: Princeton University Press, 1984), p. 39. For the Arabic, see *Iḥyā' ʿulūm al-dīn* (Beirut: Dār Ṣādir, 2010), vol. IV, pp. 319–320. This dictum is within Book 35, which is titled 'His Oneness and Reliance upon Him' (*al-tawḥīd wa'l-tawakkul*).

47 Ormsby, *Theodicy in Islamic Thought*, p. 32.

48 Ibid., pp. 92–134.

49 Jalāl al-Dīn al-Suyūṭī, *Tashyīd al-arkān fī laysa fi'l-imkān abdaʿ mimmā kān*. This is included as an appendix in *Iḥyā'*, vol. V, pp. 369–394.

50 Ibid., vol. V, p. 371.

51 Ibid., vol. V, p. 372.

52 Ibid., vol. V, pp. 374–375.

53 *Iḥyā'*, vol. IV, p. 320. See Ormsby, *Theodicy in Islamic Thought*, p. 39.

54 Suyūṭī, *Tashyīd al-arkān*, in *Iḥyā'*, vol. V, p. 381.

55 Ibid., vol. V, p. 377.

56 Ibid., vol. V, pp. 378. This refers to the story of Moses and al-Khiḍr in Q.XVIII.71–82.

57 Ibn Taymiyya, *Risāla fī maʿnā kawn al-Rabb ʿādilan*, p. 142; Hoover, *Ibn Taymiyya's Theodicy*, pp. 226–7.

58 Hoover, *Ibn Taymiyya's Theodicy*, p. 227.

59 Ormsby, *Theodicy in Islamic Thought*, p. 109.

60 See Wael Hallaq, *Ibn Taymiyya Against the Greek Logicians* (Oxford: Oxford University Press, 1993), pp. 111–112.

61 Ibn Taymiyya, *Dar' taʿāruḍ al-ʿaql wa'l-naql* (Beirut: Dār al-Kutub al-ʿIlmiyyah, 2009), vol. III, p. 370.

62 Ibid., vol. III, p. 80–82. Ghazālī states, 'The way of moderation... [is only found by] those granted success [from God], those who perceive things with

illumination [from God] rather than only by transmitted reports. Then, when the mysteries of things as they truly are, are unveiled to them, they go back to the traditions and narrations, and affirm what accords with what they have witnessed with the light of certitude, and figuratively interpret what does not accord with it. As for the one who takes the cognition of these things from transmitted reports alone, he will not be able to secure a firm foothold in them or find a solid position... Now to disclose the proper way of moderation in these matters would require us to delve into the science of unveiling, and to speak on it at length, which we shall not do here.' See Khalid Williams (tr.), *The Principles of the Creed: Book 2 of The Revival of the Religious Sciences* (Louisville: Fons Vitae, 2016), pp. 55–56.

63 Ibn Kathīr, *al-Bidāya wa'l-nihāya* (Damascus: Dār al-Fikr, 1986), vol. XIV, pp. 234–235.

64 Ghazālī, *Iḥyā'*, vol. I, p. 22; Zeni (tr.), *Ibn Qayyim al-Jawziyya on Knowledge*, pp. 205–6.

65 See below, p. 97.

66 See below, p. 101.

67 See below, p. 204.

68 See below, p. 145.

69 See Ibn al-Qayyim, *Miftāḥ dār al-saʿāda* (Mecca: Dār ʿĀlim al-Fawā'id, 2015), pp. 991–999 and below p. 96.

70 See below, p. 15.

71 See below, p. 37.

72 Numerous references are given for such Sunni authorities by Jon Hoover, including the statement of Ījī in *Kitāb al-mawāqif*: 'The Muslims have reached a consensus that the unbelievers will abide in the Fire forever; their chastisement will not be cut off.' See Jon Hoover, 'Islamic Universalism: Ibn Qayyim al-Jawziyya's Salafī Deliberations on the Duration of Hell-fire', *The Muslim World*, vol. XCIX (2009), pp. 197–8.

73 Mohammad Khalil, *Islam and the Fate of Others: The Salvation Question* (Oxford: Oxford University Press, 2012), pp. 46–48.

74 See also Khalil, *Islam and the Fate of Others*, pp. 92–102 and 127–129.

75 Hoover, 'Islamic Universalism: Ibn Qayyim al-Jawziyya's Salafī Deliberations on the Duration of Hell-fire', pp. 181–182.

76 See Albānī's introduction to Muḥammad al-Ṣanʿānī, *Rafʿ al-astār li-ibṭāl adillat al-qā'ilīn bi-fanā' al-nār* (Beirut: al-Maktab al-Islāmī, 1984), in general and pp. 48-49 specifically.

77 Q.XI.107.

78 Q.XI.108.

79 See below, p. 192.

80 The verse is Q.XL.7. See below, pp. 340-341.

81 See below, p. 185.

82 See below, p. 191.

83 See below, p. 193.

84 See Ibn al-Qayyim, *Miftāḥ dār al-saʿāda*, pp. 27–87. The discussion in the *Miftāḥ* is quite lengthy and repetitive as Ibn al-Qayyim brings forth the arguments of each viewpoint, and then presents their respective rebuttals. Ibn al-Qayyim clearly believes that the Garden was in Paradise, as he states, 'God (Glory be to Him) did not remove Adam from it except that He willed to return him to it in a more perfect state.' *Miftāḥ dār al-saʿāda*, p. 26. He also says, 'Now, God had predestined before He had created Adam that he would descend from the Garden [in Paradise] and be settled on this [earth]. This predestination occurred through causes [in order to attain certain] wise purposes… Yet praiseworthy and intended outcomes predicated on Adam's descent from Paradise did follow from these causes. Further causes were then arranged to lead to outcomes that accounted for other wise purposes. One of these outcomes is that Adam and the believers will return [to Paradise] in the most perfect state.' See below, p. 143. Ibn al-Qayyim states that the objective 'Is to recount some of the wisdoms and benefits that occur as a result of Adam's exit from the Garden and being settled onto this earth, which is the abode of tribulation and testing. The objective is to refute those who say that God's wisdom is inconsistent with allowing Adam to commit a sin that results in his exit from the Garden or that there is no benefit in that. It is also to refute those who negate [God's] wisdom and [claim that humanity's exit from the Garden] occurred solely because God had willed it.' *Miftāḥ dār al-saʿāda*, p. 36.

85 Ibn al-Qayyim, *Mukhtaṣar al-Ṣawāʿiq al-mursala ʿalā'l-Jahmiyya wa'l-Muʿaṭṭila* (Beirut: Dār al-Kutub al-ʿIlmiyyah, 1993), p. 217. The tradition is found in Tirmidhī 2599 and Ibn Abī al-Dunyā 59. It is 'weak' according to Albānī (*Silsilat al-aḥādīth al-ḍaʿīfa wa'l-mawḍūʿa* 1977). One should also note that there is no mention within this tradition as to the nature of those two individuals, that is, whether they were sinful believers or disbelievers. That they were sinful believers—and not disbelievers—is discussed in Ṣanʿānī, *Rafʿ al-astār*, p. 115.

86 Q.IV.137. There are two interpretations of those mentioned in this verse: 1) it refers to some of the hypocrites who may have believed twice but then disbelieved after each instance, and then increased in their disbelief; or 2) it refers to those who believed in Moses and the Torah but then disbelieved, believed in Jesus as a Prophet and the Gospel but then disbelieved, and finally became the worst disbelievers by denying the prophethood of Muḥammad and the Qur'ān. Ṭabarī prefers the latter view. Either way, it refers to a group who believed at some point in their lives but then disbelieved. See Abū Jaʿfar Muḥammad b. Jarīr al-Ṭabarī, *Tafsīr al-Ṭabarī* (Beirut: Mu'assasat al-Risāla, 2000), vol. IX, pp. 314–317.

87 Q.IX.113 (Muḥammad Asad translation). This is in agreement with the verses Q.IV.48 and 116: *God forgiveth not that a partner should be ascribed unto Him* (*yushraka bihi*). *He forgiveth* (*all*) *save that to whom He will.*

88 For Taqī al-Dīn al-Subkī's arguments, see his *al-Iʿtibār bi-baqāʾ al-janna waʾl-nār* in *al-Durra al-maḍiyya fīʾl-radd ʿalā Ibn Taymiyya* (Damascus: Maṭbaʿat al-Taraqqī, 1928).

89 See Jon Hoover, 'Against Islamic Universalism', in Birgit Krawietz and Georges Tamer (eds), *Islamic Theology, Philosophy and Law: Debating Ibn Taymiyya and Ibn Qayyim al-Jawziyya* (Berlin: De Gruyter, 2013), pp. 397–399.

90 *Zād al-maʿād* was written after both *Shifāʾ al-ʿalīl* and *al-Ṣawāʿiq al-mursala*, and was likely his last work; see Holtzman, 'Ibn Qayyim al-Jawziyyah', p. 217.

91 Ibn al-Qayyim, *Zād al-maʿād fī hadī khayr al-ʿibād* (Beirut: Mu'assasat al-Risāla, 1994), vol. I, p. 68.

92 Subkī, *Iʿtibār*, p. 78. Of note, a slightly summarized version of Subkī's treatise was provided as an appendix to the book *Reliance of the Traveller: A Classic Manual of Islamic Sacred Law*, translated by Nuh Ha Mim Keller (Beltsville: Amana Publications, 1994), pp. 995–1002. The above quote in Arabic is '*man qāl bi-fanāʾ al-jannah waʾl-nār aw aḥadihima fa-huwa kāfir*,' which Keller translates as 'Whoever says that heaven or hell perish is an unbeliever,' p. 1002.

93 Of note, Ghazālī does not discount the rational possibility of individuals being annihilated, although his statements on creed affirm the eternality of Hell. Ghazālī states, 'We claim that if God (Exalted is He) assigns obligations to His servants and they obey Him, then it is not obligatory for Him to reward them; rather if He wants to, He may reward them, punish them, or even annihilate them and never resurrect them; that He does not care whether He forgives all the infidels and punishes all the believers; and that this is not impossible in itself, nor does it contradict any of the divine attributes.' See Yaqub (tr.), *Al-Ghazālī's Moderation in Belief*, p. 180. Ghazālī also mentions this in the nineteenth discussion in Marmura (tr.), *The Incoherence of the Philosophers*. Therefore, a similar argument could be made about Hellfire or a portion thereof being annihilated. In conclusion, maintaining that possibility regarding Hellfire should not indicate disbelief.

94 Q.XI.107: *Abiding there so long as the heavens and the earth endure save for that which thy Lord willeth. Thy Lord is doer of what He will.*

95 Ibn Ḥajar, *al-Durar al-kāminah fī aʿyān al-māʾata al-thāminah* (Hyderabad: Maṭbaʿat Majlis Dāʾirat al-Maʿārif al-ʿUthmāniyyah, 1972), vol. V, p. 139.

Chapter One

1 This is a reference to the *ḥadīth*, 'There will always exist a group from my Community upon the truth. They will not be harmed by those who have forsaken or opposed them until God's decree comes.' Muslim 4950; Tirmidhī 2229; Abū Dāwūd 4252; Ibn Māja 10.

2 Iblīs is one of the names of the Devil or Satan (*Shayṭān*). It is derived from the word *ablasa*, which means 'to despair of all hope or goodness'.

3 This is a reference to Q.LIII.3–4.
4 This is a reference to Q.V.54.
5 Q.VIII.37.
6 Q.II.30.
7 Q.II.105.
8 Aḥmad 7160; Bayhaqī (*Sunan*) 13,327; Ibn Ḥibbān 6365; *Ḥilya*, v.III, 256. It is 'authentic' according to Albānī (*Silsilat al-aḥādīth al-ṣaḥīḥa* 1002).
9 Q.XVII.1.
10 Q.LXXVII.19.
11 Q.II.23.
12 Abū ʿAbd Allāh Muḥammad b. Ismāʿīl b. Ibrāhīm b. al-Mughīrāh al-Bukhārī (d. 256/870) was born in the city of Bukhara. Imām Bukhārī went on to collect the most authentic book of *ḥadīths* known as *Ṣaḥīḥ al-Bukhārī*, which is comprised of 7275 *ḥadīths* with repetition or 2230 without repetition.
13 Abū al-Ḥusayn Muslim b. al-Ḥajjāj b. Muslim b. Ward al-Naysābūrī (d. 261/875) was a student of Imām Bukharī and Imām Aḥmad. *Ṣaḥīḥ Muslim* is comprised of 7563 *ḥadīths* with repetition or 3033 without repetition.
14 Bukhārī 4472; Muslim 475; Tirmidhī 3148; Ibn Māja 4312; Aḥmad 15.
15 Q.LI.56.
16 Q.XXVI.8–9.
17 Q.XXXIX.75.
18 Aḥmad (*Musnad* 21,232 and *Zuhd* 256); Ḥākim 3255; Bayhaqī (*Shuʿab*) 4128. It is 'sound' according to Albānī (*Mishkāt* 122).
19 Q.LXXV.36.
20 Q.XXIII.115–116.
21 Bukhārī 6308; Muslim 6955; Aḥmad 3627.
22 See Chapter Fifteen.
23 Tirmidhī 2530; Ibn Māja 4331; Aḥmad 22,738; Ibn Ḥibbān 4612; Ḥākim 267; Bayhaqī (*Sunan*) 18,494. It is 'authentic' according to Albānī (*Silsilat al-aḥādīth al-ṣaḥīḥa* 921, 922, 1913). Of note, the *ḥadīths* present in Bukhārī (7423), Muslim (4879) and Nasā'ī (3134) specify these one hundred levels for those who wage battle/strive for God's sake.
24 Q.XLIII.72.
25 Q.XVI.32.
26 Bukhārī 6467; Muslim 7122; Aḥmad 24,941.
27 Zayd b. Thābit (d. 40/660) was a Companion and scribe of the Prophet. He was charged by Abū Bakr al-Ṣiddīq to collect the Qur'ānic scripts into one assembled text.
28 Ḥudhayfa b. al-Yamān (d. 35/656) was a Companion of the Prophet. He participated in all the battles after Uḥud. He was known as the 'Keeper of the Secret of the Messenger of God', as the Prophet told him the identities of the Hypocrites.
29 Ibn Māja 77; Abū Dāwūd 4699; Aḥmad 21,589; Ibn Ḥibbān 727; Bayhaqī

(*Sunan*) 20,874. It is 'authentic' according to Albānī (*Ṣaḥīḥ al-Jāmiʿ* 5244). This was narrated also by ʿAbd Allāh b. Masʿūd and Ubayy b. Kaʿb.

30 Q.II.30.

31 Q.VI.165.

32 Q.VII.129.

33 Q.XXI.37.

34 Q.XVII.11.

35 ʿAbd al-Raḥmān b. Ṣakhr al-Azdī, known as Abū Hurayra (d. 61/681), was a pre-eminent Companion. He narrated 5374 *ḥadīth*s with repetition (or about 1500 without repetition).

36 Bukhārī 6408; Tirmidhī 3600; Aḥmad 7424.

37 This is derived from Q.VIII.42.

38 Q.XVI.7.

39 Q.II.197.

40 Q.IX.111.

41 This phrase is used by some scholars, such as Ibn al-Qayyim and Ibn Kathīr. See a discussion of this by Muḥammad b. Ṣāliḥ b. al-ʿUthaymīn (fatwa.islamweb.net #136957).

Chapter Two

1 Q.III.26.

2 Muslim 1812; Tirmidhī 3422; Abū Dāwūd 760; Nasāʾī 898; Aḥmad 803.

3 All of these Beautiful Names are included in verse Q.LIX.23.

4 Q.II.30.

5 Abū Jaʿfar Muḥammad b. Jarīr b. Yazīd al-Ṭabarī (d. 310/923) was a jurist and scholar well known for his exegesis of the Qurʾān, *Tafsīr al-Ṭabarī*. He also wrote *Tārīkh al-rusul wa'l-mulūk*, otherwise known as *Ṭārīkh al-Ṭabarī*.

6 See *Tafsīr al-Ṭabarī*, vol. I, p. 475.

7 Abū Ṣāliḥ Dhakwān b. ʿAbd Allāh al-Sammān (d. 101/719) was a Successor. He was born during the Caliphate of ʿUmar b. al-Khaṭṭāb. He encountered and gained knowledge from many of the Companions, including Ibn ʿAbbās, Abū Hurayra, Saʿd b. Abī Waqqās and ʿĀʾisha.

8 Mujāhid b. Jabr al-Makhzūmī (d. 104/722) was one of the Successors. He studied the exegesis of the Qurʾān with Ibn ʿAbbās. He was a source for the exegeses of Sufyān al-Thawrī and Ṭabarī.

9 Q.II.30.

10 Abū Ayyūb Maymūn b. Mihrān al-Raqqī (d.117/735) was one of the Successors. He gained knowledge from Abū Hurayra, as well as ʿĀʾisha.

11 ʿAbd Allāh b. ʿAbbās b. ʿAbd al-Muṭṭalib (d. 68/687) was a pre-eminent Companion and cousin of the Prophet. He was known as the expert interpreter (*tarjumān*) of the Qurʾān. He also narrated nearly 1700 *ḥadīth*s.

12 Qatāda b. Diʿāma b. Qatāda al-Sadūsī (d. 117/735) was an exegete and one of the prominent Successors. Although born blind, he had an excellent memory and managed to become one of al-Ḥasan al-Baṣrī's students.

13 Muqātil b. Sulaymān b. Bashīr al-Balkhī (d. 150/767) was a Successor of the Successors. He wrote what is most likely the oldest surviving exegesis of the Qur'ān. Nonetheless, he was not considered to be a reliable source of *ḥadīth* by Bukhārī and others. See Abū ʿAbd Allāh Shams al-Dīn Muḥammad b. Aḥmad al-Dhahabī, *Siyar aʿlām al-nubalā'* (Beirut: Mu'assasat al-Risāla, 1985), vol. VII, pp. 201–202.

14 Abū Isḥāq Ibrāhīm b. Sahl b. al-Sārī al-Zajjāj (d. 311/923) was a prominent linguist, grammarian and exegete. See his exegesis *Maʿānī al-Qur'ān wa-iʿrābuhu* (Beirut: ʿĀlam al-Kutub, 1988), vol. V, p. 151, for this discussion.

15 See Chapter Fourteen.

16 This is derived from Q.XXXIX.55: *And follow the better (guidance) of that which is revealed unto you from your Lord.*

17 Q.LXVII.3.

18 Q.LV.29.

19 This is discussed at length in Chapter Six (Point 24).

20 This is a reference to the *ḥadīth* whereby the Prophet (may God bless him and grant him peace) related that God (Exalted is He) will punish ninety-nine out of every one hundred in Hellfire. Bukhārī 6529; Aḥmad 12,824. It is 'authentic' according to Albānī (*Silsilat al-aḥādīth al-ṣaḥīḥa* 3307).

21 Ibn al-Qayyim discusses the issue of child suffering in *Miftāḥ dār al-saʿāda*, pp. 777–780, wherein he states, 'The pain that children suffer, in addition to its causes and effects, are necessary concomitants of the human [condition] and formation. It is like heat and cold, hunger and thirst, fatigue and hardship, distress and sorrow, weakness and incapability. Had children been exempt from [suffering] they would not have been human, but rather angels or some other creature. The suffering of children is not greater than that of adults, but since the latter have become accustomed to it they find it to easier to withstand. Again, this is a requisite of being a human.'

22 Unfortunately, Ibn al-Qayyim does not subsequently address the Antichrist (*al-Masīḥ al-Dajjāl*) in *Shifā' al-ʿalīl* or *Miftāḥ dār al-saʿāda*. He does discuss the Antichrist in *Hidāyat al-ḥayārā*, vol. I, pp. 315 and 337; *Ṭarīq al-hijratayn*, p. 400; and *Zād al-maʿād*, vol. I, pp. 136 and 434–435, as well as vol. III, p. 86—but these discussions do not include the wisdom of allowing the Antichrist to exist.

23 These groups include the Qadariyya, who deny that He possesses wisdom; the Jabriyya, who maintain divine compulsion and deny causality; the Ashʿariyya, who minimize the role of His wisdom, claiming that would connote a need on His part; and Ibn Sīnā, along with other philosophers, who claim that God's acts emanate from Him in the absence of His free choice or will. See Ibn Taymiyya, *Majmūʿ al-fatāwā* (Medina: Mujammaʿ al-Malik Fahd li-Ṭibāʿat al-Muṣḥaf al-Sharīf, 1995), vol. VIII, pp. 82–83.

24 Q.III.191.
25 Q.XXIV.38–39.
26 Q.XXXVIII.27.
27 Q.XXIII.115–116.
28 Q.LXV.12.
29 Q.V.97.
30 Q.XXVII.88.
31 Q.XXXII.7.
32 Q.LXVII.3.
33 Q.II.30.
34 Q.II.32.
35 Q.II.33.

36 Abū ʿAbd Allāh Muḥammad b. ʿUmar Fakhr al-Dīn al-Rāzī (d. 606/1209) began as an Ashʿarī, but later tried to synthesize between speculative theology and philosophy and thus held eclectic views. This excerpt is taken from *al-Mabāḥith al-mashriqiyya fī ʿilm al-ilāhiyyāt wa'l-ṭabīʿīyyāt* (Qom: Intishārāt Bīdār, 1950), in a chapter titled 'Inclusion of Evil in the Divine Decree,' pp. 519–523. Rāzī was a prolific writer who wrote a long exegesis of the Qur'ān named *al-Tafsīr al-Kabīr*, and other significant works like *al-Arbaʿīn fī uṣūl al-dīn* and *Muḥaṣṣal afkār al-mutaqaddimīn wa'l muta'akhkhirīn*. See Shihadeh, *The Teleological Ethics of Fakhr al-Dīn al-Rāzī*, for further discussion.

37 By bringing up pre-eternity and temporal origination, i.e. that the universe is pre-eternal, Rāzī is essentially towing the line of Ibn Sīnā who maintains that God's acts emanate necessarily from Him. See Inati, *The Problem of Evil*. Of note, Rāzī ends the *Mabāḥith* (on pages 523–524) by affirming the need for prophethood. Yet as Ibn al-Qayyim mentions, Rāzī's doctrine, which also upholds crass determinism, neglects fundamentals of the Qur'ān and Sunna. Ibn al-Qayyim quotes him in Zeni (tr.), *Ibn Qayyim al-Jawziyya on Knowledge*, pp. 206-207, as recognizing the futility of philosophy and thus abandoning it, and affirming that certainty only results from the Qur'ān; but this occurred only at the end of Rāzī's life.

38 They are the followers of Abū Muḥriz Jahm b. Safwān al-Samarqandī (d. 128/746) who, along with al-Jaʿd b. Dirham (d. 118/736), founded this doctrine. It denied and negated all of the Attributes of God (*taʿṭīl*), including His ability to speak. Jahm denied that God spoke to Moses. The Jahmiyya doctrine only affirmed God's ability to create and His power. It also claimed that humans do not have free choice, but rather are subject to divine compulsion (*jabr*). This doctrine was also the first to maintain that the Qur'ān was created, which was later adopted by the Muʿtazila. Finally, it maintained that both Paradise and Hellfire will become annihilated.

39 The Qadariyya claimed that humans create their own destiny, actions and will, and that these may occur outside of God's will and creative power. They

also denied His predestination, claiming that God is not aware of human actions until after they occur. The Qadariyya existed mostly during the time of the Umayyad caliphate; but after holding the Caliphs accountable for their political actions and errors to God, they supported a revolt, which failed and led to their demise.

40 That the Qadariyya are the Zoroastrians of this Community is in accordance with a *ḥadīth*. See Abū Dāwūd 4691; Ibn Māja 92; Aḥmad 5584; Ḥākim 286; Bayhaqī (*Sunan*) 20,869. It is 'sound' according to Albānī (*Ṣaḥīḥ al-Jāmiʿ* 4442). The Zoroastrians believe in the existence of two deities: one was the creator of good and the other the creator of evil. Therefore, the Qadariyya who believe that humans are the creators of evil have resembled those like the Zoroastrians who believe in another deity to create evil.

41 Bukhārī 3401; Muslim 6163; Tirmidhī 3149; Aḥmad 21,114.

42 Q.XXXI.27.

43 Muslim 1090; Tirmidhī 3493; Abū Dāwūd 879; Ibn Māja 1179; Nasāʾī 1748; Aḥmad 751.

44 Bukhārī 6382; Tirmidhī 480; Abū Dāwūd 1538; Ibn Māja 1383; Nasāʾī 3255; Aḥmad 14,707.

45 Q.II.30.

46 Q.II.216.

47 Q.XVII.85.

48 Q.V.109.

49 Abū ʿAbd Allāh Naʿīm b. Ḥammād b. Muʿāwiya al-Khuzāʿī (d. 228/842) was a traditionist scholar, and one of the teachers of Imam Bukhārī.

50 Muḥammad b. Ismāʿīl al-Bukhārī, *Khalq afʿāl al-ʿibād wa'l-radd ʿalā'l-Jahmiyya wa-aṣḥāb al taʿṭīl* (Riyadh: Dār al-Maʿārif, 1978), vol. 1, p. 85.

51 Q.XXXI.15.

52 Q.VII.39.

53 Q.XXII.10.

54 Q.XLII.30.

55 Q.LXXIX.24.

56 Q.LXXVIII.26.

57 Q.IV.160–161.

58 Q.IV.155–157.

59 Q.V.13.

60 Q.III.159.

61 Q.XL.22.

62 Q.II.275.

63 Q.XLVII.3.

64 Q.LXXIX.10.

65 Q.XXIII.48.

66 Q.LXXIII.16.

67 Q.XCI.14.
68 Q.XLIII.55–56.
69 Q.L.9.
70 Q.VII.57.
71 Q.V.16.
72 Q.IX.14.
73 Q.V.38.
74 Q.XXIV.2.
75 Q.VII.170.
76 Q.XVI.88.
77 Q.VIII.29.
78 Q.XIV.7.
79 This represents the doctrine of occasionalism, which many of the Ashʿariyya espoused.
80 Q.XVIII.84 (Muḥammad Asad translation).
81 See *Tafsīr al-Ṭabarī*, vol. XVIII, p. 94.
82 ʿAbd al-Raḥmān b. Zayd b. Aslam al-ʿAdawī (d. 182/798) wrote an exegesis of the Qur'ān. He was, however, considered to be a weak narrator of *ḥadīth*.
83 ʿAbd al-Malik b. ʿAbd al-ʿAzīz b. Jurayj (d. 150/767) was Successor to the Successors. He studied under ʿAṭā' b. Abī Rabāḥ (d. 115/733), who was a pre-eminent Successor. The latter himself was a student of the Companions Ibn ʿAbbās and Ibn ʿUmar.
84 Abū al-Qāsim al-Ḍaḥḥāk b. Muzāḥim al-Hilālī (d. 102/720) was one of the prominent Successors to the Successors. He was a traditionist and exegete.
85 Abū al-ʿAbbās Muḥammad b. Yazīd al-Mubarrad (d. 286/898) was born in Basra. He became a prominent grammarian. His greatest work was the *Kāmil*.
86 Q.XVIII.85.
87 Mujāhid b. Jabr al-Makhzūmī (d. 104/722) was one of the Successors. He studied the exegesis of the Qur'ān with Ibn ʿAbbās, and was a source for exegesis of Sufyān al-Thawrī and Ṭabarī.
88 Q.XL.36–37.
89 Q.XXII.15.
90 Q.II.166.

Chapter Three

1 Q.LIV.5.
2 Q.IV.113.
3 Q.II.269.
4 Q.V.97.
5 Q.LXV.12.
6 Q.V.97.
7 Q.IV.165.

8 Q.IV.105.
9 Q.LVII.29.
10 Q.II.143.
11 Q.LXII.27–28.
12 Q.VIII.11.
13 Q.VIII.8.
14 Q.III.126.
15 Q.XVI.102.
16 Q.LXXIV.31.
17 Q.II.143.
18 Q.XVI.44.
19 Q.XIV.52.
20 Q.LVII.25.
21 Q.VI.75.
22 Q.XVI.8.
23 The Ashᶜariyya deny *lām al-taᶜlīl* and only affirm *lām al-ᶜāqiba*. See Ibn Taymiyya, *Majmūᶜ al-fatāwā*, vol. VIII, p. 44.
24 Q.XXVIII.8.
25 Q.XXVIII.8.
26 Q.VI.53.
27 Q.VI.53.
28 Q.XXII.53.
29 The believers are discussed in the next verse, Q.XXII.54: *And that those who have been given knowledge may know that it is the truth from thy Lord, so that they may believe therein and their hearts may submit humbly unto Him. God verily is guiding those who believe unto a right path.*
30 Q.III.7. The entire verse is: *He it is Who hath revealed unto thee (Muḥammad) the Book wherein are clear revelations—they are the substance of the Book—and others (which are) allegorical. But those in whose hearts is doubt pursue, forsooth, that which is allegorical seeking (to cause) dissension by seeking to explain it. None knoweth its explanation save God. And those who are of sound instruction say, We believe therein; the whole is from our Lord. But only men of understanding really heed.*
31 Q.XXII.52 states, *Never sent We a messenger or a prophet before thee but when He recited (the message) Satan proposed (opposition) in respect of that which he recited thereof. But God abolisheth that which Satan proposeth. Then God establisheth His revelations. God is omniscient, most wise.*
32 Q.III.7.
33 Q.XXII.52.
34 Q.XI.1.
35 Q.XXII.53.
36 Q.VIII.42.
37 This is referring to the Battle of Badr.

38 Q.XXXVI.69.
39 Q.VI.113. The rest of the verse reads *and that they may take pleasure therein, and that they may earn what they are earning*. The verse preceding it is: *Thus have We appointed unto every prophet an adversary—devils of humankind and jinn who inspire in one another plausible discourse through guile. If thy Lord willed, they would not do so; so leave them alone with their devising.*
40 Q.LIX.7.
41 Q.LVII.22–23.
42 Q.XVI.89.
43 Q.XXVI.208.
44 Q.LXXVII.5.
45 Q.VI.154.
46 Q.L.6–8.
47 Q.VI.156. The verse preceding it is: *And this is a blessed Book which We have revealed. So follow it and ward off (evil), that ye may find mercy.*
48 Q.XXXIX.56. The three verses preceding it are: *Say: O My servants who have been prodigal to their own hurt! Despair not of the mercy of God, Who forgiveth all sins. Lo! He is the All-Forgiving, the Merciful. Turn unto your Lord repentant, and surrender unto Him, before there come unto you the doom, when ye cannot be helped. And follow the better (guidance) of that which is revealed unto you from your Lord, before the doom cometh on you suddenly when ye know not.*
49 Q.VII.172.
50 Q.VI.70.
51 Q.V.32.
52 *Tafsīr al-Ṭabarī*, vol. X, pp. 234–235.
53 Q.II.21.
54 Q.II.183.
55 Q.XX.44 (Muḥammad Asad translation).
56 Q.XVII.89-90.
57 Q.LI.15-16.
58 Q.XII.24.
59 Q.VII.170.
60 Q.V.38.
61 Q.XXIV.2.
62 Q.XXIV.4.
63 Q.LI.15.
64 Q.II.277.
65 Q.XLIII.33.
66 Q.XLII.27.
67 Q.VI.8.
68 Q.XVII.59.
69 Q.II.22.

70 Q.XVI.80–81.
71 Q.XXX.21.
72 Q.XIV.32–33.
73 Q.XLV.12.
74 Q.XVI.68–69.
75 Q.XVI.5–8.
76 Q.XXIII.115.
77 Q.LXXV.36.
78 Q.XLIV.38–39.
79 Q.III.191.
80 Q.XXXVIII.27.
81 Q.LXVIII.35-36.
82 Q.XXXVIII.28.
83 Q.XLV.21.
84 Q.III.142.
85 Q.II.214.
86 Q.IX.16 (Yusuf Ali translation).
87 Q.IV.69.
88 Q.IX.67.
89 Q.III.195.
90 Q.XII.22.
91 Q.XLVII.10.
92 Q.XVII.77.
93 Q.XLVIII.23.
94 Q.LVIII.5.
95 Q.XXXIX.1.
96 Q.V.38.
97 Q.V.118.
98 Q.VI.96.
99 Also see Q.XXXVI.38 and Q.XLI.12.
100 Q.XXVI.9.
101 Q.V.50.
102 Q.IV.125.
103 Q.LXXVII.23.
104 Q.XXIII.14.
105 Q.LXVII.3.
106 Q.XI.56.
107 Q.XVI.76.
108 See Zajjāj, *Maʿānī al-Qurʾān*, vol. III, p. 58.
109 Abū Bakr Muḥammad b. al-Qāsim b. Bashshār b. al-Anbārī (d. 328/940) was prolific grammarian and exegete who lived in Baghdad. He wrote *al-Kāfī* and *al-Waqf wa'l-ibtidā'* in addition to numerous other works.

110 Q.XI.56.
111 Q.XXXIII.4.
112 Q.XVI.81.
113 Q.II.150.
114 Q.V.6.
115 Ibn al-Qayyim does not directly respond here, but states later, 'As for the benefits for the heart and the spirit due to pain and diseases, it is a matter which is not sensed except by those who are [spiritually] alive. The benefits of diseases have been recounted and they are more than 100.' See below p. 160. Also consider that the Prophet said, 'No fatigue, nor disease, nor sorrow, nor sadness, nor hurt, nor distress befalls a Muslim, even if it were the prick he receives from a thorn, but that God expiates some of his sins for that.' Bukhārī 5641; Aḥmad 8027.
116 Q.II.30.
117 This refers to Q.II.32: *They said, Be glorified! We have no knowledge saving that which Thou hast taught us.*
118 Q.VI.124.
119 Q.VI.53.
120 Q.XXI.81 (Muḥammad Asad translation).
121 Q.V.97.
122 Q.XLVIII.26.
123 Q.VIII.22–23.
124 Q.III.179.
125 Q.VIII.33.
126 Q.IX.115.
127 Q.XI.117.
128 Q.XXVIII.59.
129 Abū al-Maʿālī Ḍiyāʾ al-Dīn ʿAbd al-Malik b. Yūsuf al-Juwaynī (d. 478/1085) was born in Juwayn, Iran. He later taught in Mecca and Medina (thus becoming known as *Imām al-Ḥaramayn*, or 'the Imam of the Two Holy Sanctuaries') before moving to Nishapur. He was a major figure in early Ashʿarī thought.

Chapter Four

1 See Muḥammad b. ʿUmar Fakhr al-Dīn al-Rāzī (Beirut: Dār al-Kutub al-ʿIlmiyyah, 2009), *al-Arbaʿīn fī uṣūl al-dīn*, p. 245. This is Rāzī's first argument (*al-hujja al-ūlā*) in Chapter 16: 'The Impermissibility of God's Actions and Rulings (Exalted is He) being due to any Reason.' Rāzī also uses this line of thinking in many of his works, such as *al-Maḥṣūl* (Beirut: Mu'assasat al-Risāla, 1997), vol. v, p. 132, and *Mafātīḥ al-ghayb* (Beirut: Dār Iḥyāʾ al-Turāth al-ʿArabī, 1999), vol. II, p. 379.
2 Q.XVI.17.

3 Q.XVI.75–76 (Muḥammad Asad translation).

4 See Rāzī, *Arbaʿīn*, p. 245.

5 They are the followers of Abū ʿAbd Allāh Muḥammad b. Karrām (d. 255/869) who preached in Khurasan. They affirmed predestination and His wisdom, but adopted an ethical rationalism much like the Muʿtazila. They claimed that God is corporeal (*jism*), and therefore anthropomorphized Him. They also claimed that faith is only associated with affirmation in speech, and is not connected to sincerity within one's heart or in one's works. A corollary of this is that in their doctrine there is no such person as a hypocrite. See Zysow, 'Karrāmiyya', pp. 252–262.

6 See Q.VII.54: *His verily is all creation and commandment.*

7 Q.XLVIII.26.

8 Q.VI.53.

9 Q.VIII.23.

10 Q.XLIX.7–8.

11 Q.LVII.28–29.

12 Q.LXII.2–4.

13 Q.V.54.

14 Q.XIV.11.

15 Q.XLIII.31–32.

16 Bukhārī 7533; Tirmidhī 2871; Aḥmad 4508.

17 Q.IV.69–70.

18 Abū al-Ḥusayn ʿAlī Sayf al-Dīn al-Āmidī (d. 631/1233) was a famous jurist and speculative theologian. Ibn al-Qayyim discusses some of his arguments regarding deeming actions good or repugnant in *Miftāḥ dār al-saʿāda*, pp. 924–926. Āmidī wrote the significant *Kitāb al-iḥkām fī uṣūl al-aḥkām* in jurisprudence. See Dhahabī, *Siyar aʿlām al-nubalāʾ*, vol. XXII, pp. 364–367, and Bernard Weiss, *The Search for God's Law: Islamic Jurisprudence in the Writings of Sayf al-Dīn al-Āmidī* (Salt Lake City: The University of Utah Press, 2010).

19 See Rāzī, *Arbaʿīn*, pp. 245–246.

20 See Rāzī, *Arbaʿīn*, p. 246.

21 Abū Hudhayl al-ʿAllāf (d. 235/850) was a prominent founder of the Basran Muʿtazilī school. He likely originated the 'five principles' of the Muʿtazila, and he was one of the first Muʿtazila to introduce the concept of atomism (*jawhar*). See David Bennett, 'The Muʿtazilite Movement' (p.146), and Ulrich Rudolph, 'Occasionalism' (pp. 349–351), in *The Oxford Handbook of Islamic Theology*. ʿAllāf claimed that movements within Paradise and Hellfire will ultimately cease. This is discussed by Ibn al-Qayyim later in Chapter Seven.

Chapter Five

1 See this chapter, Points 18 and 20.

2 See this chapter, Point 23.

3 See Chapter Six, Point 24.
4 See Chapter Six, Point 26.
5 See Chapter Six, Point 27. This was also discussed previously in Chapter One.
6 See Chapter Six, Point 36.
7 See Chapter Seven.
8 See Chapter Six, Points 32-34 and Chapter Eight, Point 37.
9 See Chapter Eight, Point 38.
10 Abū al-Ḥasan ʿAlī b. Ismāʿīl b. Abū Bishr Isḥāq al-Ashʿarī (d. 324/936) was born in Basra, as a descendent of the Companion Abū Mūsā al-Ashʿarī. He remained a Muʿtazilī until forty years of age when it was said he disavowed their doctrine after debating Jubbā'ī, as mentioned above. He wrote two major works: *Kitāb al-Lumaʿ fī'l-rad ʿalā ahl al-ziyagh wa'l-bidʿa* and *Ibāna ʿan uṣūl al-diyāna*. The most prominent proponents of the Ashʿarī doctrine after the eponymous founder were Bāqillānī, Juwaynī, Ghazālī, Rāzī and Subkī.
11 Abū ʿAlī Muḥammad b. ʿAbd al-Wahhāb (d. 303/915) and Abū Hāshim ʿAbd al-Salām b. Abū ʿAlī al-Jubbā'ī (d. 321/933) were father and son proponents of the Muʿtazilī doctrine. They resided in Baghdad and the latter wrote *al-Jāmiʿ al-kabīr*. The Muʿtazila claimed that God is obligated to act in a manner that is beneficial and most advantageous (*al-ṣalāḥ wa'l-aṣlaḥ*). They also claimed that a Muslim who commits a major sin and does not repent is neither a Muslim nor a disbeliever; but occupies an intermediary position, and is punished in Hellfire forever, yet to a lesser degree than the disbelievers.
12 Q.XXIX.21
13 Q.II.284
14 Q.XXI.23
15 Ibn al-Qayyim refutes astrology in *Miftāḥ dār al-saʿāda*, pp. 1173–1472.
16 Ibn al-Qayyim discusses these and responds to them in *Miftāḥ dār al-saʿāda*, pp. 991–999. He discusses the Muʿtazilī claim that God is obligated to act in a manner that is beneficial and most advantageous (*al-ṣalāḥ wa'l-aṣlaḥ*); and he enumerates eighteen necessary concomitants of that claim and shows how they are inconsistent with the Qur'ān, the Sunna, reason and reality. Ibn al-Qayyim ultimately maintains that God's actions are consistent with His wisdom, mercy, beneficence and justice. In summary, the presence of Iblīs (Point 5) and allowing him to deceive humanity (7) until the Day of Judgment (6); the punishment of Hellfire (3); the death of the prophets and messengers (8); the presence of afflictions, hardships (11) and pains that are not apparently beneficial (13); and that children grow up to become disbelievers (12), not just believers (14 and 10)—these all reveal the inconsistencies of that doctrine. In addition, if God was obligated to only do that which was beneficial and most advantageous then He must ensure the guidance of all of humanity (15), and that His beneficence, kindness and grace must be granted to all in an equal fashion (16), yet higher degrees of benefit or advantage can always be postulated (17). Ibn al-Qayyim also

maintains that the Muʿtazila anthropomorphize God to His creation (1), and that by obligating Him to act in such a manner God is not deemed as praiseworthy because His actions would no longer be freely chosen (4). Finally, since God is the Most Just and Most Wise, it is not appropriate to question God as to the requisites of His actions (18)—instead only humans are held accountable.

17 Q.XXI.23.

18 Ibn al-Qayyim is likely referring to Q.XI.119: *And the Word of thy Lord hath been fulfilled: Verily I shall fill Hell with jinn and humankind together.*

19 Q.XVI.38–39.

20 Q.XXXIX.75.

21 Q.II.30.

22 Q.XVI.62: *And they assign unto God that which they (themselves) dislike, and their tongues expound the lie that the better portion will be theirs. Assuredly theirs will be the Fire, and they will be abandoned.*

23 Abū Saʿīd al-Ḥasan b. Abī al-Ḥasan Yasār al-Baṣrī (d. 110/728) was a pre-eminent Successor. He was born in Medina. He later moved to Basra, Iraq. He was a devoted ascetic and scholar attracting large numbers to his teaching circle. See Dhahabī, *Siyar aʿlām al-nubalā'*, vol. IV, p. 563.

24 Q.I.2.

25 Q.XVIII.1.

26 Q.VI.1.

27 Q.XXXIV.1.

28 Q.XXX.17–18.

29 Q.XXXII.7.

30 Q.XXVII.88.

31 Aḥmad (*Musnad* 21,232 and *Zuhd* 256); Ḥākim 3255; Bayhaqī (*Shuʿab*) 4128. It is 'sound' according to Albānī (*Mishkāt* 122). All of these narrations include Adam as the questioner, not Moses. This *ḥadīth* was previously mentioned by Ibn al-Qayyim in Chapter One with Adam as the questioner.

32 See Q.II.102: *They followed what the evil ones gave out (falsely) against the power of Solomon: the blasphemers were, not Solomon, but the evil ones, teaching men magic, and such things as came down at Babylon to the angels Harut and Marut. But neither of these taught anyone (such things) without saying, We are only for trial; so do not blaspheme. They learned from them the means to sow discord between man and wife. But they could not thus harm anyone except by God's permission. And they learned what harmed them, not what profited them. And they knew that the buyers of (magic) would have no share in the happiness of the Hereafter. And vile was the price for which they did sell their souls, if they but knew!* Unfortunately, there are no authentic *ḥadīth*s regarding Hārūt and Mārūt. See Albānī's *Silsilat al-aḥādīth al-ḍaʿīfa wa'l-mawḍūʿa* 34, 170, 910, 912, 913, 1306, 5401 and 6656. All of these are either 'fabricated' or 'weak'. Albānī considers many of them to be false Israelite traditions.

33 Q.IX.40: *But the Word of God is exalted to the heights: for God is almighty, most wise.*

34 Muslim 6965; Tirmidhī 3539; Aḥmad 8082.

35 These wisdoms are mentioned in more detail in Chapter Fifteen.

36 Q.XIV.5–6.

37 See Q.XXXVIII.41: *And make mention (O Muḥammad) of Our bondman Job, when he cried unto his Lord (saying), The Devil doth afflict me with distress and torment.*

38 Q.XXXIII.72.

39 The Prophet was rejected by the disbelievers of Ta'if and sought the protection of al-Muṭʿim b. ʿAdī. This was after the death of the Prophet's uncle Abū Ṭālib, who had provided him with protection during his life. See *Tafsīr al-Ṭabarī,* vol. XIII, p. 504; Ibn Kathīr, *Bidāya*, vol. III, p. 137.

40 Q.II.216.

41 Q.V.50.

42 Ibn al-Qayyim discusses Sūrat al-Fātiḥa further in his book *Madārij al-sālikīn bayn manāzil iyyāk naʿbudu wa-iyyāka nastaʿīn* (Beirut: Dār al-Kitāb al-ʿArabī, 1996), vol. I, p. 31–54.

43 Ibn al-Qayyim now discusses some wisdoms of the prayer in detail. Although beneficial, this forms a digression from the twenty-second aspect. For example, he says, 'It is as if the bowing is a preface and preliminary step to the prostration. Therefore, one goes from one type of submission to a more perfect, complete and greater one.' *Shifā'*, vol. III, p. 1160. 'Had we remained in prostration from the time we were created until our death, we could not fulfill the Lord's rights upon us. God commanded us to say therein, "Glory be to the Lord, the Most High," therefore we remember God's exaltedness while we are in the lowliest position, and declare Him to be infallible from a similar position as ours. The One Who is above everything is infallible from any type of lowliness; He is the Most High, and this includes every meaning of exaltedness. Since prostration is the ultimate in humility, submissiveness and brokenness, it is where we are closest [spiritually] to the Lord.' *Shifā'*, vol. III, p. 1159–1160.

44 Muslim 577; Tirmidhī 2; Aḥmad 8020.

45 Muslim 578; Aḥmad 476.

46 Q.XIII.4.

47 Q.XXX.22.

48 Q.XXIV.45.

49 Q.XVI.8.

50 Q.LXIX.38–39.

51 Q.LIII.42.

52 Ibn al-Qayyim discusses in detail many aspects of God's beautiful creation of nature. As this represents a digression though, it is largely omitted here.

53 Q.LVI.71–73.

Chapter Six

1 This twenty-fourth point has also been translated by Hoover in 'God's Wise Purposes in Creating Iblīs', pp. 127–134.

2 Tirmidhī 2955; Abū Dāwūd 4693; Aḥmad 19,582; Ibn Ḥibbān 6160; Bayhaqī (*Sunan*) 17,708; *Ḥilya*, vol. III, p. 104. It is 'authentic' according to Albānī (*Silsilat al-aḥādīth al-ṣaḥīḥa* 1630).

3 Q.III.179.

4 Ibn al-Qayyim may be suggesting through this juxtaposition that iron is used in weaponry, and therefore results in the death of the body; yet air, on the other hand, is necessary for bodily sustenance. In addition, air carries sound, and therefore it allows the transmitted revelation to be conveyed by the Prophet, which then leads to spiritual life. See other possible interpretations for iron and air being considered as opposites in Hoover, 'God's Wise Purposes in Creating Iblīs', pp. 128–129.

5 Q.XLII.11.

6 Bukhārī 6099; Muslim 7080; Aḥmad 19,589.

7 This is derived from Q.CXII.1–4.

8 Bukhārī 3193; Nasā'ī 2080; Aḥmad 8220.

9 *Ḥilya*, vol. VIII, p. 92.

10 Bayhaqī (*Shuʿab*) 4563. It is 'weak' according to Albānī (*Silsilat al-aḥādīth al-ḍaʿīfa wa'l-mawḍūʿa* 2371).

11 *Ḥilya*, vol. IV, p. 27. This tradition is relayed by Wahb b. Munabbih (d. 110/728), who was a prominent Successor. He wrote *Kitāb al-Isrā'īliyyāt*.

12 Muslim 6965; Tirmidhī 3539; Aḥmad 8082.

13 *Ḥilya*, vol. IV, p. 60. This tradition is relayed by Fuḍayl b. Iyāḍ from Wahb b. Munabbih.

14 Abū al-Ṭayyib Aḥmad b. Husayn al-Kūfī al-Kindī (d. 354/965) was otherwise known as al-Mutanabbī, as he claimed that he was a prophet at one time, but later recanted. One of the great Arab poets, he accrued much wealth as a result of his praise of rulers like Sayf al-Dawla and Ibn al-ʿAmīd. He was ultimately killed by someone he had criticized in his poetry.

15 Q.XVII.62.

16 Q.XVI.99–100.

17 This section from *Shifā' al-ʿalīl* is very similar to Chapter One, which is derived from *Miftāḥ dār al-saʿāda*. Therefore, the majority of this point was abridged.

18 Abū al-Wafā' ʿAlī b. ʿAqīl b. Muḥammad al-Baghdādī (d. 513/1119) was a Ḥanbalī scholar who adopted some Muʿtazilī tendencies, which he later abandoned. He wrote *Kitāb al-funūn*, most of which is not extant.

19 Q.XL.16.

20 Q.XXV.26.

21 Q.LXXXII.19.

22 Q.VI.53.
23 Q.XXV.20.
24 Q.XXVIII.70.
25 Q.XXIX.1–6.
26 Q.XXIX.5.
27 Q.XXIX.6.
28 Q.III.179.
29 This is mentioned in the next verse, i.e. Q.XXIX.7: *And as for those who believe and do good works, We shall remit from them their evil deeds and shall repay them the best that they did.*
30 See Q.XXIX.8: *We have enjoined on man kindness to parents; but if they strive to make thee join with Me that of which thou hast no knowledge, then obey them not. Unto Me is your return and I shall tell you what ye used to do.*
31 See Q.XXIX.10: *Of humankind is he who saith, We believe in God, but if he be made to suffer for the sake of God, he mistaketh the persecution of humankind for God's punishment; and then, if victory cometh from thy Lord, will say, We were with you (all the while). Is not God best aware of what is in the bosoms of (His) creatures?*
32 See Q.XXIX.14–40 for these stories.
33 See Q.XXIX.45–55.
34 See Q.XXIX.56: *O my bondmen who believe! My earth is spacious. Therefore, serve Me only.*
35 See Q.XXIX.58–59.
36 See Q.XXIX.60.
37 See Q.XXIX.68–69. Thus ends Sūrat al-ʿAnkabūt.
38 The text here has been lost in all editions of the book. The Muʿtazila, though, contend that animals who suffered will be compensated in some manner in the Hereafter, or used as an instrument to torment the denizens of Hellfire. See Cüneyt M. Şimsek, 'The Problem of Animal Pain: An Introduction to Nursi's Approach', in Ibrahim M. Abu-Rabiʿ (ed.), *Theodicy and Justice in Modern Islamic Thought: The Case of Said Nursi* (Surrey: Ashgate Publishing, 2010), p. 113.
39 Q.II.30.
40 Q.IV.102 (Muḥammad Asad translation).
41 Q.XCIV.5–6.
42 Ḥākim 3176. It is 'weak' according to Albānī (*Silsilat al-aḥādīth al-ḍaʿīfa wa'l-mawḍūʿa* 4342). It has been narrated as a saying by ʿUmar b. al-Khaṭṭāb in *Muwaṭṭa' Mālik* 6.
43 Q.VI.1.
44 Q.XXXIX.75.
45 Aḥmad 23,355; Bayhaqī (*Shuʿab*) 4088; Haythamī 16,888. The attribution of this exact formulation to the Prophet (may God bless him and grant him peace) is deemed 'weak' according to Albānī (*Ḍaʿīf al-targhīb wa'l-tarhīb* 963).

Chapter Seven

1 Ibn Sīnā, as mentioned in the Introduction, claimed that this world was pre-eternal and emanated from the Lord—God is exalted above such claims. See Marmura, *The Metaphysics of the Healing*, p. xxi.

2 Ibn Taymiyya mentions that 'most of the Muʿtazila and Ashʿariyya, amongst others, affirm the creative ability of the Originator, but state that there is no need for a renewed temporal cause.' See Ibn Taymiyya, *Dar' taʿāruḍ*, vol. IV, p. 155. In response, Ibn Taymiyya and Ibn al-Qayyim held that God (Exalted is He) has been perpetually creating from pre-eternity for wise purposes, which are beloved to Him. Hoover states regarding this issue, 'In order to safeguard God's sufficiency apart from the world, Ashʿarī Kalām theologians deny that God wills to create the world on account of causes or wise purposes. There is no reason why God created the world in time out of nothing when He did... Muʿtazilī Kalām theologians agree that God has no need for this world and that He created the world *ex nihilo*... God created the world to benefit humankind, but God's wise purpose in creation has no impact on Him.' Ibn Taymiyya, on the other hand, 'locates the cause in God's essence,' and that 'God's willing of something to happen [is not eternal but rather] occurs at the time that it happens... [yet] God has been willing and acting from eternity.' See Hoover, *Ibn Taymiyya's Theodicy of Perpetual Optimism*, pp. 70, 78, 85–87. I would like to thank Jon Hoover and Yahya Michot for the insight they personally provided into this passage.

3 Hoover explains that according to the 'Jahmīs and the Muʿtazilīs... attributes cannot subsist in God's essence. For the Kullābīs, and, we may add, the Ashʿarīs, God's attributes subsist in God's essence, but eternally without any link to God's power and will... Ibn Taymiyya identifies his own definition of voluntary attributes [as those] which subsist in His essence (*taqūmu bi-dhātihī*) by His will (*mashī'a*) and His power (*qudra*), such as His speech, His hearing, His sight, His will, His love, His good pleasure, His mercy, His anger, and His wrath, and such as His creating, His beneficence, His justice... [But] as for the Kullābīs and the Ashʿarīs, he [Ibn Taymiyya] observes that they subsume the voluntary attributes under the rubric of "the occurrence of temporally originating events (*ḥulūl al-ḥawādith*)" and insist that originating events cannot subsist in God.' Interestingly, Hoover explains, Rāzī 'abandons his early event-denying stance and argues in al-*Maṭālib al-ʿāliyya* that all Muslim groups, despite their disavowals, must admit originating events in God'. Finally, Ibn Taymiyya affirms that God 'has been qualified with attributes of perfection from eternity and He is still thus. He has not changed.' See Jon Hoover, 'God Acts by His Will and Power: Ibn Taymiyya's Theology of a Personal God in his Treatise on the Voluntary Attributes' in Yossef Rapoport and Shahab Ahmed (eds.), *Ibn Taymiyya and his Times* (Karachi: Oxford University Press, 2010), pp. 55–77.

4 Ibn al-Qayyim does not respond to this further here as he discussed it earlier in the same work, where he states, 'Whoever believes that the ability to create was impossible for God (Exalted is He) for some unspecified time, but then that creative ability transformed from being essentially impossible to possible without the occurrence of a cause nor anything that transpired within the Agent's [Essence], he has shown himself to be irrational in front of everyone. For if reason would allow this then it becomes permissible to state that this world transformed from non-existence to existence in the absence of an agent. Since that is irrational, then characterizing the possibility of an act transforming from essentially impossible to possible in the absence of a cause is likewise [irrational].' See Ibn al-Qayyim, *Shifāʾ al-ʿalīl*, vol. II, p. 889.

5 This is referring to the monists who believe in *waḥdat al-wujūd*, or 'the unity of existence', in strictly pantheistic terms.

6 Q.XIV.10.

7 Bukhārī 6535; Aḥmad 11,095.

8 Q.XXXIX.73.

9 Q.IX.120.

10 Q.III.141.

11 Q.IV.123.

12 Aḥmad 68; Ḥākim 4450; Bayhaqī (*Sunan*) 6536. It is 'authentic' according to Albānī (*al-Taʿlīqāt al-ḥisān ʿalā Ṣaḥīḥ Ibn Ḥibbān* 2915).

13 Q.XLII.30.

14 Tirmidhī 2626; Ibn Māja 2604; Aḥmad 775; Ḥākim 7678; Bayhaqī (*Sunan*) 17,593. It is 'weak' according to Albānī (*Ḍaʿīf al-Jāmiʿ* 5423); but there is a part of it that is contained in an authentic *ḥadīth*, which is narrated in Bukhārī (7213); Muslim (4463); Tirmidhī (1439); Nasāʾī (4166); and Aḥmad (22,678): 'Whoever perpetrates [a major] sin and his legal punishment is quickened for him [in this worldly life], then this expiates him. Otherwise, his matter is at God's discretion.'

15 Ḥākim 104; Bayhaqī (*Sunan*) 17,595; Ibn ʿAbd al-Barr 1553. Part of the tradition is 'I do not know if Dhū al-Qarnayn was a Prophet or not. I do not know if the legal punishments expiate those people [who perpetrated major sins] or not.' It is 'authentic' according to Albānī (*Silsilat al-aḥādīth al-ṣaḥīḥa* 2217).

16 Bukhārī 6784; Muslim 4461; Ibn Māja 2603.

17 Bukhārī 5641; Muslim 6568; Tirmidhī 966; Aḥmad 8027.

18 Tirmidhī 2399; Aḥmad 9811; Ibn Ḥibbān 2913; Ḥākim 1281; *Ḥilya*, vol. VIII, p. 212; Bayhaqī (*Sunan*) 6543. It is 'authentic' according to Albānī (*Silsilat al-aḥādīth al-ṣaḥīḥa* 2280).

19 Tirmidhī 2086; Ḥākim 41; Bayhaqī (*Shuʿab*) 9381; Ibn Ḥibbān 808. It is 'fabricated' according to Albānī (*Silsilat al-aḥādīth al-ḍaʿīfa wa'l-mawḍūʿa* 6437).

20 Muslim 6570; Ibn Māja 3469.

21 Muslim 6570.

22 Muslim 6556.

23 See Bukhārī 3885; Muslim 515; Aḥmad 11,058.

24 See Q.XL.46: *The Fire; they are exposed to it morning and evening; and on the day when the Hour upriseth (it is said), Cause Pharaoh's folk to enter the most awful doom.*

25 Q.XXXII.21.

26 Q.IV.147.

27 Q.XV.49–50.

28 Q.VII.167.

29 Q.LXXXV.12 and Q.LXXXV.13–14.

30 Q.XL.1–3.

31 See Tirmidhī 3507. It is 'weak' according to Albānī (*Ḍaʿīf al-Jāmiʿ* 1945).

32 Q.VI.12: *He hath prescribed for Himself mercy*; and Q.VI.54: *Your Lord hath prescribed for Himself mercy, that whoso of you doeth evil through ignorance and repenteth afterward thereof and doeth right, (for him) lo! He is forgiving, merciful.* The Prophet (may God bless him and grant him peace) said, 'When God decreed that He would create He inscribed in His Book that is present above the Throne, "My mercy prevails (*ghalabat*) over My wrath."' Bukhārī 3194; Tirmidhī 3543; Aḥmad 7500. In some narrations it is: 'My mercy precedes (*sabaqat*) My wrath.' Bukhārī 7422; Muslim 6970; Ibn Māja 189; Aḥmad 9159.

33 Q.XI.106–107.

34 Q.VI.128. Of note, Pickthall translates part of this verse as: *save him whom God willeth (to deliver)*. Since the Qur'ānic verse does not explicitly state (*to deliver*), which some may imply as universal salvation, this was not included. Yusuf Ali translates it as, *except as God willeth*, while Muḥammad Asad translates it as, *unless God wills it otherwise*.

35 Saʿīd b. Mālik Sinān al-Khazrajī al-Khudrī, known as Abū Saʿīd (d. 74/693), was a Companion of the Prophet. He narrated 1170 *ḥadīths*.

36 See *Tafsīr al-Ṭabarī*, vol. XV, p. 483; Ḥarb b. Ismāʿīl al- Kirmānī, *Masā'il Ḥarb: al-nikāḥ ilā niyāyat al-kitāb* (Mecca: Jāmiʿat Umm al-Qurā, 2001), vol. III, p. 1157; Bayhaqī (*al-Asmā' wa'l-Ṣifāt* 336).

37 ʿAbd Allāh b. Masʿūd (d. 29/650) was a pre-eminent Companion as he was the sixth man to accept Islam. He was considered to be the pre-eminent reciter of the Qur'ān. He also narrated 848 *ḥadīths*.

38 See *Tafsīr al-Ṭabarī* 18,580 in vol. XV, p. 484; al-Ḥusayn b. Masʿūd al-Baghawī, *Tafsīr al-Baghawī* (Beirut: Dār Iḥyā' al-Turāth al-ʿArabī, 1999), vol. II, p. 467. It is considered to have unknown narrators within its chain (*muẓlim*) according to Albānī (*Rafʿ al-astār*, p. 75).

39 Q.XI.108.

40 See *Tafsīr al-Ṭabarī* 18,582 in vol. XV, p. 484; *Tafsīr al-Baghawī*, vol. II, p. 467.

41 Q.XI.128.

42 Q.XI.130.

43 Q.VI.128.

44 Q.VII.27.

45 Q.VI.128.
46 Q.VI.128.
47 Q.XI.106–108.
48 Q.XLVIII.6–8.
49 Q.III.106–107.
50 Q.LXXII.23.
51 Q.IV.14.
52 Q.II.95.
53 Q.XLIII.77.
54 Q.XXXVIII.54.
55 Q.XI.108.
56 Q.LXXXIV.25.
57 Q.II.167.
58 Q.XV.48.
59 Q.XXXV.36.
60 Q.XXXII.20. The other similar verse is Q.XXII.22.
61 Q.IV.56.
62 Q.LII.7–8.
63 Q.XXV.65.
64 Abū Umāma Ṣudayy b. ʿAjlān al-Bāhilī (d. 81/700) was a Companion of the Prophet. He narrated 250 *ḥadīth*s and was the last of the Companions to die in Syria.
65 Haythamī 18,449; al-Khaṭīb al-Baghdādī (*Tārīkh Baghdād*) 4691. It is 'fabricated' according to Albānī (*Silsilat al-aḥādīth al-ḍaʿīfa wa'l-mawḍūʿa* 607).
66 Abū Muḥammad Ḥarb b. Ismāʿīl b. Khalaf al-Kirmānī (d. 280/893) was a traditionist and Ḥanbalī scholar. His book *Masā'il* encompasses the viewpoints of Imam Aḥmad b. Ḥanbal and Isḥāq b. Rāhawayh, whom Ḥarb encountered directly. Only sections of the *Masā'il* are extant and published. Ḥarb also wrote *Kitāb al-Sunna*, which has been published.
67 See Kirmānī, *Masā'il Ḥarb*, vol. III, pp. 1157–1163, for this entire discussion.
68 Isḥāq b. Ibrāhīm b. Mukhlid al-Ḥanẓalī, known as Isḥāq b. Rāhawayh (d. 238/853), was a prominent Khurāsānī traditionist and scholar. He was a contemporary of Aḥmad b. Ḥanbal and one of the teachers of Bukhārī. Ḥarb relays the opinions of Isḥāq and Imam Aḥmad in many of his books.
69 Q.XI.107.
70 Jābir b. ʿAbd Allāh b. ʿAmr b. Ḥarām (d. 78/697) was a Companion of the Prophet. He witnessed *bayʿat al-riḍwān*. He was also present at the treaty of Ḥudaybiya. He ultimately narrated 1560 *ḥadīth*s. Jābir's father was martyred in the Battle of Uḥud.
71 Abū Muḥammad al-Muʿtamir b. Sulaymān b. Ṭarkhān al-Taymī (d. 187/802) was a trustworthy scholar who lived in Basra. Ibn al-Mubārak and Sufyān al-Thawrī gained knowledge from him.

72 ʿAbd Allāh b. ʿAmr b. al-ʿĀṣ (d. 65/684) was a Companion of the Prophet, as was his father. He narrated 700 *ḥadīths*. In one notable instance his father, ʿAmr b. al-ʿĀs, notified the Prophet that he was fasting every day and praying every night. The Prophet advised him to 'fast three days out of the month, and since each good deed is multiplied tenfold, it will be as if you fasted continually'; however, ʿAbd Allāh wanted to do more. The Prophet then said, 'Fast like David (may God bless him) but no more than that,' which was every other day. When ʿAbd Allāh became old he wished that he had taken the Prophet's initial advice to fast three days out of the month. See Bukhārī 1975 and Muslim 2729.

73 Kirmānī, *Masā'il Ḥarb*, vol. III, p. 1159. A statement similar to this was relayed from Ibn Masʿūd in *Tafsīr al-Baghawī*, vol. II, p. 467. It is 'weak' according to Albānī (*Rafʿ al-astār*, pp. 80–81).

74 Kirmānī, *Masā'il Ḥarb*, vol. III, pp. 1159–1160. The verse is Q.XI.105–106.

75 Abū Muḥammad ʿAbd b. Ḥumayd b. Naṣr al-Kashshī (or al-Kassī) (d. 249/863) was a scholar and traditionist. Bukhārī and Muslim deemed him to be a reliable narrator, and they were both students of his. See Dhahabī, *Siyar aʿlām al-nubalā'*, vol. XII, pp. 235–238. He wrote an exegesis, a section of which has been published as *Qiṭʿa min tafsīr al-imām ʿAbd b. Ḥumayd* (Beirut: Dār Ibn Ḥazm, 2004). Unfortunately, it only includes an exegesis of *sūras Āl ʿImrān* and *Nisā'*—not *Anʿām* or *Hūd*, which are of concern here.

76 Ḥammād b. Salama b. Dīnār al-Baṣrī (d. 167/783) was a Successor to the Successors who lived in Basra. He gained knowledge from Thābit, Qatāda, and many others. He was a trustworthy narrator of *ḥadīth*. See Dhahabī, *Siyar aʿlām al-nubalā'*, vol. VII, pp. 444–456.

77 Abū Muḥammad Thābit b. Aslam al-Banānī (d. 127/744) encountered many Companions, like ʿAbd Allāh b. ʿUmar and ʿAbd Allāh b. al-Zubayr. He was a trustworthy narrator and a devout worshiper. See Dhahabī, *Siyar aʿlām al-nubalā'*, vol. V, pp. 220–225.

78 See Albānī's comments in *Rafʿ al-astār* pp. 48–9. Albānī discusses this further in *Silsilat al-aḥādīth al-ḍaʿīfa wa'l-mawḍūʿa* 607, and states that since al-Ḥasan did not encounter ʿUmar, this tradition cannot be used as a proof.

79 ʿAlī b. Abī Ṭalḥa (d. 143/760) was a Successor to the Successors. He was a client of Banū ʿAbbās but did not meet Ibn ʿAbbās, although he narrated much from him. It is most likely through Mujāhid that ʿAlī narrated those traditions. Ibn al-Qayyim refers to ʿAlī b. Abī Ṭalḥa's opinion once in *Madārij al-sālikīn* regarding the major sins (*kabā'ir*): 'They are those sins which God has promised Hellfire, His wrath, His damnation or punishment for.'

80 Q.VI.128.

81 See ʿAlī b. Abī Ṭalḥa, *Tafsīr Ibn ʿAbbās al-musammā ṣaḥīfat ʿAlī b. Abī Ṭalḥa* (Beirut: Mu'assasat al-Kutub al-Thaqāfiyya, 1991), p. 214.

82 See *Tafsīr al-Ṭabarī*, vol. XII, p. 118, for both ʿAlī b. Abī Ṭalha's narration from Ibn ʿAbbās and the latter's subsequent statement.

83 Ismāʿīl b. ʿAbd al-Raḥmān al-Suddī (d. 127/744) was a prominent Successor. He wrote an exegesis of the Qur'ān named *Tafsīr al-Suddī al-kabīr*.

84 Q.LXXVIII.23.

85 Q.XV.48.

86 Q.II.39.

87 *Ṭafsīr al-Ṭabarī*, vol. XV, p. 484.

88 Saʿīd b. al-Musayyab (d. 96/715) was one of the pre-eminent Successors. He famously refused to marry his daughter (born out of his marriage to one of Abu Hurayra's daughters) to the son of the Caliph ʿAbd al-Malik and was punished for that. He later lived to the Caliphate of ʿUmar b. ʿAbd al-ʿAzīz who would consult with him.

89 Q.XI.107.

90 *Ṭafsīr al-Ṭabarī*, vol. XV, p. 484.

91 Abū ʿAmr ʿĀmir b. Sharḥīl al-Hamadānī al-Shaʿbī (d. 104/722) was one of the most knowledgeable Successors for he met 500 Companions. Sufyān b. ʿUyayna said, 'There was no one like Ibn ʿAbbās in his time, nor like al-Shaʿbī in his time, nor like [Sufyān] al-Thawrī in his time.' See Dhahabī, *Siyar aʿlām al-nubalā'*, vol. III, p. 352.

92 *Ṭafsīr al-Ṭabarī*, vol. XV, p. 484. After this discussion, Abū Jaʿfar Muḥammad b. Jarīr al-Ṭabarī states that he agrees with the opinion of Qatāda and al-Ḍaḥḥāk mentioned on pp. 482–483: 'This exception applies to those Muslims who had perpetrated major sins.'

93 Bukhārī 7439; Muslim 451; Tirmidhī 2557; Aḥmad 8817. The *ḥadīth* in Bukhārī is: 'God will gather all the people on the Day of Judgment and will say, "Whoever worshipped something should follow that thing..." Whoever used to worship false deities will follow those deities. And there will remain only this Community, and God will come to them and say, "I am your Lord." They will say, "You are our Lord," so they will follow Him.'

94 See Q.XXXV.36: *But as for those who disbelieve, for them is fire of Hell; it taketh not complete effect upon them so that they can die, nor is its torment lightened for them. Thus, We punish every ingrate.*

95 See Q.V.37: *They will wish to come forth from the Fire, but they will not come forth from it. Theirs will be a lasting doom.*

96 See Bukhārī 4730; Muslim 7181; Tirmidhī 3156; Ibn Māja 4327; Aḥmad 7546.

97 See Q.VII.40: *Lo! they who deny Our revelations and scorn them, for them the gates of heaven will not be opened nor will they enter the Garden until the camel goeth through the needle's eye.*

98 Q.VI.28.

99 Q.VI.28.

100 Q.VI.27–28.

101 Bukhārī 1358; Muslim 6755; Tirmidhī 2138; Abū Dāwūd 4716; Aḥmad 7181.

102 ʿIyāḍ b. Ḥimār b. Muḥammad al-Tamīmī al-Mujashiʿī (d. 50/670) was a Companion of the Prophet. He narrated thirty *ḥadīths*.

103 Muslim 7207; Aḥmad 17,484.

104 Q.VIII.23.

105 Bukhārī 7510; Muslim 454. The *ḥadīth* in Bukhārī refers to the degree of faith as the 'slightest, slightest, slightest atom's weight of faith'.

106 See Muslim 6766; Tirmidhī 3150; Abū Dāwūd 4705; Aḥmad 21,121.

107 Q.LXXI.27. The exegetes maintain that Noah's statement came after God notified him that no further people would believe. See Q.XI.36: *And it was inspired in Noah, (saying), No-one of thy folk will believe save him who hath believed already. Be not distressed because of what they do.*

108 Tirmidhī 2191; Aḥmad 11,143; Ḥākim 8543; Bayhaqī (*Shuʿab*) 7936. It is 'weak' according to Albānī (*Silsilat al-aḥādīth al-ḍaʿīfa wa'l-mawḍūʿa* 2927).

109 Q.XV.49–50.

110 Q.VII.167.

111 Q.V.98.

112 Q.VII.156: *With My punishment I visit whom I will; but My mercy extendeth to all things. That (mercy) I shall ordain for those who do right, and practise regular charity, and those who believe in Our signs* (Yusuf Ali translation).

113 See Bukhārī 7422, Muslim 6970, Ibn Māja 189 and Aḥmad 9159 for the *ḥadīth* with the wording 'My mercy precedes My wrath' (*raḥmatī sabaqat ghaḍabī*).

114 Q.VII.156.

115 Q.XL.7.

116 Bukhārī 4712; Muslim 480; Tirmidhī 2434; Aḥmad 9623.

117 Bukhārī 6410; Muslim 6809.

118 Muslim 265.

119 Tirmidhī 2799. It is 'weak' according to Albānī (*Ḍaʿīf al-Jāmiʿ* 1596).

120 Aḥmad 3977; Ḥākim 8155; Bayhaqī (*Sunan*) 17,612. It is 'authentic' according to Albānī (*Silsilat al-aḥādīth al-ṣaḥīḥa* 1638).

121 See Abū Dāwūd 4012; Nasā'ī 406; Aḥmad 17,970; Bayhaqī (*Sunan*) 956; Tabrīzī, 447. It is 'sound' according to Albānī (*Ṣaḥīḥ al-Jāmiʿ* 1756).

122 Q.III.146: *Allah loveth the steadfast.*

123 The work by Ibn Taymiyya is *al-Radd ʿalā man qāl bi-fanā' al-jannah wa'l-nār* (Riyadh: Dār Balansiyya, 1995).

124 ʿAlī b. Abī Ṭālib (d. 40/660) was a cousin of the Prophet and the first of the youth to accept Islam. He later married the Prophet's daughter, Fāṭima, and became the fourth Rightly-Guided Caliph. He was one of the ten promised Paradise. He narrated 537 *ḥadīths*.

125 Ibn al-Qayyim also refers to this statement in *Ḥādī al-arwāḥ ilā bilād al-afrāḥ* (Beirut: Dār Ibn Ḥazm, 2011), pp. 387–388 and *Mukhtaṣar al-Ṣawāʿiq al-mursala*, p. 219. That said, the original source for it could not be found.

126 Q.VI.128.

127 Q.XI.107.

128 Q.XI.108.

129 Q.XI.108.

130 See Ibn al-Qayyim, *Ḥādī al-arwāḥ*, pp. 352–354, as well as Ibn Taymiyya, *al-Radd ʿalā man qāl bi-fanāʾ al-janna waʾl-nār*, pp. 42–46, for a more detailed discussion.

131 Q.XII.103.

132 Q.XXXIV.13.

133 Q.XXXVIII.24.

134 Q.VI.116.

135 This is based on the *ḥadīth* in Bukhārī (3348); Muslim (532); Tirmidhī (3168); and Aḥmad (11,284).

136 Commenting on the *ḥadīth* of '999 out of every 1000', Ghazālī states that 'the meaning it imparts is not that they are Unbelievers who will abide forever in the Hellfire. Rather, they will simply enter the Hellfire, be exposed to it and left there for a period commensurate with the magnitude of their sins.' See Sherman A. Jackson (tr.), *On the Boundaries of Theological Tolerance in Islam: Abū Ḥāmid al-Ghazālī's Fayṣal al-Tafriqa Bayna al-Islām wa al-Zandaqa* (Karachi: Oxford University Press, 2002), p. 125.

Chapter Eight

1 This is derived from Q.XXII.11: *And among humankind is he who worshippeth God upon a narrow marge so that if good befalleth him he is content therewith, but if a trial befalleth him, he falleth away utterly. He loseth both the world and the Hereafter. That is the sheer loss.*

2 Q.III.137 (Yusuf Ali translation).

3 Q.III.175.

4 Q.III.179.

5 Q.XXIII.115.

6 Q.LXXV.36.

7 Abū ʿAbd Allāh Muḥammad b. Idrīs al-Shāfiʿī (d. 204/820) was the eponymous founder of the Shāfiʿī school of jurisprudence. Shāfiʿī was a descendant of the Banū Muṭṭalib tribe of Quraysh. He was born in Gaza in 150/767, and at the age of 2 his mother took him to Mecca. He later moved to Medina to study under Mālik b. Anas (the eponymous founder of the Mālikī school of jurisprudence). He is also famous for writing the *Risāla*, which is the earliest surviving documentation of Islamic jurisprudence that is relatively elaborate.

8 Q.LI.56.

9 Q.LXV.12.

10 Q.V.97.

11 Q.XXIII.116.

12 Q.VI.91.

13 Q.XIV.28.

14 Q.III.164.
15 Q.LXII.2–4.
16 Q.XXI.107.
17 Q.X.58.
18 Q.V.3.
19 Q.II.231.
20 Q.XLIX.7–8 (Yusuf Ali translation).
21 Q.IV.113.
22 Q.III.18 (Yusuf Ali translation).
23 Q.XXIX.21.
24 Q.II.284.
25 Q.IIIV.8.
26 Q.XXI.23.
27 Q.XXI.23.
28 Q.XXI.21–23.

Chapter Nine

1 See Q.II.251: *So they routed them by God's leave and David slew Goliath; and God gave him the kingdom and wisdom, and taught him of that which He willeth. And if God had not repelled some men by others the earth would have been corrupted. But God is a Lord of kindness to (His) creatures.*

Chapter Ten

1 Q.XI.34.
2 Q.VI.125.
3 Q.XVII.16.
4 Q.IV.27.
5 Q.II.185.
6 Abū Muḥammad al-Ḥusayn b. Masʿūd b. Muḥammad al-Farrā' al-Baghawī (d. 516/1122) was a prominent scholar and ascetic who lived in Khurāsān. He wrote *Sharḥ al-Sunna* and *Maʿālim al-tanzīl*. He was given a title of 'Reviver of the Sunna'. See Dhahabī, *Siyar aʿlām al-nubalā'*, vol. XIX, p. 439–443.
7 Q.XI.107.
8 Q.CXIII.1–2. Yusuf Ali translates Q.CXIII.2 as *From the mischief of created things*, while Muḥammad Asad translates it as *From the evil aught that He has created.*
9 Q.LXXII.10.
10 Q.XVI.78–80.
11 Q.XVIII.79.
12 Q.XVIII.82.
13 Q.I.6–7. Here, firstly, God is not mentioned as the agent. Secondly, evil is

ascribed to His creatures' actions, and it is for that reason that they deserve His anger. Thirdly, and finally, it is due to the evilness of the creatures that they have gone astray.

14 Q.III.26.

15 Bukhārī 7419; Muslim 2308; Tirmidhī 3045; Ibn Māja 197.

16 Muslim 1812; Tirmidhī 3422; Abū Dāwūd 760; Nasā'ī 898; Aḥmad 803.

17 Q.VII.180 (Yusuf Ali translation).

18 Q.II.165.

19 Q.LI.58.

20 Q.XI.14.

21 Muslim 445; Ibn Māja 195; Aḥmad 19,632.

22 Bukhārī 7385.

23 Muslim 1090; Tirmidhī 3566; Ibn Māja 1179; Abū Dāwūd 879; Nasā'ī 169; Aḥmad 751.

24 Nasā'ī 1307; Aḥmad 18,325; Ibn Ḥibbān 1971; Ḥākim 1923. It is 'authentic' according to Albānī (*Ṣaḥīḥ al-Jāmi*ᶜ 1301).

25 Muslim 6899; Aḥmad 2748.

Chapter Eleven

1 Muslim 1090; Tirmidhī 3566; Abū Dāwūd 879; Ibn Māja 1179; Nasā'ī 169; Aḥmad 751.

2 Abū Dāwūd 5090; Aḥmad 20,430; Ibn Ḥibbān 970; Ḥākim 2000. It is 'sound' according to Albānī (*Silsilat al-aḥādīth al-ṣaḥīḥa* 227).

3 Muslim 6899; Aḥmad 2748.

4 Imam Aḥmad, as well as other scholars of Ahl al-Sunna, used this to prove that the words of God are not created.

5 See Bukhārī 5013; Muslim 1886; Tirmidhī 939; Ibn Māja 3787; Abū Dāwūd 1461; Nasā'ī 996; Aḥmad 6613.

6 Q.II.255: *God! There is no deity save Him, the Ever-Living, the Self-Subsisting. Neither slumber nor sleep overtaketh Him. Unto Him belongeth whatsoever is in the heavens and whatsoever is in the earth. Who is he that intercedeth with Him save by His leave? He knoweth that which is in front of them and that which is behind them, while they encompass nothing of His knowledge save what He will. His Throne includeth the heavens and the earth, and He is never weary of preserving them. He is the Most High, the Great.*

7 Q.XXXIX.67: *And they esteem not God as He hath the right to be esteemed, when the whole earth is His handful on the Day of Judgment, and the heavens are rolled in His Right Hand. Glorified is He and High Exalted from all that they ascribe as partner (unto Him).*

8 Q.II.102.

9 Bukhārī 6313; Muslim 6882; Tirmidhī 3423; Abū Dāwūd 5046; Aḥmad 18,515.

10 Q.III.128.

11 Q.III.154.

12 Q.XXXIX.38.
13 Q.VI.17.
14 Q.XXXV.2.

Chapter Twelve

1 Aḥmad 3712; Ibn Ḥibbān 972; Ḥākim 1877. It is 'authentic' according to Albānī (*Silsilat al-aḥādīth al-ṣaḥīḥa* 199).
2 Q.XLVII.19.
3 Haythamī 17,574. It is 'fabricated' according to Albānī (*Silsilat al-aḥādīth al-daʿīfa wa'l-mawḍūʿa* 5560).
4 Bukhārī 6346; Muslim 6921; Tirmidhī 3435; Aḥmad 2012.
5 Tirmidhī 3505; Aḥmad 1462; Ḥākim 1862; Bayhaqī (*Shuʿab*) 611. It is 'authentic' according to Albānī (*Ṣaḥīḥ al-Jāmiʿ* 3383). The verse is Q.XXI.87.
6 Muslim 6572; Aḥmad 21,420.
7 Q.XX.112.
8 Q.XL.31.
9 Q.L.29.
10 Q.XI.56.
11 This is derived from Q.XX.112: *And he who hath done some good works, being a believer, he feareth not injustice nor begrudging (of his wage).*
12 Q.XI.56.
13 Q.XVI.76.
14 Bukhārī 6410; Muslim 6809; Tirmidhī 3506; Aḥmad 8146.
15 Abū Muḥammad ʿAlī b. Aḥmad b. Saʿīd b. Ḥazm (d. 438/1064) was a scholar and prolific writer of Muslim Spain. He codified literalist Ẓāhirī thought (founded by Dāwūd al-Ẓāhirī (d. 270/884)) and was its most well-known adherent. Unfortunately, Ibn Ḥazm held some irrational views, such as: if God had willed He could punish the righteous and reward the wretched. See James Pavlin, 'Sunni *Kalām* and Theological Controversies', in Seyyed Hossein Nasr and Oliver Leaman (eds.), *History of Islamic Philosophy* (London: Routledge, 1996), p. 109. Ibn Ḥazm held other beliefs which would render God to be unwise—God is infallible and holy above that. That said, Ibn Ḥazm wrote over four-hundred volumes, including *al-Faṣl fi'l-milal wa'l-niḥal* and *al-Īṣāl ilā fahm kitāb al-khiṣāl*. See Dhahabī, *Siyar aʿlām al-nubalā'*, vol. XVIII, pp.184–212.
16 Tirmidhī 3544; Ibn Māja 3858; Abū Dāwūd 1495; Nasā'ī 1301; Aḥmad 12,611; Ibn Ḥibbān 893; Ḥākim 1857. It is 'authentic' according to Albānī (*Silsilat al-aḥādīth al-ṣaḥīḥa* 3411).
17 Tirmidhī 3475; Ibn Māja 3857; Abū Dāwūd 1493; Nasā'ī 1302; Aḥmad 22,952; Ibn Ḥibbān 891; Ḥākim 1858; Bayhaqī (*Sunan*) 2366. It is 'authentic' according to Albānī (*Ṣaḥīḥ al-targhīb wa'l-tarhīb* 1640).

18 Nasā'ī 1307; Aḥmad 18,325; Ibn Ḥibbān 1971; Ḥākim 1923. It is 'authentic' according to Albānī (*Ṣaḥīḥ al-Jāmiʿ* 1301).
19 Q.VII.180 (Yusuf Ali translation).
20 Q.VI.122.
21 Q.XLII.52.
22 Q.II.17-20.
23 Q.XXIV.35.
24 Ibn al-Qayyim mentions the three *sūras* in his book *Ijtimāʿ al-juyūsh al-islāmiyya ʿalā ḥarb al-Muʿaṭṭila wa'l-Jahmiyya* (Mecca: Dār ʿĀlam al-Fawā'id, 2010), p. 75, and they are *sūras* Baqara, Nūr and Raʿd (not Hūd). See Q.XIII.17. He discusses this verse in Zeni (tr.), *Ibn Qayyim al-Jawziyya on Knowledge*, pp. 38–39.

Chapter Thirteen

1 This has been narrated by Ṭabarānī (*al-Muʿjam al-kabīr*), vol. XXII, p. 320. It is 'very weak' according to Albānī (*Silsilat al-aḥādīth al-ḍaʿīfa wa'l-mawḍūʿa* 505).
2 Q.II.216.
3 Q.XXXIX.7.
4 Q.IV.108.
5 Q.II.205.
6 Q.IV.22.
7 Q.XLVII.28.
8 Q.LXI.3.
9 Q.IX.46.
10 Q.XVII.38. The evils are outlined in Q.XVII.22–37, starting with the notion of worshipping other than God.

Chapter Fourteen

1 Q.XXXIV.14.
2 Q.XXXIX.69.
3 Q.XVII.23.
4 Q.XXI.112.
5 Q.LX.10.
6 Q.V.1.
7 Q.XVIII.26 (Muḥammad Asad translation).
8 Q.XI.107.
9 Q.XVII.16.
10 Q.XI.34.
11 Q.XXVIII.5.
12 Q.II.185.
13 Q.IV.27.

14 This is discussed further in Chapter Fifteen, Point 30.
15 Q.LVIII.21.
16 Q.XXI.105.
17 Q.XXII.4.
18 Q.II.183.
19 Q.IV.23.
20 Q.IV.24 (Muḥammad Asad translation).
21 Q.V.45.
22 Q.XXXVI.82.
23 Q.LIV.50.
24 Q.IV.47.
25 Q.XIX.21.
26 Q.XVII.16. Of note, Asad's translation is: *But when it is Our will to destroy a community, We convey our last warning to those of its people who have lost themselves entirely in the pursuit of pleasures; and [if] they [continue to] act sinfully, the sentence [of doom] passed on the community takes effect.*
27 Q.XI.117.
28 Q.XVI.90.
29 Q.IV.58.
30 Q.II.102.
31 Q.LIX.5.
32 Q.X.59.
33 Q.XLII.21.
34 Q.XXXVI.8–9.
35 Q.X.100.
36 Q.XVI.72.
37 Q.V.103 (Muḥammad Asad translation). Asad then comments on this verse by stating that the literal translation is 'God has not ordained anything [in the nature] of a *baḥīrah,* nor a *sā'ibah,* nor a *waṣīlah*, nor a *ḥām,*' and adds: 'These expressions denote certain categories of domestic animals which the pre-Islamic Arabs used to dedicate to their various deities by setting them free to pasture and prohibiting their use of slaughter. They were selected mainly on the basis of the number, sex, or sequence of their offspring; but the lexicographers and commentators are by no means unanimous in their attempts at definition. For this reason—as well as because of their inherent complexity—the above four terms cannot be translated into any other language; consequently, I am rendering them in the text as "certain kinds of cattle marked out by superstition and set aside from the use of man": this being, in the consensus of all authorities, the common denominator of the four categories. It is obvious that their mention at this place (as well as, by implication, in 6 [Sūrat al-Anʿām, verses]: 138–139 and 143–144) serves as an illustration of the arbitrary invention of certain supposedly "religious"

obligations and prohibitions.' See Muḥammad Asad, *The Message of the Qur'ān* (Bristol: The Book Foundation, 2003), pp. 191 and 222–224.

38 Q.V.97.

39 Q.X.33.

40 Q.VII.137.

41 Aḥmad 15,461; Mālik 3500; Bayhaqī (*Shuʿab*) 4385; Haythamī 17,056; Tabrīzī 2479. It is 'authentic' according to Albānī (*Silsilat al-aḥādīth al-ṣaḥīḥa* 840). In Muslim 6878, the Prophet (may God bless him and grant him peace) said, 'Whoever enters a house and then says, "I seek refuge in God's perfect words from any evilness He has created," he will not be harmed by anything while he remains therein.' In Muslim 6880, the Prophet recommends that this be said in the evening.

42 Q.IX.6.

43 Muslim 2950; Abū Dāwūd 1905; Ibn Māja 3074; Aḥmad 20,695.

44 Q.IV.3.

45 Q.LXVI.12.

46 Q.XVII.5 (Muḥammad Asad translation).

47 Q.V.31.

48 Q.LXII.2.

49 Q.II.213.

50 Q.XIX.83.

51 Q.XXV.48.

52 Q.IX.33.

53 Q.LXXIII.15.

54 Q.XXVIII.12.

55 Q.V.26.

56 Q.XXI.95.

57 Q.IV.23.

58 Q.V.3.

59 Q.V.96.

60 Q.II.275.

61 Q.II.247.

62 Q.III.26.

63 Q.IV.54.

64 Q.LIX.7.

65 Q.II.63.

66 Q.II.269.

Chapter Fifteen

1 This book is not extant; however, Ibn al-Qayyim discusses this in an expanded fashion, comprising thirteen viewpoints, in *Madārij al-sālikīn*, vol. I, pp. 403–432.

2 See the *ḥadīth* of the Prophet in Muslim 6965; Tirmidhī 3539; Aḥmad 23,515.

3 See Chapter Three, p. 45.
4 This is according to the *ḥadīth* which says, 'God is more pleased with the repentance of His servant than anyone of you is pleased with finding his camel which he had lost in the desert.' Bukhārī 6309; Muslim 6952; Tirmidhī 2498; Ibn Māja 4249; Aḥmad 3627. This was mentioned also in Chapter One.
5 Q.XX.118–119.
6 Q.XX.122.
7 Q.XXXIII.73.
8 See *Ḥilya*, vol. IV, p. 53.
9 Ibn al-Qayyim here alludes to certain Sufi concepts which he investigates in greater detail throughout *Madārij al-sālikīn*. Essentially, Ibn al-Qayyim is stating that an individual such as this abandons all of his desires, recognises his utter servitude to the Holy Lord and therefore submits his will perfectly to God's religious will.
10 Muslim 6909; Nasā'ī 5540; Aḥmad 19,308.
11 See *Ḥilya*, vol. VIII, p. 92, for a similar tradition attributed to Fuḍayl b. ʿIyāḍ.
12 Q.XXXV.41.
13 Q.XIX.90–91.
14 The Prophet (may God bless him and grant him peace) said, 'No fatigue, nor disease, nor sorrow, nor sadness, nor hurt, nor distress befalls a Muslim, even if it were the prick he receives from a thorn, but that God expiates some of his sins for that.' Bukhārī 5641; Aḥmad 8027.
15 Muslim 3997; Tirmidhī 1307; Aḥmad 17,083.
16 Bayhaqī (*Shuʿab*) 6868, Haythamī 17,948. It is 'sound' according to Albānī (*Ṣaḥīḥ al-Jāmiʿ* 5303).
17 Q.XI.114: *Good deeds annul ill-deeds. This is reminder for the mindful.*
18 This is also a *ḥadīth* in Aḥmad 8940; Haythamī 452. It is 'sound' according to Albānī (*Silsilat al-aḥādīth al-ṣaḥīḥa* 3586).
19 *Ḥilya*, vol. X, p. 267.
20 There is a similar *ḥadīth* of the Prophet: 'The laws of Islam will be stripped away layer by layer; and then after each law is stripped away, people will go after the next. The first to be stripped away are His rulings and the last is [the obligatory] prayer.' Aḥmad 22,160; Ḥākim 7022; Ibn Ḥibbān 6715; Bayhaqī (*Shuʿab*) 7118. It is 'authentic' according to Albānī (*Ṣaḥīḥ al-Jāmiʿ* 5075).
21 Tirmidhī 2499; Ibn Māja 4251; Aḥmad 13,049; Dārimī, 2769; Hākim, 7617; Bayhaqī (*Shuʿab*) 6725. It is 'sound' according to Albānī (*Ṣaḥīḥ al-Jāmiʿ* 4515).
22 See Bayhaqī (*Shuʿab*) 6750 and *Ḥilya*, vol. III, p. 242, for similar traditions.
23 Q.II.30.
24 There are no authentic ḥadīths regarding Hārūt or Mārūt. See Albānī's (*Silsilat al-aḥādīth al-ḍaʿīfa wa'l-mawḍūʿa* 34, 170, 910, 912, 913, 1306, 5401, and 6656). All of these are either fabricated or weak. Albānī considers many of them to be false Israelite traditions.

25 Ḥākim 3655 and Bayhaqī (*Shuʿab*) 6270 mention this as being stated by Ibn ʿAbbās.

26 See Bayhaqī (*Shuʿab*) 6829.

27 Q.XVII.3.

28 Q.XVI.123: *And afterward We inspired thee (Muḥammad, saying), Follow the religion of Abraham, as one by nature upright.* Also see Q.III.95, Q.IV.125 and Q.VI.161, among many other verses of similar import.

29 See Abū Jaʿfar Muḥammad b. Jarīr al-Ṭabarī, *Tārīkh al-Ṭabarī: Tārīkh al-rusul wa'l-mulūk* (Cairo: Dār al-Maʿārif, 1967), vol. I, p. 485 (narrated by Wahb b. Munabbih). Of note, this text is not found in any collections or books of *Ḥadīth*. Nonetheless, the concept that David counted the Israelites is present in II Samuel 24:1–25 (King James version of the Old Testament).

30 Q.III.164.

31 Q.V.3 (Yusuf Ali translation).

32 Q.V.3.

33 Although Ibn al-Qayyim did not mention God's justice here, he includes it in many prior passages, such as, 'His actions all proceed from His wisdom, beneficence, mercy, justice and righteousness.' See p. 63 above.

BIBLIOGRAPHY

Abdul Aziz, Suraqah (tr.). *A Refined Explanation of the Sanusi Creed* [*entitled*] *The Foundational Proofs*. Rotterdam: Sunni Publications, 2013. [=Saeed Fodeh, *Tahdhīb sharḥ al-Sanūsiyya Umm al-barāhīn*]

Abū Khaliyl (tr.). *English Translation of Jāmiᶜ at-Tirmidhī*. Riyadh: Darussalam Publications, 2007. [=Tirmidhī, Abū ᶜĪsā Muḥammad b. ᶜĪsā al-Sulamī, al-. *Jāmiᶜ al-Tirmidhī*]

Abū Zayd, Bakr b. ᶜAbd Allāh. *Ibn Qayyim al-Jawziyya: ḥayātuhu āthāruhu mawāriduhu*. Riyadh: Dār al-ᶜĀṣima, 1995.

Adem, Rodrigo (tr.). *Al-Māturīdī and the Development of Sunnī Theology in Samarqand*. Leiden: Brill, 2015. [=Ulrich, Rudolph. *Al-Maturidi und die sunnitische Theologie in Samarkand*]

Aḥmad b. Ḥanbal. *Al-ᶜIlal wa-maᶜrifat al-rijāl li-Aḥmad: riwāyat ibnih ᶜAbd Allāh*. Riyadh: Dār al-Khānī, 2001.

———. *Al-Radd ᶜalā'l-zanādiqa wa'l-Jahmiyya*. Ed. Daghash b. Shabīb al-ᶜAjamī. Kuwait City: Ghirās, 2005.

———. *Al-Zuhd*. Ed. Muḥammad ᶜAbd al-Salām Shāhīn. Beirut: Dār al-Kutub al-ᶜIlmiyyah, 1999.

———. *Musnad al-Imām Aḥmad*. Eds. Shuᶜayb al-Arna'ūṭ and ᶜĀdil Murshid. Beirut: Mu'assasat al-Risāla, 2001.

Albānī, Muḥammad Nāṣir al-Dīn, al-. *Silsilat al-aḥādīth al-ḍaᶜīfa wa'l-mawḍūᶜa wa-atharuhā al-sayyi' fi'l-umma*. Riyadh: Maktabat al-Maᶜārif, 1992.

———. *Silsilat al-aḥādīth al-ṣaḥīḥa wa-shay' min fiqhihā wa-fawā'idihā*. Riyadh: Maktabat al-Maᶜārif, 1995.

Ali, Abdullah Yusuf. *The Holy Qur'an: Text, Translation, and Commentary*. Lahore: Sheikh Muḥammad Ashraf Publishers, 1938.

ᶜAlī b. Abī Ṭalḥa. *Tafsīr Ibn ᶜAbbās al-musammā ṣaḥīfat ᶜAlī b. Abī Ṭalḥa*. Ed. Rāshid ᶜAbd al-Munᶜim al-Rajjāl. Beirut: Mu'assasat al-Kutub al-Thaqāfiyya, 1991.

Anjum, Ovamir. *Politics, Law, and Community in Islamic Thought: The Taymiyyan Moment*. New York: Cambridge University Press, 2012.

———. 'Sufism without Mysticism? Ibn Qayyim al-Ǧawziyyah's

Objectives in *Madāriğ al-Sālikīn*'. In Caterina Bori and Livnat Holtzman (eds), *A Scholar in the Shadow: Essays in the Legal and Theological Thought of Ibn al-Qayyim al-Ğawziyyah*. Rome: Istituto per l'Oriente C. A. Nallino, 2010, pp. 161–188.

Asad, Muḥammad (tr.). *The Message of the Qur'ān*. Bristol: The Book Foundation, 2003.

Aṣbahānī, Abū Nuʿaym Aḥmad b. ʿAbd Allāh, al-. *Ḥilyat al-awliyā' wa-ṭabaqāt al-aṣfiyā'*. Beirut: Dār al-Kutub al-ʿIlmiyyah, 1988.

Azzam, Abdul Rahman. *Saladin: The Triumph of the Sunni Revival*. Cambridge: Islamic Texts Society, 2014.

Baghawī, al-Ḥusayn b. Masʿūd, al-. *Tafsīr al-Baghawī*. Ed. ʿAbd al-Razzāq al-Mahdī. Beirut: Dār Iḥyā' al-Turāth al-ʿArabī, 1999.

Baghdādī, Abū Bakr Aḥmad al-Khaṭīb, al-. *Tārīkh Baghdād*. Ed. Bashshār ʿAwād Maʿrūf. Beirut: Dār al-Gharb al-Islāmī, 2002.

Bayhaqī, Abū Bakr Aḥmad b. al-Ḥusayn al-. *Al-Asmā' wa'l-ṣifāt*. Ed. ʿAbd Allāh b. Muḥammad al-Ḥāshidī. Jeddah: Maktabat al-Suwādī, 1999.

———. *Al-Sunan al-kubrā li'l-Bayhaqī*. Ed. Muḥammad ʿAbd al-Qādir ʿAṭā'. Beirut: Dār al-Kutub al-ʿIlmiyyah, 2003.

———. *Shuʿab al-īmān*. Ed. ʿAbd al-ʿAlī ʿAbd al-Ḥamīd Ḥāmid. Riyadh: Maktabat al-Rushd, 2003.

Bennett, David. 'The Muʿtazilite Movement (II): The Early Muʿtazilites'. In Sabine Schmidtke (ed.), *The Oxford Handbook of Islamic Theology*. Oxford: Oxford University Press, 2016, pp. 142–158.

Bukhārī, Muḥammad b. Ismāʿīl, al-. *Khalq afʿāl al-ʿibād wa'l-radd ʿalā'l-Jahmiyya wa-aṣḥāb al-taʿṭīl*. Ed. ʿAbd al-Raḥmān ʿUmayra. Riyadh: Dār al-Maʿārif, 1978.

Burrell, David B., and Daher, Nazih. (tr.) *The Ninety-Nine Beautiful Names of God*. Cambridge: Islamic Texts Society, 1995. [=Ghazālī, Abū Ḥāmid Muḥammad b. Muḥammad, al-. *Al-Maqṣad al-asnā fī sharḥ asmā' Allāh al-ḥusnā*]

Dārimī, Abū Muḥammad ʿAbd Allāh b. ʿAbd al-Raḥmān, al-. *Sunan al-Dārimī*. Ed. Ḥusayn Salīm Asad al-Dārānī. Riyadh: Dār al-Mughnī, 2000.

Dhahabī, Abū ʿAbd Allāh Shams al-Dīn Muḥammad b. Aḥmad, al. *Siyar aʿlām al-nubalā'*. Editor-in-Chief Shuʿayb al-Arna'ūṭ. Beirut: Mu'assasat al-Risāla, 1985.

Dughaym, Samīḥ. *Mawsūʿat muṣṭalaḥāt al-imām Fakhr al-Dīn al-Rāzī*. Beirut: Maktabat Lubnān Nāshirūn, 2001.

Fitzgerald, Michael Abdurrahman, and Slitine, Moulay Youssef (tr.). *The Invocation of God*. Cambridge: Islamic Texts Society, 2000. [=Ibn Qayyim al-Jawziyya, Abū ʿAbd Allāh Shams al-Dīn Muḥammad b. Abī Bakr. *Al-Wābil al-ṣayyib min al-kalim al-ṭayyib* (extract)]

Ghazālī, Abū Ḥāmid Muḥammad b. Muḥammad, al-. *Iḥyā' ʿulūm al-dīn*. Beirut: Dār Ṣādir, 2010.

Ḥākim, Abū ʿAbd Allāh Muḥammad, al-. *Al-Mustadrak ʿalā'l-Ṣaḥīḥayn li'l-Ḥākim*. Ed. Muṣṭafā ʿAbd al-Qādir ʿAṭā'. Beirut: Dār al-Kutub al-ʿIlmiyyah, 1990.

Hallaq, Wael B. (tr.). *Ibn Taymiyya against the Greek Logicians*. Oxford: Clarendon Press, 1993. [=Suyūṭī, ʿAbd al-Raḥmān Jalāl al-Dīn, al-. *Jahd al-qarīha fī tajrīd al-naṣīḥa* (an abridgement of Ibn Taymiyya, *Naṣīḥat ahl al-imān fī'l-Radd ʿalā'l-manṭiqiyyīn*)]

Haythamī, Abū al-Ḥasan Nūr al-Dīn ʿAlī, al-. *Majmaʿ al-zawā'id wa-manbaʿ al-fawā'id*. Ed. Ḥusām al-Dīn al-Qudsī. Cairo: Maktabat al-Qudsī, 1994.

Holtzman, Livnat. 'Ibn Qayyim al-Jawziyyah'. In Joseph E. Lowery and Devin Stewart (eds), *Essays in Arabic Literary Biography II: 1350-1850*. Wiesbaden: Harrassowitz Verlag, 2009, pp. 202-222.

Hoover, Jon. 'Against Islamic Universalism: ʿAlī al-Ḥarbī's 1990 Attempt to Prove that Ibn Taymiyya and Ibn Qayyim al-Jawziyya Affirm the Eternity of Hell-Fire'. In Birgit Krawietz and Georges Tamer (eds.) *Islamic Theology, Philosophy and Law: Debating Ibn Taymiyya and Ibn Qayyim al-Jawziyya*. Berlin: De Gruyter, 2013, pp. 377–399.

———. 'God Acts by His Will and Power: Ibn Taymiyya's Theology of a Personal God in his Treatise on the Voluntary Attributes'. In Yossef Rapoport and Shahab Ahmed (eds.), *Ibn Taymiyya and his Times*. Karachi: Oxford University Press, 2010, pp. 55–77.

———. 'God's Wise Purposes in Creating Iblīs: Ibn Qayyim al-Ǧawziyyah's Theodicy of God's Names and Attributes'. In Caterina Bori and Livnat Holtzman (eds), *A Scholar in the Shadow: Essays in the Legal and Theological Thought of Ibn al-Qayyim al-Ǧawziyyah*. Rome: Istituto per l'Oriente C. A. Nallino, 2010, pp. 113–134.

———. *Ibn Taymiyya's Theodicy of Perpetual Optimism*. Leiden: Brill, 2007.

———. 'Islamic Universalism: Ibn Qayyim al-Jawziyya's Salafī Deliberations on the Duration of Hell-fire', *The Muslim World*, vol. XCIX (2009), pp. 181–201.

Ibn ʿAbd al-Barr. *Jāmiʿ bayān al-ʿilm wa-faḍlih*. Ed. Abū al-Ashbāl al-Zuhayrī. Dammam: Dār Ibn al-Jawzī, 1994.

Ibn ʿAdī. *Al-Kāmil fī ḍuʿafāʾ al-rijāl*. Eds. ʿĀdil Aḥmad ʿAbd al-Mawjūd and ʿAlī Muḥammad Muʿawwaḍ. Beirut: Dār al-Kutub al-ʿIlmiyyah, 1997.

Ibn Ḥajar, Abū al-Faḍl Aḥmad. *Al-Durar al-kāminah fī aʿyān al-māʾata al-thāmina*. Hyderabad: Maṭbaʿat Majlis Dāʾirat al-Maʿārif al-ʿUthmāniyya, 1972.

Ibn Ḥazm, Abū Muḥammad ʿAlī. *Asmāʾ al-Ṣaḥāba al-ruwāt wa-ma li-kulli wāḥid min al-ʿadad*. Beirut: Dār al-Kutub al-ʿIlmiyyah, 1992.

Ibn Ḥibbān, Abū Ḥātim Muḥammad. *Ṣaḥīḥ Ibn Ḥibbān*. Ed. Shuʿayb al-Arnaʾūṭ. Beirut: Muʾassasat al-Risāla, 1988.

Ibn Ḥibbān, Abū Ḥātim Muḥammad, and Albānī, Muḥammad Nāṣir al-Dīn, al-. *Al-Taʿliqāt al-ḥisān ʿalā Ṣaḥīḥ Ibn Ḥibbān*. Jeddah: Dār Bawzīr, 2003.

Ibn Kathīr, Abū al-Fidāʾ Ismāʿīl ʿImād al-Dīn b. ʿUmar. *Al-Bidāya wa'l-nihāya*. Damascus: Dār al-Fikr, 1986.

Ibn Māja, Abū ʿAbd Allāh Muḥammad b. Yazīd, and Albānī, Muḥammad Nāṣir al-Dīn, al-. *Ṣaḥīḥ Sunan Ibn Māja/Ḍaʿīf Sunan Ibn Māja*. Riyadh: Maktabat al-Maʿārif, 1997.

Ibn al-Qayyim, Abū ʿAbd Allāh Shams al-Dīn Muḥammad b. Abī Bakr. *Ḥādī al-arwāḥ ilā bilād al-afrāḥ*. Beirut: Dār Ibn Ḥazm, 2011.

———. *Ijtimāʿ al-juyūsh al-islāmiyya ʿalā ḥarb al-Muʿaṭṭila wa'l-Jahmiyya*. Ed. Zāʾid b. Aḥmad al-Nashirī. Mecca: Dār ʿĀlam al-Fawāʾid, 2010.

———. *Madārij al-sālikīn bayn manāzil iyyāka naʿbudu wa-iyyāka nastaʿīn*. Beirut: Dār al-Kitāb al-ʿArabī, 1996.

———. *Miftāḥ dār al-saʿāda wa-manshūr wilāyat al-ʿilm wa'l-irāda*. Ed. ʿAbd al-Raḥmān b. Ḥasan b. Qāʾid. Mecca: Dār ʿĀlim al-Fawāʾid, 2015.

———. *Miftāḥ dār al-saʿāda wa-manshūr wilāyat al-ʿilm wa'l-irāda*. Eds. Sayyid b. Ibrāhīm b. Ṣādiq ʿImrān and ʿAlī Muḥammad. Cairo: Dār al-Ḥadīth, 1994.

———. *Mukhtaṣar al-Ṣawāʿiq al-mursala ʿalā'l-Jahmiyya wa'l-Muʿaṭṭila*, abridged by al-Mawṣilī, Muḥammad. Ed. al-ʿAlawī, al-Ḥasan b. ʿAbd al-Raḥmān. Beirut: Dār al-Kutub al-ʿIlmiyyah, 1993.

———. *Shifāʾ al-ʿalīl fī masāʾil al-qaḍāʾ wa'l-qadar wa'l-ḥikma wa'l-taʿlīl*. Eds. Aḥmad b. Ṣāliḥ b. ʿAlī al-Ṣamʿānī and ʿAlī b. Muḥammad b. ʿAbd Allāh al-ʿAjlān. Riyadh: Dār al-Ṣamayʿī, 2013.

———. *Ṭarīq al-hijratayn wa-bāb al-saʿādatayn*. Ed. Aḥmad Ibrāhīm Zahwa. Beirut: Dār al-Kitāb al-ʿArabī, 2005.

———. *Zād al-maʿād fī hadī khayr al-ʿibād*. Beirut: Muʾassasat al-Risāla, 1994.

Ibn Rajab, Zayn al-Dīn ʿAbd al-Raḥmān. *Dhayl ṭabaqāt al-Ḥanābila*. Ed. ʿAbd al-Raḥmān b. Sulaymān al-ʿUthaymīn. Riyadh: Maktabat al-ʿUbaykān, 2005.

Ibn Taymiyya, Taqī al-Dīn Aḥmad b. ʿAbd al-Ḥalīm. *Al-Radd ʿalā man qāl bi-fanāʾ al-jannah waʾl-nār*. Ed. Muḥammad b. ʿAbd Allah al-Samharī. Riyadh: Dār Balansiyya, 1995.

———. *Darʾ taʿāruḍ al-ʿaql waʾl-naql*. Ed. ʿAbd al-Laṭīf ʿAbd al-Raḥmān. Beirut: Dār al-Kutub al-ʿIlmiyyah, 2009.

———. *Majmūʿ al-fatāwā*. Ed. ʿAbd al-Raḥmān b. Muḥammad b. Qāsim. Medina: Mujammaʿ al-Malik Fahd li-Ṭibāʿat al-Muṣḥaf al-Sharīf, 1995.

———. *Risāla fī maʿnā kawn al-Rabb ʿādilan wa-fī tanzīhih ʿan al-ẓulm* in *Jāmiʿ al-rasāʾil li-Ibn Taymiyya*. Ed. Muḥammad Rashād Sālim. Riyadh: Dār al-ʿAṭāʾ, 2001.

Inati, Shams. *The Problem of Evil: Ibn Sīna's Theodicy*. Binghampton: Globe Publications, 2000.

Jackson, Sherman. *Islam and the Problem of Black Suffering*. Oxford: Oxford University Press, 2009.

——— (tr.). *On the Boundaries of Theological Tolerance in Islam: Abū Ḥāmid al-Ghazālī's Fayṣal al-Tafriqa Bayna al-Islām wa al-Zandaqa*. Karachi: Oxford University Press, 2002.

Keller, Nuh Ha Mim (tr.). *The Reliance of the Traveller: A Classic Manual of Islamic Sacred Law*. Beltsville: Amana Publications, 1994. [=Ahmad ibn Naqib al-Misri, *ʿUmdat al-sālik*]

Khalil, Mohammad. *Islam and the Fate of Others: The Salvation Question*. Oxford: Oxford University Press, 2012.

Khān, Muḥammad Muḥsin (tr.). *The Translation of the Meaning of Ṣaḥīḥ al-Bukhārī*. Riyadh: Darussalam Publications, 1997. [=Bukhārī, Abū ʿAbd Allāh Muḥammad b. Ismāʿīl, al-. *Ṣaḥīḥ al-Bukhārī*]

Khaṭṭāb, Nāṣiruddīn, al- (tr.). *English Translation of Ṣaḥīḥ Muslim*. Riyadh: Darussalam Publications, 2007. [=Naysābūrī, Abū al-Ḥusayn Muslim b. al-Ḥajjāj, al-. *Ṣaḥīḥ Muslim*]

——— (tr.). *English Translation of Sunan Ibn Mājah*. Riyadh: Darussalam Publications, 2007. [=Ibn Māja, Abū ʿAbd Allāh Muḥammad b. Yazīd. *Sunan Ibn Māja*]

——— (tr.). *English Translation of Sunan an-Nasāʾī*. Riyadh: Darussalam Publications, 2007. [=Nasāʾī, Abū ʿAbd al-Raḥmān Aḥmad b. Shuʿayb, al-. *Sunan an-Nasāʾī*]

Kirmānī, Ḥarb b. Ismāʿīl, al-. *Masā'il Ḥarb: al-nikāḥ ilā niyāyat al-kitāb*. Ed. Fāyiz Aḥmad b. Ḥāmid Ḥābis. Mecca: Jāmiʿat Umm al-Qurā, 2001.

Krawietz, Birgit, and Tamer, Georges (eds). *Islamic Theology, Philosophy and Law: Debating Ibn Taymiyya and Ibn Qayyim al-Jawziyya*. Berlin: De Gruyter, 2013.

Mālik b. Anas. *Muwaṭṭa' al-Imām Mālik*. Ed. Muḥammad Fu'ād ʿAbd al-Bāqī. Beirut: Dār Iḥyā' al-Turāth al-ʿArabī, 1985.

Marmura, Michael E. (tr.). *The Incoherence of the Philosophers*. Provo: Brigham Young University Press, 2000. [=Ghazālī, Abū Ḥāmid Muḥammad b. Muḥammad, al-. *Tahāfut al-falāsifa*]

——— (tr.). *The Metaphysics of the Healing*. Provo: Brigham Young University Press, 2005. [Ibn Sīnā, *Kitāb al-shifā'* (extract)]

Mundhirī, Abū Muḥammad ʿAbd al-ʿAẓīm b. ʿAbd al-Qawī, al-. *Al-Targhīb wa'l-tarhīb min al-Ḥadīth al-sharīf*. Ed. Ibrāhīm Shams al-Dīn. Beirut: Dār al-Kutub al-ʿIlmiyyah, 1996.

Mundhirī, Abū Muḥammad ʿAbd al-ʿAẓīm b. ʿAbd al-Qawī, al-, and Albānī, Muḥammad Nāṣir al-Dīn, al-. *Ṣaḥīḥ al-Targhīb wa'l-tarhīb/Ḍaʿīf al-Targhīb wa'l-tarhīb*. Riyadh: Maktabat al-Maʿārif, 2000.

Mustafa, Abdul-Rahman. *On Taqlīd: Ibn al-Qayyim's Critique of Authority in Islamic Law*. New York: Oxford University Press, 2013.

Nasā'ī, Abū ʿAbd al-Raḥmān Aḥmad b. Shuʿayb, al-, and Albānī, Muḥammad Nāṣir al-Dīn, al-. *Ṣaḥīḥ Sunan al-Nasā'ī/Ḍaʿīf Sunan al-Nasā'ī*. Riyadh: Maktabat al-Maʿārif, 1999.

Ormsby, Eric. *Theodicy in Islamic Thought: The Dispute over al-Ghazālī's "Best of All Possible Worlds"*. Princeton: Princeton University Press, 1984.

Pavlin, James. 'Sunni *Kalām* and Theological Contraversies'. In Seyyed Hossein Nasr and Oliver Leaman (eds.), *History of Islamic Philosophy*. London: Routledge, 1996.

Pickthall, Muḥammad Marmaduke (tr.). *The Meaning of the Glorious Qur'an*. London: Allen & Unwin, 1976.

Publisher (ed. and tr.). *Provisions for the Hereafter* (*Mukhtaṣar Zād al-Maʿād*). Riyadh: Darussalam, 2003. [=At-Tamimi, Muḥammad ibn Abdul Wahhab. *Zād al-Maʿād*]

Publisher (tr.). *The Names and Attributes of Allah According to the Doctrine of Ahl-us-Sunnah wal Jamaʿah*. Suffolk: Jamʿiat Ihyaa' Minhaaj Al-Sunnah, 1999. [=a work by ʿUmar Sulaiman al-Ashqar]

Qadhi, Yasir. 'The "*Unleashed Thunderbolts*" of Ibn Qayyim al-Ǧawziyyah: An Introductory Essay'. In Caterina Bori and Livnat Holtzman (eds),

A Scholar in the Shadow: Essays in the Legal and Theological Thought of Ibn al-Qayyim al-Ǧawziyyah. Rome: Istituto per l'Oriente C. A. Nallino, 2010, pp. 135–149.

Qadhi, Yasir, and al-Khattab, Nasiruddin (tr.). *English Translation of Sunan Abu Dawud*. Riyadh: Darussalam Publications, 2008. [=Sijistānī, Abū Dāwūd Sulaymān b. al-Ashʿath al-Azdī, al-. *Sunan Abī Dāwūd*]

Rāzī, Muḥammad b. ʿUmar Fakhr al-Dīn al-. *Al-Arbaʿīn fī uṣūl al-dīn*. Beirut: Dār al-Kutub al-ʿIlmiyyah, 2009.

———. *Al-Maḥṣūl*. Ed. Ṭāhā Jābir Fayyāḍ al-ʿUlwānī. Beirut: Mu'assasat al-Risāla, 1997.

———. *Al-Mubāḥith al-mashriqiyya fī ʿilm al-ilāhiyyāt wa'l-ṭabīʿiyyāt*. Qom: Intishārāt Bīdār, 1950.

———. *Tafsīr al-Rāzī* or *al-Tafsīr al-kabīr* or *Mafātīḥ al-ghayb*. Beirut: Dār Iḥyā' al-Turāth al-ʿArabī, 1999.

Rudolph, Ulrich. 'Occasionalism'. In Sabine Schmidtke (ed.), *The Oxford Handbook of Islamic Theology*. Oxford: Oxford University Press, 2016, pp. 347–363.

Ṣanʿānī, Muḥammad, al-. *Rafʿ al-astār li-ibṭāl adillat al-qā'ilīn bi-fanā' al-nār*. Ed. Muḥammad Nāṣir al-Dīn al-Albānī. Beirut: al-Maktab al-Islāmī, 1984.

Schmidtke, Sabine (ed.). *The Oxford Handbook of Islamic Theology*. Oxford: Oxford University Press, 2016.

Shihadeh, Ayman. 'Theories of Ethical Value in Kalām: A New Interpretation'. In Sabine Schmidtke (ed.), *The Oxford Handbook of Islamic Theology*. Oxford: Oxford University Press, 2016, pp. 384–407.

———. *The Teleological Ethics of Fakhr al-Dīn al-Rāzī*. Leiden: Brill, 2006.

Sijistānī, Abū Dāwūd Sulaymān b. al-Ashʿath al-Azdī, al-, and Albānī, Muḥammad Nāṣir al-Dīn, al-. *Ṣaḥīḥ Sunan Abī Dāwūd/Ḍaʿīf Sunan Abī Dāwūd*. Riyadh: Maktabat al-Maʿārif, 1998.

Şimsek, Cüneyt M. 'The Problem of Animal Pain: An Introduction to Nursi's Approach'. In Ibrahim M. Abu-Rabiʿ (ed.), *Theodicy and Justice in Modern Islamic Thought: The Case of Said Nursi*. Surrey: Ashgate Publishing, 2010, pp. 111–134.

Subkī, Taqī al-Dīn ʿAlī b. ʿAbd al-Kāfī, al-. *Al-Iʿtibār bi-baqā' al-janna wa'l-nār* in *al-Durra al-maḍiyya fī'l-radd ʿalā Ibn Taymiyya*. Damascus: Maṭbaʿat al-Taraqqī, 1928.

Suyūṭī, ʿAbd al-Raḥmān Jalāl al-Dīn, al-. *Tashyīd al-arkān fī laysa fī'l-imkān abdaʿ mimmā kān*, as an addendum to Ghazālī, *Iḥyā' ʿulūm al-dīn*. Beirut: Dār Ṣādir, 2010

Suyūṭī, ʿAbd al-Raḥmān Jalāl al-Dīn, al-, and Albānī, Muḥammad Nāṣir al-Dīn, al-. *Ṣaḥīḥ al-Jāmiʿ al-ṣaghīr wa-ziyādatih/Ḍaʿīf al-Jāmiʿ al-ṣaghīr wa-ziyādatih*. Beirut: Al-Maktab al-Islāmī, 1988.

Ṭabarānī, Sulaymān, al-. *Al-Muʿjam al-kabīr*. Ed. Ḥamdī b. ʿAbd al-Majīd al-Salafī. Cairo: Maktabat Ibn Taymiyya, 1994.

Ṭabarī, Abū Jaʿfar Muḥammad b. Jarīr, al-. *Tafsīr al-Ṭabarī* or *Jāmiʿ al-bayān fī ta'wīl al-Qur'ān*. Eds. Aḥmad Muḥammad Shākir and Maḥmūd Shākir. Beirut: Mu'assasat al-Risāla, 2000.

———. *Tārīkh al-Ṭabarī: Tārīkh al-rusul wa'l-mulūk*. Ed. Muḥammad Abū al-Faḍl Ibrāhīm. Cairo: Dār al-Maʿārif, 1967.

Tabrīzī, Muḥammad b. ʿAbd Allāh al-Khaṭīb, al-. *Mishkāt al-maṣābīḥ*. Ed. Muḥammad Nāṣir al-Dīn al-Albānī. Beirut: al-Maktab al-Islāmī, 1985.

Ṭayālisī, Abū Dāwūd Sulaymān, al-. *Musnad Abī Dāwūd al-Ṭayālisī*. Ed. Muḥammad b. ʿAbd al-Muḥsin al-Turkī. Giza: Dār Hijr, 1999.

Tirmidhī, Abū ʿĪsā Muḥammad b. ʿĪsā al-Sulamī, al-, and Albānī, Muḥammad Nāṣir al-Dīn, al-. *Ṣaḥīḥ Sunan al-Tirmidhī/Ḍaʿīf Sunan al-Tirmidhī*. Riyadh: Maktabat al-Maʿārif, 1998.

Williams, Khalid (tr.). *The Principles of the Creed: Book 2 of The Revival of the Religious Sciences*. Louisville: Fons Vitae, 2016. [=Ghazālī, Abū Ḥāmid Muḥammad b. Muḥammad, al-. *Iḥyā' ʿulūm al-dīn* (Book I)]

Yaqub, Aladdin M. (tr.). *Al-Ghazālī's Moderation in Belief*. Chicago: The University of Chicago Press, 2013. [=Ghazālī, Abū Ḥāmid Muḥammad b. Muḥammad, al-. *Al-Iqtiṣād fī'l-iʿtiqād*]

Zajjāj, Ibrāhīm b. Sahl, al-. *Maʿānī al-Qur'ān wa-iʿrābuhu*. Ed. ʿAbd al-Jalīl Shalabī. Beirut: ʿĀlam al-Kutub, 1988.

Zaghlūl, Muḥammad al-Saʿīd b. Basyūnī. *Mawsūʿat aṭrāf al-Ḥadīth al-nabawī al-sharīf*. Beirut: Dār al-Kutub al-ʿIlmiyyah, 2008.

Zeni, Tallal (tr.). *Ibn Qayyim al-Jawziyya on Knowledge*. Cambridge: Islamic Texts Society, 2016.[=Ibn Qayyim al-Jawziyya, Abū ʿAbd Allāh Shams al-Dīn Muḥammad b. Abī Bakr. *Miftāḥ dār al-saʿāda wa-manshūr wilāyat al-ʿilm wa'l-irāda* (extract)]

Zysow, Aron. 'Karrāmiyya'. In Sabine Schmidtke (ed.), *The Oxford Handbook of Islamic Theology*. Oxford: Oxford University Press, 2016, pp. 252–262.

INDEX

Aaron, 259
ʿAbd Allāh b. ʿAbbās, 192
ʿAbd Allāh b. ʿAmr, 180
ʿAbd Allāh b. Masʿūd, 176
ʿAbd al-Raḥmān b. Zayd b. Aslam, 176, 192
Abel, 51
ablution: dry ablution/*tayammum*, 64; an obligation, 123; purification, 64, 120, 122–3; wisdom and benefits, 122–3
Abraham, 41, 45, 113, 133, 153, 206, 259; leader of the believers, 114; patience, 257–8; trial: sacrificing his son, 231, 258
Abū Bakr al-Ṣiddīq, 170
Abū Hudhayl al-ʿAllāf, 92, 183, 193
Abū Hurayra, 15, 122, 176, 180, 185
Abū Isḥāq al-Zajjāj, 22, 42, 62–3, 178
Abū Saʿīd al-Khudrī, 176, 178, 179, 192
Abū Ṣāliḥ, 21
Abū Ṭālib, 172
Abū Umāma, 179
Abū al-Wafā' b. ʿAqīl, 143
ʿĀd, prophet, 111, 153
Adam, 11; created with intellect and desires, 9; creation of, 5, 8, 9, 131; fall, 131, 132, 137, 239; gratitude, 132; Paradise, 17–18; predestination, 18, 143; repentance, 131, 137, 239, 257; Satan, refusal to prostrate to Adam, 205; sin, 111; viceroy on Earth, 5–6, 15, 65; see also Adam, wisdom in his descent from the Garden
Adam, wisdom in his descent from the Garden, 3–18, 31–2, 94, 116; achieving the greatest reward, 3–4; attaining God's love, 6; attaining/perfecting faith, 5, 142–3; blessing/bliss, 6, 8, 9, 11, 16–17, 142; commandment, 4, 6, 11–12; differentiating good from evil, 5; disclosing God's knowledge 5–6; establishing messengers, prophets and martyrs, 142; God's love for the repentant, 12–13; God's sovereignty, 4–5; humility and submission, 11; learning to avoid sins, 9; longing for Paradise, 15–16; manifesting Divine Names and Attributes, 4, 17, 145–6; manifesting God's praiseworthy Essence, 10–11; manifesting/perfecting love for God, 6–7, 9–10; nearness to God after trials on Earth, 4; Paradise, levels of, 13–15; perfecting humankind, 3, 18, 143; perfecting servitude to God, 7–8; trial and tribulation, 3, 4, 8, 9–10, 12, 94, 142–3, 257; worship, 7, 8, 142; see also Adam
Ahl al-Sunna, 74, 104, 204, 219
ʿĀ'isha bint Abī Bakr, 208
alcohol, 51
ʿAlī b. Abī Ṭalḥa, 180
ʿAlī b. Abī Ṭālib, 192
al-Āmidī, Abū al-Ḥusayn, 86
angel, 5–6, 53, 132, 135, 138, 147, 190, 263; Angel of Death, 259; asking

forgiveness for humankind, 256; conquest of Mecca, 114; fear of the Satanic fall, 130; gratitude, submission and humility of, 108; *ḥadīth*, 246–7; messengers, 44; *nuqaddisu* statement, 20–1; Paradise, 15, 17; perfection, 30; a soul that desires only good, 156; wisdom of creating humanity, 5, 33, 37, 65, 99, 143–4, 158, 256; worship by, 6, 144
anger, 8; evil and, 26–7; trial and tribulation, 253
animal, 25, 30, 32, 63, 90, 124–5; God's wisdom, 125; pain, 157, 158, 160, 161, 162
Antichrist, 32
ʿ*aql*, see reason/intellect
al-Ashʿarī, Abū al-Ḥasan: debate on the three hypothetical brothers, 95, 198–9
Ashʿariyya, 45, 76, 164, 198, 199–200; Divine decree and determination, 226, 227–8; God's wisdom, negation of, 68–9
association (of any partner with God), 17, 27, 111, 174
astray (going astray), 3, 46, 96, 217; 'I seek refuge with Your glory from You sending me astray', 208, 209
atheist, 96, 166
Attributes, see Divine Attributes
awliyā', see saints
ʿ*ayb*, see fault

al-Baghawī, Ibn Masʿūd: *Sharḥ al-Sunna*, 204
Battle of Badr, 112
beauty, 126; opposites and, 108–109, 195
Bedouins, 61
belief: false beliefs, 29; true belief/ *ḥunafā'*, 185
believer, 8, 17, 46, 149; bliss of Paradise, 143; concealing/remitting the believer's sins, 152, 171, 240, 245; differentiating believers from disbelievers, 148–9, 152, 155; Hellfire, punishment in, 172, 181, 183, 186
blasphemy, 89, 134–5, 207, 208, 220, 260
blessing, 11, 162, 261; Adam, wisdom in his descent from the Garden, 6, 8, 9, 11, 16–17, 142; blessings should not be bestowed upon those who are unsuitable, 83–4; Creation, blessings upon, 64; denial of, 69; gratitude for, 11, 14, 46, 66, 108, 196, 261; the greatest blessings, 160; not acknowledging the blessings of God, 250; our good deeds are insignificant compared to God's blessings, 243–4, 250; sin, God's wisdom in allowing it, 248, 249–50
bliss, 8, 243; hardship and, 115–16; Paradise, 12, 16, 145, 155, 178, 181
body, 123, 126
Books, 11, 35, 36, 38
al-Bukhārī, Muḥammad: *Khalq afʿāl al-ʿibād*, 38; *Ṣaḥīḥ al-Bukhārī*, 7

Cain, 51
causality, 71; 'The cause belongeth wholly to God', 212; commandment, 40–1, 52–3; Divine decree and determination, 39; Divine Law, 39; evidence, 41; God's actions, 53; God's wisdom, 43, 71, 129; innate disposition, 41; *lām*, 47; ontology, 12–13, 39, 52–3; polytheism, 41; Qur'ān, 39–41, 42; reason, 41; reason for an ac-

tion and its cause, 50; religion, 39; Sunna, 41; see also causality, negation of
causality, negation of, 32, 39, 53, 58, 60, 63, 164; affirmation of Oneness, 41–2; attributing faults to God, 74; Hellfire, punishment in, 164–5; Jabriyya, 35, 104; punishment, 70; speculative theology, 34–5, 70; see also causality
cause (*sabab*), 42, 46
celestial bodies, 76, 96, 106, 127–9; see also moon; star; sun
chastity, 29, 105, 147, 160, 254
child, 32, 94, 95, 96
Children of Israel, 51, 234, 258
commandment (God's commandment), 39, 54, 55, 71, 145; Adam, wisdom in his descent from the Garden, 4, 6, 11–12; causality, 40–1, 52–3; commanding is based upon attaining what is purely advantageous, 98; commandments are all merciful, benevolent and curative, 117, 118; creating/commanding distinction, 83; God's assistance to carry out His commandments, 83–4; God's wisdom and purpose, 57–8, 59–60, 70, 71, 100, 151–2; goodness of, 23; mercy, 65; pleasure and, 117; predestination, 51; religious allowance, 233–4, 235; religious appointment, 234; religious bestowal, 236; religious commandment, 233; religious decree, 224, 229–30, 240; religious fate, 236; religious prescription, 231; religious prohibition, 235; religious sending, 235; religious ruling, 40, 52–3, 230; religious will, 230, 231, 236; Satan's disdain for, 6; solely due to God's power and will, 57, 60; tribulation, 155; see also Divine Law; ontology; religion
Community (*umma*), 1, 37, 119, 123
Companions of the Prophet, 179, 182, 183, 187, 192, 193, 243; the most knowledgeable, 251–2
consensus, 204, 227; attributing/rejecting any faults from God, 68–9, 74–5; God's wisdom, 68–9, 74; Hellfire, eternal punishment, 180, 183
contentment (*riḍā*), 204, 223, 243; contentment with Divine decree, 223–6
courage, 29, 147, 160
Creation, 18, 71; all that God has created exists to result in perfection and completion, 28, 33; blessings upon, 64; the Creator is superior to creation, 76–7; Divine Names and Attributes, 55, 56, 102, 144–5, 199; elite of, 5; every created entity is intended for itself, and not for another, 81; God's magnanimity and grace are vaster than the needs of the creation, 127; God's wisdom, 54–7, 60, 62, 70, 71, 100; mercy, 65; objectives and purposes of, 55–7, 60, 62, 97, 129, 155, 166, 191 (Divine Oneness, 125–6; enlightening and remembrance of God, 50, 55; witnessing that God alone is their God, 56; worship, 8, 55, 125–6, 167, 195–6); ontology, 56; ordered existence in the most perfect and beautiful manner, 126; origin of, 60; perfection of, 29, 62, 74, 76, 90, 126 ('Thou canst see no fault in the Beneficent's creation', 28, 33, 62); purpose of any being is to attain pleasure or

to avoid distress and grief, 87, 90; tribulation, 155; truth, 55, 56, 166; variety in, 167
creation (process of), 28, 33; Adam, creation of, 5, 8, 9, 131; creating/commanding distinction, 83; creating, Divine Attribute, 28, 56, 57, 60, 102, 220; creating is based upon attaining what is purely advantageous, 98; creating opposites, 101, 115, 132, 133, 157, 161; creation of this world in six days, 97; the Creator/*al-Khāliq*, 22, 23, 38, 115, 126, 166–7, 241; evil, creation of, 20, 203–204; the good, creation of, 20; gradual creation, 75–6; heresy on, 166; humankind, 158–9; intermediaries, creation of, 88; praise, 162; speculative theology, 35; stages and types, 7, 144; wisdom of creating humanity, 5, 33, 37, 65, 99, 143–4, 158, 256

al-Ḍaḥḥāk b. Muzāḥim, 42
David, prophet, 258
Day of the Great Return, 145–6
Day of Judgment, 2, 5, 37, 50–1, 61, 97, 134, 146
Day of Resurrection, 120–1, 168
death, 168; child, 32, 95, 198, 199; death leads to the perfection of every believer, 141–2; pain from, 168, 170; perpetrating one major sin and dying without repenting, 165, 219
deficiency (*naqṣ*), 20, 103, 162; any deficiency is due to lack of acceptance, or to privation, 28, 83; defects can be harmful or evil, 28; God is high above any deficiency, 22; God's infallibility from any deficiency, 37–8, 103, 104, 195
desire, 8–9; evil and, 26–7; false desires, 29; Hellfire, 116, 160, 161; struggle against desire and temptation, 5–6, 10, 143, 149, 151, 154
Devil, see Satan
devils, 48, 104; as soul that desires only evil, 156; wisdom in creating devils, 94, 115, 131–2; see also Satan
devotion (*iḥsān*), 196, 223
dhikr, see remembrance
Dhū al-Qarnayn, 42
disbelief, 17, 27, 48, 54, 165; due to disobeying the prohibitions of God, 98; Hellfire, 169; punishment, 51; wisdom in allowing disbelief, 109, 110, 111–12
disbeliever, 48, 134, 149; differentiating believers from disbelievers, 148–9, 152, 155; Hellfire, punishment in, 172–3, 177–8, 183–4, 193; innate disposition, 186–7; killing of, 201; wisdom in allowing the existence of, 115
disease, 25, 168, 175, 214–15, 251; benefits of, 160, 201; fever, 171; visiting the ill, 171
disobedience: evil, 98; ontological determination of, 110–11; predestination as excuse for disobedience, 236; punishment for, 55; Satan's disobedience as warning and lesson, 130–1; submissiveness resulting indirectly from disobedience, 243
Divine Attributes: Almightiness, 60–1; beneficence, 64, 133, 136, 240, 263 (God's Essence, 83); benevolence, 64, 136, 240, 261; clemency, 245; creating, 28, 56, 57, 60, 102, 220; eternity, 38; generosity, 135, 245; goodness, 19, 20, 24, 30, 63, 161, 186, 203, 204, 206, 212; grace, 10,

19, 55, 127; Holiness, 99–100, 114, 145, 146, 196; lordship, 12, 17, 56, 121, 157, 220; magnanimity, 3, 127, 135, 136, 138, 189, 240; majesty, 10–11; might, 22; omnipotence, 56, 60–1, 62, 63, 71, 99, 102, 262; omniscience, 10–11, 36, 38, 49, 56, 262; patience, 134; perfection, 38, 73–4, 75, 83; 90, 91, 97, 103, 131, 162, 176; praiseworthiness/praiseworthy Essence, 10, 11, 55, 57, 61, 63, 64, 105–107, 133–4, 138, 144, 162–3; sovereignty, 4–5, 19, 37, 39, 102, 133, 144, 163; truth/truthfulness, 63, 166–7; see also Divine Attributes, ideas related to; forgiveness; God's knowledge; God's wisdom; justice; mercy; wrath

Divine Attributes, ideas related to, 12, 55, 74, 97, 120, 145–6, 210; Adam, wisdom in his descent from the Garden, 4, 17, 145–6; created opposites and Divine Attributes, 101–102, 103; Creation, 55, 56; Divine Attributes are eternally existent, 209; Divine decree and determination, 224–5; Divine Names derive from Divine Attributes, 207–208, 220; God loves His Names and Attributes, 190; God's actions, 125, 208; Jahmiyya, 207, 208; manifesting Divine Names and Attributes, 4, 12, 17, 102, 133, 135–6, 144–6, 199, 220, 224–5, 238, 240–1; Muʿaṭṭila, 41; negation of, 58, 68, 104, 105, 156, 198, 207, 208; perfect Attributes, 21, 58, 76, 105, 138, 161, 189, 198, 212, 262; Qadariyya, 35–6; Qur'ān, 61, 207–208; some Attributes are superior to others, 210; Sunna, 207–208; see also Divine Attributes

Divine decree and determination, 145, 201, 211, 212, 237, 238, 239, 241; Ashʿariyya, 226, 227–8; beloved and pleasing from one aspect, yet disliked from another, 225; causality, 39; contentment with, 223–6 (it is obligatory, 223, 224; it is preferable 223, 224); Divine Law and, 23; faith in, 217, 223; contentment with God's ontologic decree of disbelief, wickedness and sinfulness, 225–8; God's decree is just, 217–18; Jabriyya, 223–4; a manifestation of His Attributes, 224–5; negation of, 227, 228; ontological decree, 211, 216, 224, 226, 229–30, 232–3, 236, 240, 242, 248 (there is no escaping His ontological decree, 241); ontological ruling, 230; Pharaoh, 45–6; Qadariyya, 223–4, 228; religious decree, 224, 229–30, 240; sin, 223–4, 237 (ontological determination of sin, 110–11, 219, 240); see also predestination; 'Your judgment upon me…'

Divine Essence, 125, 210, 262; God's actions emanate from His Essence according to Ibn Sīnā and others, 32, 34, 38, 87; mercy, 83; praiseworthy Essence, 10, 11

Divine Law, 11, 55, 163, 261, 262; causality, 39; determination and, 23; established within people's innate disposition and intellect, 12; as manifestation of Divine Names and Attributes, 12; obligation to thank God, 107; origin of, 60; Qur'ān, 12, 64; reason, 12; wisdom in, 69–70, 89, 117–19, 122,

124; see also commandment
Divine Names, 12, 55, 120; the Administrator/*al-Mudabbir*, 225; the All-Forgiving/*al-Ghafūr*), 4, 174, 188, 241; the All-Hearing/*al-Samīʿ*, 17, 74, 133, 151, 241; the All-Seeing/*al-Baṣīr*, 17, 74, 133; the Almighty/*al-ʿAzīz*, 20, 22, 60–1, 64; the Aware/*al-Khabīr*, 107; Beautiful Names, 4, 12, 20, 22, 69, 97, 145–6, 207, 221, 238, 240, 241; the Benefactor/*al-Mannān*, 91; the Benefactor/*al-Walī*, 244; the Beneficent/*al-Raḥmān*, 53, 91, 146; the Creator/*al-Khāliq*, 22, 23, 38, 115, 126, 166–7, 241; the Effacer (of sins)/*al-ʿAfū*, 4, 102, 238; the Eminent/*al-ʿAzīz*, 5; the Ever-Living One/*al-Ḥayy*, 141; the Fashioner/*al-Muṣawwir*, 241; the Forbearing/*al-Ḥalīm*, 4, 91, 215, 238; the Full of Loving-Kindness/*al-Wadūd*, 174; the Great/*al-ʿAẓīm*, 215; the Great One/*al-Kabīr*, 22; His greatest Name/*ism Allāh al-aʿẓam*, 221; the Holy/*al-Quddūs*, 20; the Inheritor/*al-Wārith*, 4; the Invincible/*al-Qahhār*, 146; the Irresistible/*al-Jabbār*, 20; the Just Ruler/*al-Ḥakam al-ʿadl*, 219, 220; the King/*al-Malik*, 103–104, 133, 138–9; the Life-Giver/*al-Muḥyī*, 4; the Life-Taker/*al-Mumīt*, 4; Lord/*Rabb*, 225; Lord of the Worlds/*Rabb al-ʿālamīn*, 11, 136, 162, 262; the Magnanimous/*al-Jawād*, 18, 23, 91, 127, 135, 245; the Merciful/*al-Raḥīm*, 4, 7, 173, 174, 188, 241; the Most Benevolent/*al-Muḥsin*, 23; the Most Generous/*al-Karīm*, 18, 245; the Most Glorious/*al-Jalīl*, 135; the Most High/*al-ʿAlī*, 22; the Most High Friend/*al-Rafīq al-aʿlā*, 141; the Most Just/*al-ʿAdl*, 23, 133; the Most Kind/*al-Ra'ūf*, 102; the Most Merciful/*arḥam al-rāḥimīn*, 65; the Most Praiseworthy/*al-Ḥamīd*, 18, 22, 60, 220; the Most Wise/*al-Ḥakīm*, 8, 17, 18, 23, 60–1, 64, 74, 99, 107, 126, 133, 136, 262–3; the Omniscient/*al-ʿAlīm*, 5, 8, 17, 18, 74, 151; the One/*al-Aḥad*, 221; the One/*al-Wāḥid*, 146; the One full of Forgiveness/*al-Ghaffār*, 91, 238; the One Who abases/*al-Mudhill*, 4, 91, 102, 103, 133; the One Who advances/*al-Muqaddim*, 102; the One Who avenges/*al-Muntaqim*, 174; the One Who bestows/*al-Wahhāb*, 91, 102; the One Who causes harm/*al-Ḍārr*, 102; the One Who constricts/*al-Qābiḍ*, 91, 103; the One Who defers/*al-Mu'akhkhir*, 102; the One Who elevates/*al-Rāfiʿ*, 4, 91, 103, 133; the One Who grants/*al-Muʿṭī*, 102; the One Who grants benefit/*al-Nāfiʿ*, 102; the One Who honours/*al-Muʿizz*, 4, 91, 102, 103, 133; the One Who is faultless and bestows peace/*al-Salām*, 20, 21–2; the One Who is kind with His servants/*al-Laṭīf*, 91; the One Who is munificent/*al-Bāsiṭ*, 91, 103; the One Who lowers/*al-Khāfiḍ*, 4, 91, 103, 133; the One Who takes retribution/*al-Muntaqim*, 133; the One Who withholds/*al-Māniʿ*, 102; the Originator/*al-Bāri'*, 241; the Originator/*al-Fāṭir*, 115; the Patient One/*al-Ṣabūr*, 4; the Proud/*al-Mutakabbir*, 20, 22; the Provider/*al-Razzāq*, 91, 241; the

Relenting/*al-Tawwāb*, 238, 241; the Righteous Doer of Good/*al-Barr*, 7; the Ruler/*al-Ḥakam*, 23, 133; the Self-Sufficient/*al-Ghanī*, 18, 90, 135, 151, 162, 220; the Self-Sufficient Master/*al-Ṣamad*, 221; the Sovereign Owner/*Mālik*, 225

Divine Names, ideas related to, 12, 55, 120; Adam, wisdom in his descent from the Garden, 4, 17, 145–6; Creation, 55, 56; Divine Names are not created, 220–1; Divine Names derive from Divine Attributes, 207–208, 220; God loves His Names and Attributes, 190; God's actions, 125, 208; 'I ask You by every Name of Yours…', 220; manifesting Divine Names and Attributes, 4, 12, 17, 102, 133, 135–6, 144–6, 199, 220, 224–5, 238, 240–1; ninety-nine Names, 221; 'Or have kept hidden within Your knowledge of the Unseen', 221; Qadariyya, 35–6; Qur'ān, 61, 207–208; Sunna, 207–208

Divine providence, 35, 53, 69, 92, 196

effectiveness (*fāʿiliya*), 76

Emigrants, 114

enemy, 109; destruction of, 108; enemies of the messengers, 35, 36, 42, 70, 149; fleeing from, 154; trial and tribulation, 149, 152–3; see also enemy, overpowering the saints

enemy, overpowering the saints, 95, 137, 152–3; enemy's punishment, 195; martyrdom, 194; purification, 194; *Sūrat Āl ʿImrān*, 194–5; virtues, 195; wisdom in, 194–5; see also enemy; saints

enlightenment (*tabṣira*), 50

Eve, 31, 94

evidence: attributing faults to God, 68, 75; causality, 41; Hellfire, punishment in, 169, 173; mercy, 64; transmitted evidence, 75, 86, 129, 158, 166, 169, 173, 227; wise purpose, 65

evil, 158, 161; absolute essential evil, 24, 25, 27, 30, 175; the best provision is to ward off evil, 18; causes of, 20, 24, 25–6, 27, 28–9; created by God, 20, 203–204; created by humans according to the Qadariyya, 203; defects can be harmful or evil, 28; definition, 25, 98; desire and, 26–7; devil, a soul that desires only evil, 156; difference between the determination being good/evil or pleasing/painful, 202; differentiating good from evil, 5, 131, 139, 207, 262; disobedience, 98; *ḥadīth*, 20; heavenly world is devoid of evil, 31; ignorance, 24, 25; injustice, 24, 25, 26; lack of connection with God, 20, 24; non-existence and, 24–5, 26, 30; occurrence of a lesser evil is preferable to a greater evil, 159; ontology, 201, 211; privation and 28–9; punishment, 5; relative evil, 25–7, 201; types of entities according to good/evil preponderance, 29, 30–1; wisdom in the existence of, 24, 31–2, 94–5, 115, 158–9, 175; see also evil, God's infallibility from

evil, God's infallibility from, 19, 20–4, 98, 186; evil cannot be attributed to God, 19–20, 201, 205, 206–207; God does not intend or carry out evil, 203, 205; God wills and performs evil according to the

Jabriyya, 203–205; Qadariyya, 203; see also evil

fāʿiliya, see effectiveness
faith, 143, 147; attaining/perfecting faith, 5, 142–3; Day of Judgment, 5; devotion, 223; Divine decree and determination, 217, 223; trial and tribulation, 148, 153; the Unseen, 5
the faithful, 56, 193, 231
falsehood, 2, 17, 40, 89, 109, 167, 200; people of falsehood/*ahl al-bāṭil*, 199; Satan, 47; sinner, 56
faqr, see poverty
fault (*ʿayb*), 29; attributing/rejecting faults to God, 68–9, 74–5, 76, 79; causality, negation of, 74; God's infallibility from any, 22, 64, 74–5, 195; recognizing our own faultiness, 244; 'Thou canst see no fault in the Beneficent's creation', 28, 33, 62
fire, 25, 41; benefits and harms, 27, 31, 34, 133; wisdom in, 129
fiṭra, see innate disposition
forgiveness, 14, 61, 103, 110, 135–6, 209–210, 245; angel, asking forgiveness for humankind, 256; *ḥadīth*, 246–7; sin, God's wisdom in allowing it, 238, 254 (asking forgiveness for others, 255–6)
fornication, 51
Fuḍayl b. ʿIyāḍ, 135

Gabriel, 7, 97, 114, 132; Holy Spirit/*rūḥ al-qudus*, 20
glorification (*tasbīḥ*), 21, 27, 56, 196; prayer, 120; see also praise
gnosis, 38, 50, 101, 121, 122
gnostic, 113, 159, 239
God: anthropomorphism, 35, 58, 104, 134, 156; dislike/absence of God's love, 90–1, 98, 134, 144, 190–1, 224, 226–7; God is the greatest/*Allāh akbar*, 33; God's existence, proofs for, 69; Hands, 149, 163, 186, 206–207 (His other Hand, 206, 210; Right Hand, 30, 206, 210); there is no deity but God/*lā ilāh illā Allāh*, 2, 12, 33, 56, 196, 198, 212, 215; see also the entries below for God; Divine Attributes; Divine Names
God, nearness to, 219; after trials, 4; attempting to become proximate to God, 243–4; sin, God's wisdom in allowing it, 242, 252–3; struggle against temptations and desires, 5–6
God's actions, 55, 263; causality, 53; difference between God's actions and that what He enacts, 204–205, 210, 224; Divine Attributes and Names, 125, 208; emanate from His Essence according to Ibn Sīnā and others, 32, 34, 38, 87; God's will and, 38, 63–4, 71, 86–7, 199–200, 204–205; God's wisdom, 43, 54, 63–4, 71, 74, 89, 99, 200, 263 (God's wisdom is eternal, then His action should be pre-eternal, 87); goodness in, 19, 24, 63, 203, 204; *lām al-ʿāqiba*, 45, 239; *lām al-ḥikma*, 45; *lām al-taʿlīl*, 45, 48, 239; perfection, 91; perpetual action, 86; some actions are superior to others, 210; temporally originated, 81, 93, 166; wise purpose and objectives of, 57–8, 59–60, 63–4, 65, 69, 71, 73, 75, 77–9, 82, 93, 98
God's knowledge, 17, 33, 36–7, 61, 70, 162, 261; angels and wisdom of creating humanity, 5, 33, 37,

65, 99, 143–4, 158, 256; disclosing God's knowledge 5–6; God's knowledge/human knowledge comparison, 70; God's omniscience, 10–11, 36, 38, 49, 56, 262; perfect knowledge, 99; Prophet Muḥammad and, 37; see also God's wisdom
God's love, 90–1; for the grateful, 6, 11, 12; for the humble, submissive, 11; for the patient, 12; for the repentant, 12–13, 239; for those who wage battle in His path, 12; God loves His Names and Attributes, 190; the highest type of honour, 6; see also love for God
God's will (*irāda*), 35, 212; attributing the structure and events of this universe to God's will only, 32, 65–6, 70, 164, 199–200; difference between God's will and His will enacted by His servants, 204–205; claim that God cannot do anything out of His free will, 32, 34; God only wishes well-being for His servants, 262; God's actions, 38, 63–4, 71, 86–7, 199–200, 204–205; Hellfire, eternal punishment, 178–180, 182; justice, 62–3; negation of, 35, 64, 68, 87; ontological will, 51, 191, 204, 230, 231, 236; perpetual will, 83, 86; Qadariyya, 35, 36, 105, 216–17; reason, 38; religious will, 230, 231, 236; speculative theology, 70; wise purposes and objectives, 87; see also Divine decree and determination
God's wisdom, 10–11, 14, 17, 19, 33, 261; accident, claim that wise purposes occur by accident, 60–2, 63, 65, 128; the Almighty/*al-ʿAzīz*, 60–1, 64; causality, 43, 71, 129; commandment, 57–8, 59–60, 70, 71, 100, 151–2; consensus, 68–9, 74; creating, 56, 57, 60; creating opposites, 101, 133; Creation, 54–7, 60, 62, 70, 71, 100; criticism of, 37; dazzling wisdom, 46, 56, 97, 100, 101, 111, 120, 127–8, 131, 133, 136, 163, 194, 261; Divine Law, 69–70, 89, 117–19, 122, 124; evidence, 65, 86; God's actions, 43, 54, 63–4, 71, 74, 81, 89, 99, 200, 263; God's praiseworthiness, 55, 57, 61, 63, 64; God's wisdom is self-subsisting, 74; human intellect is inadequate to understand God's wisdom, 38, 70, 136, 142, 263; infallibility above carrying out actions inconsistent with His wisdom, 67–8, 79; innate disposition and, 43, 56, 68, 69, 75, 86; intermediaries, 76, 87–91; *lām*, 47, 49 (*lām al-ḥikma*, 45; *lām al-taʿlīl*, 45, 48, 49, 239; the Most Wise/ *al-Ḥakīm*, 8, 17, 18, 23, 60–1, 64, 74, 99, 107, 126, 133, 136, 262–3); perfection of, 84; placement (right placement), 11, 22–3, 26, 27, 56, 61, 97, 200; Qur'ān, 43–67, 69; reason, 43, 56, 68, 69, 75, 86; rulings, 62 (ontological and religious rulings, 52–3); Sunna, 43, 52; wise purpose and objectives, 57–8, 59–60, 63–4, 65, 69, 71, 73, 75, 77–9, 83, 97, 263; see also Divine Attributes; God's knowledge; God's wisdom, negation of
God's wisdom, negation of, 32, 34, 53, 55, 60, 63–5, 70, 157, 164; accepting ambiguity of God's wisdom as any ambiguity of recognised masters and imams, 101; 'any agent who performs something

for a purpose possesses a deficient essence', 72–3, 78; Ash^cariyya, 68–9; in allowing disbelief, wickedness and sin, 94; claim that God's actions do not entail wisdom and wise purposes, 77, 78, 79, 156; Hellfire, punishment in, 164–5; infinite regress, 92; intermediaries, 87; Jabriyya, 35, 104–105; Jahmiyya, 65; Mu^ctazila, 35; perpetually occurring wisdoms can never lead to desired ultimate outcomes, 82–3; praise/wisdom relationship, 104–105, 107, 138, 157; pre-eternal/temporally originated wisdom, 79–80; punishment, 70; the purpose of any being is either to attain pleasures or to avoid distress and grief, 87, 90; Qadariyya, 35, 36, 105, 216–17; speculative theology, 70; wise purpose, 73–4; see also God's wisdom; al-Rāzī, Fakhr al-Dīn

the good/goodness, 158; absolute/pure good, 29–30, 31, 175; 'all good is derived from existence and its necessary requisites', 24–5; angel, a soul that desires only good, 156; commandment, 23; creation of, 20; difference between the determination being good/evil or pleasing/painful, 202; differentiating good from evil, 5, 207, 131, 139, 262; Divine Attribute, 19, 20, 24, 30, 63, 161, 186, 203, 204, 206, 212; entity wherein good predominates over evil, 30, 175; God prefers the causes that lead to greater goods, 159; God's actions, 19, 24, 63, 203, 204; God's commandments, 23; goodness predominates in all that exists, 31; obligation, goodness of, 196–7; opposites and, 108–109; 'Thou canst see no fault in the Beneficent's creation', 28, 33, 62; types of entities according to good/evil preponderance, 29, 30–1

good/righteous deed, 116, 159, 164, 167, 212, 215; God replaces evil sins with good deeds, 135; a good deed is followed by another pious deed, 257; our good deeds are insignificant compared to God's blessings, 243–4, 250; Paradise and, 14, 15, 254

gratitude, 54, 55; Adam, 132; angel, 108; differences between the servants, 107–108; for God's blessings, 11, 14, 46, 66, 108, 196, 261; God's love for the grateful, 6, 11, 12; *ḥadīth*, 135; Noah, 257; obligation to thank God, 107; Paradise, 58–9, 108; prophets, 108; Satan, wisdom in allowing the existence of, 132; thanking God is the most beloved thing to Him, 107

guidance, 1–2; commanded to follow the best guidance, 24; enlightenment and remembrance, 50; God's guidance through the Prophet, 2, 3

ḥadīth, 7, 180; Adam, creation of, 5, 131; angel, 246–7; evil, 20, 206–207; forgiveness, 246–7; God's omniscience, 36; gratitude, 135; Hellfire, 168, 179, 182, 187; Hereafter, 140; humankind, 135; 'I seek refuge with Your glory from You sending me astray', 208, 209; innate disposition, 185–6; jinn, 135; 'O Ever-Living; O Self-Subsisting…', 209; Para-

dise, 14, 15; People of the Book, 85; polytheism, 135; praise, 163; pride, 248; repentance, 13, 254; sin, 110, 135, 171, 246–7, 248, 254; suffering, 137; 'There is no refuge or safe haven from You except with You', 211–12; wrath, 190; see also 'O God, I seek refuge in Your pleasure from Your wrath...'; 'Your judgment upon me...'
Hāmān, 42, 153, 227
Ḥammād b. Salama, 180
Ḥanbalīs, 223
hardship, 25, 49; ablution, 123; adversities indirectly lead to pleasures and goodness, 116; bliss, luxury and relaxation, 115–16; 'But with hardship goeth ease', 161; distress, sorrow and grief, 214–16; a mercy for God's servants, 246; a method for perfecting humankind, 3, 159–60; not to grieve in case of, 49–50; Paradise and, 116, 160, 161; patience in, 50, 116, 151; predestination, 49; reasons for, 159; remedy for, 215–16; supplication that relieves of calamities, 215; types of, 214; wisdom in, 95, 159–60; worship, 215; see also pain; suffering; trial and tribulation
Hārūt, 108, 256
al-Ḥasan al-Baṣrī, 106, 180
heart: distress, sorrow and grief, 214–16; false desires and beliefs, 29; God is always with those whose hearts are broken, 171; types of, 48 (diseased heart, 47, 48; hardened heart, 48; humble heart, 48); unveiling one's heart, 215
Hellfire, 32, 115, 129; abode of justice, 187, 188; abode of pain, suffering, calamities and evils, 145, 168–9; denizens of Hellfire, 94, 95, 96, 174, 193; desires and temptations, 116, 160, 161; entrance into, 106, 184, 192; the faster of the two abodes to be populated, 182; tree of *Zaqqūm*, 115; see also the entries below for Hellfire
Hellfire, eternal punishment, 164, 175–6, 178–93; *aḥqāban*, 181; arguments in favour of, 183; consensus, 180, 183; differences between Paradise and Hellfire, 187–91; God's will, 178–180, 182; inconsistent with God's wisdom and mercy, 169–70, 173, 187, 189–90; *khulūd*, 178, 183; see also Hellfire; Hellfire, punishment in
Hellfire, punishment in: believer, 172, 181, 183, 186; degrees of punishment, 172; denial of God's wisdom and causality, 164–5; difference between the worldly punishment and that of the Hereafter, 179; disbelief, 169; disbeliever, 172–3, 177–8, 183–4, 193; evidence, 169, 173; God's judgement on, 164–5; *ḥadīth*, 168, 179, 182, 187; in-between Paradise and Hellfire, 172; innate disposition, 169, 175, 185–6 (the only entity left after a disbeliever is absolved of all of his evilness, 169; returning back to the original innate disposition, 167–9, 185); Jabriyya, 165; a means to an objective, 175; mercy, 172, 173–4, 189–90, 193; perpetrating one major sin and dying without repenting, 165, 219; polytheism, 169, 182; purification, 168–9, 172, 184; Qadariyya, 165; Qur'ān, 176, 177–82, 185; reason and, 169, 173; Sunna,

179, 181, 183; *Sūrat al-Anʿām*, 176–7; warning of Hellfire is only to make us fearful, 165; wisdom in, 173, 174–6, 184; wrath, 174, 188, 190; see also Hellfire; Hellfire, eternal punishment
Hereafter: abode of recompense and reward, 146; *ḥadīth*, 140; manifestation of God's mercy in the Hereafter is far greater, 172; pain in, 161; see also Hellfire; Paradise
heresy, 100, 165–6, 183, 198
ḥikma, see wisdom
Hippocrates, 123
Holy Mosque, Jerusalem, 20
the Hour, 2
Hūd, prophet, 62, 218
Ḥudhayfa, 14
humankind, 1, 30; anger, 253; created for the purpose of attaining their perfection, 195; created with intellects and desires, 9; creation of, 158–9; elite of, 254; God's assistance to carry out His commandments, 83–4, 237, 241–2; *ḥadīth*, 135; mutual assistance, 126; pain, 162; perfecting humankind, 3, 18, 143, 159–60; soul desiring both good and evil, 155, 156; temptation, 253; variety of characteristics among, 107–108, 127; weakness and shortsightedness, 15; wisdom of creating humanity, 5, 33, 37, 65, 99, 143–4, 158, 256; worship, 195–6; see also Adam
humility, 47; angel, 108; God's love for the humble, 11; humble heart, 48; Muḥammad, a servant-Prophet, 7; sin, God's wisdom in allowing it, 242–3, 244, 248, 254–5
hypocrite, 59, 172, 239
Iblīs, see Satan
Ibn ʿAbbās, 21, 42, 180–1, 182
Ibn al-Anbārī, 63
Ibn ʿArabī, 193
Ibn Ḥanbal, Aḥmad, 108, 180
Ibn Ḥazm, 221
Ibn Jurayj, 42
Ibn Masʿūd, 182
Ibn al-Qayyim al-Jawziyya, 123, 156, 182; *al-Futūḥāt al-qudsiyya*, 237; poetry, 16
Ibn Sīnā, 36, 165
Ibn Taymiyya, 96, 191–2, 255–6; *al-Radd ʿalā man qāl bi-fanāʾ al-jannah wa'l-nār*, 192
Ibn Zayd, ʿAbd al-Raḥmān, 42
idol/idolatry, 27, 234, 239–40
ignorance, 37, 69, 162; evil and, 24, 25
iḥsān, see devotion
infinite regress (*tasalsul*), 77, 80, 82, 92
injustice, 20, 69, 150; equating two opposites/differentiating between two same entities, 58, 59, 102–103; evil and, 24, 25, 26; God, infallible from any injustice, 20, 21, 22, 57–8, 217; the greatest injustice, 37; Jabriyya 217–18; Qadariyya, 219; as treating something inappropriately, 218–19
innate disposition (*fiṭra*), 35, 38, 262; causality, 41; corruption of, 167, 168, 169, 185, 186; a created entity universal to all humans, 167, 185–6; the Creator is superior to creation, 76–7; disbeliever, 186–7; Divine Law, 12; God is high above any fault, 74–5; God's wisdom, 43, 56, 68, 69, 75, 86; *ḥadīth*, 185–6; Hellfire, punishment in, 169, 175, 185–6 (the only entity left after a disbeliever is absolved of all of his evilness, 169;

returning back to the original innate disposition, 167–9, 185); messengers and, 167–8; obligation, 107, 198
innovation, 1, 2, 150, 151, 180, 228
intellect, see reason/intellect
intercession, 212; Prophet Muḥammad, 7, 260
intermediaries, 76, 87–91
irāda, see God's will
Isaac, 113
Isḥāq b. Ibrāhīm/Isḥāq b. Rāhawayh, 179
Ishmael, 231, 258
Islam, 1, 68, 95, 115, 119, 183, 251, 260; 'This day have I perfected your religion…', 197, 261–2; see also religion
isrā', see Night Journey
ʿIyāḍ b. Ḥimār al-Mujāshiʿī, 185–6

Jābir b. ʿAbd Allāh, 179
Jabriyya, 216; Divine decree and determination, 223–4; evil, God's infallibility from, 203–204; God's wisdom, negation of, 35, 104–105; Hellfire, punishment in, 165; injustice, 217–18; negation of causality and wisdom, 35, 104
Jacob, 113
Jahm b. Safwān, 65, 92, 183, 193
Jahmiyya, 35, 82, 97, 207, 208, 235; Divine Attributes, negation of, 207, 208; God's wisdom, negation of, 65
Jesus, 7, 39, 61, 259
jinn, 1, 6, 135, 195, 206
Job, 113
Jonah, prophet (Dhū al-Nūn), 215
Joseph, 113
al-Jubbā'ī, Abū Hāshim: debate on the three hypothetical brothers, 95, 198–9
justice: God's justice, 10, 11, 19, 55, 62–3, 136, 162, 198 (God's decree is just, 217–18; the Just Ruler/ *al-Ḥakam al-ʿadl*, 219; 'Your judgment upon me will be carried out, and Your decree upon me is just', 216–19); Hellfire, abode of justice, 187, 188; Jabriyya, 218; Qadariyya, 218, 219; sin, God's wisdom in allowing it, 246; as treating things appropriately, 218
al-Juwaynī, Abū al-Maʿālī Ḍiyā' al-Dīn, 68, 74

Kaʿba, 33, 44, 64, 66, 111, 234
Karrāmiyya, 81
al-Kashshī, ʿAbd b. Ḥumayd, 180, 192
al-Khiḍr, 36, 186, 206
al-Kindī, Aḥmad b. Ḥusayn (al-Mutanabbī), 138–9, 160
al-Kirmānī, Ḥarb b. Ismāʿīl: *Masā'il Ḥarb*, 179–80
knowledge, 8, 37, 85; Dhū al-Qarnayn, 42; enlightenment, 50; human knowledge, inadequate to understand God's wisdom, 38, 70, 136, 142, 263; lack of knowledge about something does not render it to be non-existent, 99
Korah, 153, 227

laylat al-qadr, see Night of Power
lisān al-qadar, see predestination
Lot, prophet, 153
love for God: manifesting and perfecting our love for God, 6–7, 9–10; 'My heart's love for God brings about obedience to Him…', 243; Satan, wisdom in allowing the existence of, 136–7; submissiveness due to love, 243; trial and, 10

magic, 32
marriage, 234–5
martyr, 17, 109, 115; elite of Creation, 5–6; martyrdom, 194; nearness to God, 4
Mārūt, 108, 256
Maymūn b. Mihrān, 21
Mecca: conquest of, 114, 116, 137; emigration from, 114, 137
mercy, 14, 17, 61, 95, 162, 261, 263; commandment, 65; Creation, 65; evidence, 64; God's Essence, 83; Hellfire, punishment in, 172, 173–4, 189–90, 193; His mercy encompasses everything, 189, 193; His mercy precedes His wrath, 161, 173, 174, 187, 189, 193, 210; manifestation of God's mercy in the Hereafter is far greater, 172; the Merciful/*al-Raḥīm*, 4, 7, 173, 174, 188, 241; the Most Merciful/ *arḥam al-rāḥimīn*, 65; negation of, 65; Paradise, 14, 188; a requisite of His Names and Attributes, 188; trial and tribulation, 246, 257
messengers, 11, 17, 44, 45, 60, 61, 85, 131, 138, 149, 152; angel and, 44; attributing false doctrines and corrupt viewpoints to, 165–6; bliss of Paradise, 143; elite of Creation, 5; enemies of the messengers, 35, 36, 42, 70, 149; God's favouring and selection of, 66; innate disposition, 167–8; message, 16, 65–6; nearness to God after trials on Earth, 4; speaking softly and being gentle with disbelievers, 135; truthfulness, 69, 111
monism, 244–5
monotheism, 42, 58, 78, 121, 215, 237–8
moon, 89, 100, 117; wisdom in, 128
Moses, 15, 17, 36, 41, 97, 108, 112, 113, 132–3; patience, 259; predestination, 45–6; trial and tribulation, 259
Muʿaṭṭila, 41, 97
al-Mubarrad, Abū al-ʿAbbās Muḥammad, 42
Mujāhid b. Jabr, 21, 42, 51
mulk, see sovereignty
Muqātil b. Sulaymān, 22
muqwīn, 129
murder, 51
Muslim b. al-Ḥajjāj: *Ṣaḥīḥ Muslim*, 7, 19–20, 123
al-Muʿtamir b. Sulaymān, 179
Muʿtazila, 35, 82, 96, 184, 198–9
al-Muṭʿim b. ʿAdī, 116

Naʿīm b. Ḥammād, 38
naqṣ, see deficiency
Night Journey (*isrā'*), 7, 231, 259
Night of Power (*laylat al-qadr*), 21, 115
Noah, prophet, 111, 132, 153, 186; perfect patience and gratitude, 257
non-existent/non-existence, 28, 29, 75–6, 86, 125; anything that God does not will to exist remains non-existent by definition, 24, 35; evil, 24–5, 26, 30; lack of knowledge about something does not render it to be non-existent, 99; non-existence is nothing, 98; objectives and purposes, 73; Paradise and Hellfire, 183

'O God, I seek refuge in Your pleasure from Your wrath…', 208, 209–13; Divine Attributes are eternally existent, 209; Divine decree and determination, 211, 212; Divine Essence, 210; 'I cannot praise You enough; You are as You have praised Yourself', 212–13; 'I seek

refuge in You from Yourself', 210; Oneness, 210, 212, 213; seeking refuge, 209, 210, 211–12
obedience, 4, 8, 59; 'My heart's love for God brings about obedience to Him…', 243
obligation, 95, 119, 149, 195; ablution, 123; abode of obligations, 12, 143; a blessing, favour, grace and mercy, 197–8; goodness of, 196–7; innate disposition, 198; Islam, faith and devotion to God, 196; prayer, 122; reason, 198; worship, 109
Oneness, 17, 56, 107, 162, 210, 212, 213, 215; affirmation of, 41–2, 120, 121; Creation, 125–6; Divine Attributes, 198
ontology, 110; causality, 12–13, 39, 52–3; Creation, 56; evil, 201, 211; the ontological/*kawnī*, 23–4, 224; ontological allowance, 233; ontological appointment, 234; ontological bestowal, 235–6; ontological command, 232; ontological decree, 211, 216, 224, 226, 229–30, 232–3, 236, 240, 242, 248 (there is no escaping His ontological decree, 241); ontological determination of sin, 110–11, 219; ontological fate, 236; the ontological is attached to God's creating, 229; ontological prescription, 231; ontological ruling, 39, 52–3, 216, 229, 230; ontological sending, 235; ontological will, 51, 191, 204, 230, 231, 236; the ontologically forbidden, 235

pain, 150, 160, 162; animal pain, 157, 158, 160, 161, 162; death, pain from 168, 170; difference between the determination being good/evil or pleasing/painful, 202; Hereafter, 161; in the transient abode and the Hereafter, 150–1; lasting pain, 202; patience, 170; pleasure and, 24, 150, 151, 159, 161, 162; purification, 170; the purpose of any being is either to attain pleasures or to avoid distress and grief, 87, 90; Qur'ān, 170; Sunna, 170; wisdom in, 161, 170, 201; see also hardship; suffering; trial and tribulation
Paradise, 3, 115; abode of grace, 187, 188; Adam, 17–18; adversity and hardship, 116, 160, 161; angel, 15, 17; bliss and pleasure, 12, 16, 145, 155, 178, 181; differences between Paradise and Hellfire, 187–91; entrance into Paradise, 14, 18, 59, 106, 137–8, 168, 192; 'a gift unfailing', 176, 177, 178, 187, 192; good deed and, 14, 15, 254; gratitude in, 58–9, 108; *ḥadīth*, 14, 15; *ḥaẓirat al-quds*, 20; inhabitants of, 193; levels, 13–15; longing for, 15–16; lotus tree, 115; mercy, 14, 188; patience, 58–9; reward, 13, 18; trial, 58–9, 257
Path (Straight Path), 3, 115; God is upon the Straight Path, 62–3, 218; *Sūrat al-Fātiḥa*, 121, 206
patience, 6, 29; Abraham, 257–8; Divine Attribute, 134; God's love for the patient, 12; hardship and pain, 50, 116, 151; Jesus, 259; Moses, 259; Noah, 257; pain and, 170; Paradise, entry into, 58–9; Prophet Muḥammad, 259–60; reward for, 154; trial and tribulation, 152, 154, 155, 170, 257–61
People of the Book, 37, 44, 84, 153, 177; *ḥadīth*, 85

perfection: all that God has created exists to result in perfection and completion, 28, 33; angel, 30; Creation, 29, 62, 74, 76, 90, 126 ('Thou canst see no fault in the Beneficent's creation', 28, 33, 62); death leads to the perfection of every believer, 141–2; a Divine Attribute, 38, 73–4, 75, 83, 90, 91, 97, 103, 131, 162, 176; Divine Attributes, perfection of, 21, 58, 76, 105, 138, 161, 189, 198, 212, 262; everything asks God to grant it perfection, 30; humankind, 3, 18, 143, 159–60, 195; messenger, 30; repentance, 239–40; striving for, 116–17, 244; see also virtue
Pharaoh, 40, 42, 45, 153, 226–7, 259; Pharaoh's people, 172; wisdom in allowing the existence of, 46, 111, 112
philosopher, 71, 76, 97, 123; enemy of the messengers and Islamic doctrine, 35, 36, 70
pilgrimage, 128, 235
plant, 30, 124
pleasure, 161; commandment, 117; difference between the determination being good/evil or pleasing/painful, 202; eternal pleasure, 117, 202; faith and, 5; God's pleasure 13, 14, 109, 137, 141, 142; the greatest pleasure, 149, 160; pain and, 24, 150, 151, 159, 161, 162; the purpose of any being is either to attain pleasures or to avoid distress and grief, 87, 90; temptation and, 149; trial and tribulation, 8, 151, 154
polytheism, 27, 109, 153, 174; causality and, 41; *ḥadīth*, 135; Hellfire, punishment in, 169, 182; parents and, 152; wisdom in allowing the existence of, 112, 114
portent, 54, 124
poverty (*faqr*), 243, 248
praise, 56, 104, 106–107, 262; command to praise God, 63; creation, 162; a creature cannot praise God in a manner befitting Him, 262; God's praiseworthiness/praiseworthy Essence, 10, 11, 55, 57, 61, 63, 64, 105–107, 133–4, 138, 144, 162–3 (praise of God's Attributes is more beloved than sins, 138); *ḥadīth*, 163; *al-ḥamd li'llāh*, 33; 'I cannot praise You enough; You are as You have praised Yourself', 212–13; Jabriyya, stripping God of the praise due to Him, 104–105; the Most Praiseworthy/*al-Ḥamīd*, 18, 22, 60, 220; praise/wisdom relationship, 104–105, 107, 138, 157; prayer, 120; Prophet Muḥammad, 37, 262; *subḥān Allāh*, 21, 33, 37; *Sūrat al-Fātiḥa*, 120, 121; types of praise that God is deserving of, 162; see also glorification
prayer, 143; body/extremities involvement in, 123; conditions for, 120–1; glorification, 120; Holy Mosque, Jerusalem, 20; an obligation, 122; the occasion of prayer, 7; Oneness, affirmation of, 120, 121; praise, 120; purification, 120; *Sūrat al-Fātiḥa*, 120–1; timing and repetition of, 123; wisdom and benefits in, 120, 122–4; see also supplication; worship
pre-eternity/pre-eternal (*qadīm*), 34, 75–6, 105, 166, 244–5; God's wisdom is eternal, then His action should be pre-eternal, 87; God's wisdom is pre-eternal, yet the

action is temporally originated, 81; pre-eternal/temporally originated wisdom, 79–80
Predecessors, 14, 93, 201–202, 251, 254, 255, 256, 257, 262
predestination (*lisān al-qadar*), 143; Adam, 18, 143; commandment, 51; contentment with, 201–202; as excuse for disobedience, 236; hardship, 49; Moses, 45–6; negation of, 97; Pharaoh, 45–6; prophets, 49; Satan, 141; wise purpose, 143; see also Divine decree and determination; God's wisdom
pride, 46, 67, 130, 144; *ḥadīth*, 248; sin, God's wisdom in allowing it, 242, 247–8, 254, 256
the prohibited, 2, 4, 6, 131, 152; the ontologically forbidden, 235
Prophet Muḥammad, 2–3, 261; Mecca, conquest of, 114, 116, 137; Mecca, emigration from, 114, 137; God's guidance through, 2, 3; God's knowledge, 37; intercession by, 7, 260; the occasion of challenging, 7; the occasion of prayer, 7; patience, 259–60; praise, 37, 262; prophethood, 118–19; revelation, 84, 114; seal of the Prophets, 69; a servant-Prophet, 7; supplication, 19–20, 212, 216, 244; trial and tribulation, 153, 259–60
prophethood, 16, 118–19
prophets, 2, 17, 37, 61, 138; bliss of Paradise, 143; death of, 96, 139, 141; elite of Creation, 5; false prophet, 60; gratitude, 108; message of, 118–19; nearness to God after trials on Earth, 4; predestination, 49; veracity of, 69
prostration, 27, 205
punishment, 4, 8, 12, 51, 95, 147; causality, negation of, 70; disbelief, 51; disobedience, 55; evil and, 5; fleeing trial and testing, 154; God's wisdom, negation of, 70; purification, 191; Satan, 140; suffering, 170–1; wise purpose, 191
purification, 6, 20; ablution, 64, 120, 122–3; enemy, overpowering the saints, 194; Hellfire, punishment in, 168–9, 172, 184; pain and, 170; prayer, 120; punishment, 191; sin, God's wisdom in allowing it, 244; suffering, 170, 171

qabīḥ, see repugnant/repugnant act
Qadariyya, 184, 198, 216–17; anthropomorphism, 156; Divine Attributes and Names, negation of, 35–6, 156; Divine decree and determination, 223–4, 228; evil, God's infallibility from, 203; Hellfire, punishment in, 165; injustice, 219; negation of Divine will and wisdom, 35, 36, 105, 216–17; negation of God's sovereignty, 105; sin, 237; Zoroastrians, 35, 237
qadīm, see pre-eternity/pre-eternal
Qatāda b. Diʿāma, 22, 42, 192
qibla, 44, 120
al-qidam wa'l-ḥudūth, see temporal origination
Qur'ān, 10; abrogated verse, 48, 181; allegorical verse, 47; causality, 39–41, 42; clear-cut verse, 47; Divine Attributes and Names, 61, 207–208; Divine Law, 12, 64; evil, God's infallibility from, 205–206; God's wisdom, 43–67, 69; Hellfire, punishment in, 176, 177–82, 185; mistaken interpretation of, 165; pain, 170; Q.xi.107: 'Thy

Lord is doer of what He will', 176, 177, 178–9, 180, 192, 230; recitation, 122, 143; revelation, 47, 60–1, 84–5; *Sūrat Āl ʿImrān*, 194–5; *Sūrat al-Anʿām*, 176–7; *Sūrat al-ʿAnkabūt*, 148–55; *Sūrat al-Baqara*, 222; *Sūrat al-Fātiḥa*, 120–1, 206; *Sūrat Hūd*, 218, 222; *Sūrat al-Ikhlās*, 210; *Sūrat al-Naḥl*, 64, 218; *Sūrat al-Nūr*, 222; *Sūrat al-Shuʿarā'*, 61; *Sūrat Tabbat*, 210; 'That You make the Qur'ān the life of my heart, the light of my chest', 221–2; Verse of the Throne/*āyat al-kursī*, 210

Quraysh, 54, 112, 114

Ramadan, 33, 44, 66

al-Rāzī, Fakhr al-Dīn, 34–5, 68, 74, 86; 1st argument, 72–9; 2nd argument, 79–87, 92; 3rd argument, 87–91; 4th argument, 91–3; *al-Arbaʿīn fī uṣūl al-dīn*, 72; *al-Mabāḥith al-mashriqiyya*, 34

reason (*taʿlīl*), 49; definitive reason, 52; *lām al-taʿlīl*, 45, 48, 49, 239; reason for an action and its cause, 50–1

reason/intellect (*ʿaql*), 8–9, 262; attributing faults to God, 68, 75; causality, 41; clear reason/*ṣarīḥ al-ʿaql*, 35; the Creator is superior to creation, 76; Divine Law, 12; God's will, 38; God's wisdom, 43, 56, 68, 69, 75, 86; Hellfire, punishment in, 169, 173; human knowledge, inadequate to understand God's wisdom, 38, 70, 136, 142, 263; obligation, 198

religion, 2, 3, 11–12, 229, 261–2; causality, 39; the religious is connected to God's divinity and Divine Law, 229; true religion/*al-dīn al-ḥanīf*, 185–6; see also commandment; Islam; Divine Law

remembrance (of God/*dhikr*), 30, 50, 55, 56–7, 262

repentance, 6, 135; Adam, 131, 137, 239, 257; 'Every child of Adam sins, and the best of the sinners are the repentant', 254; God's happiness for, 110, 239, 240; God's love for the repentant, 12–13, 239, 249; *ḥadīth*, 13, 254; joy of the heart, 249; the perfect and ultimate objective of all of humanity, 239; perfection is only achieved through repentance, 239–40; perpetrating one major sin and dying without repenting, 165, 219; sin, God's wisdom in allowing it, 239–40, 245–6, 249

repugnant/repugnant act (*qabīḥ*), 22, 37, 68, 78–9; Jabriyya on, 104

resurrection, 2; heresy, 165, 166; negation of, 97, 134, 165

reward, 3–4, 12, 147; Paradise, 13, 18; patience, 154; righteousness, 55; suffering, 157

riḍā, see contentment

ruling, see commandment

sabab, see cause

sage, 82, 101, 116–17, 120, 156, 160, 191

Saʿīd b. al-Musayyab, 182

saints (*awliyā'*), 17, 22, 48, 59, 138; elite of Creation, 5; God's friendship, 16; nearness to God after trials on Earth, 4; trial and tribulation, 260; see also enemy, overpowering the saints

Ṣāliḥ, prophet, 111

Satan (Devil, Iblīs), 1, 27, 108, 226–7; basis and root of all wickedness and evil, 114, 140; Day of

Judgment, 94; disdain for God's commandments, 6; falsehood, 47; father of the jinn, 6, 131; fight against God, 6; the most wicked, filthiest and most evil spirit, 114; predestination, 141; refusal to prostrate to Adam, 205; punishment, 140; Satanic calumny, 47, 48; wearing out the Devil, 251; whisperings of, 48–9, 143, 215; see also devils; Satan, wisdom in allowing the existence of
Satan, wisdom in allowing the existence of, 30–1, 94, 113; the righteous attaining the highest levels of worship and virtues, 130, 132, 137, 147; fear and caution from the Satanic fall, 130; goodness becomes more apparent in contrast to evilness, 132; seeking God's refuge from Satan, 138–9; keeping Satan on Earth until the Day of Judgment, 96, 139–40; manifesting some of the Divine Names and Attributes, 133, 135–6, 144–5; manifesting some of God's signs, 132–3; manifesting some of God's wisdoms, 133, 135–6; indirectly leads to repentance, 131, 135, 137; Satan as touchstone when differentiating the wicked from the good people, 131, 139; Satan's disobedience as warning and lesson, 130–1; trial and tribulation, 47, 136–7, 139, 146–7; waging battle for God's sake, 132; see also devils; Satan
self-restraint (*taqwā*), 66, 84
senses, 41, 53, 89, 123
sexual intercourse, 27, 159
al-Shaʿbī, Abū ʿAmr, 182
al-Shāfiʿī, Muḥammad b. Idrīs, 195
Shuʿayb, prophet, 153
sin: ablution, 122–3; Adam, 111; avoiding sin, 9; a barrier between the heart and God's guidance, 2; concealing, remitting the believer's sins, 152, 171, 240, 245; degree of sinfulness, 51; Divine decree and determination, 223–4, 237 (ontological determination of, 110–11, 219, 240); Divine decree/human free choice and will, 239; due to disobeying the prohibitions of God, 98; *ḥadīth*, 110, 135, 171, 254; major sin, 171; Qadariyya, 237; a sin is followed by another sin, 257; see also the entries below for sin
sin, viewpoints on, 237–9; animalistic viewpoint, 237; deterministic viewpoint, 237; free-will viewpoint, 237; monotheistic viewpoint, 237–8; viewpoint of Divine Names and Attributes, 238; viewpoint of need, poverty, inability and weakness, 237; viewpoint of those who are knowledgable and faithful, 237; viewpoint of wise purposes, 238; see also sin; sin, God's wisdom in allowing it
sin, God's wisdom in allowing it, 238; appreciating God's blessings, 248, 249–50; asking forgiveness, 238, 254; asking forgiveness for others, 255–6; brokenness, 243, 244, 248; to avoid criticizing others, 255; deeming own good deeds to be insignificant, compared to God's blessings, 243–4, 250, 254; desisting from vengeance, 247; indirectly leads to fear, awe, reverence, 248; gaining experience and knowledge about evil, 251–2;

ḥadīth, 246–7, 248; indirectly leads to humility, 242–3, 244, 248, 254–5; knowing that there is no salvation except through God's forgiveness and mercy, 245; making a servant wake up, 250–1; manifesting Divine Names and Attributes, 238, 240–1; manifesting God's justice, 246; peace of mind, 255; perfecting worship, 242; poverty, 243, 248; pride, 242, 247–8, 254, 256; purification, 244; reaching a special proximity to God, 242, 252–3; recognizing our need of God's assistance, 241–2; recognizing our own faultiness, 244; recognizing that sins and doing evil are intrinsic to human beings, 247; repentance, 239–40, 245–6, 249; righteousness, 248–9; seeking refuge in God, 242; striving for perfection, 244; submission, 242–3, 244, 248; supplication for forgiveness, 255–6; treating others as God has treated the sinner, 246–7; see also sin; sin, viewpoints on
slavery, 109, 110
Solomon, 66
soul, 158; angel, soul that desires only good, 156; devil, soul that desires only evil, 156; free will and choice, 158; human being, soul desiring both good and evil, 155, 156
sovereignty (*mulk*), 19, 212; Divine Attribute, 4–5, 19, 37, 39, 102, 133, 144, 163; Qadariyya, 105
speculative theology, 71, 76, 93, 100, 104; causality, negation of, 34–5, 70; creation, 35; God's wisdom, negation of, 70
star, 89, 128, 258
struggle against desire and temptation, 5–6, 10, 143, 149, 151, 154; see also waging battle for God's sake
submission, 47; angel, 108; God's love for the submissive, 11; remembrance, 50; sin, God's wisdom in allowing it, 242–3, 244, 248; submissiveness due to love, 243; submissiveness resulting indirectly from disobedience, 243
Successors, 180, 187, 192, 193
al-Suddī, Ismāʿīl b. ʿAbd al-Raḥmān, 181
suffering: child, suffering and death, 32, 94, 95, 96; *ḥadīth*, 137; punishment for our sins, 170–1; purification, 170, 171; reasons for, 159; reward for, 157; wisdom in, 94, 96, 113, 136–7; see also hardship; pain; trial and tribulation
Sufism, 251
sun, 29, 38, 89, 100, 117; similitudes, 37, 70; wisdom and benefits, 127–8
sunna: God's custom, 24, 59; God's methodology, 24, 59
Sunna, 262; causality, 41; Divine Attributes and Names, 207–208; evil, God's infallibility from, 205; God's wisdom, 43, 52; Hellfire, punishment in, 179, 181, 183; mistaken interpretation of, 165; pain, 170
Sunnis, 183
supplication, 111, 134, 135, 214, 215–16, 257; Divine Names and Attributes, 221; forgiveness, 255–6; Prophet Muḥammad, 19–20, 212, 216, 244; supplication that relieves of calamities, 215; see also prayer
Supporters, 114

al-Ṭabarī, Ibn Jarīr, 21, 180, 182
Tablet/Preserved Tablet, 36, 49
tabṣira, see enlightenment
Ta'if, 116
taʿlīl, see reason
taqwā, see self-restraint
tasalsul, see infinite regress
tasbīḥ, see glorification
temporal origination (*al-qidam wa'l-ḥudūth*), 34, 81, 86, 124, 166
temptation, 9, 69; following the temptation, 149; Hellfire, 116, 160, 161; struggle against desire and, 5–6, 10, 143, 149, 151, 154; trial and tribulation, 253
Thābit, 180
Thamūd, 111, 153
al-Tirmidhī, Abū ʿĪsā, 131
trial and tribulation: abode of tribulation, 131, 146, 155; Abraham, 231, 258; Adam, wisdom in his descent from the Garden, 3, 4, 8, 9–10, 12, 94, 142–3, 257; anger, 253; commandment, 155; Creation, 155; differentiating believers from disbelievers, 148–9, 152, 155; faith, 148, 153; fear of trial and testing, 148–9; fleeing trial and testing, 148–9, 154; God's wisdom and praiseworthiness, 147; a mercy for God's servants, 246, 257; Moses, 259; nearness to God after trials on Earth, 4; need of, 9; as objective of God's creation and commandment, 155; Paradise, 58–9, 257; patience, 152, 154, 155, 170, 257–61; perfecting the believer, 257; pleasure, 8, 151, 154; Prophet Muḥammad, 153, 259–60; recompense in the Hereafter, 154, 155; returning back to the original innate disposition, 168; saints, 260; Satan, wisdom in allowing the existence of, 47, 136–7, 139, 146–7; *Sūrat al-ʿAnkabūt*, 148–55; temptation, 253; transient nature of, 151; tribulation of some by others, 46, 146–7; wisdom in, 257–61; worship in time of, 10; see also hardship; pain; suffering
truth/truthfulness, 63, 173; Creation, 55, 56, 166; Divine Attribute, 63, 166–7; each truth (or bearer thereof) has one who stubbornly rejects it, 97; messengers, 69, 111

ʿUbāda, 171
ʿUmar b. al-Khaṭṭāb, 176, 180, 182, 251
umma, see Community
the Unseen, 5, 67, 208, 220, 221, 261
ʿUthmān b. ʿAffān, 123

virtue, 195; see also perfection

waging battle for God's sake, 109, 115, 136, 143, 151, 225; God's love for those who wage battle, 12; the apex of worship, 109, 132, 193; Satan, wisdom in allowing the existence of, 132
will: God's will/*irāda*, 204; ontological will, 51, 191, 204, 230, 231, 236; religious will, 230, 231, 236; see also God's will
wisdom (*ḥikma*): effective wisdom, 43; knowledge and deeds, 43; see also God's wisdom
worship, 143–4; abode of tribulation, 146; Adam, wisdom in his descent from the Garden, 7, 8, 142; angel's worship, 6, 144; Creation, 8, 55, 125–6, 167, 195–6; God loves to be worshipped in all manners, 146; hardship, 215; in times of joy and

hardship, 10; obligation to worship God, 109; types of, 109–10, 115, 132, 146; as ultimate objective of God's actions and commandments, 125–6; waging battle for God's sake, apex of worship, 109, 132, 193; worshipping God by free choice as the best grade of worship, 7, 144; see also prayer
wrath, 90, 99, 161, 250; Day of Judgment, 190; *ḥadīth*, 190; Hellfire, punishment in, 174, 188, 190; His mercy precedes His wrath, 161, 173, 174, 187, 189, 193, 210; see also 'O God, I seek refuge in Your pleasure from Your wrath…'

'Your judgment upon me…', 214–22; distress, sorrow and grief, 214–16; 'I ask You by every Name of Yours…', 220; Jabriyya, 216, 217–18; 'My forelock is in Your Hand', 216; ontological decree and determination, 216, 217, 219; 'Or have kept hidden within Your knowledge of the Unseen', 221; Qadariyya, 216–17; 'Relief from my grief, and deliverance from my distress and sorrow', 222; 'That You make the Qur'ān the life of my heart, the light of my chest', 221–2; 'Your judgment upon me will be carried out, and Your decree upon me is just', 216–19

Zachariah, 52
Zayd b. Thābit, 14
Zoroastrian, 35, 237